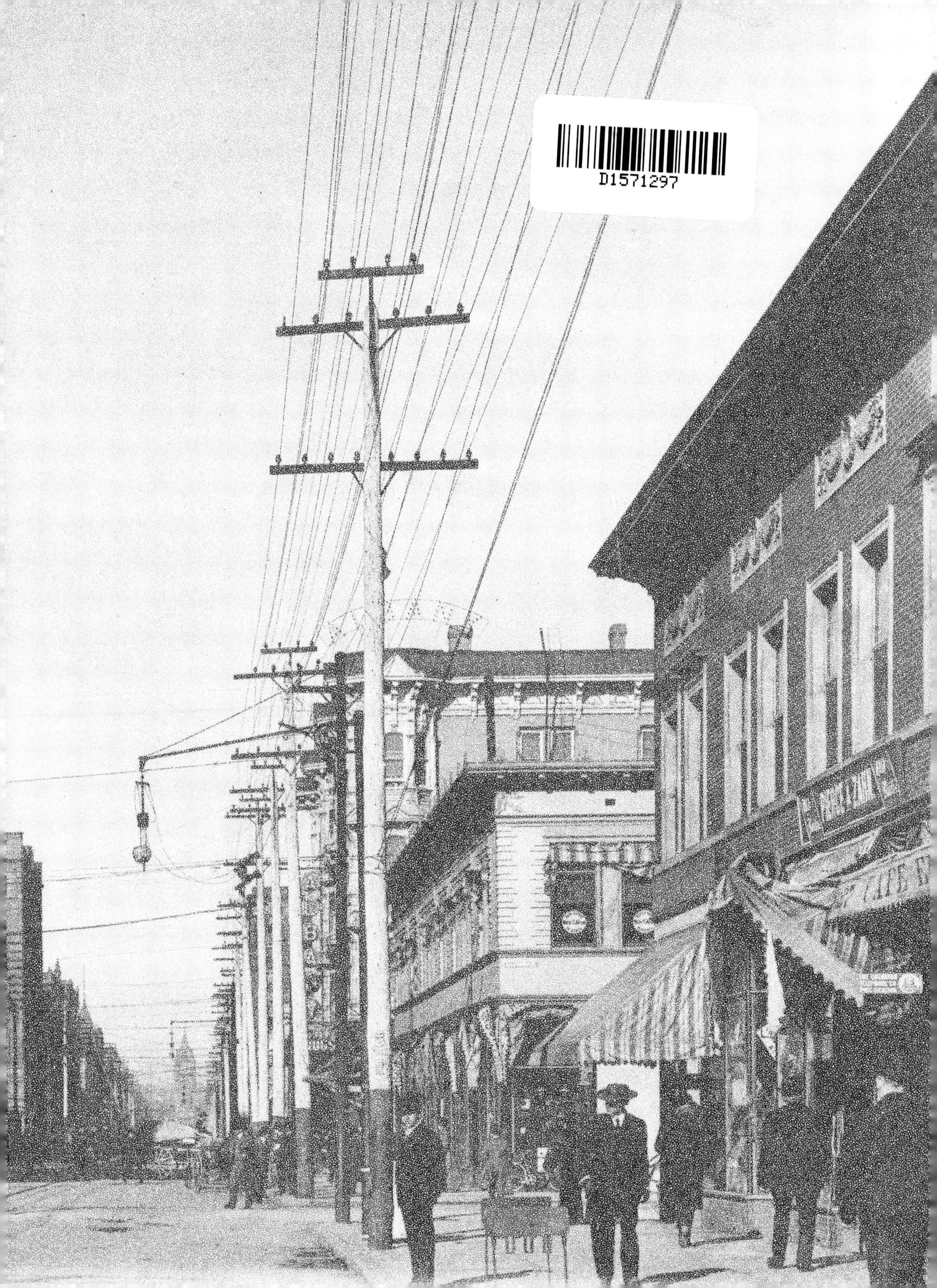

COAL, CINDERS AND PARLOR CARS:

A Century of Colorado Passenger Trains

476

COAL, CINDERS AND PARLOR CARS:

A Century of Colorado Passenger Trains

Colorado Rail Annual No. 19

A Journal of Railroad History in the Rocky Mountain West

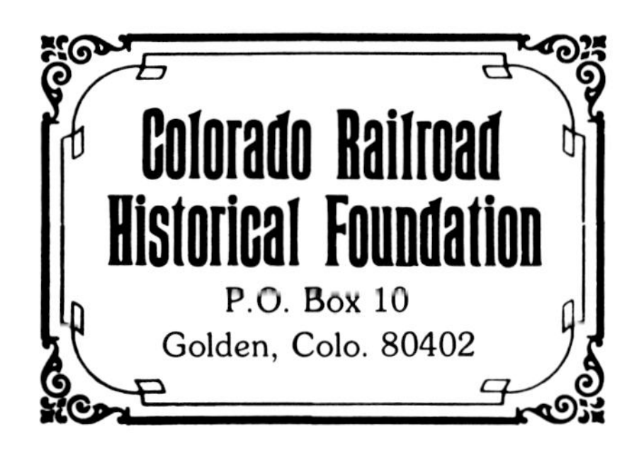

The Colorado Railroad Museum was established in 1958 to gather and preserve a tangible historic record of Colorado's fascinating railroad era. The Museum's invaluable collection of records, artifacts and equipment was begun in 1949, and the accumulation of important material is still continuing. The Museum is now operated by the non-profit Colorado Railroad Historical Foundation, Inc., in which your support and participation are cordially invited.

Colorado Rail Annual
No. 19

EDITORS

Charles Albi
R.C. Farewell
William C. Jones

Published and distributed by
Colorado Railroad Museum
Box 10, Golden, CO 80402

PRINTED ON ACID FREE PAPER

ISBN 0-918654-19-X
Library of Congress Catalog Card
No. 70-102682

Printed and bound in the United States of America by Johnson Publishing Company, Boulder, Colorado. Layout and production by the editors.

(Title page) The West Elk Mountains have witnessed the passage of Silverton-bound narrow gauge passenger trains for over a century. (R.C. Farewell)

Editors' Preface

(Cornelius W. Hauck collection)

Passenger trains have served the Colorado Rockies for 120 years. From the October morning in 1871 when the first Denver & Rio Grande narrow gauge train set out for Colorado Springs, right up to the present time, railroads have met a variety of transportation needs for the citizens of the Centennial State. In years past a large number of narrow and standard gauge routes, most of which have been long-abandoned, were the only means of getting from one place to another through the canyons and over the high passes. Even then, however, tourists from across the nation and around the world had discovered the magnificent Colorado mountain scenery. Such travelers comprised a large part of the patronage throughout the great era of train travel. Today, riding trains for pleasure and scenery has become a big part of the state's tourism industry and is shared by such diverse entities as Amtrak, Georgetown Loop and Manitou & Pikes Peak.

In *Colorado Rail Annual No. 19,* we have an opportunity to compare two railroads of the past and present. First, William F. Gale gives a detailed analysis of the scheduling of the Colorado Midland—one of the most fondly remembered of abandoned mountain railroads. He describes how the CM served such famous communities as Cripple Creek, Leadville and Aspen. We can see how schedules were adjusted to reflect changing conditions from boom times through the decline in mining. The reader can understand how intertwined were the destinies of the railroad and the territory it served. We have tried to enhance Bill's fine text with a selection from the vast amount of advertising material published by the Colorado Midland to lure patronage away from its competitors—the South Park and the Denver & Rio Grande.

The other major feature of this *Annual* describes the evolution of the Silverton train from a little used and nearly abandoned branch line in the 1940s into what is today perhaps Colorado's best known train. This story is told from three different perspectives. Bob Richardson, one of the most respected rail historians, tells about the years 1941-1962 and the role he played in developing support for the train during a time when it was little appreciated by the communities it served. John S. Walker Jr. goes on to explain the key role of one individual in the modern revival of *The Silverton.* Alexis McKinney was certainly the right person in the right place at the right time. Finally, R.C. Farewell continues the narrative with a description of innovations and improvements made by Charles E. Bradshaw Jr. under the banner of the Durango & Silverton Narrow Gauge Railroad.

We are delighted that Bob Richardson has provided us with a great number of his own photographs which never before have been published. Rich Farewell has carefully printed these from the original negatives to insure the best possible reproduction and has used many of his own sparkling images to complete the illustration.

As an *entr' acte* to the above, we are pleased to present an informative essay on another form of rail passenger service, that of urban street railways. Thomas J. Noel is one of those rare people who combines good scholarship with good writing. In his description of how the neighborhoods of Denver were developed and served by its electric trolley system, we can appreciate how this technology, now known as "light rail transit," could once again be an asset to metropolitan living.

Finally, Ron Hill reminds us that Colorado has no monopoly on narrow gauge railroads. It is interesting to compare his pioneer steam enthusiast trek to Zimbabwe in 1990 with Bob's similar venture to Colorado years ago. At the time, the San Juan Mountains were perhaps almost as remote to an Ohioan as Africa seems to us today. At any rate, enthusiasm for steam and smoke knows no boundaries.

At this point we wish to acknowledge and thank several individuals, in addition to those cited by each author, who were most generous in sharing their time and talent in order to make publication of *Colorado Rail Annual No. 19* possible. We could not have done our job without them: Richard Cooley; Amos Cordova of the Durango & Silverton Narrow Gauge Railroad; the Farewell family—Herbert, Virginia, Neil, R.C. Jr., and Pauline; E.J. Haley; Cornelius Hauck; Jerry Johnson, Cindy Schumacher, and Michel Reynolds of Johnson Publishing Company; Richard H. Kindig; Erwin Krebs; A.D. Mastrogiuseppe of the Denver Public Library Western History Department; Richard H. Mathews; S. Mazzucca; Alexis McKinney; Eric Paddock and Judy Steiner of the Colorado Historical Society and Richard Ronzio. Finally, we wish to thank our authors for the privilege of publishing their manuscripts. By relinquishing the royalties they would have received from other publishers, they have enhanced our ability to preserve history at the Colorado Railroad Museum.

The Editors

This fanciful artist's rendering of Hell Gate appeared on the cover of a promotional booklet issued circa 1908. (Museum collection)

Table of Contents

COAL, CINDERS AND PARLOR CARS: A Century of Colorado Passenger Trains

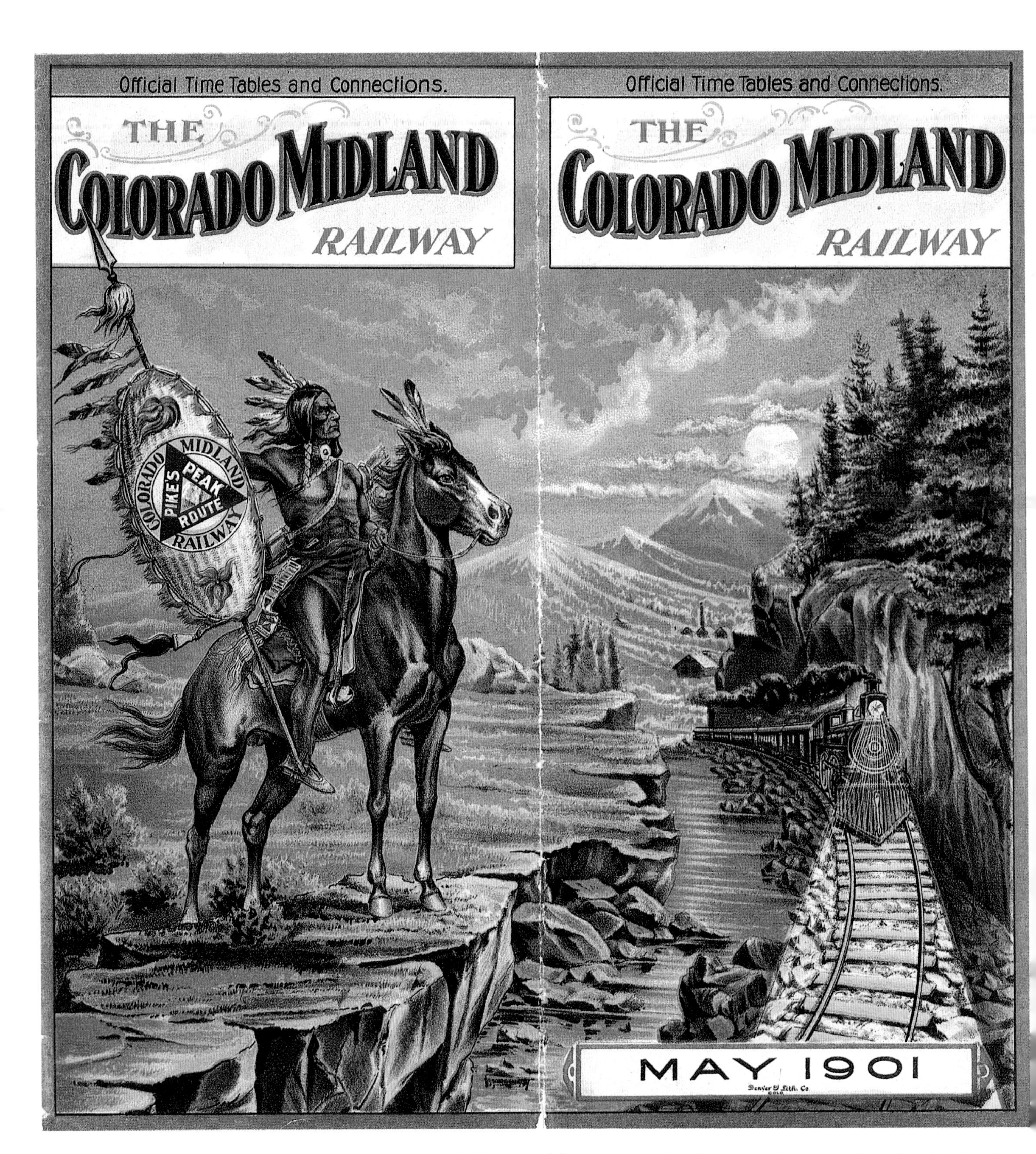

At the turn of the century Colorado's competing mountain railroads printed literally tons of colorful material to lure patronage to their individual routes. This Midland timetable cover, with a version of its trademark tribal warrior, is an outstanding example of the era's advertising art. (Museum collection)

COLORADO MIDLAND PASSENGER SERVICE 1887-1918

by William F. Gale

PREFACE and ACKNOWLEDGMENTS

The Colorado Midland first came to my attention at the age of 14 when an article appeared in the August 1936 issue of *Railroad Stories* about the fabled Colorado railroad. The interest thus raised has never flagged and continues to an acute degree to this day.

Other articles appeared in *Railroad Magazine* and *Trains* as well as Carl Graves' book-length history of the Colorado Midland published by the Railway & Locomotive Historical Society in its Bulletin No. 36, in 1936. But the real "Bible" for all Colorado Midland aficionados is Morris Cafky's *Colorado Midland* which was published by the Rocky Mountain Railroad Club of Denver in 1965. It is my opinion that this book is one of the finest histories in the growing field of railroad literature.

After the publication of *Colorado Midland*, the collecting of passenger schedules became a serious matter for me, and I made a trip in 1967 to the Library of the Association of American Railroads in Washington, D.C., which, at one time, had almost a complete collection of Official Guides. By the time of my visit, however, much of it had been returned to the publishers for their own purposes, with just two issues per year retained by the AAR. These were made available, and in the days before the universal use of photocopiers, a number of early schedules were copied by hand from the Guides available, in addition to the engineers' pay scales for 1897 and 1907.

In later years, after I was employed by the Interstate Commerce Commission and received several temporary assignments in the Washington office, it was found that there was an almost complete collection of Official Guides located in the Commission's own library. The issues that were published during the years of the Colorado Midland's lifetime form the basis for the study of the passenger schedules for that railroad and are included herein.

During the 1950s, I carried on a long and comprehensive correspondence with Ernie Peyton with respect to Colorado railroading in general, and in connection with the Pikes Peak region railroads in particular. While thus engaged, Ernie furnished a great deal of specific information relating to the operations of the railroads under discussion, which included copies of train orders, line-ups, schedules, operating practices, and some of his own experiences in riding over some of the lines. He had acquired the timeslips of a former Colorado Midland engineer, Edward W. Hartzog, had arranged them in chronological order, and had transcribed them so as to make up a complete listing of Engineer Hartzog's career. Ernie generously lent these lists and the great bulk of them were copied on 65 legal sized sheets as a first-hand record of one man's life as a CM engineer, as well as a wealth of information relating to the operations of the Colorado Midland.

Mr. Hartzog was an engineer from 1906 to the last days of the road, having hired out as a fireman about 1900. He did not get too many opportunities to handle passenger trains as a road engineer, because his seniority usually limited him to the handling of freight and helper assignments. When he did handle passenger trains, and they are appropriate to this study, his records have been included.

The career of this engineer would make a story in itself, as he ran every engine the CM owned, except for No. 35, which had blown up in 1896 at Basalt, and No. 101, which was primarily assigned to the west end division points at Basalt and Cardiff. Ed Hartzog was assigned to the First District between Colorado Springs and Leadville, although he made occasional trips over the Second District as far as Cardiff (and once to Aspen) during his career. In addition to CM engines, Ed also ran engines from "foreign" lines, such as the D&RG, C&S, MT and CS&CCD, which were rented by the Colorado Midland during periods of heavy traffic. I owe a great debt to Ernie Peyton for furnishing these records, as well as many other items he contributed with respect to the operations on a number of long-gone railroads in Colorado.

The October 1972 issue of *The Timetable Collector* contained an article by Robert S. Ash dealing with the collection of Colorado Midland timetables, and he indicated that there were known to be 73 public timetables in existence at that time, which represented 23 years of the railroad's lifetime. No doubt more have turned up since (I have one, dated November 1908, which was not included in the count). But there is still a scarcity of CM public folders, and even if one had access to all of those extant, the record of passenger services scheduled by the road would be incomplete. Hence, the basic tool used in this study is the various schedules as published in the Official Guide. I have attempted to present as complete a picture of the railroad's passenger service as possible.

A number of Official Guides were available for the earlier years of the railroad's operation, but, unfortunately, a number of the Colorado Midland schedules had been cut from the Guides by some inconsiderate, selfish individual. As a result, it is possible that a number of historically important schedules have been lost, or that important changes can no longer be definitely determined. We trust that most of the important changes have been documented within a month or two of their happening, but the record is necessarily incomplete because of someone's little razor blade.

In addition to Ernie Peyton, I owe a great deal of gratitude to others who have assisted me over the years with the accumulation of data used in this study. Harry L. Eddy, librarian for the Association of American Railroads was especially helpful in the 1960s when much of this material was secured. Helen Rowland, librarian of the AAR in more recent times, was also very helpful at a critical point in securing certain schedules. Denise L Ryan, librarian of the Interstate Commerce Commission, has also been of great assistance, and has made available much material that would have been extremely difficult, if not impossible, to obtain.

Thanks are also due to the National Railway Publishing Company, New York, for permission to include certain schedules of the excellent Official Guide reprints that have been published in recent years for June 1893 and June 1916. That firm has published the Official Guide for 100 years, thus providing almost the only complete source of passenger schedules during the period for all railroads.

The Colorado Midland's city ticket office in Denver was located in the California Building at 17th and California Streets. This night view from about 1910 highlights the CM's emblem and its direct service to points throughout the West, with large framed photographs depicting many of the locations. Camera artists William Henry Jackson, Louis Charles McClure and Harry Hale Buckwalter all did work for the Midland. (Denver Public Library Western History Dept.)

The wildflower excursions were an integral part of the Colorado Midland legend. This postcard was mailed home to Abilene, Kansas by a tourist who wrote, "Hello Sis, I am seeing some sights." Observation car 111 is now a prized exhibit at the Colorado Railroad Museum. (Cornelius W. Hauck collection)

AN OVERVIEW OF COLORADO MIDLAND SCHEDULES

A legitimate question could well be asked as to why anyone would want to study the passenger train schedules during the lifetime of the Colorado Midland. After all, many people consider railway timetables to be rather dull reading, something akin to watching paint dry. The true devotee does not see a timetable as just figures opposite station names and a confusing garble of reference marks; instead, he can convert those figures in the schedule columns into a mental image of a real train of cars hauled by a steam locomotive, traveling along steel rails winding through some of the most fabulous scenery on this continent. The equipment lists that accompany the schedules also provide a mental picture of the type of cars carried, so that the picture of the train is complete.

The history of the scheduled passenger service is chosen because it was the activity of the railroad that has always been most visible to the public at large. Granted that the CM's passenger revenues usually amounted to 10% of the total revenue of the railroad, the "varnished cars" contributed a much larger percentage to the reputation of the railroad, and the esteem, or lack of it, that it had in the eyes of the public.

While it is true that freight revenue overshadowed that of passenger service, it is also true that freight operations are extremely difficult to define over a long period of time. They are generally subject to a greater degree of fluctuation than passenger operations—particularly at a time when the passenger train was the primary method of travel in the Rocky Mountain region. Freight trains are generally operated when sufficient tonnage is available; even though a freight is scheduled in the timetable, it may be annulled if there is insufficient tonnage. On the other hand, during periods of good business, it may be necessary to operate additional sections of regular freight trains or to run extras to move the available traffic.

In the Colorado Midland operating timetables that have come to light, the CM scheduled from one to four freight trains each way over the various districts of the railroad. Even when there was only one freight train scheduled each way, indications are that a number of extra trains were operated on a daily basis. Since the CM was a mountain railroad, most freight trains were quite short as viewed by present day eyes, with 950 tons constituting a heavy train requiring several helpers on the most severe grades.

Unlike the fluctuations of freight train operations, passenger trains ran every day they were scheduled. When business was very good, a second section could well be run. If a large group was involved, requiring a full train to handle, it could be operated as a second section of a regular train, or it could be run "special," independent of the regular train. It should be noted that the practice of the day was to identify such a train as "special" rather than using the term "passenger extra" which is more generally favored in the modern era.

When business was poor, passenger trains continued to operate as scheduled, until the trend was duly noted by management, and adjustments were made in the schedule, either by a consolidation of trains or by taking them off altogether. Thus it can be seen that passenger services can be defined more readily than freight operations, and, in the case of the Colorado Midland, it will be seen that the mountain railroad contained a kaleidoscope of passenger trains during its lifetime.

What is the mystique that still attracts devotees to this railroad that has been out of operation for 73 years—longer than most of us have been alive? The Colorado Midland ran for only a few days more than 31 years, it was in continual financial hot water, it was never able to

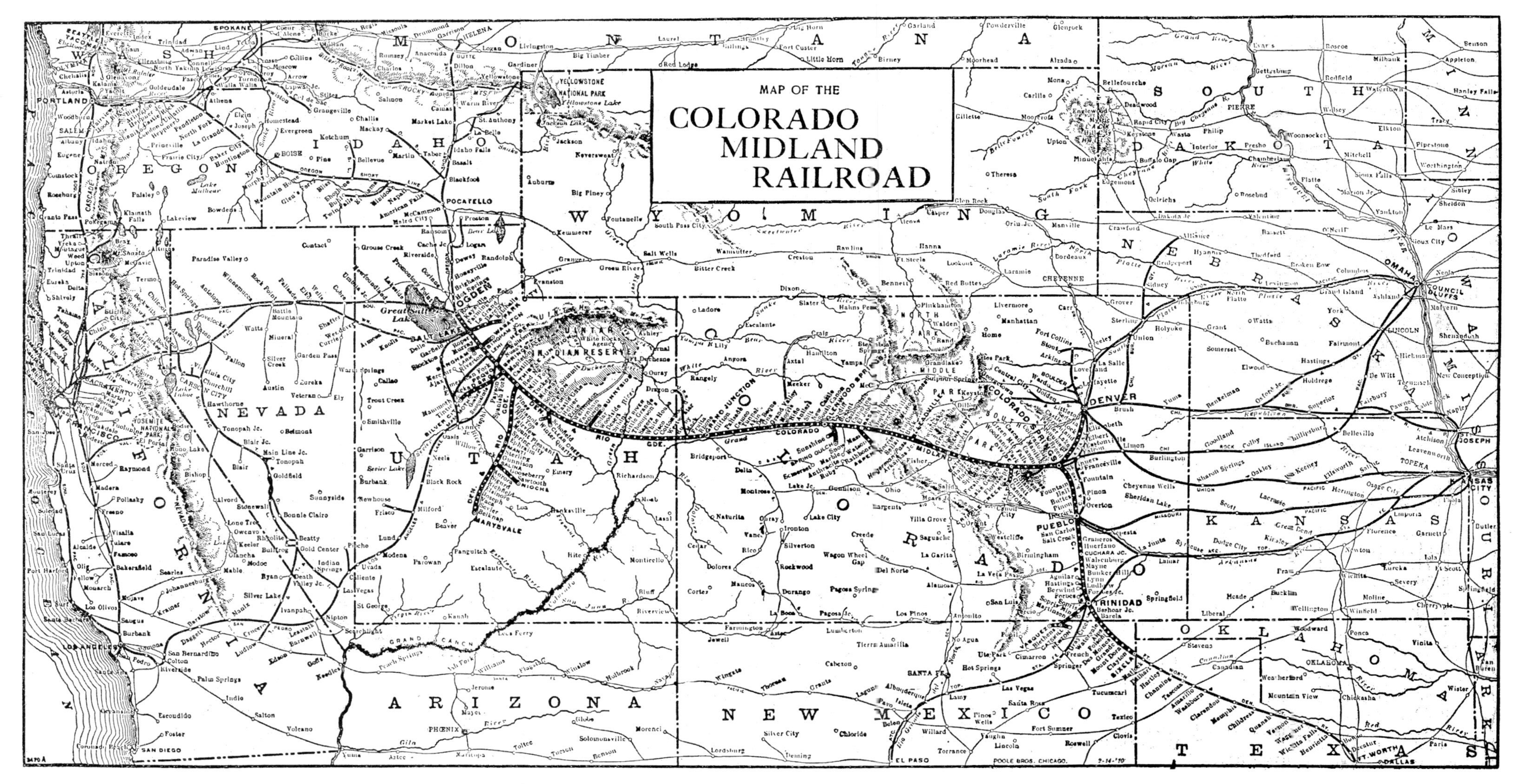

This 1910 timetable map illustrates the Colorado Midland's route in relation to its major connections east and west. Note how the competing line of the Denver & Rio Grande is almost obscured between Pueblo, Leadville and Grand Junction and then is transformed into the CM's connection west of the latter point. (Museum collection)

extend its line further west of Grand Junction in order to tap a more productive territory, its equipment was virtually the same when it ended operations as when it had started (making it a 19th Century anachronism well into the 20th Century), and it served a relatively sparsely populated region, punctuated by mining boom towns. Certainly, this does not seem to create a railroad of which legends are made, yet there are almost as many legends about the Colorado Midland as there were passengers hauled during its lifetime.

After all, the Colorado Midland was the first standard gauge railroad to penetrate the Rocky Mountain fastness of Colorado, it had some of the most magnificent scenery along its rails, it was associated with great mining camps such as Leadville, Aspen and Cripple Creek, it was an engineering marvel for its time, its lifetime spanned the most "romantic era" of American railroading, and it became one of the most famous lost causes in railroad history when it was abandoned. This is the stuff of which legends are made.

Another thing that separates the Colorado Midland from such storied roads as the Denver South Park & Pacific (later the narrow gauge lines of the Colorado & Southern), the Denver Northwestern & Pacific (later the Denver & Salt Lake), and the Colorado Springs & Cripple Creek District was the fact that the Colorado Midland was not a dead end railroad. Through its connections on the east at Colorado Springs, and on the west with the Rio Grande Western at Grand Junction, the Colorado Midland was able to participate in through routes for both passenger and freight traffic. Sleeping cars that originated at off-line stations traveled over the CM to points beyond, and, for years, the railroad handled tourist sleepers that were enroute between Chicago and other Midwestern cities and points on the west coast. At one time, the Colorado Midland even had a sleeper from Denver to Portland, Oregon.

The Colorado Midland was also known as an excursion railroad, and countless numbers of special trains were handled over its storied rails during the years of its existence. There are probably more photos extant of such excursion trains than there are of the regularly scheduled trains, yet it was the latter that handled the bulk of the Colorado Midland's passenger, mail and express traffic over the years. Not only were there many special trains operating over the length of the railroad, but the CM was also famous for its own local excursions, principally the heralded Wildflower Special that ran daily during the summer between Colorado Springs and Spinney for many years. Other specials ran between Aspen and Glenwood Springs on weekends so that the families of the mining community could soak in the healing waters at Glenwood, and for innumerable picnics and holidays.

While the Colorado Midland solicited through passenger and freight business, it did not neglect local traffic that was available in its region. With a double daily service during most of its years, the CM provided sleeping car service to the on line points of Leadville and Grand Junction. It also ran a sleeping car line that has to be one of the shortest such operations ever, between Colorado Springs and Cripple Creek, 57 miles! In later years, it offered the amenities of dining car service on its principal trains.

Even though the Midland Terminal, which supplied the connection on the Colorado Midland at Divide with the great gold camp at Cripple Creek, was a separate organization, it was originally backed by Santa Fe interests at the same time that the Santa Fe had control of the Colorado Midland. The two roads entered into an operating agreement that called for the Colorado Midland to provide the motive power, rolling stock and crews on all of the through trains between Colorado Springs and Cripple Creek. At one time, after the Midland Terminal had become part of the Associated Lines in the Cripple Creek area, an attempt was made to breach the contract, but the Colorado Midland management refused to allow this to happen, so that the arrangement continued in effect almost to the last when the Midland Terminal was granted trackage rights over the CM by a management that controlled both roads. Because of the contractual relationship, this survey of Colorado Midland schedule passenger service includes the through Colorado Springs–Cripple Creek services, and, in this context, treats the Midland Terminal as a branch line passenger operation of the Colorado Midland.

Some historians, in their treatment of the Colorado Midland, have considered the Rio Grande Junction Railway to be outside the scope of the Midland story and have neglected this aspect of the CM's operations. Since the RGJ was a joint ownership of the Colorado Midland and the Denver & Rio Grande, and actually provided nothing more than a track and roadbed over which each railroad operated its own passenger and freight trains, similar to the operation of many a terminal railroad, it is considered in this survey to be part and parcel of the Colorado Midland. The CM used its own motive power, equipment and crews to operate over the RGJ between Rifle and Grand Junction, and had access to all of the stations and industries in that territory, as well as terminal rights on the D&RG at Grand Junction, and trackage rights over the D&RG between Gramid (New Castle) and Rifle. Even after the D&RG spirited away the Colorado Midland's 50% ownership of the RGJ in 1912, the CM still maintained the right to traffic at stations and industries until the very end. For these reasons the Rio Grande Junction is treated in this survey as an integral part of the Colorado Midland.

Purists in the timetable collecting field may argue that the Official Guide representations are inadequate, as collectors are generally more interested in securing a publication direct from the railroad involved for its own sake, rather than for the subject matter that it contains. The schedules shown in the Official Guide are furnished to the publisher by the railroads, who pay for the space used, so that the information contained in the railroad's individual representation is the first hand data as supplied by the railroad itself. These schedules are often somewhat condensed, but the Colorado Midland's representations are fortunately complete enough to provide a clear picture of the road's passenger services.

For this survey 72 different schedules, as published in the Official Guide and other sources, have been used to show the progression in the schedules themselves and the various changes that were made over the years, as well as the equipment that was handled in each of the trains, when it has been listed. There is at least one schedule for every year that the railroad operated, and when important changes were made, both the before and after schedules have been used when available. For instance, when the Colorado Midland had its disagreement with the Busk Tunnel Company, both the last schedule showing the use of the Busk Tunnel, and the first schedule showing the operation over Hagerman Pass and through the Hagerman Tunnel have been included. Again, when the railroad went back to using the Busk Tunnel, the last schedule through the Hagerman Tunnel and the first one of the return to the Busk Tunnel are shown. Others have been used for their possible historical interest, such as the schedule in effect at the turn of the century on January 1, 1900, and when there have been unusual operations.

Because of the importance of the Cripple Creek business to the Colorado Midland, a number of schedules have been used to show the progress of the Midland Terminal as it built from Divide to the great gold camp, and how the passenger service was changed to meet the expanding construction of the MT. Likewise, when the Colorado Springs & Cripple Creek District was built, some of the schedules of that famous old railroad are included, in order to show the competitive situation between the CM-MT and the Short Line routes, as well as in the years when the two routes cooperated in the operation of tourist trains.

Although the Denver & Rio Grande and the Colorado Midland competed directly for traffic between Denver, Colorado Springs, Leadville, Aspen, Glenwood Springs and points along the Rio Grande Junction, this study does not concern itself with the comparable schedules of the D&RG. Even though the Colorado Midland was considerably shorter than the D&RG route, the latter road's schedules were very competitive and were not much more than an hour or so longer than the Midland timings. For instance, the Colorado Midland connection from Denver might leave an hour later than the D&RG train, but they both made the same connection with the Rio Grande Western at Grand Junction. Eastbound service was about the same, with the D&RG time somewhat longer than the Colorado Midland, but there were times, however, when the overall schedules of both roads were virtually identical. It was felt that a continual reference to the competitive D&RG schedules over the years would clutter up the study of the Colorado Midland and would

This folder described personally conducted tours out of Chicago via the Chicago Milwaukee & St. Paul to Omaha, the Rock Island to Colorado Springs and Denver, the CM/Rio Grande Western to Ogden and the Southern Pacific to San Francisco. (Museum collection)

Tourist Pullman cars, with rattan instead of upholstered seats, were not as luxurious as their first class counterparts but provided comfortable accommodations at more moderate fares. (H.H. Buckwalter, Colorado Historical Society; right, Museum collection)

Tourist Car Berth Rates

BETWEEN CHICAGO AND		BETWEEN OMAHA AND	
Denver or Colorado Springs,	$2.50	Denver or Colorado Springs,	$1.50
Ogden, Utah, - -	4.00	Ogden, Utah, - -	3.00
Salt Lake City, -	4.00	Salt Lake City, -	3.00
Sacramento, - -	6.00	Sacramento, - -	5.00
San Francisco, -	6.00	San Francisco, -	5.00

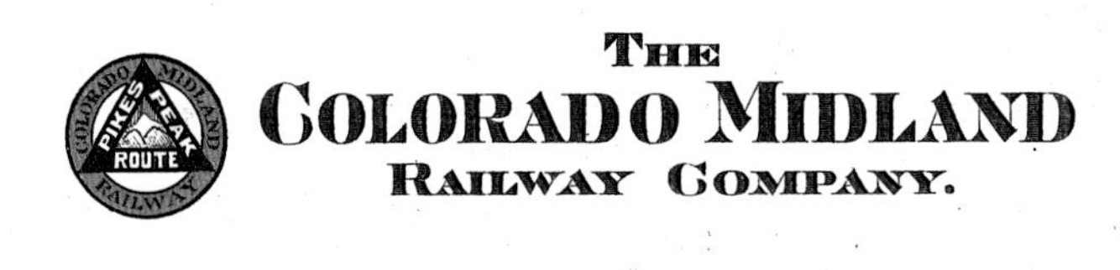

PASS Mrs. G. W. Kramer & Daughters-

1903

GENERAL MANAGER.

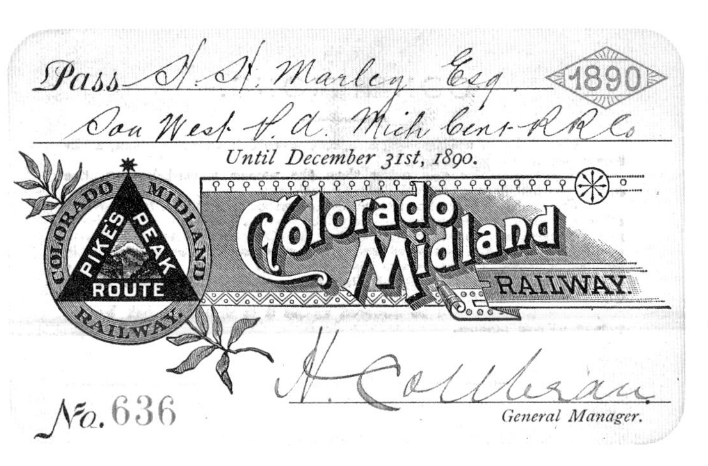

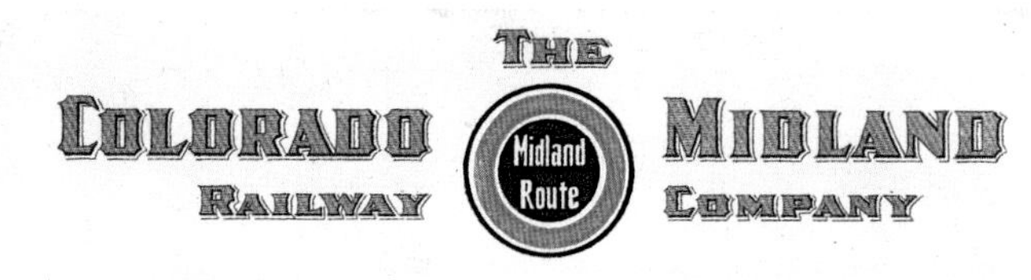

PASS **Mr. C. E. Hedrix,**

Train Master, St. J. & G. I. Ry.

UNTIL DECEMBER 31ST 1906 UNLESS OTHERWISE ORDERED.

GENERAL MANAGER.

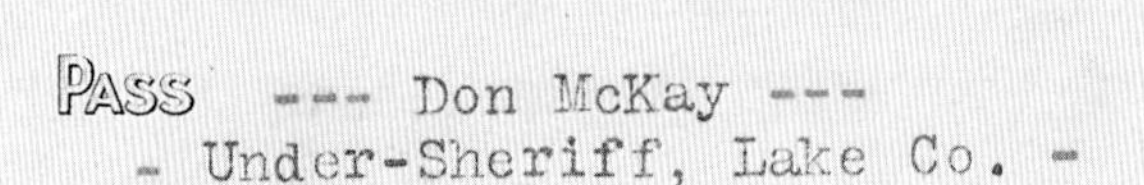

UNTIL DECEMBER 31ST 1908 UNLESS OTHERWISE ORDERED

THE

COLORADO MIDLAND

RAILWAY COMPANY

PASS Mr. J. J. Hagerman, -

- And Party in Special Car-

President, P. V. & N. R'y.

UNTIL DECEMBER 31ST 1900 UNLESS OTHERWISE ORDERED.

PRESIDENT.

A 267

PASS John Ward and 8 men

ACCOUNT Wreckers

UNTIL DECEMBER 31, 1918 BETWEEN ALL STATIONS

UNLESS OTHERWISE LIMITED BELOW SUBJECT TO CONDITIONS ON BACK

LIMITED (TERRITORY OR TIME):
BETWEEN COLORADO SPRINGS
AND NEWCASTLE

VALID WHEN COUNTERSIGNED BY MYSELF OR H. W. CONARD

COUNTERSIGNED BY

GENERAL MANAGER

Established in the summer of 1906, the Midland's dining car service equalled that of carriers many times its size. Observe that each place setting included seven pieces of silver flatware. (L.C. McClure, Denver Public Library Western History Dept.) On the opposite page is a selection of the many varieties of annual passes issued over the years. The 1900 pass is made out to CM founder J.J. Hagerman, who was by then president of the Pecos Valley & Northeastern in Texas. (Museum collection)

only prove what has already been said about them. The Rio Grande passenger schedules and services have been adequately covered in Jackson Thode's excellent article, entitled "A Century of Passenger Trains" published in the Brand Book of the Denver Westerners in 1972.

Mention should be made of the Colorado Midland's other rail passenger competitor, the famous old narrow gauge Denver South Park & Pacific—later the Denver Leadville & Gunnison and finally, the Colorado & Southern. This line was the shortest route between Denver and Leadville at 151 miles, but it had some horrendous four percent grades and surmounted the Continental Divide twice in its journey between the two terminals.

During Colorado Midland days, this narrow gauge line traditionally operated a daily passenger train between Denver and Leadville, leaving its respective terminals between 8 AM and 8:40 AM, and arriving at the other end from nine to ten hours later. Lunch was obtained by the passengers during the division point stop at Como.

In the early years, when passenger service was still being offered on the Como–Gunnison District, connections in both directions were maintained with these trains at Como. In 1892, for instance, a passenger from Denver at 8:30 AM could change at Como and arrive in Buena Vista at 5 PM. In the opposite direction, he could leave Buena Vista at 9 AM, and arrive Denver nine hours later. During most of the CM years, however, service on this line was composed of mixed trains, on a schedule that was inconvenient for much more than a purely local type of passenger travel.

Colorado Midland schedules in the Official Guide were published in two different styles over the years. From 1887 through the end of Santa Fe control in 1895, there were two station columns showing westbound and eastbound schedules separately, with the times of all trains reading down. After the summer of 1895 until the railroad ceased operations in 1918, there was a single column of stations, in the center of the table, with westbound trains reading down, and eastbound trains reading up. The Midland's own timetables often continued to show two station columns, with all trains reading down, regardless of direction.

The study of Colorado Midland schedules over the years often raises more questions than it answers, and the published timetables seem to contain inconsistencies and contradictions that just do not provide sound reasons or solutions for what is printed in them. Frequently, the schedules listed for various trains and the equipment listed for them do not agree, or equipment is listed for trains that are no longer shown in the schedule columns. There were times when there were more trains scheduled in one direction than in the other; in the case of the Colorado Springs–Cripple Creek trains this was true one year, but the next year the imbalance was reversed, and no ready explanation for this operation has been discovered. At other times, the equipment list has shown certain types of cars being handled in one direction, but not in the opposite direction, which causes one to wonder how the equipment was actually handled.

After the dining cars were placed in operation, and particularly toward the end of operations, the scheduling of the diners leaves one to wonder just how these were actually set up. During some of the later winter seasons, when Nos. 5 and 6 were operating, each train showed having a diner in service for the evening meal only. It was impossible for one diner to cover both trains, yet it also seems questionable that the railroad, in severe financial straits at the time, would operate two diners for these trains where meals were served for only about 90 minutes.

Another question is in connection with the Jerome Park schedules. For years, the schedule would indicate that one train ran from Cardiff to Gulch, and that another train ran from Gulch to Cardiff, each with a separate set of equipment. All available information, however, would indicate that these trains were always operated on a turnaround basis, from Cardiff to Gulch and return, yet the schedule, as published, contradicts this practice. The answer may lie in the fact that this was a misprint that was carried on for years before any correction was made. As pointed out in the yearly commentaries, this branch carried virtually no passengers except miners and their families, who would generally be aware of the railroad's arrangement to and from the Gulch and probably never had reason to look at the timetable.

Other errors of omission or commission are rampant through the years in these publications. Perhaps the longest lived error was that of the mileage between Arkansas Junction and Busk, which lasted in schedules for 17 years. Perhaps this was deliberate, in order to show a greater mileage in the timetable than the actual mileage, in an era when certain passenger fares were constructed on a mileage basis. This is not an unheard of practice, and in Switzerland it has been the normal thing to show both actual kilometers and "tariff" kilometers, due to the mountainous terrain that these railroads encounter.

Some of the errors and contradictions that run through Midland schedules are just plain misprints, and as this happens all the time, even in current productions, no particular concern is expressed over them. With respect to the other inconsistencies and contradictions as outlined above, when they have been uncovered in the individual schedules concerned, they are pointed out; but we make no claims that all of them have been found, and it is quite possible that some of them have escaped our attention completely. At any rate, some of these little matters will merely add to the legend of the Colorado Midland and will be grist for the mill for future discussions of the road's operations.

While we have been able to produce at least one schedule for every year that the road operated from the Official

FROM
GRAND JUNCTION
GLENWOOD SPRINGS

TO
DENVER
PUEBLO

Description of Coupon lifted, to be punched by Conductor.

FIRST O CLASS.
SECOND O CLASS.
ROUND O TRIP.
O CLERGY.
HALF O TICKET.
BAGGAGE O CHECKED.

Colorado Midland Railway — Midland Route

ISSUED BY
THE COLORADO MIDLAND RAILWAY COMPANY.
GEO. W. VALLERY, Receiver.
Account Atchison, Topeka & Santa Fe R'y.

Issued .... 19 .... *in exchange for*
.... *R. R.,*
Form .... *No.* ....

This Exchange Check entitles the holder to one passage from point punched under heading "FROM" to point punched under heading "TO" and of the class indicated by punch mark in margin.

It will not be honored after midnight of date cancelled in margin under heading "Final Limit."

34913

Form
D. E. C. 2.

General Passenger Agent.

Final Limit.		
JAN.	DAY	16
FEB.	1	17
MAR.	2	18
APR.	3	19
MAY	4	20
JUNE	5	21
JULY	6	22
AUG.	7	23
SEP	8	24
OCT.	9	25
NOV.	10	26
DEC.	11	27
1916	12	28
1917	13	29
1918	14	30
1919	15	31

On this and the next page are samples of Colorado Midland tickets. The length of a rail trip was reflected by the length of the coupon form tickets used. (Museum collection)

GOOD FOR

ONE PASSAGE

TO THE POINT AND OF THE CLASS DESIGNATED ON

COLORADO MIDLAND RAILWAY

When officially dated, stamped and presented with coupons attached.

SUBJECT TO THE FOLLOWING CONTRACT:

1st. In selling this ticket and checking baggage hereon, this company acts as agent, and is not responsible beyond its own line.

2d. It is subject to the STOP-OVER regulations of the lines over which it reads, and may be exchanged by conductors at any point for tickets or checks conforming to such regulations.

3d. It is VOID for passage if any alterations or erasures are made hereon, or if more than one date is canceled.

4th. If the coupons are punched or marked SECOND CLASS, the passenger is entitled to SECOND CLASS passage only otherwise FIRST CLASS.

5th. If limited as to time it will not be accepted for passage unless used to destination before midnight of the date canceled by "L" punch in margin hereof, and is subject to exchange, either in whole or part, at any point on the route for a continuous passage ticket or check

6th. Baggage will be transported subject to tariff regulations

7th. It is not transferable, and if presented by any other person than the original holder whose signature is hereon (in ink), it will be taken up and full fare collected.

8th. The holder will identify himself or herself as the original purchaser of this ticket by writing his or her name, or by other means if necessary, when required by conductors or agents.

NO AGENT OR EMPLOYE HAS POWER TO MODIFY THIS CONTRACT IN ANY PARTICULAR.

I hereby agree to all the conditions of the above Contract.

1933 1932 1931 1930 1929 1928 1927 1926 1925 1924 1923

16 31 | 15 30 | 14 29 | 13 28 | 12 27 | 11 26 | 10 25 | 9 24 | 8 23 | 7 22 | 6 21 | 5 20 | 4 19 | 3 18 | 2 17 | 1 DAY

JUN DEC | MAY NOV | APR OCT | MAR SEP | FEB AUG | JAN JUL

Purchaser

Witness

FORM 333 R.H. Wallace
Passenger Traffic Manager

COLORADO MIDLAND RAILWAY

DENVER or COLORADO SPRINGS

—TO—

Station Stamped or Written in Margin of this Coupon

On conditions named in contract ★

Destination

FORM 333 | FIRST CLASS Unless Stamped, Punched or Marked Otherwise NOT GOOD IF DETACHED

Via CRI&P, CM

CHIC., ROCK ISLAND & PACIFIC RY.

OMAHA or KANSAS CITY

—TO—

DENVER or COLORADO SPRINGS

On conditions named in contract. ★

FORM 333 | FIRST CLASS Unless Stamped, Punched or Marked Otherwise NOT GOOD IF DETACHED

Via CRI&P, CM

ISSUED BY COLORADO MIDLAND R.R.
Geo. W. Ristine, Receiver.

GOOD FOR ONE ADMISSION TO

LEADVILLE ICE PALACE.

Form SPECIAL 1.

VOID IF DETACHED from Railroad Ticket and after expiration of time limit of same.

ISSUED BY COLORADO MIDLAND R.R.
Geo. W. Ristine, Receiver.

GOOD FOR ONE ADMISSION TO

LEADVILLE ICE PALACE.

Form SPECIAL 1.

VOID IF DETACHED from Railroad Ticket and after expiration of time limit of same.

ISSUED BY

COLORADO MIDLAND RAILROAD.

GEO. W. RISTINE, Receiver.

GOOD FOR

One FIRST CLASS CONTINUOUS Passage

FROM

Station Stamped on Back

—TO—

LEADVILLE, Colo.

AND RETURN.

ACCOUNT

Crystal Carnival

1896

When Officially Stamped and presented with Coupons attached, subject to the following contract:

This ticket is not transferable, and if presented by other than the original purchaser, conductor will take it up and collect full fare. The holder will establish identity by signature or otherwise when so requested. This ticket will be honored for continuous passage only in each direction, going passage to begin not later than one day from date of sale stamped on back, and will be void for return passage after

....1896.

POSITIVELY NO STOP-OVERS WILL BE ALLOWED.

This ticket will be void should any alterations or erasures be made upon it, and no agent or other employe has the authority to change or waive any of the conditions of this contract.

Baggage liability limited to wearing apparel not exceeding one hundred dollars in value.

W.F. Bailey
Gen'l Pass'r Agent.

ISSUED BY COLORADO MIDLAND R.R.
Geo. W. Ristine, Receiver.

COLORADO MIDLAND RAILROAD.

LEADVILLE, Colo.

TO

Station Stamped on Back.

ON CONDITIONS NAMED IN CONTRACT.

FIRST CLASS CONTINUOUS PASSAGE.

Special 1. | Not good if Detached.

Via CM.

Guides, we have checked a great deal many more than that in an effort to determine when certain changes were made in schedules and equipment. There is one thing that is certain about the Colorado Midland—it was not static with respect to its schedules. Quite often, the road would change a schedule within a month of its publication, and, in some cases, these changes were of a significant nature and would have had a considerable effect on either the timings of the trains or the equipment that was carried by them. Some roads can have a pretty stable passenger operation for long periods of time, but this was certainly not true of the Colorado Midland, as schedules were constantly being adjusted. This policy, of course, merely adds to the fascination of the railroad, and the constantly changing panorama of its schedules adds spice to the survey of its passenger operations.

Just how fast did Colorado Midland passenger trains get over their mountainous route between Colorado Springs and Grand Junction? The slowest timing in the road's history was in 1891, when the one eastbound train took over 18 hours to make the trip, an average speed of about 17.3 MPH. The fastest ever schedule was just nine years later, when No. 6 managed to cover the railroad in just under 11 hours, for an average of 27 MPH, which was certainly a remarkable performance when all things are considered. As a rule of thumb, the Colorado Midland maintained schedules for a number of years that flirted with 12 hour running times. This produced an average speed of 24.8 MPH, and was not too shabby for the period.

SAVE ONE BUSINESS DAY

IMPORTANT TIME CARD CHANGES

THE COLORADO MIDLAND RAILWAY

WILL OPERATE COMMENCING MAY 7TH AND
EASTBOUND ON MORNING TRAIN MAY 8TH

DOUBLE DAILY PASSENGER TRAIN SERVICE

EASTBOUND LEAVE Leadville, 8:55 AM and 9:45 PM

Arrive Colorado Springs 3.00 P. M. and 3.50 A. M.
Arrive Denver 5.50 P. M. and 7.00 A. M.

WESTBOUND LEAVE Leadville 5:00 AM and 6:50 PM

Arrive Grand Junction 12.30 Noon and 2.30 A. M. Trains Westbound Leave Denver 9.00 A. M. and 7.45 P.M. Leave Colorado Springs 12.20 Noon and 10.45 P. M.

DINING CARS—CHAIR CARS—PULLMAN SLEEPING CARS
Let us explain this excellent new service by telephone, letter or a personal call.

C. B. Carter,
Agent,
Leadville, Colo.

This handbill announced the resumption of two trains daily out of Leadville in each direction in the spring of 1916. No one could have foreseen that the demise of the Colorado Midland was just two years away. (Museum collection)

Included in this study is an attempt to show the chronological development of the passenger car fleet, as well as the locomotive roster, especially in connection with the passenger service engines. Much of the car fleet was purchased in the first year of the road's operations, but it underwent a number of rebuildings as conditions changed, and the requirement for certain types of cars also changed. These have been documented as much as possible for the individual years that such rebuildings or conversions took place. It should be noted that the Colorado Midland was essentially a "wooden" railroad—all of its passenger cars were built of wood and only in its last years did it construct steel underframe cars, no doubt at the insistence of the post office authorities. The Midland did handle all-steel baggage and express cars belonging to other railroads, but passenger-carrying cars were of wooden construction. Even the Pullman sleeping cars that operated over the line were usually made of wood, although in later years, steel underframe Pullmans were used, as well as the tourist sleepers that the road handled for many years. Mel McFarland, in *The Midland Route*, lists at least 34 Pullman sleepers by name that were moved over Midland rails, primarily from repair records of cars that had been damaged on the CM, so it is quite certain that a great many more than this were operated during the lifetime of the railroad. The most famous cars assigned to the Midland in the early years of the Twentieth Century were no doubt the *Tryphena* and *Tryphosa*, observation sleeping cars that operated between Denver and Ogden, usually in trains No. 5 and 4. The Midland itself, however, never owned any sleepers, but relied on the Pullman Company for its cars.

The locomotive fleet is also shown in chronological order, and includes the changes made to the individual engines in the year that these occurred, particularly with respect to the engines used in passenger service.

CORPORATE HISTORY

This survey makes no pretensions to being a history of the Colorado Midland, as that subject has been adequately covered by both Morris Cafky and Mel McFarland in their respective books on the CM and its history. It might be well, however, to sketch the corporate history of the railroad, if for nothing more than being able to determine when the terms "Railroad" and "Railway" were applicable during the course of this study, and it is set out in the table at right:

No.	Name	Incorporated	Succession	Note
1.	Colorado Midland Railway Company (1883)	11/23/83	Consolidated 12/1/93 with No. 2 to form No. 3	A
2.	Aspen Short Line Railway Company	11/15/88	Consolidated 12/1/93 with No. 1 to form No. 3	B
3.	The Colorado Midland Railroad Company (1893)	12/1/93	Sold at foreclosure on 9/8/97: Property conveyed to No. 5 on 10/30/97	C
4.	The Busk Tunnel Railway Company	6/16/90	Sold 1/2/1900 to No. 5	D
5.	The Colorado Midland Railway Company (1897)	10/11/97	Sold at foreclosure on 4/21/17 and reorganized on 5/31/17 as No. 6	E
6.	The Colorado Midland Railroad Company (1917)	5/31/17	Operation discontinued on 8/5/18. Divide – Gramid abandoned and taken up in 1921. Company dissolved 5/21/22	F

Note A – AT&SF acquired majority of common stock by agreement signed September 5, 1890 and controlled CM Ry. (1883) until 12/1/93, when it was consolidated with No. 2 to form CM RR (1893). AT&SF continued in control until the time shown in Note C.

Note B – The Aspen Short Line Railway constructed a new line from Crystal Lake for 6.6 miles to a junction with the original mainline 3.8 miles west of Leadville, which was completed early in 1889. This junction was named Arkansas Junction, and was destined to become an important operating location on the CM. The Aspen Short Line Railway was consolidated on 12/1/93 with the original Colorado Midland Railway (1883), to become The Colorado Midland Railroad (1893).

Note C – Colorado Midland Railroad (1893) was operated by its own organization under the control of the AT&SF, until 2/2/94. From that date until 5/1/95, it was operated by receivers of the AT&SF, who were also appointed to the same position on the CM. On 5/1/95, the AT&SF receivers were discharged with respect to the CM, and a new receiver appointed who was solely responsible for the property of the CM (1893).

Note D – The property of the Busk Tunnel Railway Company was operated by the CM Ry (1883) and successors from October 1893 to the date of sale, 1/2/00, except for the period from 11/1/97 to 6/25/99, when it was not operated.

Note E – CM Ry. (1897) was operated by its own organization until 12/13/12, and by a receiver from that date to the date of reorganization on 5/31/17. After the cancellation of the lease with the Busk Tunnel Railway, CM Ry. (1897), 9.83 miles of track from Busk to near Ivanhoe, via Hagerman Pass was operated from 11/1/97 to 6/25/99, and CM Ry. (1897) purchased the Busk Tunnel Railway on 1/2/00. Control of CM Ry. (1897) was acquired jointly by the Colorado & Southern, and the Rio Grande Western, on 7/2/00. The Denver & Rio Grande acquired control of the Rio Grande Western, 7/01, thus becoming a half-owner of CM Ry. (1897).

Note F – CM RR (1917) was operated by its own organization 5/31/17 to 6/30/18. A receiver was appointed 7/1/18 and operated the property until 8/5/18 when its operation was discontinued by court order. CM RR (1917) was dissolved 5/21/22.

It should also be noted that Colorado Midland Railway and Denver & Rio Grande Railway jointly incorporated the Rio Grande Junction Railway in June 1889. The RGJ constructed 62.091 miles of line between Rifle and Grand Junction in 1890, and the trains of both railroads were operated over this line. By agreement, both of the owning roads had access to the industries served by the RGJ, and, in all respects, each road operated over the RGJ as though it was its own track. The CM also obtained trackage rights from the D&RG from Gramid, just west of New Castle, to Rifle, as well as trackage rights within the terminal area of Grand Junction, for a total of 14.46 miles. For operating convenience, the RGJ controlled and dispatched all trains between New Castle and Grand Junction, and trackage between those points will be treated and referred to as the Rio Grande Junction in this study. The CM Ry. (1897) sold its interest in the RGJ to the D&RG on 11/13/12, but retained all rights of operation and access to traffic as before. The RGJ remained in existence until 1947, when it was merged into the Denver & Rio Grande Western.

PHYSICAL CHARACTERISTICS

The Colorado Midland was truly a mountain railroad, and this was no more apparent than right from its beginning at Colorado Springs and its proximity to the Front Range of the Rocky Mountains. From an elevation of 6000 feet at Colorado Springs, the line started to climb on a grade of 1.20% up to its yard, engine house and operating headquarters at Colorado City, milepost three from Colorado Springs. From the yards, the grade immediately increased to three percent as it progressed up the Fountain Creek Valley toward Manitou. After passing the station at Manitou, which was on the south side of the valley well above the rest of the town, the line went through tunnels one and two and then curved over the large Engelmann Canon viaduct to the station at Manitou Iron Springs.

At the Iron Springs the line started up the most severe mainline grade it was to encounter—four percent for the next 4.6 miles to Cascade Canon. This portion of the road also went through six tunnels while it struggled up Ute Pass. The grade eased somewhat after Cascade Canon to a mere 2.23% to Green Mountain Falls, then increased to a three percent climb from there to Divide, at an elevation of 9198 feet.

From Divide the road dropped down a three percent grade to Florissant, where a helper station was maintained during the lifetime of the CM. The line continued downgrade at a 1.64% clip to Lake George before it started up through Eleven Mile Canon in grades ranging between two and 2.15% to Idlewild, where it emerged from the canon and entered the wide expanse of South Park. Although the maximum grade between Idlewild and Spinney was 1.10%, the balance of the road across South Park varied between .50% and .95%, relatively minor gradients, as it ascended the river grade of the South Platte. At Haver, however, the line climbed at a rate of two percent up to Bath over Trout Creek Pass, crossing the narrow gauge line of the Denver South Park & Pacific (later Denver Leadville & Gunnison and Colorado & Southern). From Bath, at an elevation of 9516 feet, the line descended into the Arkansas River Valley on a grade of 1.65%, past the station for Buena Vista, high on the side of the hill east of town, and thence into Wild Horse at the foot of the grade. This was another helper station for the CM in both directions. From Wild Horse the line ascended the grade of the Arkansas River, varying between 1.42% and 1.65%, to Crystal Lake (later called Snowden). As the D&RG had already taken the line of least resistance along the river, the CM was forced to build on a higher level, and this portion of the road included four tunnels within a distance of .36 mile. At Granite, the CM crossed both the river and the D&RG on a bridge, and then went up the west side of the river to Crystal Lake. At this point the original mainline again crossed back to the east side of the valley and the D&RG, winding along the hillside as it climbed up to the cloud city of Leadville, on

Reproduced here and through page 26 is a station-by-station route guide handed out to train passengers. These folders are an interesting amalgam of factual information and advertising hyperbole. (Museum collection)

ALTITUDES OF COLORADO MOUNTAINS.

Field work by the United States Geological Survey during the past summer has made some changes in the former figures giving the elevations of the principal mountains of the state. The following table shows the most recent measurements, with the authority for same:

MOUNTAIN	ALT	AUTHORITY	MOUNTAIN	ALT.	AUTHORITY
Mt. Massive	14,424	U. S. Geol.	Mt. Yale	14,187	Hayden
Mt. Elbert	14,421	U.S.C.G.S.	Mt. Ross	14,184	Not Known
Gray's Peak	14,411	Hayden	Old Baldy	14,176	Hayden
Sierra Blanca	14,400	U. S. Geol.	Goat's Peak	14,132	Not Known
Mt. Harvard	14,375	Hayden	Democrat Mt.	14,125	Not Known
La Plata Mt	14,342	U. S. Geol.	Pike's Peak	14,108	U.S.C.G.S.
Mt. Rosalie	14,340	Hayden	San Luis Peak	14,100	Hayden
Torrey's Peak	14,336	Hayden	Red Cloud Peak	14,092	Wheeler
Mt. Evans	14,330	Hayden	San Miguel Mt.	14,075	Not Known
Mt. Sopris	14,300	U. S. Geol.	Wetterhorn	14,069	Wheeler
Mt. Lincoln	14,297	Hayden	Culebra Peak	14,069	Hayden
Uncompahgre Peak	14,289	U.S.C.G.S.	Simpson Peak	14,065	Wheeler
Mt. Wilson	14,280	U. S. Geol.	R. G. Pyramid	14,055	Hayden
Long's Peak	14,271	Hayden	Mt. Æolus	14,054	Hayden
Quandary	14,266	U. S. Geol.	Needle Mt.	14,051	Not Known
Castle Peak	14,259	U. S. Geol	Humboldt Peak	14,041	Not Known
Mt. Antero	14,245	Hayden	Stewart Peak	14,032	Hayden
Mt Sneffles	14,240	Not Known	Handies' Peak	14,008	U.S.C.G.S.
Mt. Shavano	14,230	Hayden	Mt. Sherman	14,008	U. S. Geol.
Creston Peak	14,233	Hayden	Mt. Holy Cross	14,006	U. S. Geol.
Mt. Princeton	14,190	Not Known	Maroon Peak	14,003	U. S. Geol.
			Cameron Mt.	14,000	Not Known

Some of the well-known peaks below 14,000 feet are given new readings:

MOUNTAIN	ALT	AUTHORITY	MOUNTAIN	ALT	AUTHORITY
Mt. Ouray	13,956	U.S.C.G.S.	E. Spanish Peak	12,708	U. S. Geol.
Silver Heels	13,855	U. S. Geol.	W. Spanish Peak	13,622	U. S. Geol.
Mt. Arkansas	13,807	U. S. Geol.	Homestake Peak	13,227	U. S. Geol.

OBJECTS OF INTEREST

DENVER Altitude, 5,200 feet.

Capitol of the State. Many objects and points of interest, all reached by electric cars. Magnificent view of over 200 miles of mountain ranges. Colorado Midland trains leave from commodious union station in center of city. All car lines transfer to this point without extra charge.

SKIRTING THE RANGE

Between Denver and Colorado Springs the train runs for seventy-four miles in sight of a gorgeous array of the lofty monarchs of the Rockies. Long's, Gray's, Torrey's, Pike's and the Spanish Peaks are all in plain view, and the traveler is not for one moment out of sight of eternal snow.

PALMER LAKE Altitude, 7,200 feet.

The track from Denver to Palmer Lake is a gradual ascent, scarcely noticed by the passenger. The lake is a pretty sheet of water on the divide just above Colorado Springs. The drop to the latter place is somewhat more lively, and the train rushes rapidly to the base of Pike's Peak.

COLORADO SPRINGS Altitude, 6,000 feet.

A famous all-the-year health resort, the home of hundreds of very wealthy men and women, who find here certain relief from asthmatic and lung affections. The home of succesful mining men, who operate not only in Cripple Creek, but all over the United States. Pike's Peak, Cheyenne Mountain, Bald Mountain, Cameron's Cone and the Rampart Range in full view.

COLORADO CITY Altitude, 6,085 feet.

"Old Town," first capitol of the state. Colorado Midland shop and yards are located here. Large chlorination works on left just after leaving depot Here the gold is extracted from the low-grade Cripple Creek ores. Other reduction works and smelters also located here.

GARDEN OF THE GODS Altitude, 6,410 feet.

Just after passing the reduction works the train runs in sight of the famous Garden of the Gods, where the awful forces of nature have played strange pranks with the rocks.

MANITOU Altitude, 6,442 feet.

World-famed health and summer resort, where hundreds of springs of highly carbonated water bubble and gush from the ground. The largest soda spring in the world just below station. Fine hotels open all the year. Magnificent drives and rambles through canons.

MANITOU IRON SPRINGS Altitude, 6,552 feet.

Several large groups of ice-cold water, from which carbonic gas splashes and bubbles. Fine pavilion and hotel. Cog road depot just above Colorado Midland "High Bridge." Iron springs on left and Manitou on right of train.

UTE PASS Altitude, 6,600 to 9,000 feet.

From Manitou Iron Springs to Woodland Park the line is built on solid rock roadbed, dug, mainly, on the left, or southern, side of the narrow gorge. "Horseshoe Curve" in Ute Pass carriage road on right, a mile above Iron Springs station. "Lion's Head Cut" on left, at narrowest point in canon. Road ascends on grade of four per cent., or 211 feet to the mile. The Fountaine Qui Bouille (boiling water), a mountain stream, fed by the snows on Pike's Peak, descends the Pass.

CASCADE CANON Altitude, 7,421 feet.

Summer resort. Hotel Ramona, Cascade House and canon to the left. Starting point of carriage road to top of Pike's Peak, distance eighteen miles.

UTE PARK Altitude, 7,511 feet.

Summer resort. Artificial lake on right, numerous cottages on both sides.

GREEN MOUNTAIN FALLS Altitude, 7,734 feet.

Summmer resort near head of the Pass. One of the most beautiful points in the West. Three streams descend the precipitous sides of the canon to the bottom, a fall of over 2,000 feet. Comfortable hotels, numerous cotages, and long rows of tents for the accommodation of the summer tourist.

PIKE'S PEAK Altitude, 14,108 feet.

Northern side in full view, to the left, after leaving Green Mountain Falls. A glorious sight.

WOODLAND PARK Altitude, 8,484 feet.

On the mesa at the head of the Ute Pass. Woodland Hotel to the right; splendid view of the mountains, including Pike's Peak.

MANITOU PARK Altitude, 8,500 feet.

Six miles from Woodland Park station, to the right; Concord stage, four-in-hand, meets train.

grades averaging about 1.8% to an elevation of 10,103 feet.

From Leadville, the line dropped back down to the Arkansas River Valley on a grade of three percent. At the foot of this hill was the location of Arkansas Junction, which came into being with the construction of the Aspen Short Line Railroad in January 1889, from Crystal Lake (Snowden). Grades on the Aspen Short Line reached a maximum of 1.65% up to Arkansas Junction. This short cut eliminated 4.8 miles of mainline running for through traffic, as well as 1206 feet of rise and fall via Leadville. One thing the CM did not need was another hill to climb.

Arkansas Junction was the beginning of the climb over the Continental Divide, and the line ascended at a rate of 3.24% up to Busk. It then continued up on a looping route that included the great curved wooden trestle and numerous snowsheds, past Rogers Spur, and on up to Hagerman Tunnel at an elevation of 11,528 feet. The grade from Busk to Hagerman station just west of the tunnel appears to work out to an average of 2.57%, probably compensated for all of the curvature encountered on this climb. Hagerman Tunnel was 2060 feet in length and was the highest point reached by the Colorado Midland. From Hagerman, the road dropped down on another

EDLOWE Altitude, 8,923 feet.
Near the summit of Hayden Divide. Noted for its beautiful wild flowers. Magnificent view to the left, with Pike's Peak in the distance.

DIVIDE Altitude, 9,198 feet.
From Divide the Midland Terminal Railroad leads to Cripple Creek gold camp, all trains making close connections.

CRIPPLE CREEK Altitude, 9,396 feet.
The most noted mining camp of this day. Thirty miles south of Divide, reached via the Midland Terminal Railway. A beautiful ride through the Pike's Peak region.

FLORISSANT CANON Altitude, 8,200 feet.
Descent from (Hayden's) Divide to South Platte River. Some beautiful rocky views, full of interest. Wonderful shale beds on left of train, where petrified and fossiled leaves, ferns, bugs and flowers may be gathered in a few minutes' search.

FLORISSANT Altitude, 8,194 feet.
To right on leaving station. Forest of petrified wood and wonderful crystal and agate formations, from Nature's laboratory, near road. Source of the famous Florissant Topaz. Enormous petrified stump of redwood tree, four miles south of track.

LAKE GEORGE Altitude, 8,085 feet.
To the right. A beautiful mountain lake, formed in bend of South Platte River, right at entrance to

ELEVEN-MILE OR GRANITE CANON
Altitude, 8,085 feet.
One of the most picturesque canons in the West. Along the Platte River, Dome Rock on right, about half way. Note the granite walls and boulders, seamed and seared as they were from the day of upheaval.

IDLEWILD Altitude, 8,477 feet.
Entrance to the "South Park," the Bayou Salada of the fur traders. Formerly the home of countless thousands of fur-bearing animals. A great treeless plain with mountain ranges on all sides.

FRESHWATER Altitude, 8,571 feet.
Station in the rich and fertile South Park or Platte Valley, producing minerals of all kind, lime and lumber, and sustaining great herds of cattle. A great stock country. Magnificent water-fowl shooting in fall and autumn; good trout fishing in the summer. Stage from here to the Freshwater mining district, sixteen miles south.

SPINNEY Altitude, 8,652 feet.
Great hay and cattle shipping point, on the Platte River. Note the number of times the railroad crosses the river.

HARTSEL
In South Park. Noted hot springs with great curative powers. Spring and river to left, and hotel on right. Stage from here to Alma and Fairplay.

HAVER Altitude, 8,991 feet.
New mining district to the left, known as Badger Creek and Whitehorn. Crossing the ridge from the South Park and Platte Valley to Trout Creek Valley.

BATH Altitude, 9,528 feet.
Notice the altitude. View of Buffalo Peaks and Park range to the right.

NEWETT Altitude, 9,105 feet.
Mining town; inexhaustible supply of limestone, used by smelters for fluxing.

BUENA VISTA Altitude, 8,248 feet.
In the valley of the Arkansas River, to the left, Collegiate Range; Mt. Princeton, 14,190 feet, Mt. Yale, 14,187 feet; Mt. Harvard, 14,375 feet, back of the town and easily distinguished. Cottonwood Springs and Lake at base of peaks, eight miles away. A noble view of the beautiful valley of the Arkansas.

WILD HORSE Altitude, 8,081 feet.
On the rise to Leadville, along the Arkansas River. Sphinx Rock, a wonderful monolith, rises from the plain on the left of the track, about three miles west of Buena Vista station.

BARRE Altitude, 8,597 feet.
Lumber, agricultural and cattle lands; lime burning, etc., in the vicinity. Mining in the mountains, of which there are fine views from here.

GRANITE Altitude, 8,959 feet.
Mining town in the Arkansas Valley. Great placer mines; signs of sluice and hydraulic mining can be seen.

TWIN LAKES Altitude, 9,333 feet.
Ten miles distant from station of same name. Largest lakes in the mountains; fine fishing and attractive summer resort. Good hotel accommodations during the season.

LEADVILLE Altitude, 10,103 feet.
Greatest mining camp in the world. Production of gold and silver up to January 1, 1907, $389,000,000. A wonderful view of the mountains, mines and smelters in every direction. Two miles above sea level.

EVERGREEN LAKES Altitude, 10,000 feet.
Five miles west of Leadville, reached by a magnificent boulevard. Fine fishing and boating. Famous iron and soda springs. United States fish hatcheries and grounds, the most complete in the world.

MT. MASSIVE Altitude, 14,424 feet.
The highest mountain in Colorado, near to and in plain view of Leadville, easy of access, and summit never known to have been without its covering of snow.

ARKANSAS JUNCTION Altitude, 9,706 feet.
Foot of mountains on the head waters of the Arkansas River. The climb over the Continental Divide commences here.

TURQUOISE LAKE Altitude, 10,000 feet.
To the right of the train. Highest artificial lake in the world, contains six billion gallons of water for use in great C. F. & I. steel works at Pueblo, over 150 miles away. Reservoir contains 2,200 acres.

BUSK Altitude, 10,805 feet.
Eastern end of the two-mile-long Busk Tunnel. From here the waters find their way into the Gulf of Mexico through the Arkansas and Mississippi rivers.

looping route to Ivanhoe, on grades averaging 2.84%. The High Line over Hagerman Pass was only used for about six years, until the Busk-Ivanhoe Tunnel was placed in service late in 1893. Due to a dispute with the tunnel company, the High Line was again placed in service from late 1897 until June 1899. After the tunnel company was purchased by the CM in 1900, the High Line was abandoned and torn up later in the year.

The Busk Tunnel was 1.78 miles in length and on a rising grade of 1.41% from Busk to Ivanhoe, with the latter becoming the new high point on the railroad at an elevation of 10,944 feet. The total mileage of the Busk Tunnel Railway was 2.9 miles.

Helper engines from both directions were cut off at Ivanhoe and, after turning, went back to their terminals at Arkansas Junction or Basalt. The rising grade through the tunnel for westbound trains caused many problems with smoke and gas, and the tunnel was notoriously slow in clearing after a train had passed through.

From Ivanhoe the line descended on grades varying between 2.50% and 3.01% all the way to Basalt, past Hell Gate, the coking village of Sellar, around the loop at Nast

IVANHOE Altitude, 10,944 feet.
Western end of Busk Tunnel, on the western slope of the Rockies; Loch Ivanhoe, one of the highest lakes in the land, on the left; source of Frying Pan River, the great trout stream, which empties in the Pacific.

HELL GATE Altitude, 10,540 feet.
One of the most magnificent views in the world. Rugged chasm in the mountains, with cliffs 2,000 feet sheer descent. The train goes around fourteen miles in order to descend one-half mile.

SELLAR Altitude, 9,616 feet.
Numerous charcoal pits. Grand view on the left of Mt. Nast and the valley of the Frying Pan.

NAST—NORRIE Altitude, 8,454 feet.
Mountain points on the Frying Pan River. Excellent hunting and fishing, with mining in the mountains. Lumber regions; timber cut largely for fuel and charcoal. Hotel and cottages at Nast afford good accommodations for tourist.

THOMASVILLE Altitude, 8,003 feet.
Smelter to right of train. Noted for its great variety of wild flowers. Great lumber point. Fine fishing and hunting. Lime rock in inexhaustible quantities, which is shipped to Leadville and Aspen and used for fluxing purposes by smelters.

WOOD'S LAKE Altitude, 9,200 feet.
Eight miles north of Thomasville. Beautiful resort situated at foot of mountain peaks over 14,000 feet high. Finest fishing in state. Deer, bear, duck and other fowel in abundance.

RUEDI HOPKINS SLOANE
Altitude, 7, 585 feet. Altitude, 7,184 feet.
Magnificent scenery; massive red granite cliffs towering on either side of the narrow canon, with the brawling mountain stream at their foot. The railroad closely follows the windings of the river.

RED ROCK CANON Altitude, 7,500 feet.
A most magnificently colored canon; mountains on either side, towering towards the skies, their slopes covered with bright green, broken by cliffs of red granite. Scenery mainly on the right, with Frying Pan River winding through.

PEACH BLOW Altitude, 6,800 feet.
Wonderful quarries of finest building stone in the world. So called on account of the delicate coloring of the rocks.

SEVEN CASTLES Altitude, 7,400 feet.
Three miles from Peach Blow and on right of train. Massive cliffs of red sandstone, shaped like ancient castles.

BASALT Altitude, 6,614 feet.
Where Frying Pan and Roaring Fork Rivers meet. Snow Mass Mountain in plain view on the right. Junction with branch line to Aspen, eighteen miles distant. Dining room and lunch counter.

ASPEN Altitude. 7,950 feet.
The greatest silver mining camp in Colorado. The location of the two richest silver mines in the world—Mollie Gibson and Smuggler mines.

WHEELER—BRYANT Altitude, 6,371 feet.
On the Roaring Fork. Elk Mountain on left; agricultural and lumber country; proposed branch line to Elk Mountains starts from Bryant.

CARBONDALE Altitude, 6,200 feet.
Beautiful little mountain town, nestling at the foot of Mount Sopris. The outfitting point for the Crystal River country. Daily train to Crystal. Elegant trout fishing; deer, elk and bear hunting in easy reach.

MOUNT SOPRIS Altitude, 14,300 feet.
Artists have declared that no more impressive view of mountain scenery exists in the world than the sight of Mount Sopris from the car windows of the Colorado Midland—the peak being in plain view and but ten miles distant.

CARDIFF Altitude, 5,940 feet.
Great coke ovens to left; coal shafts and mines on all sides. Coaling point for Colorado Mindland Railway.

JEROME PARK
Reached only by branch line of the Colorado Midland from Cardiff; one of the finest of the natural parks in the State; scenery unsurpassed; coal-mining country.

GLENWOOD SPRINGS Altitude, 5,800 feet.
Greatest hot springs in the world; at Junction of Roaring Fork and Grand River. Bath house cost $500,000; swimming pool 700 feet long and 110 feet wide, all warm water. Good hotels and splendid resort. Through passengers will do well to stop over here for a rest. Stop-over privileges given on both railroad and Pullman tickets.

SOUTH CANON Altitude, 5,033 feet.
Along the Grand river. Some of the largest coal mines in the West are located here. Train follows river in its windings through the mountains.

NEW CASTLE Altitude, 5,574 feet.
Great coal mines and thriving little city; home of the famous "Sunshine" coal, and one of the outfitting points for the hunting and fishing grounds on White River. Here we practically leave the mountains for the plains of the Grand River Valley.

SILT—ANTLERS Altitude, 5,350 feet.
On plains of valley of Grand river, the home of the most productive orchards in the world.

AKIN—TUNNEL—CAMEO Altitude, 4,800 feet.
Growing towns which are made rich by irrigation of once barren lines in this section of the state.

RIFLE Altitude, 5,310 feet.
On right bank of Grand River. White River plateau, sixty miles to north, with stages from Rifle. Lumber, mining and agriculture. Great hunting country. Bear, deer, elk and mountain sheep.

GRAND VALLEY Altitude, 5,400 feet.
Great fruit country; under irrigation; the "Little Book Cliffs" to the right.

and down the valley of Frying Pan Creek through Thomasville, Ruedi, Peach Blow and Basalt. This was not only a helper station but also a division point until November 1907 and the junction for the branch to Aspen. From Basalt the line descended the Roaring Fork on grades of 1.25% to 1.15% through Cardiff, which became the division point in November 1907, and on to West Glenwood. Here a spur, with the switch facing west, crossed the Roaring Fork to the station at Glenwood Springs. Because the switch faced west, westbound trains backed from West Glenwood to the station, while eastbound trains headed into the station and then reversed to the junction switch on the other side of the Roaring Fork.

Leaving West Glenwood, the line followed the south side of the Grand River, descending at a rate varying between 1.25% and .74%, to a point just east of New Castle. Here it crossed the river and the D&RG at grade into the joint station at New Castle, at an elevation of 5574 feet, the lowest point on the CM proper. At a point .8 mile west of the station at New Castle, the CM joined the D&RG at Gramid (a contraction of "Grande" and "Midland"). From this point, the CM had trackage rights over

DE BEQUE — Altitude, 4,945 feet.

Fine peach and apple orchards, with other fruits. Irrigation ditches on all sides. Finest deer hunting in the world on the mesa twenty miles north. Stage to the Plateau Valey, south.

GLEN BEULAH PARK — Altitude, 6,000 feet.

Twenty miles north of De Beque, at the base of the Little Book Cliffs, lies a natural park, in which hundreds of head of deer are breeding. On mesa above, thousands of deer roam and make finest sport imaginable. Bear, elk and mountain lions in fair supply for those who care for that kind of game. Horses, wagons and guides may be hired, at reasonable rates, at De Beque.

PALISADE — Altitude, 4,741 feet.

Thriving and up-to-date community in center of rich fruit growing country. Note results achieved in this country by use of irrigation.

GRAND JUNCTION — Altitude, 4,580 feet.

Western terminus of Colorado Midland Railway, at the junction of the Grand and Gunnison rivers. Center of the fruit plains of the Grand River Valley; a thriving little city with all modern improvements.

RIO GRANDE WESTERN RAILWAY.

FRUITA — Altitude, 4,542 feet.

In the Grand Valley; noted for great fruit growing district.

CREVASSE

Entrance to the mountains along the Grand River. The scenery on both sides is very fine.

UTAH LINE — Altitude, 4,758 feet.

Here the train crosses from Colorado into Utah. On the right, high up on the bluff, is painted the striking sign, COLORADO-UTAH.

WESTWATER — COTTONWOOD — Altitude, 4,602 feet.

The edge of the desert is now reached and the river is lost to sight. Book Cliffs to the right and snow caps in the distance.

AGATE — CISCO — THOMPSON'S — Altitude, 5,140 feet.

Interesting points on the sand plains. At Thompson's, the water, which is brought six miles, has made a beautiful oasis of the spot.

GREEN RIVER — Altitude, 4,060 feet.

An oasis in the desert, with the majestic river on its way to join the Grand and form the great Colorado River.

DESERT — LOWER CROSSING — Altitude, 4,630 feet.
WELLINGTON — PRICE — Altitude, 5,547 feet.

There are many interesting sights between these points—mountains on all sides and the great plains between. The Wasatch Range, with its snow caps, looms up in the distance. Water is scarce and vegetation scant.

HELPER — Altitude, 5,857 feet.

On Price River—end of second division. Dining station. The ascent of the canons of the Price River commences here.

CASTLE GATE — Altitude, 6,257 feet.

Large coal mines, which supply the road. Above the town is the wonderful Castle Gate, one of the greatest sights in the West. The best view is from the rear platform.

P. V. JUNCTION — Altitude, 7,177 feet.

Branch line, eighteen miles to Pleasant Valley coal mines.

SOLDIER'S SUMMIT — Altitude, 7,465 feet.

The highest point between Grand Junction and Salt Lake. Upon the mountain, nearly 10,000 feet above the sea level, lies buried one of Albert Sidney Johnston's soldiers who fell in the "Mormon war."

THISTLE JUNCTION — Altitude, 5,050 feet.

San Pete ranch of the Rio Grande Western Railway to the quarries and ranches of the San Pete Valley.

CASTILLA SPRINGS — Altitude, 4,920 feet.

Bath houses and hotels on the right; wonderful springs. A great health resort.

SPRINGVILLE — UTAH LAKE

Through the beautiful Utah Valley. Provo is an important manufacturing point. The largest woolen mills in the West are located here. Rich and fertile country. On the left the beautiful Utah Lake can be seen stretching westward for miles, with the Wasatch Mountains on the far side.

SALT LAKE CITY — Altitude, 4,220 feet.

The Mormon Zion. Capitol of Utah. One of the most beautiful cities in the world. The great Temple is seen for miles before the city is reached; glimpses of the Great Salt Lake are caught from time to time. Population, 55,000. There are many points of interest to be visited here.

OGDEN — Altitude, 4,286 feet.

Terminus of the line. Population, 20,000, and a live, go-ahead city, appropriately called the "Marvel of the Desert." It lies on th edge of the alkali plains of the Great American Desert.

Full information will be furnished upon application to any of the agents of the Company, or to

G. W. Vallery, General Manager............Denver, Colo.
H. C. Bush, Traffic Manager...............Denver, Colo.
C. H. Speers, General Passenger Agent......Denver, Colo.
E. D. Whitley, C. T. A., 17th st., cor. Calif..Denver, Colo.
J. J. Killeen, C.P.A., 17th st., cor. California.Denver, Colo.
P. J. Murphy, C. F. A., 17th st., cor. Calif., Denver, Colo.
N. L. Drew, G. A., 9 N. Tejon st...Colorado Springs, Colo.
C. D. Simonson, G. E. A., 425 Broadway, New York, N. Y.
Herbert Bonsor, T.F.& P.A., 425 Br'dway, New York, N.Y.
H. W. Jackson, Gen. Agt., 107 Adams st......Chicago, Ill.
A. E. Brown, T. F. & P. A., 107 Adams st....Chicago, Ill.
F. S. Kingore, C. F. & P. A., 107 Adams st.....Chicago, Ill.
O. F. Spindler, D.F.& P.A., 522 Park Bldg...Pittsburg, Pa.
J. H. Davis, D. F. & P. A., 839 Pierce Bldg., St. Louis, Mo.
F. L. Feakins, Gen. Agt., 219 So. 14th st.....Omaha, Neb.
M. R. Sutton, G. A., 566 Sheidley bldg...Kansas City, Mo.
C. M. Keck, Passenger Agent.....Glenwood Springs, Colo.
R. E. Vickery, General Agent.......Grand Junction, Colo.
L. H. Harding, G. A., 77 W. 2nd So. st., Salt Lake, Utah.
W. B. Throckmorton, T.F.&P.A., 77 W. 2d So. st., Salt Lake.
W. H. Davenport, Gen. Agt., 695 Market st., San Francisco.
C. L. Brown, C. F. & P. A., 695 Market st., San Francisco.
C. L. O'Brien, Ticket Agt., 685 Market st...San Francisco
Malone Joyce, D.F.&P.A., 609 S. Spring st., Los Angeles, Cal.
C. F. A. Scholz, C.P.A., 609 S. Spring st., Los Angeles, Cal.
C. S. Browne, T.F.&P.A., 609 S.Spring st., Los Angeles, Cal.

the D&RG to Rifle, which was the beginning of the Rio Grande Junction Railway. The RGJ followed the north bank of the Grand River all the way to Grand Junction on grades ranging from .6% to one percent. Grand Junction was at an altitude of 4553 feet, the lowest point visited by CM trains. It was also the western terminus of the railroad. It should be noted that the name of the Grand River was not changed to the Colorado River until July 1921; for the lifetime of the CM, it was always known as "The Grand River."

The Aspen Branch left the junction at Basalt and proceeded on a two percent grade up to the crossing of the D&RG's Aspen Branch, which was one of only two grade crossings with another railroad on the CM, the other being at New Castle on the mainline. The line continued to climb on grades ranging from 1.84 to two percent to the depot at Aspen, 18.4 miles from Basalt at an elevation of 7950 feet. The line continued around the mountain for about one mile to a connection with the D&RG with several intermediate sidings serving various mines.

The Jerome Park Branch, also known as the Coal Branch, left the main line at Cardiff and climbed immedi-

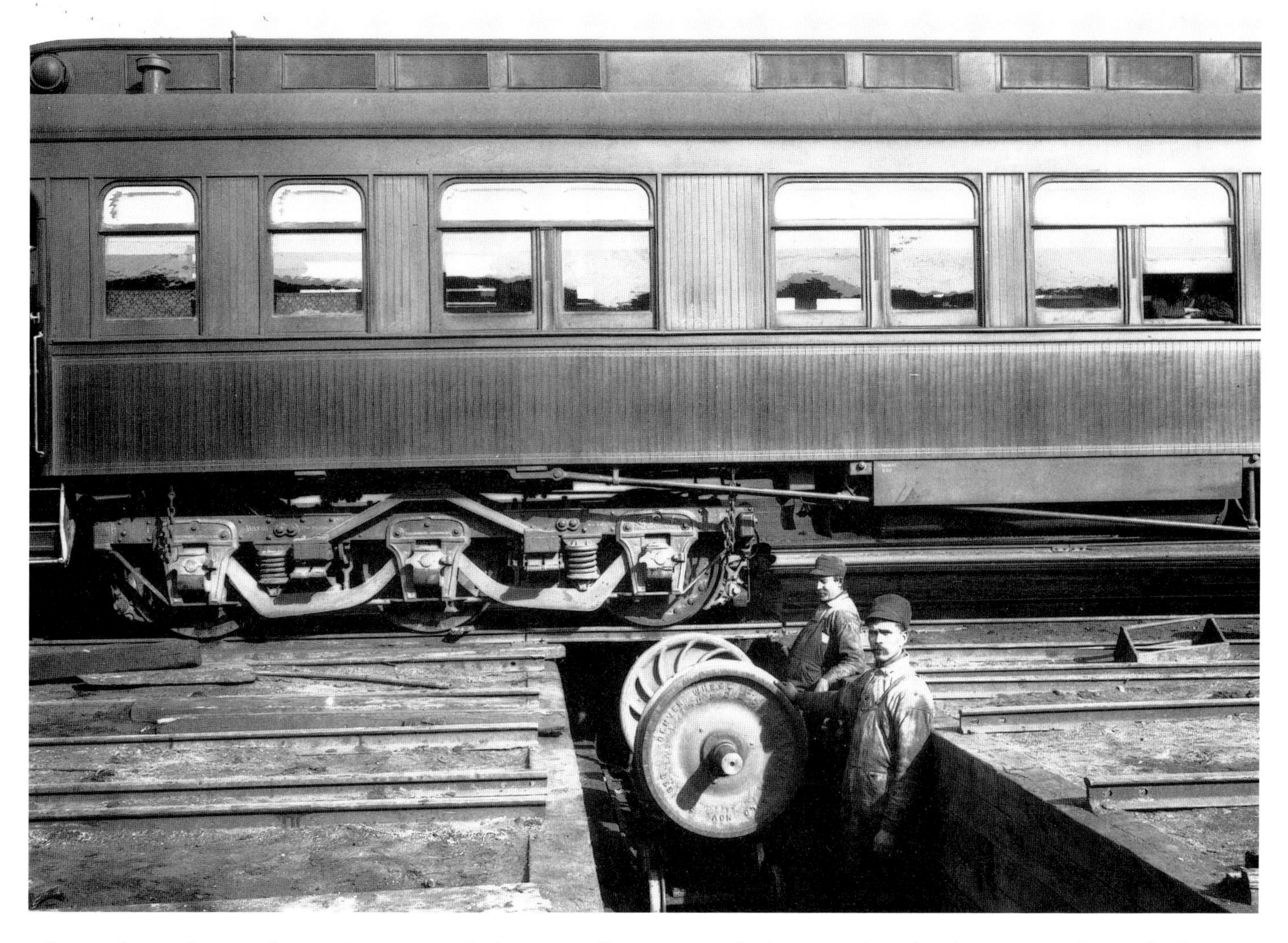

Two somber workers are about to change out a wheel set on a Pullman car over the drop pit at the Colorado City car yard. Note the three-rail track at left to handle narrow gauge cars and the lack, by today's standards, of occupational safety conditions. (H.H. Buckwalter, Colorado Historical Society)

ately at a steady four percent for approximately 10.2 miles. It then ran level for a little over two miles before going up another grade of three percent to Spring Gulch (or just "Gulch") 15.01 miles from Cardiff. Although this line is shown in passenger schedules at various times over the years, it was the practice to carry passengers in the cabooses of freight trains, since the grade was so steep and the need to move empty coal cars up the hill was so great. The only passengers likely to use the service were miners and their families who worked at the various mines along the branch, as it was nothing more than an industrial spur.

COLORADO MIDLAND MILEAGES

Mileages shown by the Colorado Midland in its timetables and listings in the Official Guide were often confusing in the way that they were changed. In one case, an error in the timetable mileage was continued for 17 years before it was corrected. It will be attempted here to sort out the various mileages that were shown over the years, indicate how they came to be and to determine the correct mileage.

As built in 1887, the mileage was shown to be 221.0 from Colorado Springs to Glenwood Springs via the original mainline through Leadville and over Hagerman Pass. By 1888, the distance from Colorado Springs to Glenwood Springs was increased to 221.3. This appears to have been caused by some minor adjustments to the mileages shown west of Leadville. When the CM was completed to New Castle in 1889, the mileage to that point was shown as 233.5. This continued to be the end of line until the RGJ was constructed to Grand Junction by the end of 1890.

With completion of the line to Grand Junction and the acquisition of control by the Atchison Topeka & Santa Fe, the Official Guide listing now showed mileage from Denver to Colorado Springs as 74 even miles. This resulted in

New Castle being 307 miles from Denver (233 from Colorado Springs) and Grand Junction 384 from Denver (310 from Colorado Springs). In 1891 the timetable also showed the results of the construction of the Aspen Short Line, with the listing of Arkansas Junction for the first time at mile 213 (139 from Colorado Springs) via Snowden and Leadville.

The 1892 employee timetable shows Colorado Springs to Snowden as 127.9 miles. From Snowden via the original mainline through Leadville to Arkansas Junction, the distance was 11.2 miles. From Snowden to Arkansas Junction via the Aspen Short Line was listed as 6.6 miles, or a saving of 4.6 miles, in addition to the considerable rise and fall via Leadville. The 1892 timetable continues to show Arkansas Junction at milepost 139.1 via Leadville, Busk at milepost 147.3, Hagerman at milepost 152.8 and Ivanhoe at milepost 156.8. Other important points on the west end were shown at Aspen Junction 197.8, New Castle 233.5 and Grand Junction 310.4. These mileages agree essentially with the even mileages as shown in the 1891 public schedules.

By 1895 the Busk Tunnel had been completed, with its saving of 7.4 miles over Hagerman Pass, and the employee timetable reflects this important change. The distance through the tunnel between Busk and Ivanhoe was now shown as 2.1 miles, instead of 9.5 miles over the pass, and Aspen Junction was now at milepost 190.5, New Castle at 226.2 and Grand Junction at 303.1. There was a difference of .4 mile between the 1892 timetable and the 1895 timetable due to a change in the reported mileage between Colorado Springs and Colorado City; in 1892 it was shown as 3.3 but in 1895 was shown as 2.9 miles. This .4 mile was reflected in all distances west of Colorado City in the 1895 timetable.

Later in 1895, the Official Guide mileage to Arkansas Junction was changed to show the shorter route via the Aspen Short Line and was now listed at 208 from Denver (134 from Colorado Springs). The mileage at Busk, however, was still shown as 221 from Denver, the same as when the distance was computed via the original mainline through Leadville. Busk was actually 8.2 miles from Arkansas Junction, but the public timetable continued to indicate that there was a 13-mile difference between the two points. All the mileages west of Busk were similarly distorted, to Grand Junction which showed as 377 from Denver, rather than 372 that it should have been. This error was perpetrated until late in 1912, when the method of showing mileages reverted to the listing of miles and tenths from Colorado Springs.

In 1896, the Official Guide distance between Colorado Springs and Colorado City was again changed to four miles, instead of the three miles, and this affected all mileages west of Colorado City, so that Arkansas Junction was now listed at 209 and Grand Junction at 378 from Denver.

Although the CM started operating over Hagerman Pass again on November 1, 1897, due to the dispute with

Colorado Midland Railway

LOCAL TIME CARD between DENVER, COLORADO SPRINGS and GRAND JUNCTION.

Miles from Denver	Westbound — ALL TRAINS DAILY Unless Otherwise Marked.	Altitude.	Train No. 5. Colo. Utah Ltd.	Train No. 7 The "Ute."	Train No. 9 11 Come 7	Train No. 1. Cripple Creek Accom.
0	Lv. Denver	5197	8.30AM	8:00PM	11.45PM	3.20AM
51	Ar. Palmer Lake	7237	10.12AM	9.55PM	1.50AM	5.10AM
74	Ar. Colo. Springs	5992	10.50AM	10.30PM	2.30AM	5 50AM
74	Lv. Colo. Spgs	5992	11.C0AM	10.40PM	2.45AM	7.50AM
77	" Colorado City	6085	11.13AM	10.52PM	2.53AM	8 00AM
80	" Manitou	6542	11.23AM	f11.02PM	f 3.07AM	8.08AM
81	" Manitou Iron Spgs.	6552	f11 25AM			f 8.10AM
86	Ar. Cascade Canon	7421	¶11.45AM			
86	Lv. Cascade Canon	7421	12.05PM	f11.27PM	f 3.33AM	8.28AM
88	" Ute Park	7511	f			f
89	" Green Mt. Falls	7734	12.17PM	f11.40PM	f 3.47AM	f 8.38AM
94	" Woodland Park	8484	12.35PM	f11.58PM	f 4.05AM	8.53AM
97	" Edlowe	8923	f12 45PM			f 9.00AM
101	Ar. Divide	9198	1.00PM	12.20AM	4.35AM	9.15AM
125	" Victor (via Mid. T.)	9396	2.37PM		6.06AM	10 37AM
131	" Cripple Creek "	9734	3.00PM		6.30AM	11.00AM
101	Lv. Divide	9198	1.10PM	12.20AM		
110	" Florrisant	8194	1.33PM	12.43AM		
114	" Lake George	8085	f 1.41PM	f12 49AM		
117	" Lidderdale	8200	f 1.46PM			
123	" Idlewild	8477	f 2.04PM			
127	" Freshwater	8571	2.10PM	f 1.22AM		
132	" Spinney	8652	f 2.18PM	f 1.35AM		
143	" Hartzel	8892	2.39PM	f 1.55AM		
152	" Haver	8991	f 2.55PM			
159	" Bath	9528	f 3.13PM	f 2.32AM		
165	" Newett	9105	f 3.24PM	f 2.43AM		
175	" Buena Vista	8248	3.49PM	3.10AM		
187	" Fisher	8597	f 4.11PM	f 3.38AM		
193	" Granite	8959	f 4.27PM	f 3.53AM		
195	" Twin Lakes	9333				
200	" Hayden	9500		f		
202	" Snowden	9600	f 4.45PM	f 4.14AM	Train No. 41 Mixed	
208	Ar. Arkansas Junc.	9706	5.00PM	4.30AM		
212	" Leadville	10200	5.25PM	4.55AM		
212	Lv. Leadville	10200	4.45PM	4.15AM	6.10AM	
208	" Arkansas Junc.	9706	5.10PM	4.40AM	7.05AM	
216	" Busk	10805	5.37PM	5.05AM	7.50AM	
218	" Ivanhoe	10944	5.47PM	5.15AM	8.07AM	
228	" Seller	9616	f 6.14PM	f 5.41AM	8.42AM	
236	" Norrie	8454	f 6.37PM	f 6.01AM	9.09AM	
240	" Tomasville	8000	f 6.45PM	f 6.10AM	9.21AM	
242	" Meredith	7800	f 6.48PM	f 6.14AM	9.26AM	
246	" Ruedi	7585	f 6.55PM	f 6 22AM	9.34AM	
250	" Hopkins	7250	f	f		
252	" Sloane	7000	f 7.08PM		9.53AM	
253	" Peach Blow	6800	f	f		
261	Ar. Basalt	6614	¶ 7.30PM	¶ 6.55AM	10.30AM	
265	Ar. Snow Mass	6780	f 8.05PM	f 7.30AM	11.20AM	f Flag Stop.
270	" Watson	7124	f 8.15PM	f 7.40AM	11.43AM	¶ Stop for Meals
273	" Rathbone	7680	f 8.23PM	f 7.48AM	12.05PM	
280	" Aspen	7950	8.40PM	8.05AM	12.45PM	
280	Lv. Aspen	7950	7.00PM	6.30AM		
261	Lv. Basalt	6614	7.50PM	7.15AM	11.15AM	
265	Lv. El Jebel	6526	f 7.57PM	f 7 22AM	11.27AM	
268	" Wheeler	6371	f 8.02PM	f 7.27AM	11 35AM	
269	" Catherine	6311	f 8.03PM	f 7 29AM	11.40AM	
273	" Carbondale	6200	8.11PM	f 7.36AM	12 01PM	
274	" Bryant	6008	f 8.13PM	f 7 38AM	12.05PM	
282	" Cardiff	5940	8.27PM	7.52AM	12.35PM	
286	" Glenwood	5758	8.37PM	8.02AM	1.05PM	
290	" South Canon	5633	f 8.47PM	f 8.12AM	1.19PM	
297	Ar. New Castle	5574	9.05PM	8.30AM	1.45PM	
297	Lv. New Castle	5574	9.10PM	8.34AM		
304	" Silt	5400	f 9.22PM	f 8.46AM		
307	" Antlers	5350	f 9.27PM	f 8.51AM		
311	" Rifle	5310	9.37PM	9.01AM		
320	" Morris	5207	f 9.51PM	f 9.15AM		
329	" Parachute	5104	10.04PM	9.28AM		
334	" Una	5025	f10.11PM	f 9.35AM		
342	" De Beque	4945	10.23PM	9.47AM		
349	" Cabeza	4873	f10.33PM	f 9.57AM		
354	" Tunnel	4881	f10.42PM	f10.06AM		
359	" Cameo	4809	f10.51PM	f10.15AM		
364	" Palisade	4741	f11.00PM	f10.24AM		
370	" Clifton	4660	f11.08PM	f10.32AM		
377	Ar. Grand Junction	4590	11.20PM	10.44AM		

JEROME PARK BRANCH.

DAILY EXCEPT SUNDAY.

SOUTHBOUND. Mxd. No. 61	Miles from D'n'r		NORTHBOUND. Mxd. No. 62
7.00 AM	285	Lv. Cardiff ... Ar.	1.30 PM
	293	Ar. Sunshine Spur Lv.	
11.00 AM	300	Ar. Spring Gulch. Lv.	9.30 AM

f Flag stop. ¶ Stop for meals.

This page from the November 1899 public timetable lists mileages from Denver and elevations on the mainline and Aspen Branch. (Museum collection)

the Busk Tunnel Railway about rental charges, the distance was not changed until July 1898, to reflect the added seven miles, as far as the Official Guide listing was concerned. After this date, all mileages west of Busk had seven miles added, so that Grand Junction was 384 from Denver. But it was still five miles more than the actual distance, as related above. The CM was similarly tardy in reverting the mileage after operations through the Busk Tunnel resumed on June 25, 1899. This time the change was not made until the August 12, 1900 timetable in the Official Guide. The nine miles between Busk and Ivanhoe were now finally reduced to two miles through the tunnel, and after the Busk Tunnel Railway was purchased by the Colorado Midland in 1900, the line over Hagerman Pass was abandoned and torn up.

The 1908 public timetable showed Colorado Springs–Colorado City as three miles, while the Official Guide continued to show this distance as four miles, with the difference extending all the way to Grand Junction. The employee timetable, however, lists the Colorado Springs to Colorado City mileage as 3.0.

In October 1912, the Official Guide listed distance in miles and tenths, as mentioned above, and these mileages were identical to those shown in the 1908 and 1917 employee timetables. Thus, after 1908, there does not appear to be any significant change since the employee timetables, as well as the profile and rail chart, all have identical mileages.

The distances listed for the Aspen Branch at 18.4, and the Jerome Park Branch at 15.1 remained the same through the years, until the latter was cut back to Sunlight, at 9.8 miles, late in 1917.

Although the railroad undertook some important line changes and relocations at Divide in 1904, and between Ivanhoe and Basalt in 1899-1900, these did not seem to have any major impact on mileage. To sum up, the mileage of the Colorado Midland appears to have four major phases, and can be described as follows:

Years Used	Miles from Colorado Springs to:	New Castle	Grand Junction
1887-1893	Via Leadville & Hagerman Pass	233.5	310.4
1893-1895	Via Leadville & Busk Tunnel	226.2	303.1
1895-1897	Via Arkansas Jct. & Busk Tunnel	221.1	298.0
1897-1899	Via Arkansas Jct. & Hagerman Pass	228.5	305.4
1899-1918	Via Arkansas Jct. & Busk Tunnel	221.1	298.0

It will be noted that the mileages after 1895 until the road closed in 1918 were the same with the exception of the period that the CM was forced to detour over Hagerman Pass.

There does seem to be some confusion over the actual location of one of the Colorado Midland's major scenic attractions—just where was Hell Gate? This confusion, incidentally, is caused primarily by the railroad itself in its publications. The 1902 public timetable shows Hell Gate as five miles west of Ivanhoe, while the 1908 edition shows it six miles west of Ivanhoe. The employee timetables do not show Hell Gate as a station, since there was no siding or other facility at that point. The 1908 employee timetable showed almost the same time for passenger trains at Mallon that the public timetable showed at Hell Gate, yet Mallon was listed as 5.8 miles west of Ivanhoe. If Hell Gate and Mallon were the same place, this would put Hell Gate west of tunnel 17, which appears to be contrary to all of the information available. Tunnel 17 was shown in later employee timetables between mileposts 149.0 and 149.1, while Mallon was listed as 149.5.

The Official Guide for the summer of 1915 was one of the few Guide listings that showed time for the passenger trains at Hell Gate:

3	5		4	6
6:25AM	8:15PM	143.7 Ivanhoe	12:20PM	11:55PM
6:30AM	8:20PM	149.7 Hell Gate	11:55AM	11:30PM
6:52AM	8:47PM	153.7 Sellar	11:24AM	10:57PM

This indicates that westbound trains were supposed to run the imagined six miles at something over 60 MPH, which of course, is nonsense. Eastbound trains had considerably longer to make the uphill run from Hell Gate to Ivanhoe, although there was probably time allowed in the schedule at Ivanhoe to cut off the helper and inspect the train before descending the heavy grade to Arkansas Junction. At any rate, the mileage shown for Hell Gate as 149.7 would put it .2 mile west of Mallon, based on the mileage shown in the timetable, and this appears to be patently in error.

Both Morris Cafky, in *Colorado Midland*, who shows Hell Gate as "about MP 148" and Mel McFarland, in *Midland Route*, who shows it at MP 148.0, are probably correct in their statements, regardless of what the railroad listed for one of its most important tourist attractions. Furthermore, it is difficult to pinpoint the exact location of Hell Gate, since it was more of an area than a precise location and trying to do so would be similar to defining the exact spot known as "The Royal Gorge."

THE DENVER CONNECTION

Although the Colorado Midland's eastern terminal was located in Colorado Springs, most of the passenger trains' through cars actually originated or terminated in Denver and were handled by the power and crews of connecting lines between Denver and Colorado Springs. How this worked out will be explained in this section.

At the outset of Colorado Midland operations in 1887, it is difficult to tell whether or not there were any through cars to and from Denver. The Santa Fe only secured entry into Denver that year, and the very limited equipment list for Colorado Midland trains gives little hint of where their cars originated or terminated at the eastern end of the railroad. At any rate, it is known that the Colorado Midland used the Santa Fe station in Colorado Springs, and this continued for the entire life of the railroad as far as the through trains to and from Grand Junction were concerned. The Denver & Rio Grande, naturally, was not going to foster the activities of its competitor by allowing it to use its station in Colorado Springs, thus possibly short-hauling its own passenger service.

When the Santa Fe secured control of the Colorado Midland in late 1890 and through service was established in connection with the Rio Grande Western at Grand Junction, the Santa Fe advertised a through service to Denver, and this called for operation over Santa Fe rails between Denver and Colorado Springs. The 1891 schedule listed a "solid train between Denver and Ogden." "Through Pullman sleeping cars and tourist cars between Denver and San Francisco without change" were handled under the new arrangement. Emphasis on the Denver connection was diluted to some extent in 1893, when the Santa Fe advertised sleeping cars from Chicago to Ogden via Colorado Springs, which of course, required that these cars travel via Pueblo rather than Denver. This operation did not last long, and the Colorado Midland's through cars once again originated and terminated in Denver.

After the Santa Fe lost its control over the Colorado Midland in 1895, the CM trains continued to be handled by Santa Fe power and crews between Denver and Colorado Springs. The Denver–Cripple Creek sleeper was handled by the Colorado Midland in its through trains, being set off or picked up at Divide. By July 25, 1897, however, new through trains, Nos. 9 and 10, were established between Cripple Creek and Denver, and these were operated over the Union Pacific Denver & Gulf between Colorado Springs and Denver. This route was listed as 91 miles, compared with 74 miles via the Santa Fe. The additional mileage, however, did not have much affect on the operation of these trains, as the run was so short that there was plenty of time to provide for an easy overnight service.

The through operation of train Nos. 9 and 10 continued over the UPD&G until that railroad became the Colorado & Southern in 1899. Then the trains ran under the C&S banner but still via the route through Elizabeth and Falcon. Shortly after the formation of the C&S, its new management worked out an operating agreement with the Santa Fe which established the rights of the C&S to handle its trains over the Santa Fe's line between South Denver and Pueblo, which included Colorado Springs. The note in the CM schedule indicating that Nos. 9 and 10 ran via the C&S main line was taken out of the Official Guide by the November 5, 1899 schedule, implying that these trains were now running via the Santa Fe route. The hilly, roundabout line from Denver to Pueblo formerly used by Nos. 9 and 10 was relegated to a mixed train service between Denver and Colorado Springs, with all of the through C&S trains running over the Santa Fe.

In the next move, the C&S, jointly with the Rio Grande Western, secured control of the Colorado Midland on July 2, 1900. Under this arrangement it was natural that the C&S would then handle the Colorado Midland's cars between Denver and Colorado Springs, but it did not always work out that way. In October 1902, for example, the CM's cars were handled as follows:

- C&S No. 4 leaving Denver 8:30 AM for Pueblo handled CM No. 5's cars, as well as cars for Cripple Creek.
- C&S No. 8 leaving Denver 9:30 PM for Ft. Worth handled CM No. 3's cars.
- C&S No. 3 arriving Denver 9:00 PM from Pueblo had CM No. 4's cars and the Cripple Creek connection cars.
- ATSF No. 5 arriving Denver 9:30 AM from Chicago had CM No. 6's cars.

In 1905, all of the Colorado Midland connections were handled as a straight Denver–Colorado Springs train of the C&S, indicating that there were enough cars destined to and from the CM to require a solid train. Under this arrangement C&S No. 12 became CM No. 5, C&S No. 16 became CM No. 3, CM No. 6 became C&S No. 13 and CM No. 4 became C&S No. 11. In the Santa Fe schedule, these trains were identified as C&S trains, operating only between Denver and Colorado Springs.

Looking at the C&S schedules for 1910, the same practice was in effect, in that the C&S trains were still operated only between Denver and Colorado Springs as a solid Colorado Midland connection. The C&S had changed some of its train numbers, but the service was essentially the same as shown above. The through service between Colorado Springs and Cripple Creek was a different story due to the various management changes that took place in connection with the Colorado Springs & Cripple Creek District Railway (The Short Line).

When the Colorado Midland/Midland Terminal through service began in 1895, the Santa Fe station was used in Colorado Springs, in the same manner as it was used for the through trains to and from Grand Junction. When the Short Line started operations in 1901, it used

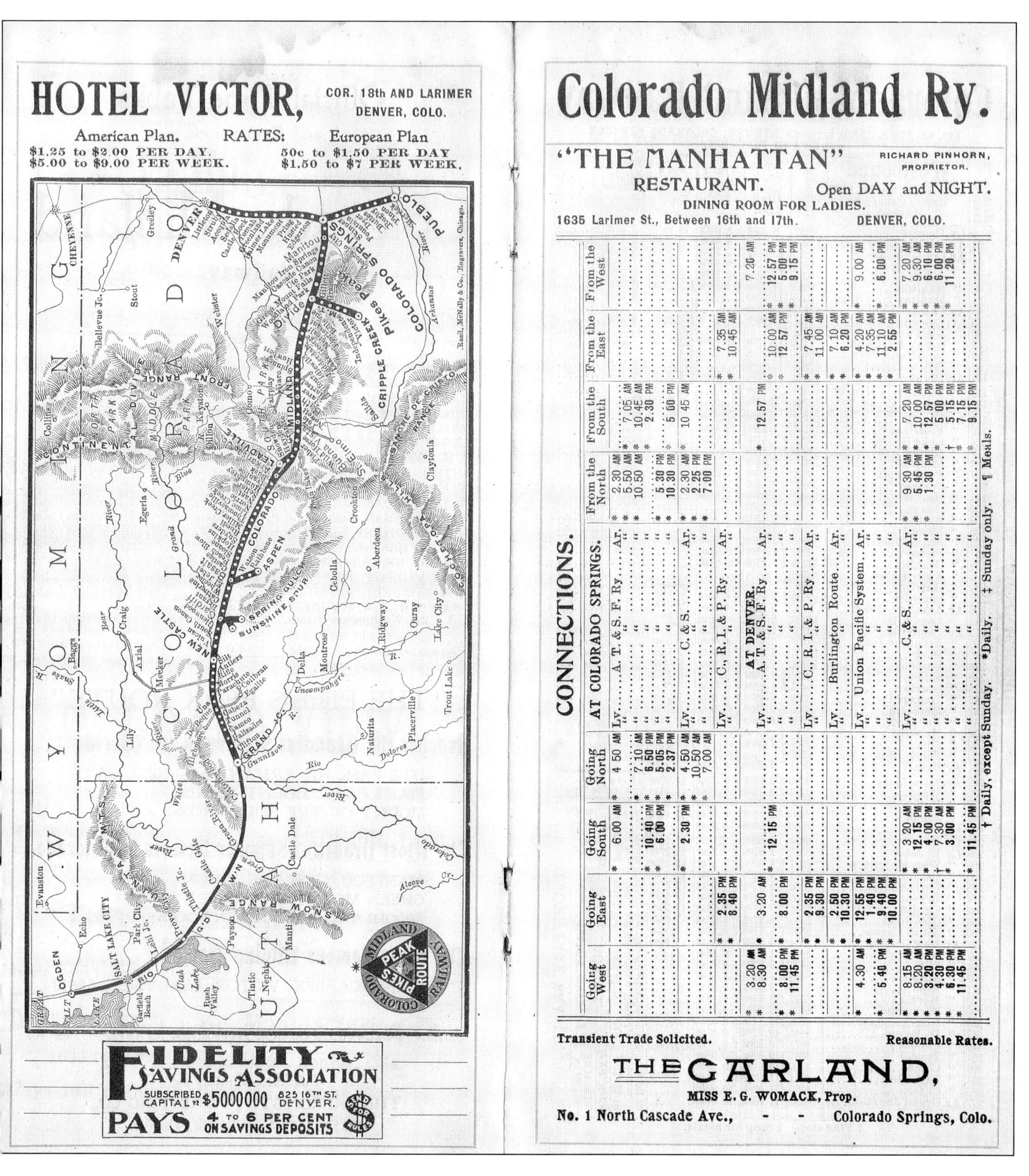

HOTEL VICTOR,

COR. 18th AND LARIMER
DENVER, COLO.

American Plan. RATES: European Plan
$1.25 to $2.00 PER DAY. 50c to $1.50 PER DAY
$5.00 to $9.00 PER WEEK. $1.50 to $7 PER WEEK.

FIDELITY SAVINGS ASSOCIATION
SUBSCRIBED CAPITAL $5000000 825 16TH ST. DENVER.
PAYS 4 TO 6 PER CENT ON SAVINGS DEPOSITS
SEND FOR RULES

Colorado Midland Ry.

"THE MANHATTAN" RICHARD PINHORN, PROPRIETOR.
RESTAURANT. Open DAY and NIGHT.
DINING ROOM FOR LADIES.
1635 Larimer St., Between 16th and 17th. DENVER, COLO.

CONNECTIONS.

Going West	Going East	Going South	Going North	AT COLORADO SPRINGS.	From the North	From the South	From the East	From the West
		* 6.00 AM	* 4 50 AM	Lv.......A. T. & S. F. Ry.....Ar.	* 2.30 AM			
				" " "	* 5.50 AM	* 7.05 AM		
			* 7.10 AM	" " "	* 10.50 AM	10.45 AM		
		* 10.40 PM	* 6.50 PM	" " "		* 2.30 PM		
		* 6.00 PM	* 5.05 PM	" " "	* 5.30 PM			
			* 2.37 PM	" " "	* 10.30 PM	* 5 00 PM		
		* 2.30 PM	* 4.50 AM	Lv.........C. & S..........Ar.	* 2.30 AM	* 10 45 AM		
			* 10.50 AM	" " "	* 2.25 PM			
			* 7.00 AM	" " "	* 7.00 PM			
	* 2.35 PM			Lv......C., R. I. & P. Ry.....Ar.			* 7.35 AM	
	* 8.40 PM			" " "			* 10.45 AM	
* 3.20 AM				AT DENVER.				7.20 AM
* 8.30 AM	* 3.20 AM			Lv.......A. T. & S. F. Ry.....Ar.		* 12.57 PM		
		* 12.15 PM		" " "			* 10.00 AM	* 12.57 PM
* 8.00 PM	* 8.00 PM			" " "			* 12 57 PM	* 5.00 PM
* 11.45 PM				" " "				* 9.15 PM
	* 2.35 PM			Lv......C., R. I. & P. Ry.....Ar.			* 7.45 AM	
	* 9.30 PM			" " "			* 11.00 AM	
	* 2.50 PM			Lv.....Burlington Route....Ar.			* 7.10 AM	
	* 10.30 PM			" " "			* 6.20 PM	
* 4.30 AM	* 12.55 PM			Lv...Union Pacific System..Ar.			* 4.20 AM	* 9.00 AM
	* 1.40 PM			" " "			* 7.35 AM	
* 5.40 PM	* 9.40 PM			" " "			* 11.10 AM	* 6.00 PM
	* 10.00 PM			" " "			* 2.55 PM	
* 8.15 AM		* 3 20 AM		Lv..........C. & S..........Ar.	* 9 30 AM	* 7.20 AM		* 7.20 AM
* 8.20 AM		* 12.15 PM		" " "	* 5.45 PM	* 10.00 AM		* 9.30 AM
* 3.20 PM		* 4.00 PM		" " "	* 1.30 PM	* 12.57 PM		* 6.10 PM
* 4.30 PM		† 7.30 AM		" " "		* 5 00 PM		* 6.00 PM
* 6.30 PM		* 3.00 PM		" " "		† 5.15 PM		* 11.20 PM
* 11.45 PM				" " "		* 7.15 PM		
		* 11.45 PM		" " "		* 9.15 PM		

† Daily, except Sunday. *Daily. ‡ Sunday only. ¶ Meals.

Transient Trade Solicited. Reasonable Rates.

THE GARLAND,
MISS E. G. WOMACK, Prop.
No. 1 North Cascade Ave., - - Colorado Springs, Colo.

The November 1899 timetable included condensed schedules over connecting lines at Colorado Springs and Denver. The map showed the Midland Terminal to Cripple Creek and Denver-Pueblo AT&SF/D&RG track as part of the CM system, although the RGW west of Grand Junction is delineated separately. (Museum collection)

the Denver & Rio Grande station in Colorado Springs, and the D&RG handled the through Denver–Cripple Creek coaches and observation cars (and the sleeper for the short time that it operated). In January 1905, the C&S purchased the Short Line, and on March 1st, the terminal was moved from the D&RG to the Santa Fe station. If no change were to be made with respect to the CM/MT trains, this would mean that all through passenger traffic between Denver and Cripple Creek would move over the C&S/Santa Fe between Denver and Colorado Springs. This would cut out the D&RG completely from participating in any through passenger business between the two points.

While the Colorado Midland was a competitor with the D&RG for passenger business between Denver and Leadville and Glenwood Springs and west, it was not a competitor for the Cripple Creek traffic, so an agreement was quickly worked out that resulted in through trains between Cripple Creek and Colorado Springs via the CM/MT route being handled by the D&RG to Denver. This arrangement was also effective on March 1, 1905, and the Colorado Springs–Cripple Creek trains of the CM/MT used the Denver & Rio Grande station in Colorado Springs until the through trains ceased operating in 1917.

Since the Colorado Midland equipment operating in and out of Denver was handled by "foreign" crews and locomotives, not much attention is given to the arrivals and departures at Denver in the yearly analyses that follow other than to indicate whether such arrivals and departures were of a convenient or inconvenient nature. The emphasis is on the schedules over the Colorado Midland between Colorado Springs and Grand Junction, and to and from Cripple Creek, as handled by Colorado Midland crews and engines. The Denver connection was only an adjunct, albeit a necessary one, of the Colorado Midland's own passenger operation.

THE LEADVILLE PROBLEM

Leadville, the largest intermediate city on the Colorado Midland, was, due to its location at an elevation of 10,103 feet high on the eastern side of the Arkansas Valley, a problem for both the Midland and the Rio Grande. The latter's mainline over Tennessee Pass never did go directly through Leadville, but served it by a loop line in early days, from Malta to Leadville to Leadville Junction. The Colorado Midland, on the other hand, built its original mainline through Leadville. From its inception in 1887 until the Aspen Short Line was completed in early 1889, all trains had to go up the steep hill from Crystal Lake to Leadville and then drop down to the Arkansas Valley before assaulting the hill up to Hagerman Pass. This was particularly onerous to the freight operation and was the principal reason for the construction of the Aspen Short Line from Crystal Lake (Snowden) to Arkansas Junction.

At the outset, the Aspen Short Line was not utilized by the passenger trains, as they continued to use the mainline through Leadville, at least through the end of 1891. In fact, Arkansas Junction was not added to the Official Guide CM schedules until February 1, 1891, and then only as the first station west of Leadville. By June 1892, when there were four mainline trains, three of them operated via Leadville, while No. 2 used the Aspen Short Line route. Under this arrangement, No. 2 ran to Arkansas Junction, where the engine cut off, and took any Leadville cars, plus a combine or other car picked up at Arkansas Junction, and ran as No. 16 to Leadville. Prior to that time, the First District engine had left Leadville with train No. 15 and run to Arkansas Junction with the local car, plus any through cars for the east. On arrival it was consolidated with the remaining cars in No. 2 from the west and proceeded towards Colorado Springs as No. 2.

With the onset of the depression of 1893, the CM was running only one train each way, and apparently these trains ran via the Leadville mainline. By the end of the year it appears that these were running via Arkansas Junction, thence to Leadville and back to Arkansas Junction, in both directions, based on the way that the running times are shown around the Leadville area. This arrangement lasted until late in 1897, when No. 7 was handled in the same fashion as No. 2 had been in 1892. The other three trains were running via Arkansas Junction into and out of Leadville and back to Arkansas Junction. By March 1898, two trains were running into Leadville from Arkansas Junction, while the other two were running through Arkansas Junction directly, with stub runs to and from Leadville. The same arrangement prevailed into the early part of 1899, but the same trains were not always involved. In June 1899, only one train ran into Leadville, while the other three were operated through Arkansas Junction, with stub runs to Leadville. In November 1899, all trains by-passed Leadville, with stub runs to and from that city, but this lasted only until May 1900, when one train was changed to run into Leadville.

During the years of 1901 and 1902, all trains ran directly via Arkansas Junction, with stub runs into and out of Leadville. As a switch, in the summer of 1903, all trains again ran into and out of Leadville, passing Arkansas Junction twice in the process. The summer of 1904 saw three trains operating directly into Leadville, with just one train by-passing that point via Arkansas Junction. This arrangement remained the same through the summer of 1905, but in the fall all four trains were again run into Leadville. The schedule for June 17, 1906 shows the same operation, but less than a month later, on July 11, the schedules were changed with the result that all four trains on the mainline now operated directly through Arkansas Junction, with stub runs to and from the Cloud City. As it developed, the June 1906, schedule was the last one where through trains operated directly into and out of Leadville. After the July 11th schedule, until the end of the railroad's operations in 1918, all mainline trains by-passed Leadville, with the stub trains providing all service to the latter point.

There have been several references in the past to the "Leadville Branch"; even the condensed rail chart and profile issued by the railroad itself mentions the line from Arkansas Junction to Leadville as the Leadville Branch. Technically, however, the road's operating timetables always showed Leadville as the eastern terminal of the Second District. After the original mainline between Snowden and Leadville had been abandoned in 1906, First District trains were given separate identities in the timetable between Arkansas Junction and Leadville. Perhaps the best way to illustrate the way this worked is to look at the operating timetable for November 22, 1908, during the zenith of the Midland's career. As shown above, all trains were operating through Arkansas Junction, by-passing Leadville, so that the stub runs were used between those two points on the Second District. The train numbers are shown below, first in the progression from east to west, and then from west to east, using symbols for the stations (C.S. for Colorado Springs, A.J. for Arkansas Junction, LE for Leadville and G.J. for Grand Junction):

Westbound

First District C.S. to A.J.	Second District A.J. to LE	Second District LE to A.J.	Second District A.J. to G.J.
3	22	3	3
5	24	5	5

Eastbound

Second District G.J. to A.J.	Second District A.J. to LE	Second District LE to A.J.	First District A.J. to C.S.
4	4	21	4
6	6	23	6

Thus it can be seen that Second District trains picked up or retained their mainline identity from or to Leadville, with the First District portion operating between Arkansas Junction and Leadville with train numbers in the "20" series. Nos. 3 and 5 from Leadville were the stub trains to meet the corresponding mainline train numbers, while in the opposite direction, Nos. 4 and 6 from Arkansas Junction to Leadville were the stub runs

The elaborately sheathed frame depot at Leadville, with ornate chimney brickwork emblazoned with two different CM heralds, was by far the most imposing on the railroad. Several people have gathered prior to the arrival of a train. The station was dismantled in 1940. (H.H. Buckwalter, Colorado Historical Society)

off the mainline trains of the same numbers. This system was used consistently until the end of operations in 1918.

When reading Colorado Midland public timetables or Official Guide listings, the clue as to how the trains were being handled at that particular time is the way the times are shown for Leadville station. When the arriving time is *earlier* than the leaving time, this indicates that the whole train ran to Leadville, made the station stop and then left on its journey (sometimes allowance is made for meals); this is true whether or not the train ran via the original mainline or via Arkansas Junction to and from Leadville. Where the time shown arriving Leadville is *later* than the leaving time, it indicates that the service to and from Leadville was provided by the stub runs, and that the through portion of the train made the station stop only at Arkansas Junction and did not run east of that point on the Second District. The times at Arkansas Junction are also a clue, as the station time seldom exceeded ten minutes at that point, except for the short period that an eating house was maintained there.

The practice of running trains directly into and out of Leadville via Arkansas Junction raises another question as to how this was actually handled by the CM. Since there were no turning facilities at Leadville, except for a 60-foot turntable at the roundhouse, passenger trains would be required to run in reverse on at least one leg of the trip to and from the Leadville station. It hardly seems likely that the CM would run a passenger train in reverse over half of the railroad, so it would seem probable that the trains had to be turned at Arkansas Junction either before they went to Leadville or on the return from that station. There is nothing mentioned in the special instructions in the operating timetables available at the time of this practice, so it is difficult to state just how it was handled, other than that the trains had to be turned at some location in order to have the equipment lined up in the proper order.

While there were three different methods of reaching Leadville with the passenger trains, the operation of freight trains by the Colorado Midland was pretty well standardized after the construction of the Aspen Short Line. In general, scheduled freight trains were handled the same as passenger trains were after July 1906, with the through cars being set off at Arkansas Junction and the Leadville cars being handled to that yard. Outbound cars from Leadville were handled by stub runs to Arkansas Junction, where they were added to the through trains. All extras originated at Leadville, the site of the roundhouse, and all terminated there as well.

Colorado Midland Ry.

STAGE CONNECTIONS.

BUENA VISTA.

Stage line to St. Elmo: Rate, Hortense Hot Springs, $1.00; St. Elmo $2.00, one way; baggage, 75c per 100 lbs. St. Elmo; 50c Hortense Hot Springs. Stage leaves Buena Vista 7 a. m. daily, arrives Hortense Hot Springs 10 a. m., Alpine 12 noon, St. Elmo 1 p. m. Returning, leave St, Elmo 7 a. m,, arrive Buena Vista 1 p. m. For Buena Vista Hot Springs: Rate 50c baggage, 25c per 100 lbs.; leaves Buena Vista 5 p. m., arrives Buena Vista Hot Springs 6 p. m.

CARBONDALE,

Crystal River Ry: Trains leave daily 9:45 a. m., for Janeway, 12 miles, Hot Springs, 14 miles, Redstone, 17 miles, $1.00; connections at Redstone daily except Sunday with stage for Marble City, 13 miles, $1.00; Crystal, 30 miles, $1.50, from Redstone. Returning trains arrive Carbondale 3 p.m.

DE BEQUE.

For Eagalite and Collbran, Colo.: Stage leaves daily except Sunday, 8 a. m; returning, arrives 6 p. m. Distance: Mesa 13 miles, Eagalite 19 miles, Collbran 20 miles. Fare: Mesa $1.25 one way, $2.00 round trip; Eagalite $1.75; Collbran $2.00 one way, $3.00 round trip; baggage free 20 lbs., excess same as stage fare. For Highmore, Colo.: Distance 14 miles, fare $1.00. Stage leaves DeBeque 8 a. m. Tuesdays and Saturdays; arrives from Highmore 4 p. m. Tuesdays and Saturdays.

GRANITE.

For Twin Lakes: Leave Granite 8 a. m. daily; leave Twin Lakes 11:15 a. m. Arrive Granite 12:45 p. m. Fare to Twin Lakes 75c; fare to Lower Lake, 50c.

HARTSEL.

For Balfour, 8 miles: Stage leaves Hartsel on arrival of No. 5 (about 1½ hours drive); leaves Balfour 12:30 p. m., arrives Hartsel 2 p. m. Rate, $1.00; baggage, 30 lbs. free; excess, 50c per 100 lbs. For Garo, Colo., (on Colo. & So. Ry.): Stage leaves Hartsel daily, 9:30 a. m. Fare $1.00; small baggage free; heavy baggage 50c per 100 lbs. Leaves Garo returning at 11:30 a. m., arrives Hartsel 2:00 p. m., connects with Nos. 5 and 6.

LAKE GEORGE.

Daily, except Sunday, stages for Puma City, Jasper and O'Brien, connect with No. 5.

LEADVILLE.

Stages for Oro, Soda Springs, Twin Lakes and Evergreen Lakes.

FRESHWATER.

For Guffey, via. Hall City (14 miles); Stage leaves daily on arrival of No. 5, arrives Guffey 6 p. m.; leaves Guffey 11 a. m.; arrives Freshwater 2 p. m. Fare $1.00 each way.

RIFLE, COLO.

Stage leaves daily 9 a. m.; arrives Meeker 7 p. m.; Axial next day noon; Craig, 7 p. m.; baggage, 40 lbs. free; excess, Meeker, 2c per lb.; Axial, 3c per lb ; Craig, 4c per lb. Fare: Meeker, $5.00, round trip, $8.00; Axial $7.50, one way; Craig, $10.00, one way.

WOODLAND PARK,

For Manitou Park stages connect with all day trains on advice to agent.

For Platt Station, Pemberton and West Creek, stage leaves at 2 p, m., daily. Fare to Pemberton $1.25; to Platt Station, $2.50.

The November 1899 timetable listed stagecoach connections to many off-line points. Some of these towns still exist; others have been ghosts for many years. (Museum collection)

Train Service

Midland Route

Midland Route

THRU passenger service both ways between Denver and Ogden, via Salt Lake City, with thru Pullman observation sleeper on daylight trains 4 and 5. Standard Pullmans on night trains 3 and 6 between Denver and Leadville and Denver and Grand Junction via Glenwood Springs. Thru trains carry dining cars for meals, service a la carte. Direct connections with other roads are made by all eastbound and westbound trains at Denver, Colorado Springs, Salt Lake City and Ogden.

The daylight trips over the Colorado Midland are unsurpassed in point of service and scenic features. Trains pass over the mountains "On Top Looking Down," giving an unobstructed view of the magnificent mountain scenery from the car windows.

Our passengers are our guests, and are so treated. Our train crews are composed of gentlemen. They know and appreciate the value of courtesy to a stranger seeking information and guidance. Ladies traveling alone or with children are accorded polite assistance. This is an inviolate Colorado Midland rule.

Copies of this and other booklets issued by the Midland Route, together with any information desired, are cheerfully forwarded upon application to any officer or representative named below:

G. W. VALLERY, Receiver	Denver, Colo.
C. H. SPEERS, General Passenger Agent	Denver, Colo.
Aspen, Colo.	W. L. Graves, Agent
Buena Vista, Colo.	H. Kirkpatrick, Agent
Chicago, Ill., 350 Marquette Bldg.	H. W. Jackson, General Agent C. E. Webb, Trav. Frt. & Pass. Agent N. B. Wood, Soliciting Frt. & Pass. Agent
Colorado Springs, Colo., 121 E. Pike's Peak Ave.	H. E. Gardner, General Agent
Denver, Colo., 714 17th Street	E. D. Whitley, City Ticket Agent C. D. Peirce, City Pass. Agent
Glenwood Springs, Colo.	C. M. Keck, General Agent S. J. Lowe, Agent
Grand Junction, Colo.	R. E. Vickery, General Agent
Kansas City, Mo., 566 Sheidley Bldg.	M. R. Sutton, General Agent
Leadville, Colo.	C. B. Carter, Agent
Los Angeles, Cal., Room 216, 702 So. Spring St.	Malone Joyce, General Agent
New York, 1322 Woolworth Bldg., 233 Broadway	F. N. Dowler, General Eastern Agent
Omaha, Neb., 411 1st Natl. Bank Blk., 13th & Farnam Sts.	Perry J. Murphy, General Agent
Pittsburgh, Pa., 838 Oliver Bldg.	C. A. Creitz, General Agent
Salt Lake City, Utah, 523 Judge Bldg.	J. H. Davis, General Agent
San Francisco, Cal., 291 Monadnock Bldg.	C. L. Brown, General Agent F. C. Thompson, T. F. & P. A.

This advertisement is from a Midland folder "Thru the Rockies," published sometime during 1913-1916, and lists offices maintained across the United States. One hopes that the train crews always lived up to their billing. (Museum collection)

PIKE'S PEAK ROUTE.

COLORADO MIDLAND RAILWAY.

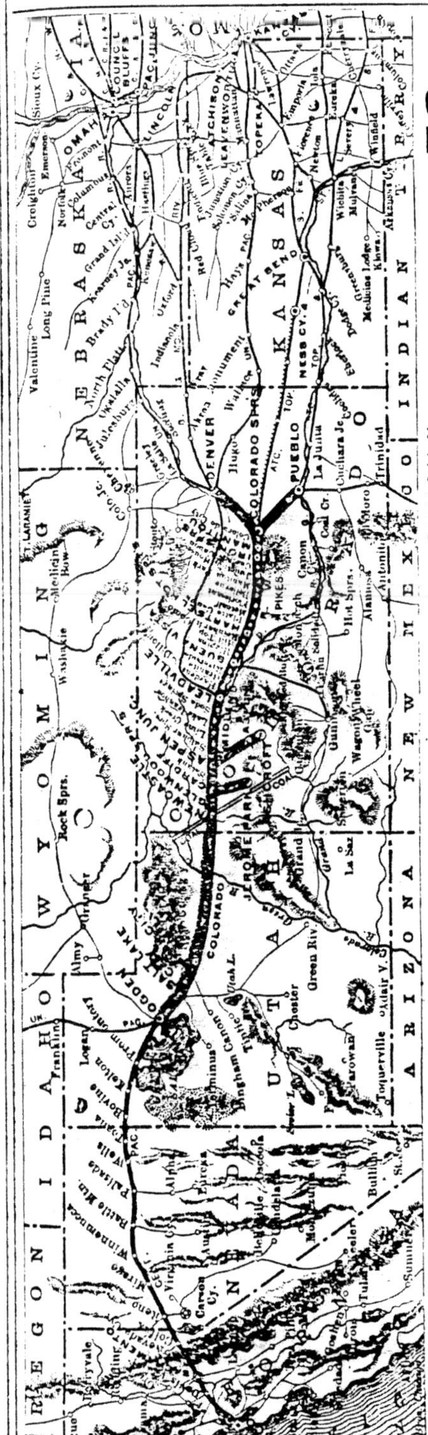

Connections made at Denver (Union Depot) and at Colorado Springs with all trains to and from the east.

N.B.—Trains marked * run daily; ‡ trains stop for meals. ♁ Telegraph stations.

THE ONLY

Standard Gauge Railroad

PENETRATING THE HEART OF THE

ROCKY MOUNTAINS.

Equipment Unsurpassed! Scenery Unequalled!

J. J. HAGERMAN, President.
T. M. DAVIS, 1st Vice-President.
D. B. ROBINSON, Gen. Manager.
C. A. LANSING, Secretary.
IRVING HOWBERT, Treasurer.
HENRY T. ROGERS, Gen. Solicitor.
G. A. CARTWRIGHT, Act'g Gen. Freight Agt.

CHAS. S. LEE, Gen. Passenger Agent.
J. J. BLOWER, Auditor.
THOS. SAUNDERS, Superintendent.
B. C. BOSWORTH, Acting Superintendent Machinery.
B. H. BRYANT, Chief Engineer.

General Offices—Colorado Springs, Col.—Traffic Department—Denver, Col.

Westward. December 18, 1887.	Mls.	No. 1 Exs.	No. 3 Exs.
		A. M.	P. M.
Denver ♁ lve.		*8 00	*9 15
[LEAVE		A. M.	
Pueblo ♁		9 10	
[LEAVE		A. M.	N'HT
Colorado Springs ♁	0	*11 15	*12 25
Colorado City ♁	3.1	11 35	12 45
Manitou	6.3	11 48	12 58
Manitou Iron Springs	7.2	11 53	1 03
Cascade Cañon	11.8	‡12 40	1 25
Culver ♁	12.8	12 43	....
Junction House	18.0	....	....
Manitou Park	20.1	1 13	2 03
Theodore ♁	23.6	1 25	2 15
Hayden's Divide	27.4	1 37	....
Bellevue	29.6	1 45	....
Florissant ♁	36.5	2 10	3 00
Metcalf	38.8	2 18	....
Lidderdale	42.8	2 32	....
Idlewild ♁	49.3	2 55	3 40
Howbert	52.7	3 03	....
Spinney ♁	58.2	3 13	4 00
Hartsel ♁	69.5	3 37	4 25
Haver	78.5	3 55	....
Hill Top ♁	85.1	4 10	5 05
Higgins	90.8	4 22	....
Buena Vista ♁	101.6	4 50	5 50
Wild Horse	104.3	5 00	....
Fisher ♁	112.7	5 19	....
Granite	119.1	5 35	6 38
Crystal Lake	127.5	5 55	7 00
Leadville ♁ arr.	135.3	6 20	7 30
Leadville ♁ lve.	135.3	P. M.	7 50
Busk	147.1		8 37
Rogers Spur	150.5		8 50
Hagerman ♁	152.8		9 00
Ivanhoe	156.6		9 15
Sellar ♁	166.1		9 50
Norrie	174.1		10 20
Ruedi ♁	182.7	15	10 50
Sloane	188.8	Exs.	11 09
Aspen Junction	197.7	A. M.	11 37
Aspen	216.7	*8 00	12 30
Aspen Junction	197.7	*9 00	*11 50
Wheeler	203.7	9 20	12 08
Sands ♁	210.2	9 42	12 28
Cardiff	217.5	10 05	12 40
Glenwood Springs	221.0	10 15	1 00
[ARRIVE		A. M.	P. M.

Eastward.	Mls.	18 Exs.	No. 4 Exs.
[LEAVE		A. M.	P. M.
Glenwood Springs	0	*10 25	*8 00
Cardiff	3.5	10 40	3 15
Sands ♁	10.8	11 01	3 35
Wheeler	17.3	11 20	3 58
Aspen Junction	23.3	11 37	4 10
Aspen	42.3	12 30	*3 30
Aspen Junction	23.3	NO'N	4 20
Sloane	32.2		4 50
Ruedi ♁	38.3		5 10
Norrie	46.9		5 45
Sellar ♁	54.9		6 17
Ivanhoe	64.4		6 54
Hagerman ♁	68.2		7 09
Rogers' Spur	70.5	No. 2	7 18
Busk ♁	73.9	Exs.	7 33
Leadville arr.	85.7	A. M.	8 30
Leadville ♁ lve.	85.7	*8 15	*8 50
Crystal Lake	93.5	8 37	9 15
Granite	101.9	8 58	9 38
Fisher ♁	108.3	9 15	....
Wild Horse	116.7	9 35	....
Buena Vista ♁	119.4	9 45	10 30
Higgins	130.2	10 15	....
Hill Top ♁	135.6	10 30	11 20
Haver	142.5	10 47	....
Hartsel ♁	151.5	11 07	12 00
Spinney ♁	162.8	11 30	12 25
Howbert	168.3	11 42	....
Idlewild ♁	171.7	11 50	12 45
Lidderdale	178.2	12 08	....
Metcalf	182.2	12 20	....
Florissant ♁	184.5	12 30	1 30
Bellevue	191.4	12 48	....
Hayden's Divide	193.6	....	....
Theodore ♁	197.4	1 03	2 15
Manitou Park	200.9	1 13	2 25
Junction House	203.0	....	....
Culver ♁	208.2	1 29	....
Cascade Cañon	209.2	‡1 55	2 47
Manitou Iron Springs	214.0	2 15	3 10
Manitou	214.9	2 20	3 15
Colorado City ♁	218.1	2 35	3 30
Colorado Springs ♁	221.0	2 50	3 50
[ARRIVE		P. M.	A. M.
Pueblo ♁		6 30	
[ARRIVE		P. M.	
Denver ♁		6 00	7 00
[ARRIVE		P. M.	A. M.

Train leaves Aspen for Glenwood Springs *3 30 p.m. Returning, leaves Glenwood Springs for Aspen *8 00 p.m.

Night Trains have Pullman Palace Sleeping Cars attached.

Day Trains have Pullman Smoking Room Coaches. No extra Charge.

COLORADO MIDLAND SCHEDULES THROUGH THE YEARS

1887

The construction of the Colorado Midland was an engineering marvel of its time. It was built in 10 sections, all starting at various dates after April 19, 1886 and all being completed to Glenwood Springs by December 18, 1887. In just 20 months, the forces of J.J. Hagerman had thrown a standard gauge railroad into the Rocky Mountains, over the Continental Divide and down the valleys for 221 miles—certainly a massive undertaking for that day and age.

The first regular passenger service was established on July 13th and provided trains between Colorado Springs and Buena Vista. The rails reached Leadville late in August, and service was extended to that point on September 1st. On October 8th, the Colorado Springs – Leadville Railway Post Office was established, which showed that the Post Office at least had confidence in the new railroad to maintain the service that the postal authorities required.

Track was laid to West Glenwood by December 9th, but the actual entry into Glenwood Springs had to wait a few days longer until the bridge over the Roaring Fork could be completed. The first through service over the fledgling railroad was effective on December 18th, and called for two trains daily each way between Colorado Springs and Leadville, with one train continuing on to Glenwood Springs. A couple of locals between Glenwood Springs and the end of track at Aspen rounded out the schedule. It should be noted that while Aspen is shown in this schedule, the CM did not reach that station until February 4, 1888, due to the fact that the bridge over Maroon Creek had not yet been completed. Until that time, the CM trains started and terminated at a temporary depot just short of the viaduct.

This first through schedule called for No. 1 to leave Colorado Springs at 11:15 AM, have lunch at Cascade Canon and arrive in Leadville at 6:20 PM. The Denver connection for this train left that city at 8 AM, with another Denver departure at 9:15 PM for CM train No. 3, which left Colorado Springs at 12:25 AM. No. 3 stopped at Leadville from 7:30 to 7:50 AM and, after passing over Hagerman Pass at 9 AM, was into Glenwood Springs at 1 PM. This 12 hour 35 minute running time for the 221 miles over a brand new railroad was not bad considering all of the difficulties that could be encountered through the mountains. No. 15 left the temporary station at Aspen at 8 AM and arrived in Glenwood Springs at 10:15 AM. No. 18 departed Glenwood Springs at 10:25 AM and arrived at the Aspen terminal at 12:30 PM.

No. 2 left Leadville at 8:15 AM, also stopping for lunch at Cascade Canon, and arrived Colorado Springs at 2:50 PM, with a Denver connection arriving at that point at 6 PM. Train No. 4 got out of Glenwood Springs at 3 PM, stopped at Leadville from 8:20 to 8:50 PM, arrived at Colorado Springs at 3:50 AM and Denver at 7 AM. A footnote in the timetable called for an additional train leaving Aspen for Glenwood Springs at 3:30 PM, and this time is also shown for Aspen as a connection for eastbound No. 4; returning, a train was listed as leaving Glenwood Springs for Aspen at 3 PM, but this was the same time as shown for No. 4's departure from Glenwood Springs. So there is something of a quandary as to how the CM originally set up these schedules on the west end of the railroad.

The only reference to the equipment carried by these trains is a note that the night trains had Pullman Palace sleeping cars attached, and that day trains had Pullman smoking room coaches at no extra charge.

This brand new railroad started business with brand new equipment. Three locomotives had been received in 1886, Class 115 2-8-0s, numbered 1 – 3. In 1887 the company received 25 more locomotives as follows:

Road Numbers	Type	Class	No. of Engines
4 – 10	2-8-0	115	7
11 – 14	4-6-0	102	4
15 – 22	4-6-0	104	8
23 – 25	4-6-0	93	3
30 – 32	0-6-0	91	3

The class 93 and class 104 engines were primarily used in passenger service, while the class 102 and class 115 were used in freight and helper service under normal conditions, but all 4-6-0s and 2-8-0s could be switched from one type of service to the other when necessary. The class 91 engines were, of course, used as yard switchers. Normally, two of these engines were assigned to Colorado City while one was assigned to Aspen Junction, the western division point at that time.

The new railroad also started out with 38 cars in the passenger fleet, as follows:

Car Type	Car Numbers	Builder	No. of Cars
Baggage	301 – 313	Pullman	13
Coach/Mail/Baggage	11 – 12	Pullman	2
First Class Coach	101 – 112	Pullman	12
Suburban Coach	113	Pullman	1
Second Class Coach	251 – 260	Pullman	10

Although the Jerome Park Branch was also completed during 1887, passenger service on that steep line was not established until 1895 as will be shown in the commentary for that year.

TIME TABLE
No. 2.
October 9, 1887.

WESTWARD.									EASTWARD.			
13 Through Freight. Second Class. Daily.	11 Way Freight. Second Class. Daily, Ex't Sunday.	3 Aspen Express. First Class. Daily.	1 Leadville Express. First Class. Daily.	Distance from Colo. Springs. Miles.	Coal and Water.	STATIONS.	Telegraph Stations.	Capacity of Sidings. No. Cars.	2 Eastern Express. First Class. Daily.	4 Denver Express. First Class. Daily.	12 Way Freight. Second Class. Daily, Ex't Sunday.	14 Through Freight. Second Class. Daily.
		11:00pm	8:00am			DENVER.			6:30pm	7:20am		
						PUEBLO.						
10:15pm		2:00 / 2:10am	11:00 / 11:20am			COLORADO SPRINGS.	T		3:30pm / 3:15	4:20am / 4:05		4:45am
						3.1						
10:40	7:00am	s 2:25	11:35 / 11:40	3.1	W C	COLORADO CITY.	N	350	s 3:00	s 3:50	7:00pm	4:20
						3.2						
10:55	7:15	s 2:37	s 11:56	6.3		MANITOU.	T	12	s 2:48	s 3:38	6:45	4:00
						0.9						
11:00	7:20	f 2:40	s 12:01pm	7.2		MANITOU IRON SPRINGS.		9	s 2:43	f 3:33	6:40	3:55
						4.6						
11:30	7:50	s 3:00	s 12:30	11.8		CASCADE CANON.	T	25	s 2:23	s 3:10	6:10	3:25
						1						
11:40	8:00	s **3:05**	f 12:35	12.8	W	CULVER.		48	f 2:20	s **3:05**	6:05 / 5:55	**3:05**
						5.2						
12:05am	8:30	3:22	f 12:52	18		JUNCTION HOUSE.		10	f 2:07	2:49	5:25	2:30
						2.1						
12:20	8:40	3:29	s 1:00	20.1		MANITOU PARK.	T	14	s 2:02	2:43	5:10	2:15
						3.5						
12:40	9:00	3:40	s 1:13	23.6		THEODORE.	T	17	s 1:52	2:33	4:50	1:55
						6						
1:15	9:25	3:58	s **1:34**	29.6		BELLEVUE.		42	s **1:34**	2:16	4:20	**1:15**
						6.9						
1:57	10:00	s 4:20	s 1:55	36.5	W	FLORISSANT.	N	15	s 1:15	s **1:57**	3:45	12:35
						2.3						
2:10	10:15	4:28	f 2:03	38.8		METCALF.		65	f 1:05	1:47	3:25	12:20am
						4						
2:30	10:35	4:38	f 2:15	42.8		LIDDERDALE.		38	f 12:53	1:34	3:05	12:00
						6.5						
3:00	11:10	f 4:55	¶ **2:35** / 2:50	49.3		IDLEWILD.	T	38	¶ 12:35 / 12:20	f 1:15	**2:35**	11:30
						3.4						
3:15	11:30	5:01	f 2:57	52.7		HOWBERT.			f 12:13	1:08	2:10	11:15
						5.5						
3:40	**12:02pm**	f 5:12	s 3:08	58.2	W C	SPINNEY.	N	56	s **12:02pm**	f 12:57	1:50	10:55
						10.5						
4:20	**1:00**	f 5:32	s 3:31	68.7		HARTSEL.	T	10	s 11:38	f 12:35	**1:00**	10:15
						4						
4:40	1:20	5:40	f 3:40	72.7		REINHART.		50	f 11:30	12:27am	12:25pm	9:55
						12						
5:35	2:20	f 6:05	s 4:05	84.7		HILL TOP.	N	35	s 10:57	f 11:54	11:20	9:05
						6						
6:00	2:50	6:20	f 4:20	90.7	W	HIGGINS.		38	f **10:40**	11:37	**10:40**	8:40
						11						
6:50	3:45	s **6:50**	s 4:50	101.7		BUENA VISTA.	T	10	s 10:10	s 11:07	9:40	7:50
						2						
7:10	3:55	7:00	f 5:00	103.7		WILD HORSE.		55	f 10:00	10:57	9:25	7:40
						8.4						
7:45	4:40	7:18	f 5:22	112.1	W	FISHER.		55	f 9:38	10:36	8:45	7:05
						6.3						
8:15	5:15	f **7:35**	s 5:37	118.4		GRANITE.	T	21	s 9:20	f 10:17	**8:15** / **7:35**	6:35
						8.4						
9:00	**6:00**	f 8:00	s **6:00**	126.8	W	CRYSTAL LAKE.	T	110	s **9:00**	f 9:55	6:55	**6:00**
						7.8						
9:40	6:45	8:25am	6:25pm	134.6	W C	LEADVILLE.	N	300	8:40am	9:30pm	6:20am	5:15pm
Daily.	Daily Ex't Sunday.	Daily.	Daily.						Daily.	Daily.	Daily, Ex't Sunday.	Daily.

Employee Timetable No. 2 was effective October 9, 1887, just after track had been laid into Leadville. The line over Hagerman Pass to the west was still under construction but had been completed to West Glenwood and Maroon Creek viaduct, just north of Aspen by December 1st, when the public timetable on this page went into effect. (opposite, Charles Albi collection; this page, Museum collection)

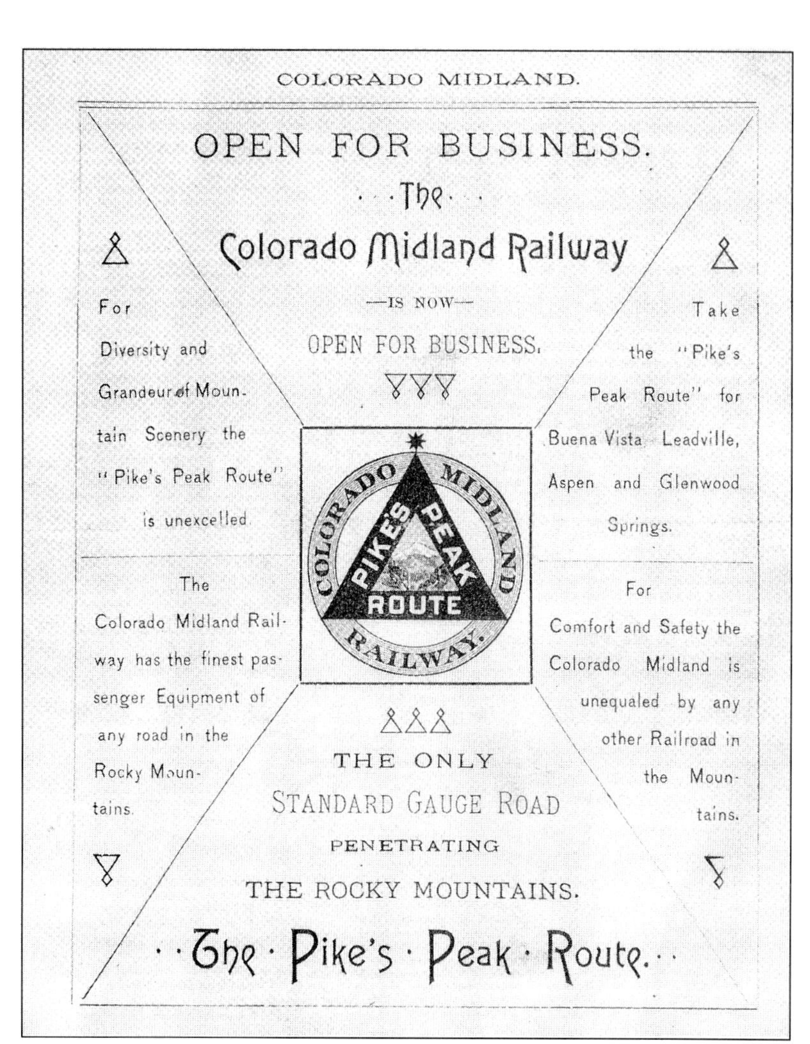

COLORADO MIDLAND.

OPEN FOR BUSINESS.

The

Colorado Midland Railway

—IS NOW—

OPEN FOR BUSINESS.

For Diversity and Grandeur of Mountain Scenery the "Pike's Peak Route" is unexcelled.

Take the "Pike's Peak Route" for Buena Vista, Leadville, Aspen and Glenwood Springs.

COLORADO MIDLAND RAILWAY. PIKE'S PEAK ROUTE

The Colorado Midland Railway has the finest passenger Equipment of any road in the Rocky Mountains.

For Comfort and Safety the Colorado Midland is unequaled by any other Railroad in the Mountains.

THE ONLY STANDARD GAUGE ROAD PENETRATING THE ROCKY MOUNTAINS.

The Pike's Peak Route.

CONNECTIONS.

ATCHISON, TOPEKA AND SANTA FE.

COLORADO SPRINGS UNION DEPOT.

EAST AND SOUTH.

Leave	12.10 a. m.	5.05 p. m.
Arrive	3.55 a. m.	11.00 a. m

BURLINGTON AND MISSOURI RIVER R. R.

DENVER UNION DEPOT.

EAST.

Leave	8.30 a. m.	12.00 noon	10.00 p. m.
Arrive	7.30 p. m.	2.30 p. m.	10.00 p. m.

UNION PACIFIC RAILROAD.

DENVER UNION DEPOT.

EAST.

Leave	8.10 a. m.	9.55 p. m.
Arrive	7.00 a. m.	2.30 p. m.

KANSAS PACIFIC RAILROAD.

DENVER UNION DEPOT.

EAST.

Leave	7.00 a. m.	8.05 p. m.
Arrive	7.15 a. m.	8.55 p. m.

Take the PIKES PEAK ROUTE

—BETWEEN—

Denver, Colorado Springs, Pueblo, Buena Vista, Leadville, Aspen and Glenwood Springs.

D. B. ROBINSON, General Manager. **CHAS. S. LEE,** General Passenger Agent.

IN EFFECT DEC. 1st. 1887.

POCKET

TIME TABLE

—OF THE—

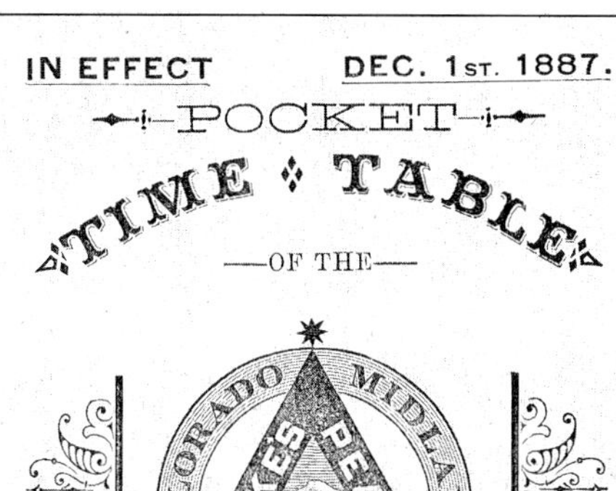

AND CONNECTIONS

TO AND FROM THE EAST.

MOUNTAIN TIME.

TICKET OFFICES:

Denver City Office, 1309 17th Street, near Larimer,
E. G. PATTERSON, Pass. & Ticket Agent.
Denver Union Depot Office,
E. F. LACKNER, Agent.
Colorado Springs City Office, Opera House Block,
S. N. NYE, Passenger Agent.
Colorado Springs Depot Office, Pikes Peak Ave.,
J. J. HOYT, Agent.
Pueblo City Office.
Pueblo Union Depot, Pueblo Stone Depot,
J. E. WATSON, Agent.
Buena Vista City Office,
M. D. POTTER, Agent.
Buena Vista Depot Office,
P. J. RYAN, Agent.
Leadville Depot, Spruce Street, Bet. 3d & 4th Sts.
GEO. W. COOK, General Agent.
H. C. BURNETT, Passenger & Ticket Agent.
Aspen City Office, Post Office,
C. C. KENDALL, Agent.
Glenwood Springs, C. M. MARSH, Agent.

1888

The through schedules for May 1st were almost a duplicate of the ones for December 1887, insofar as trains No. 1, 2, 3 and 4 were concerned. The Aspen Branch trains had their numbers changed from Nos. 15 and 18 to Nos. 21 and 22, respectively, running on the same schedule as before. There is still a footnote indicating that a train left Glenwood Springs at 3 PM (the same departure time as No. 4), and arrived at Aspen at 5:20 PM. Since the viaduct over Maroon Creek had been completed in February, this schedule now showed the trains to the Aspen station in the downtown area.

Meal stops were also shown for Leadville and Aspen Junction for the through trains, in addition to the meal station at Cascade Canon. In the Ute Pass area, suburban trains were shown as leaving Colorado Springs for Green Mountain Falls at 8:30 AM, 1:05 PM and 3:45 PM. The return trips left Green Mountain Falls at 10 AM, 2:25 PM and 6:30 PM, with all of these trains marked to run daily.

The line was completed to New Castle on October 20th, and the Aspen Short Line was incorporated late in the year to build a new line from Crystal Lake to a point west of Leadville, which would be known as Arkansas Junction. Construction was started late in the year and completed early in 1889.

The CM received 13 more locomotives during 1888; three of them were class 102 4-6-0s, Nos. 26 – 28, while the other ten were Baldwin class 102 4-6-0s, Nos. 29 – 38. The latter engines were the first Baldwin-built engines on the road, as all others up to this point had been built by Schenectady. All of the engines received this year were designed to be used primarily in freight and helper service. The only change in passenger equipment during the year was the acquisition of office car *Manitou*, (No. 99) which was built by Barney & Smith.

Several station names were changed during 1888, as follows: Junction House at milepost 18.0 in 1887 was discontinued, while Green Mountain Falls at milepost 15.0 was added. The station at Theodore (milepost 23.6) was changed to Summit Park, shown at milepost 23.8. Also, Hayden's Divide at milepost 27.4 was shortened to Divide, and the mileage changed to 27.8. Glenwood Springs was also shortened to Glenwood, temporarily as it developed.

Westward.	Mls.	No. 1 Exs.	No. 3 Exs.
May 1, 1888.		A. M.	P. M.
Denver ♁ lve.		*8 00	*9 15
[LEAVE		A. M.	
Pueblo ♁		9 10	
[LEAVE		A. M.	N'HT
Colorado Springs ♁	0	*11 15	*12 25
Colorado City ♁	3.3	11 35	12 45
Manitou	6.5	11 48	1 00
Manitou Iron Springs	7.3	11 52	1 03
Cascade Cañon	11.9	‖12 30	1 25
Culver ♁	13.0	12 33	. . .
Green Mt. Falls	15.0	12 43	1 42
Manitou Park	20.4	12 57	2 00
Summit Park ♁	23.8	1 10	2 15
Divide	27.8	1 23	. . .
Bellevue	29.7	1 28	. . .
Florissant ♁	36.7	1 50	3 00
Metcalf	38.9	2 00	. .
Lidderdale	42.0	2 10	. . .
Idlewild ♁	49.5	2 32	. . .
Howbert	52.9	2 42	3 46
Spinney ♁	58.7	2 58	4 00
Hartsel ♁	69.7	3 25	4 25
Haver	78.2	3 43	. . .
Hill Top ♁	85.5	4 03	5 05
Higgins	91.0	4 18	. . .
Buena Vista ♁	101.8	4 50	5 50
Wild Horse	104.2	5 00	. . .
Fisher ♁	113.1	5 22	. . .
Granite	119.4	5 38	6 38
Crystal Lake	128.0	6 00	7 00
Leadville ♁ arr.	135.3	6 25	‖7 30
Leadville ♁ lve.	135.3	P. M.	7 50
Busk	147.6		8 35
Rogers Spur	150.8		8 50
Hagerman ♁	152.9		9 00
Ivanhoe	156.8		9 15
Sellar ♁	165.6		9 50
Norrie	174.2		10 18
Ruedi ♁	182.9	21	10 50
Sloane	188.8	Exs.	11 08
Aspen Junction	197.8	A. M.	‖11 37
Aspen	216.2	*8 00	12 50
Aspen Junction	197.8	*9 00	*11 50
Wheeler	203.8	9 22	12 08
Sands ♁	210.5	9 42	12 28
Cardiff	217.9	10 05	12 50
Glenwood	221.3	10 15	1 00
[ARRIVE		A. M.	P. M.

Eastward.	Mls.	22 Exs.	No. 4 Exs.
[LEAVE		A. M.	P. M.
Glenwood	0	*10 25	*3 00
Cardiff	3.4	10 40	3 15
Sands ♁	10.8	11 00	3 35
Wheeler	17.5	11 18	3 53
Aspen Junction	23.5	11 37	4 10
Aspen	41.7	12 50	*3 15
Aspen Junction	23.5	NO'N	‖4 20
Sloane	32.5		4 48
Ruedi ♁	38.4		5 10
Norrie	47.1		5 45
Sellar ♁	55.7		6 16
Ivanhoe	64.5		6 55
Hagerman ♁	68.4		7 10
Rogers' Spur	70.5	No. 2	7 20
Busk ♁	73.7	Exs.	7 33
Leadville arr.	86.0	A. M.	‖8 20
Leadville ♁ lve.	86.0	*8 25	8 50
Crystal Lake	93.3	8 45	9 15
Granite	101.9	9 04	9 38
Fisher ♁	108.2	9 18	. . . .
Wild Horse	117.1	9 40	. . . .
Buena Vista ♁	119.5	9 50	10 30
Higgins	130.3	10 15	. . . .
Hill Top ♁	135.8	10 30	11 20
Haver	143.1	10 47	. . . .
Hartsel ♁	151.6	11 06	11 58
Spinney ♁	162.6	11 32	12 25
Howbert	168.4	11 44	12 37
Idlewild ♁	171.8	11 52	. . . .
Lidderdale	179.3	12 12	. . . .
Metcalf	182.4	12 20	. . . .
Florissant ♁	184.6	12 30	1 30
Bellevue	191.6	12 52	. . . .
Divide	193.9	12 58	. . . .
Summit Park ♁	197.9	1 10	2 15
Manitou Park	200.9	1 18	2 27
Green Mt. Falls	206.3	1 29	2 38
Culver ♁	208.3	1 37	. . .
Cascade Cañon	209.4	‖2 00	2 50
Manitou Iron Springs	214.0	2 22	3 11
Manitou	214.8	2 25	3 15
Colorado City ♁	218.0	2 40	3 30
Colorado Springs ♁	221.3	2 55	3 50
[ARRIVE		P. M.	A. M.
Pueblo ♁		6 30	
[ARRIVE		P. M.	
Denver ♁		6 00	7 00
[ARRIVE		P. M.	A. M.

Train leaves Glenwood *3 00 p.m., arriving at Aspen 5 20 p.m.

Trains leave Colorado Springs for Green Mt. Falls *8 3c a.m., *1 05, *3 45 p.m. Returning, leave Green Mt. Falls *10 00 a.m., *2 25, *6 30 p.m.

(opposite) Sometime during the second decade of this century, a pioneer motorist paces a Colorado Midland doubleheader, lead by 4-6-0 No. 14, as it struggles with the four percent grade, up Ute Pass west of Manitou near tunnel 8. (R.H. Kindig collection) Above a four-car passenger train is headed downgrade along the Frying Pan River somewhere east of Basalt. (H.H. Buckwalter, Colorado Historical Society)

1889

While passenger schedules during the first two years of the Colorado Midland's existence remained fairly stable, this year marked considerable experimentation and there were three distinct methods of operation during the year. With the completion of the line to New Castle late in 1888, schedules now reflected this extension, and New Castle became the western terminal of the line for all of this year.

It should also be noted that J. J. Hagerman relinquished his presidency of the CM, and this job was turned over to John Scott, although Hagerman retained actual control over the railroad.

As noted above, the Aspen Short Line was completed early in the year with its 6.6 miles of line from Crystal Lake to Arkansas Junction. This new line was primarily used at first for the benefit of freight traffic, and it did not have a great impact on passenger train routings at the time. Passenger trains continued to move between Crystal Lake and Leadville via the original mainline. Leadville was not only the major station on the railroad, but it also served as a meal station for most of the passenger trains.

The schedule for February 20th was quite similar to the ones previously mentioned, with the exception that the trains now ran to New Castle. No. 3 was still essentially a night train from Colorado Springs to New Castle, while No. 4 also was a night train on its eastbound run. Nos. 1 and 2 continued to provide a daylight service between Colorado Springs and Leadville on much the same schedule as in the past two years. No mention is made, however, of any service for the local stations between Colorado Springs and Green Mountain Falls, so this could have been strictly a summer operation the year before. Although the station at Rogers Spur (milepost 150.8) on Hagerman Pass was still listed, no time was shown for either train that passed that location.

On June 20th, considerable revamping of the schedules took place which mostly affected the through service. Train Nos. 1 and 2 between Colorado Springs and

Westward.	Mls	No. 1	No. 5
October 21, 1889.		A. M.	
Denver .... lve.		*8 00	
[LEAVE		A. M.	A. M.
Pueblo		8 30	8 05
[LEAVE		A. M.	A. M.
Colorado Springs	0	*10 50	*9 40
Colorado City	3 3	11 10	9 53
Manitou	6.5	11 22	10 04
Manitou Iron Springs	7.3	11 25	10 07
Cascade Cañon	11.9	11 46	10 30
Culver	13.0	11 50	10 33
Green Mt. Falls	15.0	11 58	10 40
Beaumont	20.4	12 35	11 10
Summit Park	23.8	12 45	11 20
Divide	27.8	12 56	11 32
Bellevue	29.7	1 01	11 37
Florissant	36.7	1 25	12 02
Metcalf	38.9	1 31	12 08
Lidderdale	42.0	1 41	12 18
Idlewild	49.5	1 58	12 38
Howbert	52.9	2 06	12 45
Spinney	58.7	2 25	1 00
Hartsel	69.7	2 47	P. M.
Haver	78 2	3 03	
Hill Top	85.5	3 26	
Higgins	91.0	3 38	
Buena Vista	101.8	4 05	
Wild Horse	104.2	4 12	
Fisher	113.1	4 31	
Granite	119.4	4 45	
Crystal Lake	128 0	5 05	
Leadville .... arr.	135.3	5 35	
Leadville .... lve.	135.3	5 55	
Busk	147 6	6 40	
Rogers Spur	150.8	....	
Hagerman	152 9	7 01	
Ivanhoe	156.8	7 16	
Sellar	165.6	7 47	
Norrie	174.2	8 14	
Ruedi	182.9	8 40	23
Sloane	188.8	8 58	P. M.
Aspen Junction	197.8	9 30	*4 40
Aspen	216.2	10 35	5 35
Aspen Junction	197.8	9 40	P. M.
Wheeler	203.8	10 10	
Sands	210.5	10 20	
Cardiff	217.9	10 40	
Glenwood	227.3	10 55	
New Castle	233.5	11 30	
[ARRIVE		P. M.	

Eastward.	Mls	No. 2	20
[LEAVE		P. M.	
New Castle	0	*2 25	
Glenwood	12.2	3 05	
Cardiff	15.6	3 20	
Sands	23.0	3 44	
Wheeler	29.7	4 05	
Aspen Junction	35.7	4 25	P. M.
Aspen	17.3	*3 30	*8 30
Aspen Junction	36.0	4 35	9 25
Sloane	44.7	5 08	P. M.
Ruedi	50.6	5 30	
Norrie	59.3	6 00	
Sellar	67.9	6 35	
Ivanhoe	76.7	7 16	
Hagerman	80.6	7 32	
Rogers' Spur	81.7	....	
Busk	85.9	7 55	
Leadville .... arr.	98.2	8 50	
Leadville .... lve.	98.2	9 15	
Crystal Lake	105.5	9 40	
Granite	114.1	10 00	
Fisher	120.4	10 17	
Wild Horse	129.3	10 37	
Buena Vista	131.7	10 45	
Higgins	142.5	11 21	
Hill Top	148.0	11 40	
Haver	155.3	11 59	6
Hartsel	163.8	12 15	P. M.
Spinney	174.8	12 35	*2 40
Howbert	180.6	12 48	2 55
Idlewild	184.0	12 55	3 02
Lidderdale	191 5	1 15	3 20
Metcalf	194.6	1 26	3 30
Florissant	196.8	1 35	3 36
Bellevue	203.8	2 02	4 00
Divide	205.7	2 10	4 05
Summit Park	209.7	2 22	4 16
Beaumont	213.1	2 35	4 26
Green Mt. Falls	218.5	2 50	4 41
Culver	220.5	....	4 47
Cascade Cañon	221.6	3 00	4 50
Manitou Iron Springs	226.2	3 20	5 07
Manitou	227.0	3 23	5 10
Colorado City	230.2	3 35	5 22
Colorado Springs	233.5	3 50	5 35
[ARRIVE		A. M.	P. M.
Pueblo			7 45
[ARRIVE			P. M.
Denver		6 45	
[ARRIVE		A. M.	

Leadville were discontinued, and 3 and 4 were also changed. New No. 1 now ran on a daylight schedule from Colorado Springs to New Castle, with the schedule time between Colorado Springs and Leadville approximating the former No. 1 that ran only between those two points. The Denver connection left that city at 7:45 AM, with No. 1 getting out of Colorado Springs at 10:50 AM, stopping at Leadville from 5:15 to 5:35 PM and arriving at New Castle at 10:55 PM, a 12 hour five minute running time. New No. 2 ran on about the same schedule as old No. 4, but left New Castle 30 minutes later at 3:30 PM, with arrival at Colorado Springs 30 minutes earlier at 3:50 AM, providing a Denver arrival at 6:45 AM. No. 2 covered the CM's 233.5 miles in 12 hours 20 minutes, a full hour faster than the previous No. 4. Two round trips were provided on the Aspen Branch, operating in the late afternoon and early evening, in order to make connections with both of the mainline trains.

This table also showed Nos. 5 and 6 operating between Colorado Springs and Manitou Park (milepost 20.4) with No. 5 leaving Colorado Springs at 7:30 AM and arriving Manitou Park at 8:50 AM. Returning as No. 6, it left Manitou Park at 9 AM and arrived in Colorado Springs at 10:15 AM. A footnote indicated that additional trains left Colorado Springs for Manitou Park at 1:20 PM and 4:40 PM, with return service leaving Manitou Park at 2:45 PM and 6:45 PM. Thus the Ute Pass local service was restored for this summer season, following the similar service of the year before. On September 9th the Colorado Springs – Leadville RPO was extended and became the Colorado Springs – New Castle RPO.

On October 21st, a new schedule was issued which lengthened the schedule of No. 1 by 35 minutes and No. 2 by one hour five minutes, possibly in anticipation of the approaching winter weather and the impending snow problems over Hagerman Pass. The primary change in this schedule, however, was the extension of Nos. 5 and 6 to a western terminal at Spinney (milepost 58.7). No. 5 left Colorado Springs at 9:40 AM and arrived Spinney at 1 PM. The return trip as No. 6 left Spinney at 2:40 PM and arrived Colorado Springs by 5:35 PM. This schedule closely approximated the famous Wildflower Specials that ran during most of the Colorado Midland's lifetime. The October timetable drops all mention of the Ute Pass locals of the summertime, with Nos. 5 and 6 providing the only service to these points, other than Nos. 1 and 2, the through trains.

It should also be noted that the station at Manitou Park (milepost 20.4) was changed to Beaumont, and the meal station was transferred to this station from Cascade

Canyon. Both Nos. 5 and 1 stopped for lunch at Beaumont, but none of the eastbound trains stopped there. It is rather curious that the CM scheduled both of its westbound trains to leave Colorado Springs within one hour ten minutes of each other, as it would appear that a more balanced schedule, such as the eastbound arrangement, would have been more effective.

Late in the year, the CM and the D&RG reached an agreement in connection with the establishment and joint operation of the Rio Grande Junction Railway, which would furnish both roads with an entry to Grand Junction and would enable the CM to effect a connection with the Rio Grande Western Ry. During the year, the CM received six more locomotives in class 102, Nos. 39 – 44, and these Tenwheelers were primarily destined for service in freight and helper duties. This acquisition brought the locomotive fleet up to 47 engines.

1890

The latter part of this year saw great changes take place on the Colorado Midland; in September, Hagerman managed to sell the CM to the Atchison Topeka & Santa Fe for $3.6 million in cash and stock, plus the Santa Fe's guarantee of $11.2 million in bonds. In the same month, the Rio Grande Junction was completed to Grand Junction. The sale of the CM bailed the investors out of a situation that appeared to be getting desperate, and they made a small profit out of the railroad. Hagerman considered it a vindication of his vision in building the line in the first place.

The completion of the Rio Grande Junction, and its connection with the Rio Grande Western at Grand Junction, made the Colorado Midland a through route able to compete for traffic beyond the confines of the Rocky Mountains. After November 14th, when trains of both the CM and D&RG began running to and from Grand Junction, the CM was no longer a "dead end" railroad. On November 15th, a lease was executed that allowed the CM to use the D&RG terminal facilities at Grand Junction. The D&RG performed all the switching service at this terminal, and the CM paid for it on a pro rata basis, using the number of road engines during a certain time period to determine each road's responsibility. Since the CM was permitted to solicit traffic and passengers at all stations on the Rio Grande Junction, this was an effective extension of CM trackage to Grand Junction.

The September 8th schedule was probably the last issued under an independent CM prior to the takeover by the Santa Fe. No. 1 still left Colorado Springs in the late morning at 10:45 AM and, after stopping at Leadville from 5:10 to 5:25 PM, arrived at New Castle at 9:55 PM, for an 11 hour ten minute trip over the road. No. 1 covered the railroad at a one hour 30 minute faster clip than in the previous year. No. 2 was out of New Castle at 4:10 PM, and was into Colorado Springs at 3:50 AM, the same as in 1889, with a similar arrival in Denver. This 11 hour 40 minute schedule was a full hour and 45 minutes faster than in 1889. It was quite remarkable to be able to cut this much time off the schedule, in both directions, considering the terrain and the type of railroad that the Midland had at that time.

Changes were made in the Ute pass area under the September 8th schedule. Nos. 5 and 6 were cut back and now terminated at Woodland Park, milepost 20.4, instead of at Spinney. No. 5 left Colorado Springs at 7:30 AM and arrived Woodland Park at 8:50 AM. No. 6 returned at 9:10 AM and was due in Colorado Springs at 10:20 AM. A footnote stated that another train left Colorado Springs at 1:20 PM for Woodland Park, with the return leaving that station at 5:20 PM. There were two new trains in the Ute Pass area. No. 12 left Florissant at 6:25 AM and was due Colorado Springs at 8:20 AM. No. 11 left Colorado Springs at 6:15 PM and made all stops to Florissant, arriving there at 8:05 PM. On the west end of the railroad, the two round trips on the Aspen Branch continued to operate during the late afternoon and early evening hours to accommodate passengers to and from the mainline trains, much as they had in the previous year.

In addition, because of the construction of the RGJ, the CM also listed train No. 41, leaving New Castle at 9:05 AM and due at DeBeque at 11:55 AM. No. 42 left DeBeque at 12:45 PM and returned to New Castle at 3:35 PM. The time consumed in running the 44 miles to DeBeque would indicate that these were mixed trains rather than straight passenger operations. Both of these trains ran daily except Sunday, while all other CM trains were listed for daily operation.

Westward.	Mls.	1	5	11
September 8. 1890.		A.M.		
Denver ... ♁ lve.		*8 00		
[LEAVE		A.M.	A.M.	
Pueblo ... ♁		9 05	8 00	
[LEAVE		A.M.	A.M.	P.M.
Colorado Springs ♁	0	*10 45	*7 30	*6 15
Colorado City ... ♁	3.3	11 05	7 42	6 25
Manitou ... ♁	6.5	11 15	7 55	6 37
Manitou Iron Springs ...	7.3	11 18	7 58	6 40
Cascade Cañon ... ♁	11.9	11 45	8 20	6 55
Ute Pass Park ...	13.0	11 48	8 24	6 58
Green Mt. Falls ... ♁	15.0	11 57	8 33	7 05
Wood and Park ... ♁	20.4	12 35	8 50	7 20
Summit Park ... ♁	23.8	12 45	A.M.	7 30
Divide ...	27.8	12 56		7 40
Bellevue ...	29.7	1 03		7 44
Florissant ... ♁	36.7	1 20		8 05
Metcalf ...	38.9	1 27		P.M.
Lidderdale ...	42.0	1 37		
Idlewild ...	49.5	1 55		
Howbert ... ♁	52.9	2 02		
Spinney ... ♁	58.7	2 15		
Hartsel ... ♁	69.7	2 34		
Haver ... ♁	78.2	2 48		
Hill Top ...	85.5	3 09		
Higgins ... ♁	91.0	3 22		
Buena Vista ... ♁	101.8	3 50		
Wild Horse ...	104.2	3 56		
Fisher ...	113.1	4 13		
Granite ... ♁	119.4	4 27		
Crystal Lake ... ♁	128.0	4 45		
Leadville ... ♁ arr.	135.3	5 10		
Leadville ... ♁ lve.	135.3	5 25		
Busk ... ♁	147.6	5 57		
Hagerman ... ♁	152.9	6 15		
Ivanhoe ... ♁	156.8	6 27		
Sellar ...	165.6	6 52		
Norrie ... ♁	174.2	7 15		
Ruedi ... ♁	182.9	7 35		23
Sloane ...	188.8	7 50		P.M.
Aspen Junction ... ♁	197.8	8 15		*6 00
Aspen ... ♁	216.2	9 10		6 45
Aspen Junction ...	197.8	8 25		P.M.
Wheeler ...	203.8	8 38		
Sands ...	210.5	8 53		
Cardiff ... ♁	217.9	9 10		
Glenwood ... ♁	221.3	9 25		A.M.
New Castle ... ♁	233.5	9 55		†9 05
Rifle Creek ...	247.0	P.M.		10 00
Parachute ...	265.0			11 05
De Beque ...	277.5			11 55
[ARRIVE				A.M.

Eastward.	Mls.	2	42	
[LEAVE			NO'N	
De Beque ...	0		*12 45	
Parachute ...	12.0		1 35	
Rifle Creek ...	30.0	P.M.	2 40	
New Castle ... ♁	44.0	*4 10	3 35	
Glenwood ... ♁	56.2	4 43	P.M.	
Cardiff ... ♁	59.6	4 55		
Sands ... ♁	67.7	5 13		
Wheeler ...	73.7	5 28	20	
Aspen Junction ...	79.7	5 45	P.M.	
Aspen ... ♁	61.3	*5 05	*7 25	
Aspen Junction ... ♁	80.0	6 00	8 10	
Sloane ...	88.7	6 28	P.M.	
Ruedi ... ♁	94.6	6 48		
Norrie ... ♁	103.3	7 15		
Sellar ...	111.9	7 45		
Ivanhoe ... ♁	120.7	8 25		
Hagerman ... ♁	124.6	8 40		
Busk ... ♁	129.9	9 02		
Leadville ... arr.	142.2	9 45		
Leadville ... ♁ lve	142.2	9 55		
Crystal Lake ... ♁	149.5	10 20		
Granite ... ♁	158.1	10 37		
Fisher ...	164.4	10 50		
Wild Horse ...	173.3	11 08		
Buena Vista ... ♁	175.7	11 15		
Higgins ... ♁	186.5	11 47		
Hill Top ...	192.0	12 03		
Haver ... ♁	199.3	12 22		
Hartsel ... ♁	207.8	13 37		
Spinney ... ♁	218.8	12 57		
Howbert ... ♁	224.6	1 03		
Idlewild ...	228.0	1 15		
Lidderdale ...	235.5	1 33		12
Metcalf ...	238.6	1 45		A.M.
Florissant ... ♁	240.8	1 55		*6 25
Bellevue ...	247.8	2 17		6 43
Divide ...	249.7	2 22	6	6 48
Summit Park ... ♁	253.7	2 35	A.M.	7 00
Woodland Park ... ♁	257.7	2 45	*9 10	7 10
Green Mt. Falls ... ♁	262.5	2 58	9 25	7 25
Ute Pass Park ...	264.5	3 02	9 32	7 32
Cascade Cañon ... ♁	265.6	3 05	9 35	7 35
Manitou Iron Springs.	270.2	3 22	9 55	7 52
Manitou ... ♁	271.0	3 25	9 58	7 55
Colorado City ... ♁	274.2	3 35	10 10	8 07
Colorado Springs ♁	277.5	3 50	10 20	8 20
[ARRIVE		A.M.	A.M.	A.M.
Pueblo ... ♁			8 00	
[ARRIVE			P.M.	
Denver ... ♁		6 45		
[ARRIVE		A.M.		

Train leaves Colorado Springs for Woodland Park *1 20 p.m. Train leaves Woodland Park for Colorado Springs *5 20 p.m.

During the year, the station at Culver (milepost 13.0) was changed to Ute Pass Park, and the station at Beaumont (milepost 20.4) was changed to Woodland Park as has already been mentioned. The eating house remained at Woodland Park as a holdover from the previous year. The station at Rogers Spur (milepost 150.8) was finally dropped from the station listings. The September 8th schedule listed the new RGJ stations at Rifle Creek (milepost 247.0), Parachute (milepost 265.0) and DeBeque (milepost 277.5) in anticipation of further extension of the RGJ line to Grand Junction, and the establishment of Nos. 41 and 42 west of New Castle.

On November 25th, the Colorado Springs & New Castle RPO was changed to the Colorado Springs & Aspen RPO. This would indicate that the RPO car now arrived on No. 1's connection at 9:10 PM at Aspen, while the eastbound car for No. 2 left Aspen at 5:05 PM.

During 1890, the CM received four more class 102 ten-wheelers for freight service, Nos. 45 to 48, bringing the fleet up to 51 engines. These would be the last locomotive purchases until 1897. The road also bought three more baggage cars, numbered 314 – 316, which were built by Barney & Smith. This brought the passenger car fleet up to 42 cars going into into the Santa Fe ownership.

1891

With the completion of the Rio Grande Junction to Grand Junction late in 1890 and the Santa Fe acquiring control of the CM in September of that year, the way was paved for a complete revamping of the CM's passenger services. That is exactly what took place.

Under the new arrangement, emphasis appeared to have been placed on through business, rather than on the local traffic that had been promoted prior to the road's access to Grand Junction and the Rio Grande Western. Two through trains were established by February 1st, with Nos. 1 and 2 operating on somewhat similar schedules as they had during the previous year. No. 1 left Colorado Springs more than two hours later than it had in 1890; its connection now left Denver at 10 AM, with departure from Colorado Springs at 1 PM. After a lunch stop at Woodland Park, the train was due in Leadville at 8:05 PM for a 20-minute dinner stop. No. 1 was at New Castle at 2:05 AM and was due in Grand Junction by 4:35 AM. Only five minutes was allowed for the change to the RGW, and arrival at Salt Lake City was listed for 4:30 PM, with Ogden at 6 PM.

No. 2's connection left Ogden at 8:45 PM and Salt Lake City at 10:05 PM, with arrival at Grand Junction at 9:45 AM. CM No. 2 did not get out of Grand Junction until 1:30 PM and then ran east of New Castle on a schedule very similar to that of No. 2 in 1890. Arrival at Colorado Springs was 4:50 AM, and the Denver connection was due in that city by 7:50 AM.

No. 3 had its Denver connection out at 7:45 PM, with CM's train leaving Colorado Springs at 10:30 PM and arrival at Grand Junction marked up for 12:45 PM the next day. The RGW connecting train did not leave Grand Junction until 2:15 PM, with arrival at Salt Lake City at 1:45 AM and Ogden at 3 AM.

The RGW connection for No. 4 left Ogden at 8:30 AM and Salt Lake City at 9:50 AM, and arrived Grand Junction by 9:30 that evening. CM No. 4 left Grand Junction at 9:40 PM, stopped in Leadville from 5:50 to 6 AM and, after a morning run, arrived Colorado Springs by 12:35 PM. The Denver connection deposited passengers in that city at 3:50 PM.

Two round trips operated on the Aspen Branch, with crews making the trip from Aspen to Aspen Junction and return. The morning trip made a connection with No. 3 for Aspen, while the afternoon trip made a connection with No. 2 for the east. No Ute Pass locals were listed, and it would be unusual to see any of these trains running during the winter season. The only reference to equipment being assigned to the through trains was the statement that the "CM Division" had a "Solid train between Denver and Ogden" and that "Through Pullman Sleeping Cars and Tourist Cars between Denver and San Francisco, without change" were being assigned.

Under the new regime, a number of station names were changed; Manitou Iron Springs was shortened to Iron Springs, Ute Pass Park was changed to Ute Park, Crystal Lake (the junction of the short line to Arkansas Junction) was now called Snowden and Hagerman was changed to Hagerman Tunnel. Peach Blow, the site of a famous stone quarry, was added to the station listing, although some stations were dropped from the Official Guide in order to make room for the additional listings for the western connections.

Since this was an entirely new operation, it might be interesting to look at the running times for the entire 712-mile run of the through trains, as well as the Colorado Midland's initial running time between Colorado Springs and Grand Junction. These times are shown below:

Train No.	Colo. Springs–Grand Jct.	Denver–Ogden
1	15 hrs. 35 mins.	32 hrs. 0 mins.
3	14 hrs. 15 mins.	31 hrs. 15 mins.
2	15 hrs. 20 mins.	35 hrs. 5 mins.
4	14 hrs. 55 mins.	31 hrs. 20 mins.

These would not be considered fast schedules today, but considering the fact that this was essentially a new mountain railroad, with the Rio Grande Western having recently been widened from narrow to standard gauge, the times were quite good. It will be noted that in later years the Colorado Midland was able to reduce its running times considerably under those shown above. It must also be remembered that the schedules were competitive with those offered by the D&RG, and this factor

Santa Fé Route.

COLORADO MIDLAND DIVISION.

THROUGH TIME-TABLE.

Westward.

February 1, 1891.	Mls	No. 1 Express.	No. 3 Express
(*Mountain time.*)			
Lve. **Denver** δ	0	*10 00 A.M.	*7 45 P.M.
Lve. **Pueblo** δ	0		11 25 P.M.
Arr. **Colorado Springs** δ	74	12 50 NO'N	10 30 P.M.
Lve. **Colorado Springs**	74	1 00 P.M.	10 30 »
» Colorado City δ	77	1 25 »	10 50 »
» **Manitou** δ	80	1 38 »	11 00 »
» Iron Springs	81	..	
» Cascade Canon δ	86	2 03 »	11 25 »
» Ute Park	87	2 08 »	11 29 »
» Green Mt. Falls δ	89	2 18 »	11 38 »
Arr. Woodland Park δ	94	‡2 37 »	11 56 »
Lve. Woodland Park	94	2 57 »	11 56 P.M.
» Florissant δ	110	3 46 »	12 44 N'HT
» Howbert δ	126	4 30 »	1 27 A.M.
» Spinney δ	132	4 46 »	1 42 »
» Hartsel δ	143	5 08 »	2 10 »
» Haver δ	151	5 25 »	....
» Hill Top	158	5 46 »	...
» Higgins δ	163	5 59 »	3 02 »
» **Buena Vista** δ	174	6 28 »	3 32 »
» Granite δ	192	7 16 »	4 24 »
» Snowden δ	201	7 40 »	4 49 »
Arr. **Leadville** δ	209	8 05 »	5 15 »
Lve. **Leadville** δ	209	8 25 »	5 25 »
» Arkansas Junction	213	8 35 »	5 37 »
» Busk δ	221	9 08 »	6 08 »
» **Hagerman Tunnel**	226	9 40 »	6 40 »
» Ivanhoe δ	230	9 55 »	6 52 »
» Ruedi δ	256	11 30 P.M.	8 07 »
» Sloane	262	....	8 23 »
» Peach Blow	263		8 26 »
Arr. **Aspen Junction**	271	12 20 NH'T	8 50 A.M.
Arr. **Aspen**	290		*9 45 A.M.
Lve. **Aspen** δ	290		*7 50 A.M.
Lve. **Aspen Junction**	271	12 30 N'HT	8 50 A.M.
» **Wheeler**	277	....	9 03 »
» Cardiff δ	291	1 24 A.M.	9 32 »
Arr. **Glenwood Springs**	295	1 37 »	9 45 »
Lve. **Glenwood Springs**	295	1 37 »	9 45 »
Arr. **New Castle** δ	307	2 05 »	10 15 »
Lve. **New Castle**	307	2 05 »	10 15 »
» Rifle Creek	321	2 32 »	10 39 »
» Parachute	338	3 05 »	11 10 »
» De Beque	351	3 29 »	11 32 A.M.
Arr. **Grand Junction**	384	4 35 »	12 45 NO'N
Lve. **Grand Junction**	384	4 40 »	2 15 »
» Fruita		4 57 »	2 33 »
» **Cisco**	439	0 35 »	....
» Little Grand	475	..	
Arr. **Green River**	489	18 30 »	15 50 »
Lve. **Green River**	489	8 50 »	6 10 »
» Lower Crossing	515	9 45 »	7 02 »
» Price	554	11 10 »	8 25 »
» **Castle Gate**	564	11 38 A.M.	8 56 »
» Pleasant Valley Junction	578	12 25 NO'N	9 15 P.M.
» Red Narrows	604	....	....
» Pole Canon	616	....	....
» **Spanish Fork**	621	2 28 P.M.	....
» Springville	625	2 38 »	12 08 N'HT
Arr. **Provo**	630	‡2 50 »	12 20 »
Lve. **Provo**	630	3 10 »	12 20 N'HT
» Battle Creek	640	3 28 »	....
» American Fork	644	3 33 »	....
» Lehi	647	3 38 »	....
» Jordan Narrows	653	3 51 »	....
» **Bingham Junction**	665	4 11 »	....
» Francklyn	668	4 17 »	....
Arr. **Salt Lake City**	676	4 30 »	1 45 A.M.
Lve. **Salt Lake City**	676	4 45 »	2 00 »
» Hot Springs	679	....	....
» Lake Shore	688	..	....
» Kaysville	695	5 24 »	....
» Layton	698		....
Arr. **Ogden**	712	6 00 P.M.	3 00 A.M.
(*Pacific time.*)			
Lve. **Ogden**		6 00 P.M.	3 00 A.M.
» **Reno**		3 00 P.M.	11 40 P.M.
» **Sacramento**		2 50 A.M.	8 40 A.M.
Arr. **San Francisco**		6 45 A.M.	12 15 NO'N

Eastward.

February 1, 1891.	Mls	No. 2 Express.	No. 4 Express.
(*Pacific time.*)			
Lve. **San Francisco**		*7 30 A.M.	*7 00 P.M.
» **Sacramento**		12 05 NO'N	11 00 P.M.
» **Reno**		10 20 P.M.	9 20 A.M.
Arr. **Ogden**		7 00 P.M.	6 30 A.M.
(*Mountain time.*)			
Lve. **Ogden**	0	*8 45 P.M.	*8 30 A.M.
» Layton	14	....	....
» Kaysville	17	....	....
» Lake Shore	24	....	....
» Hot Springs	33	....	....
Arr. **Salt Lake City**	36	9 55 »	9 40 !
Lve. **Salt Lake City**	36	10 05 »	9 50 »
» Francklyn	43	....	10 04 »
» **Bingham Junction**	47	....	10 13 »
» Jordan Narrows	59	....	....
» Lehi	65	....	10 47 »
» American Fork	68	....	10 53 »
» Battle Creek	72	....	11 00 »
Arr. **Provo**	82	11 30 »	‡11 20 »
Lve. **Provo**	82	11 35 »	11 40 »
» Springville	87	11 47 P.M.	11 52 A.M.
» **Spanish Fork**	91	....	12 03 NO'N
» Pole Canon	96	....	....
» Red Narrows	108	....	....
» Pleasant Valley Junction	134	2 10 A.M.	2 15 P.M.
» **Castle Gate**	148	2 54 »	2 55 »
» Price	158	3 22 »	3 20 »
» Lower Crossing	197	4 40 »	4 38 »
Arr. **Green River**	223	5 30 »	‡5 30 »
Lve. **Green River**	223	5 35 »	5 50 »
» Little Grand	237	....	....
» **Cisco**	273	....	7 37 »
» Fruita	....	9 20 »	9 12 »
Arr. **Grand Junction**	328	9 45 A.M.	9 30 »
Lve. **Grand Junction**	328	1 30 P.M.	9 40 »
» De Beque	361	2 35 »	10 45 »
» Parachute	374	2 59 »	11 10 »
» Rifle Creek	391	3 32 »	11 42 P.M.
Arr. **New Castle**	405	4 00 »	12 10 N'HT
Lve. **New Castle**	405	4 00 »	12 10 »
Arr. **Glenwood Springs**	417	4 30 »	12 38 »
Lve. **Glenwood Springs**	417	4 30 »	12 38 »
» Cardiff δ	421	4 43 »	12 50 N'HT
» Wheeler	434	5 15 »	1 21 A.M.
Arr. **Aspen Junction** δ	441	5 30 P.M.	1 35 A.M.
Arr. **Aspen**	456	*6 30 P.M.	
Lve. **Aspen** δ	456	*4 50 P.M.	
Lve. **Aspen Junction**	441	5 45 P.M.	1 40 A.M.
» Peach Blow	449	6 13 »	2 07 »
» Sloane	450	6 16 »	....
» Ruedi δ	456	6 36 »	2 30 »
» Ivanhoe δ	482	8 23 »	4 13 »
» **Hagerman Tunnel**	486	8 48 »	4 38 »
» Busk δ	491	9 08 »	5 00 »
» Arkansas Junction	499	9 35 »	5 37 »
Arr. **Leadville**	503	9 50 »	5 50 »
Lve. **Leadville** δ	503	10 00 »	6 00 »
» Snowden δ	511	10 25 »	6 25 »
» Granite δ	519	10 48 »	6 48 »
» **Buena Vista** δ	537	11 37 P.M.	7 36 »
» Higgins δ	548	12 12 N'HT	8 06 »
» Hill Top	553	....	8 21 »
» Haver δ	560	....	8 40 »
» Hartsel δ	568	1 13 A.M.	8 57 »
» Spinney δ	579	1 42 »	9 21 »
» Howbert δ	585	1 55 »	9 32 »
» Florissant δ	601	2 40 »	10 15 »
Arr. Woodland Park δ	617	3 30 »	11 08 »
Lve. Woodland Park	617	3 30 »	11 08 »
» Green Mt. Falls δ	622	3 44 »	11 25 »
» Ute Park	624	3 52 »	11 33 »
» Cascade Canon δ	625	4 00 »	11 42 A.M.
» Iron Springs	630	....	..
» **Manitou**	631	4 21 »	12 05 NO'N
» Colorado City	634	4 35 »	12 20 »
Arr. **Colorado Springs** δ	637	4 50 »	12 35 »
Lve. **Colorado Springs** δ	637	5 00 A.M.	12 50 NO'N
Arr. **Pueblo** δ	680		1 40 P.M.
Arr. **Denver** δ	712	7 50 A.M.	3 50 P.M.

ASPEN TO ASPEN JUNCTION.

STATIONS.	Mls	Express.	Express.
Lve. **Aspen**	0	*7 50 A.M.	*4 50 P.M.
» Maroon	2.4	....	....
» Rathbone	6.6	8 09 »	5 08 »
» Watson	10.4	8 19 »	5 17 »
Arr. **Aspen Junction**	18.4	8 40 A.M.	5 36 P.M.

ASPEN JUNCTION TO ASPEN.

STATIONS.	Mls	Express.	Express.
Lve. **Aspen Junction**	0	*9 00 A.M.	*5 45 P.M.
» Watson	8.0	9 18 »	6 03 »
» Rathbone	11.8	9 28 »	6 12 »
» Maroon	16.0	....	....
Arr. **Aspen**	18.0	9 45 A.M.	6 30 P.M.

N. B.—Trains marked * run daily ; ‡ Meals.

δ Telegraph stations.

CONNECTIONS.—In Union Depots at Denver, Colorado Springs, Pueblo and Ogden.

SOLID TRAIN BETWEEN DENVER AND OGDEN.

Through Pullman Sleeping Cars and Tourist Cars between Denver and San Francisco, without change.

546

Santa Fé Route.

COLORADO MIDLAND DIVISION.

PIKE'S PEAK ROUTE

STANDARD GAUGE.

GENERAL OFFICES:
COLORADO SPRINGS, COL.

TRAFFIC DEPARTMENT:
DENVER, COL.

ALLEN MANVEL, President, Chicago, Ill.
J. W. REINHART, Vice-President, Boston, Mass.
H. COLLBRAN, Gen. Manager, Colorado Springs, Col.
E. W. SELLS, Secretary and Auditor, Colorado Springs, Col.
CHARLES E. NOBLE, Treasurer, Colorado Springs, Col.
HENRY T. ROGERS, Gen. Solicitor, Denver, Col.
J. K. WATERMAN, Gen. Freight Agent, Denver, Col.
CHAS. S. LEE, Gen. Passenger Agent, Denver, Col.
W. J. LAWRENCE, Superintendent, Colorado City, Col.
B. H. BRYANT, Chief Engineer, Colorado Springs, Col.

The New Trans-Continental Route

BETWEEN

COLORADO, UTAH AND THE PACIFIC COAST

PASSING THROUGH

Leadville, Glenwood Springs, Grand Junction, Salt Lake City and Ogden.

TWO DAILY PASSENGER TRAINS EACH WAY.

Pullman Palace Sleeping Cars

AND

Pullman Tourist Excursion Cars

BETWEEN

DENVER AND SAN FRANCISCO

WITHOUT CHANGE.

Full page advertisements such as this appeared in the Official Guide with Colorado Midland schedules, which were included with Santa Fe listings during the 1890-1895 period when the AT&SF owned the CM.

was to play a large part in the planning of CM schedules in the future.

On June 18th, the CM Division, as it was now known in the Santa Fe family, changed the schedules again. Nos. 1 and 2 were eliminated, which would indicate that two through trains in each direction were a little more than the traffic could stand. The fact that these trains were taken off during the summer season also pointed to the fact that business was not very good at all over the new route to the west.

Under the new schedule, No. 3 operated on about the same times as before, and No. 4 ran on the times of old No. 2 to Grand Junction, with considerable earlier times east of that point. No. 3 now left Colorado Springs at 11:10 PM, with arrival at Grand Junction at 2 PM the next afternoon. No. 4 left Grand Junction at 10:15 AM and did not reach Colorado Springs until 4:17 AM, providing an early morning arrival at Denver. This schedule eliminated Woodland Park as a meal station, with Leadville as the only such stop for No. 3, while No. 4 stopped at Glenwood Springs and Leadville for this purpose. Under this arrangement, the running time of No. 3 was not appreciably changed, but the time of No. 4 was lengthened to just over 18 hours! The one hour 25 minute lunch stop at Glenwood Springs did not help in getting No. 4 over the road and contributed in no small part to making this the slowest of all CM schedules between Grand Junction and Colorado Springs.

The Aspen Branch was not affected by this change, as connections with both the westbound and eastbound through trains were maintained. The equipment listing was changed to the effect that "Through Pullman Sleeping Cars between Denver, Leadville, Aspen and Salt Lake City, without change" were being operated in the one through train each way.

Since the June 18th schedule covered the summer season, the road once again established Ute Pass local schedules, and both morning and evening service was operated between Colorado Springs and Woodland Park. There was a mid-day service to and from Florissant on schedules somewhat approximating the famous Wildflower Specials that the road ran for many years.

On November 29th, the second train in each direction over the mainline was restored, indicating that business had either picked up, or that the single train was not sufficient to handle the business that was available. Nos. 3 and 4 maintained a schedule similar to that in June, and new No. 1 left Colorado Springs at 10 AM, with a 7:20 AM connection from Denver. No. 1 stopped in Leadville from 4:52 to 5:12 PM, Aspen Junction from 8:33 to 8:43 PM and arrived in Grand Junction at 12:50 AM. Close connection was made for the west, with arrivals in Salt Lake City at 12:01 PM, and Ogden at 1:20 PM. No. 2's connection left Ogden at 8:30 AM and Salt Lake City at 9:50 AM, and arrived in Grand Junction by 9:30 that evening. CM No. 2 departed at 9:45 PM, stopped for breakfast at Leadville from 6:40 to 7 AM, and arrived in Colorado Springs at 1:45 PM, with a Denver connection into that city by 4:35 PM. Woodland Park, Leadville and Aspen Junction were still the meal stations for the through trains.

The service on the Aspen Branch doubled over its former arrangement, and there were now four round trips on the line, starting at Aspen and running to Aspen Junction and return. Because the mainline trains now had such irregular times at Aspen Junction, a connection was run for each of the four trains. There was even a train leaving Aspen at 1:05 AM and returning at 3:15 AM in order to make a connection with eastbound No. 2 which was due at Aspen Junction from 2:10 to 2:25 AM!

Although specific equipment assignments were not listed, the road now advertised "Through Pullman Sleeping Cars between Denver, Leadville, Aspen and Salt Lake City without change" and between "Manitou, Col., Colorado Springs, and Kansas City and Chicago." This would indicate that the Santa Fe's thrust was now veering toward its own long haul routes and away from the Denver connections, even though the mileages were still being shown from the Denver origin.

The only station name change was at Granite, now called Granite Gate, and there were no additions or subtractions from the locomotive or car fleets during the year.

66

Mile Scenic
Trip for

$1.00

Thru Historic Ute Pass over the Old Ute Indian Trail and thru the Beautiful Mountain Resorts of Cascade, Green Mountain Falls, Crystola and Woodland Park to Hayden's Divide (elevation 9,200 feet)

Midland Terminal Ry.

Wildflower
Excursion

Train Leaves from Santa Fe Station
9 a. m. daily

Santa Fé Route.

COLORADO MIDLAND DIVISION.

THROUGH TIME-TABLE.

PIKES PEAK ROUTE

Westward.

June 19, 1892.	MI	No. 1 Express.	No. 3 Express.
(Mountain time.)			
Lve. Denver ♂	0	*8 10A.M.	*8 05 P.M.
Lve. Pueblo ♂	0	*6 10A.M.	*3 20 P.M.
Arr.. Colorado Springs ♂	74	10 50A.M.	10 45 P.M.
Lve. Colorado Springs	74	10 55 "	10 50 "
" Colorado City ♂	77	11 12 "	11 07 "
" Manitou ♂	80	11 19 "	11 16 "
" Iron Springs	81	11 22 "	
" Cascade Canon ♂	86	11 39 "	11 40 "
" Ute Park	87	11 43 "	11 50 "
" Green Mt. Falls ♂	89	11 47A.M.	11 55 P.M.
Arr.. Woodland Park ♂	94	12 12NO'N	12 13N'HT
Lve. Woodland Park	94	12 17NO'N	12 13N'HT
" Florissant ♂	110	1 00 P.M.	1 00A.M.
" Howbert ♂	126	1 39 "	....
" Spinney ♂	132	1 51 "	1 49 "
" Hartsel ♂	143	2 09 "	2 07 "
" Haver ♂	151	....	....
" Bath	158	2 42 "	2 41 "
" Higgins ♂	163	2 55 "	
" Buena Vista ♂	174	3 22 "	3 23 "
" Granite Gate ♂	192	4 00 "	
" Snowden ♂	201	4 18 "	4 38 "
Arr.. Leadville ♂	209	4 48 "	5 15 "
Lve. Leadville ♂	209	5 03 "	5 25 "
" Arkansas Junction	213	5 13 "	5 36 "
" Busk ♂	221	5 43 "	6 09 "
" Hagerman	226	6 10 "	6 37 "
" Ivanhoe ♂	230	6 22 "	6 49 "
" Ruedi ♂	256	7 35 "	8 03 "
" Sloane	262	....	8 19 "
" Peach Blow	263	7 54 "	[illegible]
Arr.. Aspen Junction	271	8 15 P.M.	8 45A.M.
Arr.. Aspen	290	9 00 P.M.	9 55A.M.
Lve. Aspen ♂	290	7 20 P.M.	8 00A.M.
Lve. Aspen Junction	271	8 23 P.M.	9 05A.M.
" Wheeler	277	....	9 20 "
" Cardiff ♂	291	9 00 "	9 48 "
Arr.. Glenwood Springs	295	9 10 "	10 00 "
Lve. Glenwood Springs	295	9 10 "	10 00 "
Arr.. New Castle ♂	307	9 42 "	10 30 "
Lve. New Castle	307	9 45 "	10 30 "
" Rifle	321	10 10 "	10 55 "
" Parachute	338	10 42 "	11 27 "
" De Beque	351	11 05 P.M.	11 50A.M.
Arr.. Grand Junction	384	12 05N'HT	12 50NO'N
Lve. Grand Junction	384	12 35N'HT	1 10 P.M.
" Fruita	....	....	1 26 "
" Cisco	439	....	2 49 "
" Little Grand	475	....	....
Arr.. Green River	489	3 53A.M.	4 25 "
Lve. Green River	489	3 53 "	4 25 "
" Lower Crossing	515	4 42 "	5 14 "
" Price	554	5 56 "	6 25 "
" Castle Gate	564	6 29 "	
" Pleasant Valley Junction	578	7 15 "	8 05 "
" Red Narrows	604	....	
" Pole Canon	616	....	
" Vista	621	....	
" Springville	625	9 15 "	10 15 "
Arr.. Provo	630	9 25 "	10 25 "
Lve. Provo	630	9 45 "	10 25 "
" Battle Creek	640	....	
" American Fork	644	....	
" Lehi	647	....	
" Jordan Narrows	653	....	
" Bingham Junction	665	....	
" Francklyn	668	....	
Arr.. Salt Lake City	676	11 05 "	11 48 "
Lve. Salt Lake City	676	11 15A.M.	11 58 P.M.
" Hot Springs	679	....	
" Lake Shore	688	....	
" Kaysville	695	....	
" Layton	698	....	
Arr.. Ogden	712	12 15NO'N	1 00A.M.
(Pacific time.)			
Lve. Ogden		12 01NO'N	12 45N'HT
" Reno		9 00A.M.	8 40 P.M.
" Sacramento		5 45 P.M.	5 15A.M.
Arr.. San Francisco		9 45 P.M.	9 15A.M.

Eastward.

June 19, 1892.	MI	No. 4 Express.	No. 2 Express
(Pacific time.)			
Lve. San Francisco		*8 00A.M.	*6 00 P.M.
" Sacramento		11 55A.M.	10 00 P.M.
" Reno		10 20 P.M.	8 10A.M.
Arr.. Ogden		6 30 P.M.	5 15A.M.
(Mountain time.)			
Lve. Ogden	0	*8 15 P.M.	*7 00A.M.
" Layton	14	....	....
" Kaysville	17	8 48 "	....
" Lake Shore	24	....	....
" Hot Springs	33	....	....
Arr. Salt Lake City	36	9 15 "	7 50 "
Lve. Salt Lake City	36	9 25 "	8 00 "
" Francklyn	43	....	....
" Bingham Junction	47	....	....
" Jordan Narrows	59	....	....
" Lehi	65	10 15 "	....
" American Fork	68	10 20 "	....
" Battle Creek	72	....	....
Arr. Provo	82	10 44 "	9 05 "
Lve. Provo	82	10 44 "	9 25 "
" Springville	87	10 55 P.M.	9 36 "
" Vista	91	....	....
" Pole Canon	95	....	....
" Red Narrows	108	....	....
" Pleasant Valley Junction	134	1 15A.M.	11 50A.M.
" Castle Gate	148	1 34 "	12 28NO'N
" Price	158	2 22 "	12 57NO'N
" Lower Crossing	197	3 34 "	2 00 P.M.
Arr. Green River	223	4 20 "	....
Lve. Green River	223	4 20 "	....
" Little Grand	237	4 52 "	....
" Cisco	[illegible]	[illegible]	....
" Fruita	..	7 32 "	....
Arr. Grand Junction	328	7 50 "	5 50 "
Lve. Grand Junction	328	8 10 "	6 20 "
" De Beque	361	9 06 "	7 21 "
" Parachute	374	9 27 "	7 44 "
" Rifle	391	9 57 "	8 13 "
Arr. New Castle	405	10 20 "	8 40 "
Lve. New Castle	405	10 20 "	8 40 "
Arr. Glenwood Springs	417	10 51 "	9 10 "
Lve. Glenwood Springs	417	10 51 "	9 10 "
" Cardiff ♂	421	11 02 "	9 19 "
" Wheeler	434	....	....
Arr. Aspen Junction ♂	441	11 40A.M.	9 55 P.M.
Arr. Aspen	456	12 40NO'N	10 53 P.M.
Lve. Aspen ♂	456	10 55A.M.	9 15 P.M.
Lve. Aspen Junction	441	11 45A.M.	10 00 P.M.
" Peach Blow	449	12 10NO'N	....
" Sloane	450	....	....
" Ruedi ♂	456	12 30NO'N	....
" Ivanhoe ♂	482	1 52 P.M.	11 51 P.M.
" Hagerman	486	2 09 "	12 05N'HT
" Busk ♂	491	2 25 "	12 22 "
" Arkansas Junction	499	2 49 "	12 45N'HT
Arr. Leadville	503	3 00 "	1 05A.M.
Lve. Leadville	503	3 20 "	12 20N'HT
" Snowden ♂	511	3 44 "	1 05A.M.
" Granite Gate ♂	519	4 00 "	....
" Buena Vista ♂	537	4 37 "	1 58 "
" Higgins ♂	548	....	....
" Bath	553	5 15 "	2 41 "
" Haver ♂	560	....	....
" Hartsel ♂	568	5 44 "	....
" Spinney ♂	579	6 01 "	....
" Howbert	585	6 10 "	....
" Florissant ♂	601	6 45 "	4 13 "
Arr. Woodland Park ♂	617	7 30 "	4 59 "
Lve. Woodland Park	617	7 45 "	4 59 "
" Green Mt. Falls ♂	622	7 58 "	....
" Ute Park	624	....	....
" Cascade Canon ♂	625	8 12 "	5 25 "
" Iron Springs	630	....	....
" Manitou	631	8 32 "	5 45 "
" Colorado City	634	8 45 "	5 57 "
Arr. Colorado Springs ♂	637	8 55 "	6 05 "
Lve. Colorado Springs ♂	637	9 05 P.M.	6 10A.M.
Arr. Pueblo ♂	680	10 34 P.M.	
Arr. Denver ♂	712	11 45 P.M.	8 50A.M.

ASPEN BRANCH.

June 19, 1892.	M	23	25	27	29
[LEAVE		A.M.	A.M.	P.M.	P.M.
Aspen Junc.	0	*9 10	*11 50	*6 20	*10 05
Watson	8	9 30	12 11	....	10 25
Rathbone	12	9 39	12 20	....	10 35
Aspen	18	9 55	12 40	9 00	10 53
[ARRIVE		A.M.	NO'N	P.M.	P.M.
STATIONS.	M	22	24	26	28
[LEAVE		A.M.	A.M.	P.M.	P.M.
Aspen	0	*8 00	*10 55	*7 20	*9 15
Rathbone	6	8 16	11 13	7 36	....
Watson	10	8 25	11 22	7 45	....
Aspen Junc.	18	8 45	11 40	8 05	9 55
[ARRIVE		A.M.	A.M.	P.M.	P.M.

SUBURBAN TRAINS.

June 19, 1892.	5	7	9
[LEAVE	A.M.	P.M.	P.M.
Colorado Springs	*8 10	*1 15	*5 15
Colorado City	8 25	2 00	5 33
Manitou	8 34	3 09	5 42
Iron Springs	8 37	2 12	5 45
Cascade Canon	8 54	2 29	6 02
Ute Park	8 59	2 35	6 07
Green Mt. Falls	9 04	2 40	6 12
Woodland Park	9 20	2 57	6 30
Summit Park	9 29	3 07	P.M.
Divide	9 39	3 17	
Bellevue	9 44	P.M.	
Florissant	10 03		
[ARRIVE	A.M.		
STATIONS.	6	8	10
[LEAVE		A.M.	
Florissant		*10 30	
Bellevue		10 52	P.M.
Divide		10 58	*3 30
Summit Park	A.M.	11 08	3 39
Woodland Park	*6 40	11 18	3 48
Green Mt. Falls	6 54	11 34	4 01
Ute Park	6 59	11 39	4 06
Cascade Canon	7 08	11 47	4 14
Iron Springs	7 25	12 04	4 31
Manitou	7 28	12 07	4 34
Colorado City	7 37	12 15	4 43
Colorado Springs	7 50	12 30	4 55
[ARRIVE	A.M.	NO'N	P.M.

*Daily. ‡ Meals. ♂ Telegraph stations.

CONNECTIONS.

IN UNION DEPOTS

—AT—

Denver, Colorado Springs, Pueblo and Ogden.

THROUGH PULLMAN PALACE SLEEPING CARS,

Without change, between Denver, Leadville, Aspen and Salt Lake City;

Between Denver and Ogden, between Chicago and Ogden, and between Denver and Leadville, daily.

1892

While previous schedules shown in the Official Guide do not yet list the names of trains, the employee timetable for June 19th, published in the end pages of *Colorado Midland,* do show the names of each of the passenger trains operating on the mainline. It should also be noted at this time that Cripple Creek was becoming well known after the discovery of gold by Bob Womack in 1890. The big rush was already on to this greatest of American gold camps—hence, the advertising of trains as being expresses to Cripple Creek was a legitimate title. In this era, CM's trains were met by stages at Divide or Florissant and passengers were transported by these coaches to Cripple Creek and environs.

The names of the trains as listed in the employee timetable are as follows:

Westbound –No. 1 – Pacific Express
No. 3 – Utah & California Express
No. 5 – Cripple Creek Mail & Express–Florissant
No. 7 – Cripple Creek Mail & Express–Divide
No. 9 – Suburban – Woodland Park

Eastbound – No. 2 – Atlantic Express
No. 4 – Chicago Limited
No. 6 – Suburban – Woodland Park
No. 8 – Cripple Creek Mail & Express–Florissant
No. 10 – Cripple Creek Mail & Express–Divide

It will be noted that the Ute Pass local services were again established for the summer season and, with the influx of passengers to the Cripple Creek region, these trains probably did a very handsome business.

The westbound schedules were very similar to those of the previous November, but there was a considerable improvement in the eastbound running times for both Nos. 2 and 4. No. 2 now left Grand Junction at 6:20 PM, three hours 25 minutes earlier than previously, and arrived Colorado Springs at 6:05 AM, for an overall running time of 11 hours 45 minutes, quite a lot better than the 16 hours needed in November. Part of this improvement was due to the fact that this train no longer ran into Leadville, but ran via Arkansas Junction and the Aspen Short Line. This was a relatively new operation for the CM, and one of the early attempts to utilize the Aspen Short Line for passenger service improvements. In this case, the crew and engine of No. 2 on arrival at Arkansas Junction assumed the schedule of stub run No. 16 from Arkansas Junction to Leadville, handling a coach or combine plus any Leadville cars off No. 2. Prior to the arrival of No. 2 at Arkansas Junction, the First District crew and engine left Leadville with a coach or combine, plus any through cars from Leadville to the east, as train No. 15 on the Second District and ran to Arkansas Junction to meet No. 2. After the Leadville cars had been added to the through consist, this crew then departed Arkansas Junction for Colorado Springs, proceeding as No. 2.

No. 2's schedule was not the only improvement, as No. 4 was also reduced from a 16 hour 25 minute running time to 12 hours 45 minutes, and now provided almost a complete daytime ride over the CM, from 8:10 AM from Grand Junction to an 8:55 PM arrival at Colorado Springs; the arrival at Denver was a full six hours earlier than the previous November. While a rather late-in-the-evening arrival at 11:45 PM, it still allowed a night's rest in a hotel, as compared to the former arrival time of 5:45 AM.

It seems remarkable in this day and age that a schedule over the same territory, with no apparent changes in the line or equipment, could accommodate almost a 25% improvement in running time in one direction, yet this is what the summer of 1892 offered as compared to the previous winter's schedule. It does not look like it could all be attributed to winter weather conditions. Whatever brought it about, it was a dramatic improvement for eastbound trains. Four round trips were still being run on the Aspen Branch, with a connection being operated for each of the four through trains.

The Santa Fe was not reluctant to trumpet the advantages of its Colorado Midland Division with advertising claiming:

> Two daily passenger trains each way equipped with all the latest appliances known to modern railway travelers. The Colorado Midland is the shortest line by 75 miles from Denver to all Utah and Pacific Coast points via Colorado Springs, through a scenic region that has no equal in Colorado. Through Pullman Palace Sleeping Cars without change between Denver, Leadville, Aspen and Salt Lake City; between Denver and Ogden, between Chicago and Ogden and between Denver and Leadville, Daily.

There was no further mention of the Manitou sleeping car service, so presumably such passengers would have to travel all the way from Manitou to Colorado Springs in order to avail themselves of a through berth to Kansas City or Chicago. There were no changes in either the locomotive fleet or the passenger car fleet during the year.

Colorado Midland Tenwheeler 46 stops at Green Mountain Falls with a Cripple Creek to Colorado Springs train sometime in the late 1890s. This station generated a good deal of passenger revenue due to its two resort hotels and many summer homes. At nearly the end of the Midland's life, local residents protested a reduction in winter passenger service. (PUC report, Museum collection; H.H. Buckwalter, Colorado Historical Society)

BEFORE THE

Public Utilities Commission

OF THE

State of Colorado

CITIZENS OF GREEN MOUNTAIN FALLS, COLORADO, *Complainants,* v. THE COLORADO MIDLAND RAILWAY COMPANY, George W. Vallery, Receiver, *Defendant.*	Case No. 109

Submitted December 22, 1916. *Decided January 17, 1917.*

COMPLAINT against winter passenger train service afforded Green Mountain Falls and Cascade by the Colorado Midland Railway Company; complaint dismissed.

APPEARANCES:

For the Complainants, Mr. James B. Barnes.

For the Defendant, Mr. George A. H. Fraser and Mr. Chester H. Speers.

STATEMENT

By the Commission:

On the 20th day of November, 1916, the Commission received a written petition signed by twenty-seven (27) citizens of Green Mountain Falls, Colorado, requesting that trains Nos. 8 and 11,

operated by the defendant, The Colorado Midland Railway Company, George W. Vallery, Receiver, be retained and to investigate the withdrawal of same.

The petition stated that the only means of transportation since the discontinuance of trains Nos. 8 and 11 is by train No. 3, westbound, arriving Green Mountain Falls 12:05 (midnight), and train No. 6, eastbound, arriving at 3:00 o'clock A. M., completely cutting off any convenient communication with Colorado Springs and other trading points.

On the 5th day of December, 1916, the defendant corporation filed with the Commission its answer to the petition, stating that ever since December 13, 1912, the functions and activities of this defendant as a common carrier have been suspended; that upon said date Mr. George W. Vallery was appointed Receiver of this defendant by the District Court of the United States for the District of Colorado; that immediately thereafter he qualified as such Receiver, and that ever since said date he has been, and now is, the duly qualified and acting Receiver of this defendant; that all functions of the company, as a common carrier, ever since have been, and now are, discharged by said Receiver;

That on to-wit, November 19, 1916, trains Nos. 8 and 11, mentioned in said complaint, were withdrawn by said Receiver; that two passenger trains are daily operated by said Receiver through Green Mountain Falls, to-wit, train No. 3, westbound, reaching said station at 11:50 p. m., and No. 6, eastbound, reaching said station at 3:00 A. M.;

That for many consecutive years last past said trains Nos. 8 and 11 have, at about this time of year, been similarly withdrawn by reason of the fact that as the winter approaches the earnings therefrom become insufficient to pay operating expenses and that, even during a considerable portion of the time of operation of said trains each year, the same are operated at a loss;

That it has been the practice to resume operation of said trains about the month of April each year;

That at all times of the year, for many years last past, Green Mountain Falls has been merely a flag station for most passenger trains; that it is a very small community, and that passenger traffic to or from it at all times of the year has been very light and during the winter months has been, and is, so small as to be negligible; that said community has not grown or increased in size or importance for many years last past; that the winter schedule of trains has been arranged with a view to best serving the greatest number of residents located along the entire line; that it is necessary to have trains leave and arrive at terminals at such times as to make connections with the various other lines reaching such terminals; that the arrangement of train movement be made to accommodate through travel, as well as local passengers, and that

it is impossible so to schedule trains that every point will be reached at an hour convenient to the inhabitants thereof;

That similar conditions as to time of train arrivals to those at Green Mountain Falls apply on westbound traffic to all stations west of Green Mountain Falls, at least as far as Ivanhoe;

That by reason of the foregoing it is totally impracticable to continue said trains Nos. 8 and 11 during the winter months and that the inconvenience to Green Mountain Falls by reason of the suspension of said trains is necessarily incidental to the operation of the entire line.

On December 18, 1916, a written petition was received by the Commission signed by sixteen (16) citizens of Cascade, Colorado, (Cascade being situated four (4) miles southeast of Green Mountain Falls on the line of the defendant carrier), asking that an investigation be had as to the removal of trains Nos. 8 and 11 on November 19, 1916, and stating that the only means of transportation now being train No. 3, westbound, and train No. 6, eastbound, inconvenience is caused in going to and from Colorado Springs and other trading points.

Petitioners were granted the right to intervene and were made a party to this cause.

It developed from the testimony that Green Mountain Falls is mainly a tourist resort; that the business shops and merchants there are almost wholly supported by tourist trade, and that the months of June, July and August are the principal months in which business is transacted.

There is one small hotel which is closed during the winter. The principal industry is the renting of cottages or tents to tourists, and supplying them with their wants and needs during the summer season. That a number of cottages there are owned by people who occupy them only as summer residences, and that it has been the custom of the railway company for years to maintain an agency station at this point during only a portion of the year. Also it appears that part of the passenger train service has been discontinued by the defendant carrier over its line during the winter months for several years past, but that the residents of Green Mountain Falls can avail themselves of an automobile stage service which is operated at convenient hours, so that the people do not have to depend entirely on the railroad.

During the winter the population of Green Mountain Falls is about seventy-five (75); in the summer months there are one thousand (1,000) additional residents, mostly tourists. During the summer season the defendant carrier operates eight (8) passenger trains every twenty-four (24) hours, four (4) in each direction, and during the winter months the two (2) passenger trains operated are so scheduled as to serve the more densely populated communities through which the defendant carrier operates, in order to

give satisfactory service to the largest possible number of its patrons.

The Commission is of the opinion that the present passenger schedule of The Colorado Midland Railway Company, George W. Vallery, Receiver, taken in conjunction with the automobile stage service available during certain months of the winter, is sufficient to handle the business of Green Mountain Falls and Cascade and that these communities are not entitled to the same service in the winter as is afforded during the summer, or tourist season.

ORDER

IT IS THEREFORE ORDERED, That the complaint be dismissed.

The Public Utilities Commission of the State of Colorado.

(Seal)

S. S. KENDALL,
GEO. T. BRADLEY,
M. H. AYLESWORTH,
Commissioners.

Dated at Denver, Colorado, this 17th day of January, 1917.

1893

Two events occurred during this year that had a profound effect on the Colorado Midland and would change the character of the railroad for years to come. The first concerned the onset of the panic of 1893, brought on originally by the closing of the mints of India to the coinage of silver and the repeal of the bimetallic policy of the United States in favor of the gold standard. These factors had a disastrous effect on the economy of Colorado in particular, causing a virtual stand-still in the mining of silver throughout the state. The country as a whole plunged into a depression the likes of which had not been felt before. This caused severe economic problems at mining centers such as Aspen and Leadville, which were served by the CM, and also had its effect on corollary industries. Even the mighty Santa Fe was not immune to the economic malaise that spread throughout the land, as we shall see.

The other major event in the life of the Colorado Midland was the completion of the Busk-Ivanhoe Tunnel when the headings came together on October 18th. The Busk Tunnel Railway Company had been incorporated on June 16, 1890, and construction had started that year. The tunnel was completed by December 17th, and CM started to use the new bore almost immediately. The tunnel was 1.78 miles long and saved the CM 7.4 miles (9.5 miles over Hagerman Pass vs. 2.1 miles from Busk to Ivanhoe direct), as well as 575 feet in elevation (a total of 1011 feet of rise and fall) and 1,958 degrees of curvature. The line ascended westbound through the tunnel on a grade of 1.41 percent. Helpers on trains out of Arkansas Junction kept on pushing through the tunnel to Ivanhoe, where a new station was erected slightly east of the old one. a turntable as well as several auxiliary tracks were constructed, so that helpers from both directions could be turned and sent back to their starting points, either

The demeanor of this engineer and fireman leaves no doubt as to their pride in being assigned to Colorado Midland locomotive No. 1. The famed Denver photographer Harry Hale Buckwalter took their portrait at Ivanhoe, Colorado on a winter day just after the turn of the century, as they waited to return to Arkansas Junction after helping a westbound train up through the Busk Tunnel.

Arkansas Junction or Aspen Junction. The fact that trains had to work hard ascending the westbound grade in the tunnel caused considerable problem with the gasses emitted by the engines, and it took quite a while to clear the tunnel of these gasses, as satisfactory ventilation was never established. The benefits of the tunnel, however, far outweighed this problem, as will be seen.

Perhaps the Santa Fe foresaw the depression of 1893 coming over the horizon, for the CM Division's schedules were again reduced to one train daily over the road in each direction as of May 7th. No. 1 was now the only through westbound train out of Colorado Springs, and it left that station on a somewhat similar schedule to the one of the 1892 summer season. Departure was now 10 AM and, with a lunch stop at Woodland Park at 11:38 AM, it arrived in Leadville by 4:25 PM for dinner. Departure was 20 minutes later, and Grand Junction was reached at 11:55 PM. The RGW connection left at 12:10 AM, and arrival at Salt Lake City was marked for 10:20 AM, Ogden at 11:30 AM. Eastbound No. 4 operated about two hours earlier than it had the previous summer, and the RGW connection left Ogden at 6:15 PM and Salt Lake City at 7:20 PM, with arrival at Grand Junction at 5:15 AM. CM No. 4 left its western terminal at 5:30 AM, stopped at Aspen Junction for 20 minutes for breakfast (8:55 to 9:15 AM) and arrived at Leadville in time for lunch at 12:45 PM. Out of there at 1:00 PM, it ran through to Colorado Springs by 6:55 PM, with the Denver connection into that city at 9:30 PM. The Santa Fe advertised that a Palace sleeper was operated on these trains between Chicago and Ogden via Pueblo. Other mainline service included Ute Pass locals, Nos. 5 and 6, operating on a morning turnaround from Colorado Springs to Florissant.

Aspen Branch service was reduced to match the mainline reductions, and the CM now offered only two round trips a day out of Aspen to connect with train Nos. 1 and 4. The morning trains were numbered 24 and 23, connecting with No. 4, and the evening runs were numbered 22 and 21, affording a connection with westbound No. 1.

Since the operation over Hagerman Pass was about to be discontinued it might be interesting to see just what the schedule looked like over the pass at this time. Here is the way it shaped up in the summer of 1893:

No. 1		No. 4
5:26 PM	Busk	12:10 PM
5:55 PM	Hagerman	11:50 AM
6:08 PM	Ivanhoe	11:32 AM

It can be seen from the above that the overall time for No. 1 was 42 minutes, while No. 4 was listed for a 38 minute running time. When this is compared with the traditional running time of ten minutes through the tunnel, it can easily be seen what the benefit of the tunnel was to the passenger operation. As the freight trains of the period generally took twice the time of passenger trains, not to mention the effort of getting over the summit at Hagerman, the tunnel was certainly a boon of no small proportion to the CM.

The first schedule showing trains through the Busk Tunnel was in the Official Guide as of December 21st and still contained only one train each way over the railroad. No. 1 was changed to No. 5, and it left Colorado Springs at 11:10 AM from a Denver connection leaving there at 8:35 AM. Lunch was still taken at Woodland Park, and Leadville was reached at 5:58 PM. Departure was set for 6:15 PM, and the time at Busk was 7:10 PM, with Ivanhoe at 7:25 PM. Aspen Junction was reached at 9:22 PM, for a ten-minute meal stop, and arrival at Grand Junction was listed for 1:15 AM. The RGW connection was correspondingly later at Salt Lake City and Ogden. Eastbound No. 6, in lieu of old No. 4, left Grand Junction at 7:35 AM, connecting with the RGW overnight train from the Utah cities. Aspen Junction was a meal stop from 10:53 to 11:08 AM, and the time through the tunnel was Ivanhoe at 1:40 PM and Busk at 1:50 PM. No. 6 reached Leadville at 2:20 PM and departed 2:28 PM, stopping for supper at Woodland Park at 7:20 PM, with an arrival of 8:25 PM at Colorado Springs. The Denver connection got there at 11 PM, too late for much evening activity but still time to get to a hotel for a good night's rest.

Ute Pass service was cut back from Florissant to Divide, and new No. 11 made a morning trip westbound leaving Colorado Springs at 8:20 AM, arriving divide at 9:53 AM. Returning, No. 12 left Divide at 5:45 PM, just one hour ahead of No. 6, and arrived at Colorado Springs at 7:30 PM. The scheduling of this train around Woodland Park indicates that a stop was made for dinner as well as the later stop by No. 6.

Aspen Branch service still consisted of two round trips, but now the morning round trip was numbered 26 and 27 while the evening trains were Nos. 24 and 25. Connections were still made with mainline trains Nos. 5 and 6.

The equipment now shown for the through trains listed a Palace sleeper from Chicago to Leadville, Salt Lake City and Ogden without change; and a chair car from Denver to Ogden in train No. 5, with the same equipment listed in the reverse direction for No. 6. Although the CM was now operating through the Busk Tunnel, the mileages were not yet changed and would not be, in the public timetable, until the middle of 1895.

Due to the severe downturn in economic conditions during the latter part of 1893, the Santa Fe found itself overextended financially and as a result of this mighty company being unable to meet its obligations, receivers were appointed on December 23rd.

During the year, the only change to the car or locomotive fleet was the destruction of first class coach No. 102, which reduced the passenger car fleet to 41 units at the end of the year. This car would be rebuilt in 1897 but, in the meantime, it was taken off the roster.

Prior to the completion of the Midland Terminal in 1894, stagecoaches and freight wagons to the gold camp connected with the CM at Divide. (Museum collection)

1894

More momentous events would occur in this year that would shape the future of the Colorado Midland. On February 2nd, the same receivers who had been appointed for the Santa Fe in December 1893 were appointed for the Colorado Midland, since the CM was in default. These parties would direct the fortunes of the road until April 30, 1895.

The other, and more lasting event, was the completion of the Midland Terminal Railway from Divide to the Cripple Creek District. During this year, the MT would be extended from Midland to Victor in the District. This new line into the great gold camp would have a significant effect of Colorado Midland passenger service for the remainder of its lifetime. Since the through passenger trains operating between Colorado Springs and the Cripple Creek district were handled by CM crews, using CM locomotives and passenger cars until 1917, the schedules will be treated here as though they were Colorado Midland schedules and trains. Until changed by the common management in 1917, the Midland Terminal was responsible only for the operation of its local passenger, freight and switching service in the District and between there and Divide. At the latter point, freight traffic was interchanged with the CM, which handled the freight between Divide and Colorado Springs, and to and from points west of Divide, which was a considerable business in its own right.

The schedule for June 10th still listed one through train between Colorado Springs and Grand Junction, on a similar schedule as was effective the previous year. The trains were now renumbered in the Santa Fe series. No. 5 was now No. 905, with No. 6 being No. 906. This system was also used for the Ute Pass locals and the new Cripple

Creek service which now extended only as far as Midland. Nos. 907 and 911 ran from Colorado Springs to Midland, and No. 903 was the afternoon commuter from Colorado Springs to Woodland Park. Eastbound schedules from Midland to Colorado Springs were covered by Nos. 908 and 912, with the morning Ute Pass local running as No. 904. There was also a connection on the Midland Terminal between Midland and Divide, which provided a service with mainline through trains Nos. 905 and 906. Two round trips were still being operated on the Aspen Branch, each one making a connection with either No. 905 or No. 906 and still using Aspen as the home terminal for the crews.

For the first time in the Official Guide listing, detailed equipment assignments were shown with the schedules. The equipment listed in this particular schedule showed the through movement of cars from Chicago. This train handled a through Palace sleeper from Chicago to Leadville, Salt Lake City and Ogden without change and a chair car from Denver to Ogden. No. 907 carried a Pullman buffet sleeper from Denver to Midland, with a stage coach connection from there to Cripple Creek. Eastbound, the equipment was in reverse order for Nos. 906 and 908.

The Cripple Creek night train left Denver at 11:50 PM, and arrived Colorado Springs at 3:45 AM. The CM train left Colorado Springs at 4:05 AM, and the MT portion arrived Midland at 6AM. Here the CM and MT schedules differ, as the CM advertised a 7:15 AM arrival in Cripple Creek by stage, while the MT schedule listed an 8:30 AM arrival at the gold camp. The eastbound train, No. 908, had a departure from Midland at 9:05 PM with the Denver sleeper. The stage connection from Cripple Creek was still at variance, as the MT advertised a departure of 6:50 PM while the CM showed it leaving Cripple Creek at 7:30 PM. No. 908 was due at divide at 9:35 PM and, after a five minute stop, headed down the hill to Colorado Springs, being due there at 11:20 PM. The Santa Fe connection left at 1:15 AM, and was in Denver by 4:45 AM.

The other Midland Terminal running times varied between 20 and 25 minutes for the seven-mile trip between Divide and Midland. The Midland Terminal's own schedule in the Official Guide for the same period showed the through Pullman sleeper between Denver and Midland. Under the heading "Connections" it listed the ATSF Ry – Colorado Midland Division at Divide and at Midland "with the Concord coaches of the Kuykendale Transportation Co. meeting passenger trains at Midland and conveying passengers to Cripple Creek in two hours." Based on the times shown at Midland, it would appear that the MT schedule was more accurate than that of the CM with respect to the arrival and departure times of the Cripple Creek stages.

It should be noted that the meal station at Woodland Park had now been changed back to Cascade Canon, with two trains stopping there for meals in each direction—Nos. 905 and 906 on the mainline service and the two Cripple Creek day trains, Nos. 911 and 912.

The June 10th schedule discussed above was originally published in the July 1894 Guide. The August Guide also showed the schedule as being dated June 10th, but there are a few differences. The times of the CM trains were identical, but the equipment listing dropped the reference to the through sleeper between Chicago and Ogden. The only through equipment was the chair car between Denver and Ogden. The CM also adjusted the times at Cripple Creek to reflect the fact that the MT was operating to Gillett.

The Midland Terminal schedule in the August Official Guide was shown as being effective on July 4th. It was as follows:

Pas. AM	Pas. PM	Pas. AM	Miles	Stations	Pas. PM	Pas. PM	Pas. PM
5:45	1:12	10:25	0	Divide	12:40	5:30	9:35
6:05	1:38	10:45	6	Midland Jct.	12:20	5:10	9:15
6:30	2:12	11:15	15	Gillett	11:55	4:40	8:45
7:00	2:40	11:45		Cripple Creek	10.55	3:40	7:45
AM	PM	AM		(Stage)	AM	PM	PM

"Through Pullman Sleeper between Denver and Midland on trains leaving Denver 11:50 PM and leaving Gillett 8:45 PM."

The connection note now stated that "the Concord coaches of Kuykendale Transportation meet all passenger trains and convey passengers to Cripple Creek in 30 minutes."

It will be seen that there is a discrepancy in the above with respect to the operation of the sleeping car. Although the line was running through to Gillett, the note stated that the car ran only as far as Midland. It seems strange that the sleeper would be set off at Midland, thus requiring Pullman passengers for the District to change from the sleeper to a coach for the short trip to Gillett and then have to change again to the stage coach upon reaching that point. While it is true that there was a very heavy grade from Midland to Gillett and it is possible that the railroad did not want to haul the sleeper up this hill, the more plausible explanation is that the copy for the schedule changes did not keep up with the actual construction of the road. It is felt that the sleeper did, in fact, operate through to Gillett and originate at that station on its eastbound trip back to Denver. After all, once the line was completed to Victor and Cripple Creek, the sleepers were hauled up the hill and for quite a lengthy period there were at least two sleepers on the night train between Cripple Creek and Colorado Springs.

Regardless of this apparent discrepancy in the timetable, it is abundantly clear that the activities in the Cripple Creek region had a profound effect upon the passenger operations of the Colorado Midland. This effect would be felt for the rest of the railroad's existence.

THE GREAT

Wildflower Train

On COLORADO MIDLAND R'Y

Thursday, August 23, 1906

LEAVES

Colorado Springs - - -	8.30 am
Colorado City - - - -	8.40 am
Manitou - - - - -	8.50 am
Cascade Canon - - - -	9.08 am
Green Mountain Falls - - -	9.20 am
Woodland Park - - - -	9.35 am

Where It Goes

¶ Through Divide, Florissant, Lake George, Idlewild, Freshwater and through Granite Canon to Spinney, in beautiful South Park, a distance of sixty miles. Numerous stops will be made, affording passengers an opportunity to gather wildflowers.

¶ Returns to Manitou, Colorado City and Colorado Springs at 4.10, 4.20 and 4.30, respectively.

The wildflower trains apparently were unique to the Colorado Midland. In the pre-automobile age they offered a fine opportunity for a one day summer excursion into the Rocky Mountains for thousands of Colorado residents and visitors over the years. As evidenced here, management promoted the trains to a great degree, and they continued under the Midland Terminal after the CM was abandoned (see page 47). A group photograph was the highlight of each trip and provided a souvenir record of the day's harvest. These usually were taken in Eleven Mile Canon (below, H.H. Buckwalter, Colorado Historical Society), sometimes also called Granite Canon. (opposite, Museum collection)

WILDFLOWER EXCURSION TRAIN IN GRANITE CANON. (View No. 9)

Comforts

¶ First-class equipment of chair cars and coaches, also an observation car. Lunch at popular city prices will be served on the train — sandwiches, coffee, etc.

The Cost

Round trip to adults only

$1.50

Children between five and twelve, 75 cents

(Regular fare on other days, $6.30)

Buy Tickets at

COLORADO SPRINGS
Midland City Office, No. 9 N. Tejon
D. & R. G Depot, back of Antlers Hotel

COLORADO CITY
Midland Depot
509 Colorado Avenue

MANITOU
Midland Depot
100 Canon Avenue

"If you would honor my memory, put wildflowers upon my grave"

"When mountain ozone is laden with perfume of wildflowers it becomes Nature's most precious gift."

Imprint: Carson-Harper, Denver

1895

The Colorado Railroad Museum's reprint of AT&SF/Colorado Midland Division Timetable No. 66, effective January 1, 1895, provides an excellent picture of scheduled operations, both passenger and freight, at the beginning of this year. No. 905 (*Colorado and Utah Limited*) and No. 906 (*Kansas City and Chicago Limited*) ran on schedules similar to those of the previous year, with both trains operating through Arkansas Junction to Leadville and return to Arkansas Junction, thus eliminating the original mainline between Snowden and Leadville. There were also two round trips on the Aspen Branch. Nos. 976 and 973 made a morning trip connecting with eastbound No. 906; Nos. 974 and 975 made the evening round trip for a connection with No. 905 on its westbound journey. The Aspen Branch trains would continue to be numbered in the "70" series, after the Santa Fe influence disappeared, although the "900" classifications would be withdrawn.

No. 907, the *Cripple Creek Night Express*, left Colorado Springs at 3:10 AM, and arrived at Divide at 4:55 AM for further movement via the MT. Eastbound No. 908, the *Denver Night Express*, left Divide at 11:35 PM off the MT, and arrived in Colorado Springs at 1:20 AM, where connections were made for Denver.

It is unfortunate that the schedule for January 1st was not published in the Official Guide, as it is always interesting to compare the operating with the public timetable. However, the schedule that was effective November 25, 1894 was continued in the Guide until the February 1895 issue, at which time the schedule was dated January 20, 1895. Fortunately, the only change from that of the January 1st working timetable was for No. 907. Under the January 20th time, this train now left Colorado Springs at 6 AM, almost three hours later than it did under the previous schedule. Arrival at Divide was listed for 7:45 AM, with an eventual arrival at Victor at 9:15 AM on the MT. Other than this change, all times on the CM were identical in both the January 1st and January 20th schedules.

The January 20th schedule refers to the through trains as Nos. 5 and 6, although other trains are still in the "900" series. The equipment notes show that there was now a Pullman sleeper and free chair car between Denver and Ogden on these trains, so the lack of sleeping car accommodation on the through trains was relatively short-lived.

1	No. 7	No. 5	Miles	June, 1895.	No. 6	No. 8	2	4
				LEAVE] [ARRIVE			A.M.	P.M.
	*11 50 P.M.	*8 35 A.M.	0	+ ...... Denver ...... ♂	9 15 P.M.	4 40 A.M.	11 00	5 00
	11 45 P.M.	7 00 A.M.		+ .... Pueblo .... ♂	11 00 P.M.	4 35 A.M.	5 35	5 35
A.M.				LEAVE] [ARRIVE			A.M.	P.M.
*8 35	*3 20 A.M.	*11 15 A.M.	74	+ . Colorado Springs .. ♂	6 30 P.M.	2 40 A.M.	8 15	2 25
8 47	3 32 "	11 32 "	77	+ ..... Colorado City ...... ♂	6 17 "	2 28 "	8 01	2 12
8 55	3 40 "	11 40 A.M.	80	+ .... Manitou .... ♂	6 03 "	2 18 "	7 55	2 02
8 57	....	f ...	81	... Manitou Iron Springs	..	....	7 53	1 59
9 15	4 05 "	12 27 NO'N	86	..... ‖ Cascade Cañon ... ♂	5 42 "	1 55 "	7 35	1 41
9 22	4 12 "	f ..	88	.... Ute Park	....	1 46 "	7 20	1 32
9 27	4 17 "	12 40 "	89	...... Green Mt. Falls ... ♂	5 09 "	1 43 "	7 17	1 30
9 42	4 32 "	12 55 NO'N	94	.... Woodland Park .... ♂	4 58 "	1 30 "	7 04	1 17
10 05	4 55 A.M.	1 15 P.M.	101	arr .... Divide ♂ lve.	4 40 P.M.	1 07 A.M.	*6 45	12 50
10 25	5 30 A.M.	1 44 P.M.	108	arr. Midland (Mid. Term. Ry.). lve.	4 15 P.M.	11 55 P.M.	A.M.	12 30
10 55	6 15 "	2 20 "	115	.... Gillett "	3 45 "	11 05 "		12 05
11 12	6 35 "	2 35 "	121	.... Grassy "	3 28 "	10 35 "		11 50
11 20	6 47 "	2 45 "	123	.. Independence "	3 20 "	10 10 "		11 40
11 25	6 55 "	2 55 "	125	...... Victor ..... "	3 15 "	10 00 "		11 35
11 30	6 43 A.M.	3 00 P.M.	125	.. Cripple Creek .. (*Stage*) ..	*2 48 P.M.	*10 20 P.M.		*11 08
A.M.				ARRIVE] [LEAVE		—		A.M.
	4 55 A.M.	1 15 P.M.	101	lve. ...... Divide ♂ ..... arr.	4 40 P.M.	1 07 A.M.		
	5 17 "	1 39 "	110	.... Florissant .... ♂	4 05 "	12 37 N'GT		
	6 05 "	2 32 "	132	.... Spinney .... ♂	3 17 "	11 47 P.M.		
	6 25 "	2 56 "	143	.... Hartsel .... ♂	2 56 "	11 25 "		
	7 30 "	4 05 "	175	+ .... Buena Vista .... ♂	1 46 P.M.	10 17 "		
	8 37 "	5 15 "	208	...... Arkansas Junction ... ♂	12 42 NO'N	9 12 "		
	8 50 A.M.	5 30 "	209	arr. ... + ‖ Leadville ♂ .. lve.	12 25 "	*9 00 P.M.		
		5 55 "	209	lve. ... + Leadville ♂ ... arr.	12 15 "			
		6 12 "	208	lve. Arkansas Junction ♂ lve.	12 02 NO'N			
		6 55 "	221	.... Busk .... ♂	11 37 A.M.			
		7 05 "	224	.... Ivanhoe .... ♂	11 27 "			
		7 35 "	233	.... Sellar .... ♂	10 47 "			
	No. 73	8 08 "	244	.... Thomasville .... ♂	10 05 "	No. 74		
	*9 20 A.M.	9 07 P.M.	264	arr. . ‖ Basalt ♂ .... lve.	9 13 A.M.	8 45 P.M.		
	10 05 A.M.	9 55 P.M.	282	arr. ..... + Aspen ♂ .... lve.	8 20 A.M.	*7 55 P.M.		
		9 17 P.M.	264	lve. .... Basalt ♂ .... arr.	8 48 A.M.			
		10 05 "	285	+ .... Cardiff .... ♂	8 12 "			
		10 15 "	288	.... Greenwood Springs ... ♂	8 02 "			
		11 35 "	300	+ .... New Castle ..... ♂	7 35 "			
		11 57 P.M.	314	.... Rifle .... ♂	7 08 "			
		12 24 N'GT	331	.... Parachute .... ♂	6 41 "			
		12 47 N'GT	344	.... De Beque .... ♂	6 20 "			
		1 45 A.M.	377	+ .. Grand Junction ♂ lve.	*5 25 A.M.			
				ARRIVE] [LEAVE				
		1 20 P.M.	669	arr. .... Salt Lake ...... ♂	7 40 P.M.			
		2 30 P.M.	705	.... Ogden .... ♂	*6 35 P.M.			
				ARRIVE] [LEAVE				

No. 5—Daily, Pullman Sleeper and Free Chair Car Denver to Ogden, via Colorado Springs, connecting with Southern Pacific for Pacific Coast points.

No. 7—Daily, Pullman Buffet Sleeper Denver to Leadville, Grassy and Victor, via Colorado Springs. Stage Coach Grassy to Cripple Creek.

No. 1—Daily, Coaches Denver and Colorado Springs.

No. 3—Daily, to Victor.

Nos. 1 and 3 connect with stage at Grassy for Cripple Creek.

No. 6—Daily, Palace Sleeper San Francisco to Ogden. Pullman Sleeper and Free Chair Car Ogden to Colorado Springs and Denver. Solid Vestibuled train of Free Reclining Chair Cars and Palace Sleepers Denver to Chicago. Dining Cars Kansas City to Chicago.

No. 8—Daily, Pullman Buffet Sleeper Leadville, Victor and Grassy to Denver.

No. 2—Daily, Coaches from Victor to Colorado Springs and Denver.

No. 4—Daily, Coaches from Victor to Colorado Springs and Denver.

Stage from Cripple Creek connects with Nos. 2 and 4.

* Daily. + Coupon stations; ♂ Telegraph stations. ‖ Meal station. f Stops on signal.

CONNECTIONS.

Denver—With Atchison, Topeka & Santa Fé Ry., Burlington & Missouri River R.R., Chicago, Rock Island & Pacific Ry. and Union Pacific Ry. Lines, and Union Pacific, Denver & Gulf Ry., in Union Depot.

Colorado Springs—With Chicago, Rock Island & Pacific, Atchison, Topeka & Santa Fé, and Union Pacific, Denver & Gulf Rys.

Divide—With Midland Terminal Ry. for Grassy, Cripple Creek, &c.

Buena Vista—With Denver, Leadville & Gunnison Ry., and with stage lines for Buena Vista Spa and for the Tin Cup and Aspen Districts, via Cottonwood Pass.

Grand Junction—With Rio Grande Western Ry.

Manitou—With Manitou & Pike's Peak Ry.

Nos. 907 and 908, the Cripple Creek District trains, showed a Pullman Buffet Sleeper between Denver, Grassy and Victor, with the stage connection for Cripple Creek now operating via Grassy.

The Midland Terminal schedule for January 20, 1895, reads as follows:

49	7	5	Miles	Stations	6	8	46
PM	AM	PM			PM	PM	AM
7:50	7:45	1:25	0	Divide	4:30	11:25	11:30
8:55	8:35	2:15	15	Gillett	3:43	10:30	10:15
9:25	8:55	2:35		Grassy	3:26	10:15	9:25
	9:15	2:55		Cripple Creek (Stage)	3:00	9:45	
9:40	9:05	2:45		Independence	3:17	10:10	9:05
9:50	9:15	2:55		Victor	3:10	10:05	8:45
PM	AM	PM			PM	PM	AM

"Through Pullman Sleeper between Denver and Victor on Trains 7 and 8. Passengers may remain in sleeper until 7:00 AM."

Under "connections" was now stated, "At Grassy with Concord coaches of the Kuykendale Transportation Co., meeting all passenger trains and conveying passengers to Cripple Creek in twenty minutes." The time of 20 minutes via stagecoach from Grassy to Cripple Creek appears to be an optimistic estimate for, when the Short Line was built in 1901, its trains took longer than that in the run over Hoosier Pass. It should also be noted that Nos. 46 and 49 in the above schedule were no doubt mixed trains, as the running time was considerably longer than for the other passenger trains, and there was no advertised connection to and from Cripple Creek.

There is no indication as to why the night train from Denver was now held at Colorado Springs from its arrival at 2:59 AM until 6:00 AM before departing for the Cripple Creek District. A connection from Pueblo got in even earlier at 1:40 AM, so it is difficult to understand why this train should have been held for such a lengthy period. Perhaps the change was made to allow the train to serve two purposes: handle the sleeper from Denver, yet run late enough to catch the business travel going from Colorado Springs to the District. Businessmen could return in the afternoon on MT No. 6, which then connected at Divide with mainline No. 6 for a 6:30 PM arrival at Colorado Springs.

Colorado Midland bondholders had been getting increasingly restive over the performance of the AT&SF receivers and early in the year petitioned the court to discharge them and to appoint a receiver who would be responsible only for the CM's affairs. After due consideration, the court acceded to their request and appointed George W. Ristine as the receiver for the Colorado Midland on May 1st. This action effectively ended the control of the Santa Fe although the two roads continued to work closely together, and the passenger train connections between Denver and Colorado Springs were still handled by the Santa Fe.

The schedule for June 1895, the first for the independent Colorado Midland since the fall of 1890, eliminated the Santa Fe numbering system and returned all trains to their former numbering method. It also listed more detailed information relating to the assignment of equipment to the passenger trains. Nos. 5 and 6 were still the only through passenger trains scheduled between Colorado Springs and Grand Junction with western connections via the Rio Grande Western, and the schedules were similar to those of January. Nos. 7 and 8, the night trains, which had formerly run only over the CM to Divide and on to Victor over the MT, were now extended to Leadville on the mainline, providing an overnight service between Denver and the Cloud City. These trains also continued to handle the Denver – Victor sleeper, with the stage connection at Grassy being maintained for Cripple Creek passengers.

During this summer season, additional service was established between Colorado Springs and the Cripple Creek District. No. 1 left Colorado Springs at 8:35 AM and Divide and 10:05 AM for an 11:30 AM arrival at Victor. No. 3 left Colorado Springs at 5:35 PM and Divide at 7:20 PM arriving at victor by 8:35 PM. Eastbound No. 4 left Victor at 11:35 AM and Divide at 12:50 PM and arrived in Colorado Springs at 2:25 PM. Curiously, No. 2 showed on the CM schedule as running only from Divide at 6:45 AM and arriving Colorado Springs at 8:15 AM, with no connection from the MT. The equipment listing showed that the train handled coaches from Victor to Colorado Springs and Denver. So here is another of the many apparently contradictory items that appear in CM schedules from time to time.

The Midland Terminal also operated connecting schedules for the CM's mainline trains Nos. 5, 6, 7 and 8. Nos. 7 and 8, of course, handled the sleeping car between Denver and Victor, but the connections to and from Nos. 5 and 6 evidently required a change of cars at Divide, since no through cars were advertised.

Nos. 5 and 6 did include a Pullman sleeper and free chair car between Denver and Ogden, and both trains ran via the Aspen Short Line to Arkansas Junction, thence to Leadville and return to Arkansas Junction, and did not use the original mainline between Leadville and Snowden. The Aspen Branch also operated two round trips to connect with Nos. 5 and 6 at Basalt, as before.

As mentioned in the section on mileages, this schedule now showed Arkansas Junction to be 208 miles from Denver, but continued to show the improper mileage at Busk and west thereof. This continued in CM public timetables until 1912. The timetable, however, did restore Busk and Ivanhoe to the station listing, and showed mileage that reflected the use of the Busk Tunnel. Manitou Iron Springs was also restored to the station listing, but the biggest station name change was that Aspen Junc-

"Masonic Excursionists Lunching on the Platte" is the inscription on this circa 1888 view. The flatcar temporarily converted as an open-air coach was an ancestor of those in service today on the Durango & Silverton. (George E. Mellen, Colorado Historical Society)

tion was now called Basalt. It would retain this name from that time on. Basalt was the division point for the Second District where crews changed on mainline trains. The Second District included the mainline from Leadville to New Castle and the operation over the Rio Grande Junction to Grand Junction.

The schedule for November 17th again showed Nos. 5 and 6 to be the only through trains over the mainline, with essentially the same schedule as before, but No. 5 was speeded up by 45 minutes on its run to Grand Junction. The principal change on the mainline again concerned Nos. 7 and 8, as they were now extended west of Leadville to Basalt and Aspen. While still providing the overnight service between Denver and Leadville, and carrying both the Leadville and Victor sleepers, they offered a midmorning arrival and suppertime departure at Aspen. No. 1 also provided a morning service from Colorado Springs to Victor, and No. 2 showed a departure from Victor at 9:52 AM, with an arrival at Colorado Springs at 1 PM.

As the Midland Terminal had been completed as far as Anaconda in the District, the schedule now showed arrivals and departures at that point. This would indicate that the trains had been extended to that station, although the equipment listing showed the through cars operating to and from Victor. Grassy was still the connecting point with the stage line to and from Cripple Creek. This sometimes appears to have provided an earlier arrival and later departure than the train could do via Anaconda. Although the equipment listing showed Nos. 3 and 4 between Victor and Colorado Springs, no such trains were carried in the schedule columns, so presumably these trains had been discontinued for the winter months.

Another question is raised by the arrival time of No. 7's Aspen Branch connection at Aspen. The train left Basalt at 10:10 AM with arrival in Aspen at 11:55 AM. Since most trains on the branch showed a running time of 45 minutes, it appears reasonable to suspect that the arrival time in Aspen should be 10:55 AM and that the other figure was a misprint.

The Jerome Park Branch made its initial appearance in the Guide with a train from Cardiff at 7:00 AM, except Sundays, for Spring Gulch, with a return leaving at 9:30 AM. Although passengers were handled, they were carried in the caboose, as it was essentially a freight train handling coal cars to and from the mines located on the branch. Due to the severe four percent grades going up to the mines, it was not deemed economical to handle a coach or combine on the trip. The CM, however, continued to show such a passenger service in its schedules from this point until the fall of 1917. Granite, formerly

Granite Gate, also was returned to the station listing in this schedule.

The Colorado Midland issued a new schedule dated December 1st, published in the January 1896 Guide, which appeared to be slightly premature with respect to the Midland Terminal. This schedule showed through service to Cripple Creek for the first time, although records indicate that the line was not completed until December 18th. Regardless, the Midland Terminal schedule dated December 19th was identical to the times shown in the Colorado Midland timetable, so there was agreement on that point at least.

Under the December 1st schedule, the mainline trains were almost the same as they had been under the November 17th schedule, with the exception of No. 7. This train's connection now left Denver at 11:30 PM, as opposed to the 9:50 PM departure previously, and left Colorado Springs at 2:20 AM, or one hour 45 minutes later than the old schedule. Arrival at Divide was now 4 AM, with Leadville at 8:35 AM. After a 20-minute stop for breakfast, the train went on to arrive at Basalt at 11:30 AM, departing there five minutes later for a 12:20 PM arrival at Aspen. Midland Terminal No. 7 left Divide at 4:50 AM, after picking up the District sleeper and arrived in Cripple Creek at 7 AM.

Since the December 19th schedule of the Midland Terminal was the first complete schedule into and out of Cripple Creek, it is shown below. The Colorado Midland was still furnishing all crews, locomotives and passenger equipment for the through trains. In fact, the CM furnished the motive power for all Midland Terminal freight and switching operations, as the MT did not get its own locomotives until 1896. Here is the schedule with all trains operating daily:

5	1	7	Miles	Stations	2	6	8
PM	AM	AM			AM	PM	AM
1:35	9:20	4:50	0	Divide	11:05	4:42	1:40
1:54	9:37	5:10	6	Midland	10:40	4:23	1:17
2:25	10:08	5:45	14	Gillett	10:08	3:58	12:42
2:43	10:30	6:05	20	Grassy	9:50	3:42	12:22
2:47	10:34	6:10	21	Bull Hill	9:45	3:38	12:15
2:52	10:38	6:15	22	Independence	9:38	3:30	12:06
2:57	10:42	6:20	23	Portland	9:33	3:25	12:01
3:05	10:52	6:35	24	Victor	9:24	3:16	11:50
3:35	11:01	6:45	25	Elkton	9:15	3:06	11:37
3:41	11:06	6:51	27	Anaconda	9:10	3:00	11:30
3:50	11:15	7:00	29	Cripple Creek	9:00	2:50	11:15
PM	AM	AM			AM	PM	PM

"Through Pullman Sleeper between Denver and Cripple Creek on trains 7 and 8. Passengers may remain in sleeper until 7:00 AM."

It appears that the privilege of staying in the sleeper until 7 AM was an empty one, since both of the night trains were due at their terminals at 7 AM.

As far as the passenger equipment was concerned during 1895, the Colorado Midland shops at Colorado City converted second class coaches Nos. 251 through 257 into chair cars. During the year, baggage car No. 302 was destroyed in a wreck, leaving the active fleet at 40 units at the end of the year. There were no changes in motive power during the year.

1896

The summer of 1896 saw the return of two through trains all the way over the mainline between Colorado Springs and Grand Junction. The schedules of the former trains, Nos. 5 and 6, were similar to the previous year, while Nos. 7 and 8 now provided the overnight service on the CM, with western connections via the RGW, compared to the 1895 schedule which only had service as far west as Aspen. The time of No. 7 was moved up a couple of hours, in order to secure better connections at both ends of the railroad, while the time of No. 8 was set back a similar amount of time, departing from Grand Junction at 6:20 PM, with arrival at Colorado Springs at 6:15 AM. This was a little more bearable for passengers destined to Colorado Springs than the previous arrival of 4:10 AM; Denver was still reached at a respectable hour of 8:45 AM.

All four trains operated directly into Leadville. The westbound trains proceeded to Arkansas Junction, then ran up the Second District to Leadville. After the station stop the trains ran back down to Arkansas Junction and continued on their way west. The eastbound trains reversed this procedure.

Cripple Creek received the services of three trains each way daily, only one of which appears to be a through train in its own right, although some of the other trains handled through equipment. No. 1 ran through, Colorado Springs to Cripple Creek, and No. 2 was listed as the eastbound counterpart of that train. Perusal of the schedule indicates that CM No. 2 was due to leave Divide at 9:55 AM, while MT No. 2 was due to arrive five minutes later at 10:00 AM! No. 1's schedule also raises a question as to why it stayed at Divide from 9:45 AM to 10:20 AM. Possibly these trains were turns on each of the roads; MT No. 2 turned back at Divide as No. 1, while CM No. 1 turned back as No. 2. This seems unlikely, however, as the normal practice was to run through between Colorado Springs and Cripple Creek.

The MT did run trains that connected with CM's mainline trains, as in this schedule where connections were maintained for both the day and night trains. MT No. 8 handled the Cripple Creek – Denver sleeper, while No. 7 handled the car in the reverse direction. It will be noted that there was considerable delay at Divide for both of these MT trains, with No. 8 due at 1:50 AM while CM No. 8 did not arrive until 4:35 AM. In the opposite direc-

No. 1	No. 7	No. 5	Mls	December 1, 1895.	No. 6	No. 8	No. 2
				LEAVE] [ARRIVE			
	*11 30 P.M.	*8 35A.M.	0	+ ... Denver ... ☿	9 10 P.M.	7 00A.M.	5 15 P.M.
4 28A.M.		8 00A.M.		+.........Pueblo........☿	8 07 P.M.		5 30 P.M.
				LEAVE] [ARRIVE			
7 30A.M.	*2 20A.M.	*11 15A.M.	74	+ .Colorado Springs..☿	6 35 P.M.	4 10A.M.	1 00 P.M.
7 42 »	2 37 »	11 35 »	77	+.....Colorado City......☿	6 23 »	3 48 »	12 48NO'N
7 55 »	2 45 »	11 43 »	80	+.......Manitou.......☿	6 07 »	3 40 »	12 37 »
7 58 »	....	11 45A.M.	81	....Manitou Iron Springs....	6 05 »	...	12 35 »
8 20 »	3 09 »	12 25NO'N	86	.....I Cascade Cañon. ...☿	5 50 »	3 14 »	12 20NO'N
8 32 »	3 24 »	12 40 »	89	......Green Mt. Falls ☿	5 22 »	2 59 »	11 50A.M.
8 47 »	3 39 »	12 55NO'N	94	.......Woodland Park.. ☿	5 10 »	2 45 »	11 39 »
9 15A.M.	4 00A.M.	1 20 P.M.	101	arr ...... Divide ☿ lve.	4 52 P.M.	2 25A.M.	*11 20A.M.
9 20A.M.	4 50A.M.	1 35 P.M.	101	lve. Divide (Mid. Term. Ry.). arr.	4 42 P.M.	1 40A.M.	11 05A.M.
9 37 »	5 10 »	1 54 »	108	arr. Midland.. » lve.	4 23 »	1 17A.M.	10 40 »
10 08 »	5 45 »	2 25 »	115	.Gillett....... »	3 58 »	12 42N'HT	10 08 »
10 30 »	6 05 »	2 43 »	121	.Grassy...... »	3 42 »	12 22N'HT	9 50 »
10 52 »	6 35 »	3 06 »	125	.Victor...... »	3 16 »	11 50 P.M.	9 24 »
11 06 »	6 51 »	3 11 »	129	.Anaconda.. »	3 00 »	11 30 »	9 10 »
11 35A.M.	7 00A.M.	3 50 P.M.	131	.Cripple Creek »	*2 50 P.M.	*11 15 P.M.	*9 00A.M.
				ARRIVE] [LEAVE			
	4 26A.M.	1 20 P.M.	101	lve........Divide ☿.....arr.	4 52 P.M.	2 25A.M.	
	4 45 »	1 43 »	110	..........Florissant........	4 12 »	1 45A.M.	
	5 35 »	2 35 »	132	...........Spinney.........☿	3 27 »	12 58N'HT	
	5 59 »	2 54 »	143	...........Hartsel	3 03 »	12 38N'HT	
	7 08 »	4 12 »	175	+...... Buena Vista......☿	1 55 »	11 29 P.M.	
	7 44 »	4 53 »	193	.. .Granite. .....☿	1 18 P.M.	10 54 »	
	8 20 »	5 25 »	208	arr. Arkansas Junction. ☿ .lve.	12 47NO'N	10 25 »	
	8 35 »	5 45 »	212	arr...+ I Leadville ☿.. lve.	12 30 »	10 05 »	
	8 55 »	6 05 »	212	lve....+ Leadville ☿...arr.	12 20 »	9 55 »	
	9 06 »	6 17 »	208	lve..Arkansas Junction ☿ lve.	12 06NO'N	9 43 »	
	9 40 »	6 53 »	221	............Busk.........☿	11 42A.M.	9 20 »	
	9 50 »	7 03 »	224	..........Ivanhoe........☿	11 32 »	9 10 »	
	10 15 »	7 30 »	233	....Sellar. ....☿	10 43 »	8 23 »	
	10 45 »	8 00 »	244	.. Thomasville......☿	10 01 »	7 42 »	
No. 73	11 30A.M.	8 50 P.M.	264	arr..... I Basalt ☿ lve.	9 10A.M.	*6 55 P.M.	No. 74
20A.M.	11 35A.M.	9 00 P.M.	264	lve........Basalt...... arr.	9 05A.M.	6 50 P.M.	8 35 P.M.
05A.M.	12 20NO'N	9 50 P.M.	283	arr. ....+ Aspen ☿.... lve.	*8 20A.M.	*6 10 P.M.	*7 35 P.M.
		9 00 P.M.	264	lve.......Basalt ☿ ....arr.	8 50A.M.		
		9 40 »	285	+........Cardiff.........☿	8 12 »		
		9 52 »	288	..Glenwood Springs....☿	8 02 »		
		10 30 »	300	+.......New Castle..... .☿	7 35 »		
		10 52 »	314	............Rifle. ....☿	7 08 »		
		11 19 »	331	....Parachute.......☿	6 41 »		
		11 42 P.M.	344	..........De Beque........☿	6 20 »		
		[illegible]	377	[illegible] Junction ☿ lve.	[illegible]		
				ARRIVE] [LEAVE			
		12 05NO'N	669	arr......Salt Lake......☿	7 40 P.M.		
		1 15 P.M.	705	arr.......Ogden ☿ lve.	*6 35 P.M.		

JEROME PARK BRANCH.—Train leaves Cardiff †7 00 a.m. for Spring Gulch (15 miles). Returning, leaves Spring Gulch for Cardiff *9 30 a.m.

No 5—Daily, Pullman Sleeper and Free Chair Car Denver to Ogden, via Colorado Springs, connecting with Southern Pacific for Pacific Coast points.

No. 7—Daily, Pullman Buffet Sleeper Denver to Leadville, Grassy, Victor and Cripple Creek, via Colorado Springs.

No. 1—Daily, Coaches Denver and Colorado Springs.

No. 6—Daily, Palace Sleeper San Francisco to Ogden. Pullman Sleeper and Free Chair Car Ogden to Colorado Springs and Denver. Solid Vestibuled train of Free Reclining Chair Cars and Palace Sleepers Denver to Chicago. Dining Cars Kansas City to Chicago.

No. 8—Daily, Pullman Buffet Sleeper Leadville, Cripple Creek, Victor and Grassy to Denver.

No. 2—Daily, Coaches from Cripple Creek to Colorado Springs and Denver.

* Daily; † daily, except Sunday. + Coupon stations. ☿ Telegraph stations. I Meal stations.

CONNECTIONS.

Denver—With Atchison, Topeka & Santa Fé Ry., Burlington & Missouri River R.R., Chicago, Rock Island & Pacific Ry. and Union Pacific Ry. Lines, and Union Pacific, Denver & Gulf Ry., in Union Depot.

Colorado Springs—With Chicago, Rock Island & Pacific, Atchison, Topeka & Santa Fé, and Union Pacific, Denver & Gulf Rys.

Divide—With Midland Terminal Ry. for Grassy, Cripple Creek, &c.

Buena Vista—With Denver, Leadville & Gunnison Ry., and with stage lines for Buena Vista and for the Tin Cup and Aspen Districts, via Cottonwood Pass.

Grand Junction—With Rio Grande Western Ry.

Manitou—With Manitou & Pike's Peak Ry.

tion, CM No. 7 set off the Cripple Creek sleeper at 1:50 AM, but it did not leave Divide on the MT until 4:30 AM. It can be seen that MT No. 8 did connect with CM No. 7 at Divide and leaves one to believe that there was sufficient travel from Cripple Creek to points west on the CM to maintain this connection. But, as CM No. 8 was due at Divide five minutes after MT No. 7 left, this negates any such idea. These are just further examples of the vagaries of CM scheduling that are more or less consistent throughout the history of the road.

The Aspen Branch continued to maintain two round trips making connections with the mainline trains. The schedule on the mainline was such that the morning train from Aspen could make connections with both Nos. 7 and 6, while the evening round trip connected with Nos. 5 and 8.

For the first time, the Jerome Park schedule lists arriving times at Spring Gulch for the westbound and at Cardiff for the eastbound train. Here is another curiosity in CM scheduling. It was normally the practice to run turnarounds from Cardiff to the mines at Spring Gulch, yet this schedule calls for a train from Cardiff at 7 AM to arrive Spring Gulch at 11 AM, and the return to leave Spring Gulch at 9:30 AM with an arrival at Cardiff at 1:30 PM. It is possible that it was meant for the westbound train to show arrival at the Gulch at 9:30 AM, with departure from that point at 11:00 AM, but this same schedule was maintained in the timetables until August 1901. Whether or not it was an oversight is questionable, and, as has been mentioned before, very few passengers other than the miners and their families would be interested in the schedule. They would be familiar with the methods of operation and would not need a timetable. In the August 1901 table, the times did show arrival at Spring Gulch at 9:30 AM with return departure listed at 10:30 AM, so there is some reason to believe that the 1896 schedule was a misprint.

With Nos. 7 and 8 now operating through to Grand Junction, the equipment list showed that these trains handled up to three sleepers a night, at least as far west as Divide, which was no mean load for No. 7 on its westbound pull up through Ute Pass. These trains had Pullman buffet sleepers between Denver, Cripple Creek, Leadville and Ogden. Nos. 5 and 6 still carried their Pullman sleeper and chair car between Denver and Ogden and advertised Pacific Coast connections with the Southern Pacific, although these were no through cars.

Nos. 1 and 2 carried through cars between Denver and

Cripple Creek, which further confounds the scheduling of No. 2 at Divide. The CM also maintained a Ute Pass local, with a morning train daily from Divide to Colorado Springs and the return of this "commuter" leaving Colorado Springs at 5:45 PM, with arrival at Divide at 7:40 PM. No MT connections were listed for either of these runs.

Another oddity is the fact that Sunday trains were scheduled from Colorado Springs to Manitou Iron Springs, starting at 1 PM, and every hour until 5 PM, then 7 PM, and 8 PM. The return trips were scheduled to leave Manitou Iron Springs at 1:20 PM, and every hour until 4:20 PM, then 6:20 PM, 7:20 PM and 8:20 PM. If it was expected that the return trips were to be handled by the same crew, it would appear that the 20-minute schedule between Colorado Springs and Manitou Iron Springs was overly optimistic, since the best time of the regular trains between the two points was 27 minutes. Perhaps the railroad showed the time at Manitou Iron Springs so that the passengers would be there at that time and the train would not have to wait for them when it arrived from Colorado Springs. At any rate, this was an interesting arrangement for the Sundays of this summer, with a veritable interurban type service between the two stations.

A development of major proportions affecting CM passenger travel during the year was the strike of the miners at Leadville that started at 11:30 PM June 19th and lasted until March 9, 1897. This protracted strike had a disastrous effect on the economy of western Colorado, as it affected not only the passenger travel, but also the movement of ores, coal, stone and merchandise in the whole area.

In line with the mention of the labor situation, an item of interest is the attached pay schedule for locomotive engineers that was effective on January 1, 1896. This lists the various runs that were established at that time with the number of hours that were allowed to make round or one way trips and the pay for each of the runs listed, both passenger and freight. It also lists some of the other types of service, including both the Aspen and Coal Branches, and the districts over which the crews had seniority rights. This information was compiled from a booklet which was on file at the Association of American Railroads Library, Washington, DC, in 1967. By present standards CM engineers did not earn a lot of money, but for the times they were good jobs. It must be remembered that they were receiving "mountain" pay for the most part, which was somewhat higher than their brethren who worked on the prairie railroads.

The same train depicted on page 60 is seen at the front of two following sections in a view taken earlier on the same day by William Henry Jackson. These were among the earliest Colorado Midland excursions, though not yet known as wildflower trains. (Colorado Historical Society)

COLORADO MIDLAND RAILROAD CO.
Rates of Pay for Engineers, 1/1/1896

RUNS	TRIPS	IF MADE WITHIN		PAY OF ENGINEERS	
		PSGR.	FRT.	PSGR.	FRT.
BETWEEN		hrs/mins.	hrs/mins.		
Colorado City – Leadville	Single	8 00	11 15	$6.20	$7.20
Colo. City or Colo. Sprgs – Woodland Park or Divide	Double	6 00	6 00	4.00	4.00
Colo. City or Colo. Sprgs – East of Woodland Park	Double	3 00	3 00	2.00	2.00
Colo. City or Colo. Sprgs – Florissant	Double	7 00	7 00	4.50	4.50
Colo. City or Colo. Sprgs – Cripple Creek	Double	11 30	11 30	7.25	7.25
Colo. City or Colo. Sprgs – Midland	Double	7 30	7 30	4.50	4.50
Buena Vista or Wild Horse – Bath	Double	3 05	3 05	2.00	2.00
Florissant – Divide	Double	3 00	3 00	2.00	2.00
Leadville – Busk	Double	3 00	3 00	2.00	2.00
Leadville – Ivanhoe	Double	3 45	3 45	2.50	2.50
Leadville – Sellar	Double	5 17	5 17	4.15	4.15
Leadville – Thomasville	Double	7 50	7 50	6.25	6.25
Leadville – Basalt	Single	6 10	6 10	4.00	4.00
Leadville – Aspen	Single	7 00	7 00	4.85	4.85
Basalt – Thomasville	Double	3 00	3 00	2.00	2.00
Basalt – Ivanhoe – Thomasville	Single	7 00	7 00	4.80	4.80
Basalt – Ivanhoe	Double	9 13	9 13	5.80	5.80
Thomasville – Ivanhoe	Double	4 47	4 47	3.80	3.80
Basalt – New Castle	Double	6 00	6 00	4.00	4.00
Basalt – Grand Junction	Single	—	—	4.50	4.50

Other rates of pay, etc. –

Yard Engineers	–	$3.25 for 12-hour day, except at Leadville. $4.00 for 12-hour day at Leadville.
Cardiff Coal Branch	–	$6.00 for 12 hours or less for regular assigned crew. $3.00 per round trip for extra crews.
Rotary Snow Plow	–	$5.00 for 12 hours or less.
Work trains	–	$4.00 for 12 hours or less.
Aspen Branch	–	$0.85 each way, running time, 1 hour 30 minutes.
Overtime	–	$0.40 per hour for road crews. 1/10 of 1 day's pay per hour for yard crews.
DISTRICTS	–	1st – Colorado Springs to Leadville, including Midland Terminal. 2nd – Leadville to Basalt, including Aspen Branch. 3rd – Basalt to Grand Junction, including Cardiff Coal Branch.

1st District crews have rights only on 1st District. 2nd and 3rd District crews have rights on either 2nd or 3rd Districts, according to Seniority.

Pay for firemen is 65% (Sixty-Five) of Engineer's pay.

Rates based on average of about 6¢ per mile.

from booklet on file at AAR Library, Washington, DC.

During the year, the motive power fleet was reduced by one, when engine 35 blew up at Basalt on August 15th. It was so badly damaged that it was never rebuilt. The passenger car fleet also lost a couple of cars, as both baggage car No. 307 and coach No. 105 were destroyed in a wreck on December 13th. These changes reduced the locomotive fleet to 50, and the car fleet to 38, which is what the road had when it first started business in 1887.

It should also be noted that the Midland Terminal took delivery of five 2-8-0 type engines during the year, which were the first that this road had received. Up to the time of acquiring these engines, the Colorado Midland had furnished all motive power for the MT. With these five engines on the MT, that line was now able to provide its own power for the freight and switching operations demanded by the customers and mines in the Cripple Creek District, as well as its own local passenger services.

1897

Two major events occurred during this year that had a considerable effect on the Colorado Midland. One had to do with the emergence of the company from receivership, while the other was related to the argument with the Busk Tunnel Railway with respect to the charges that were being levied against the CM for the use of the tunnel.

First, however, let us examine the schedule for July 25th, which was the last timetable issued under the receivership and also the last schedule through the Busk Tunnel until the middle of 1899. This schedule was essentially the same as in the summer of 1896, although the time of No. 7 was now two hours earlier than in the previous year. The passenger department seemed to have trouble with the time for this train, as it kept bouncing back and forth like a ping-pong ball, from early evening departures to midnight departures during the preceding few years. Now the Denver connection left that point at 7:15 PM and with a Colorado Springs departure at 10 PM. The arrival at Grand Junction was set for 10:50 AM with connections for the west via the Rio Grande Western.

All four mainline trains still went into Leadville after first stopping at Arkansas Junction, and while the Cloud City was still listed as a meal station, the longest station time was only ten minutes, hardly long enough to enjoy a hot meal.

The Colorado Springs – Cripple Creek service was maintained by three trains daily, with two of them running through and one a connection at Divide with Nos. 5 and 6 on the mainline. Nos. 9 and 10 now carried two sleepers; one between Denver and the gold camp, while the other now originated and terminated at Colorado Springs. With a distance of 57 miles, this certainly has to rate as one of the shortest sleeping car lines in the nation. No doubt the businessmen of Colorado Springs wanted to have their own sleeper between the two points, so that they could spend a full business day in the Cripple Creek District and not have to waste three hours in traveling back and forth during the day. The Denver sleeper was not at all attractive to this class of travel. Although the equipment listing lumped the Denver and Colorado Springs sleepers in one statement, which could be construed that the Denver sleeper merely passed through Colorado Springs, later schedules are definite in specifying a sleeper between Colorado Springs and Cripple Creek. It is to be noted that the sleepers to and from the gold camp were now handled by a through train between Colorado Springs and Cripple Creek, rather than by a connection at Divide with Nos. 7 and 8 as had been the practice during the prior couple of years. With the additional sleeper now in service from Colorado Springs, it was evidently too much of a load for No. 7, and the institution of Nos. 9 and 10 was required to handle all the business available.

Another vagary in the equipment listing is that No. 7 showed only a sleeper and coach from Denver to Ogden (and listed the sleeper to Ogden twice). It does not show a Denver – Leadville sleeper. No. 8, however, did show the Leadville to Denver sleeper, so it is presumed that the listing for No. 7 actually should show a sleeper to Leadville, rather than the second sleeper to Ogden.

Under this schedule, service on the Aspen Branch had been increased to three round trips, due primarily to the earlier time of No. 7. Now two trips were run in the morning in order to make connections with both Nos. 7 and 8, with one evening round trip still able to make both the Nos. 5 and 6 connections. The Jerome Park Branch still had its questionable schedule. One omission in this timetable is the lack of any Ute Pass local service for this summer season, but this could be due to the fact that as there were now four trains each way between Colorado Springs and Divide, this was considered to provide adequate service to those intermediate stations.

On October 11th, the Colorado Midland *Railway* was incorporated, and took over the property of the Colorado Midland *Railroad*, thus ending the receivership of the old organization. George W. Ristine was appointed president of the new company, as he had done such a fine job during his tenure as receiver. Negotiations had been taking place, even prior to this time, with the Busk Tunnel Railway over the rental for the use of the railway and tunnel between Busk and Ivanhoe. Early on during these negotiations, it was apparent to the CM managment that the tunnel company was intractable in its demands, so arrangements were made to rehabilitate the old line over Hagerman Pass. When this was completed, the Colorado Midland cancelled its lease with the Busk Tunnel Railway and resumed operation over the original mainline. This cancellation was effective on October 31st, and a new timetable was issued on November 1st to show the operation over the Pass. The schedule mentioned above for July 25th remained in effect until the CM stopped running through the Busk Tunnel.

No. 9	No. 1	No. 7	No. 5	Mls	November 1, 1897.	No. 6	No. 8	No. 2	No. 10
P.M.	A.M.				LEAVE] [ARRIVE			P.M.	A.M.
*11 30	*3 40	*7 00 P.M.	*8 35 A.M.	0	+ Denver	9 15 P.M.	10 30 A.M.	5 00	7 00
□			7 25 A.M.		+ Pueblo	10 53 P.M.		5 20	□
A.M.	A.M.				LEAVE] [ARRIVE			A.M.	A.M.
*3 00	*8 00	*9 45 P.M.	*11 10 A.M.	74	+ Colorado Springs	6 45 P.M.	8 00 A.M.	11 10	2 55
3 15	8 10	10 05 "	11 27 "	78	+ Colorado City	6 33 "	7 47 "	10 [illegible]	2 40
3 23	8 18	10 15 "	11 37 "	81	+ Manitou	6 20 "	7 37 "	10 42	2 32
3 25	8 20	10 17 "	11 39 A.M.	82	Manitou Iron Springs	6 18 "	....	10 40	....
3 50	8 35	10 40 "	12 20 NO'N	86	Cascade Cañon	6 03 "	7 20 "	10 25	2 15
4 03	8 45	10 50 "	12 30 "	90	Green Mt. Falls	5 46 "	6 52 "	10 12	2 00
4 25	9 00	11 05 "	12 45 NO'N	95	Woodland Park	5 35 "	6 41 "	10 00	1 48
5 00	9 20	11 30 P.M.	1 10 P.M.	102	arr. Divide lve.	5 18 P.M.	6 25 A.M.	*9 45	*1 30
5 10	9 40		1 25 P.M.	102	lve. Divide (Mid. Term. Ry.). arr.	5 10 P.M.		9 34	1 05
5 28	9 58		1 43 "	108	arr. Midland " lve.	4 51 "		9 16	12 40
6 02	10 27		2 12 "	115	Gillett "	4 25 "		8 50	12 11
6 18	10 42		2 27 "	121	Grassy "	4 11 "		8 36	11 51
6 38	11 02		2 48 "	125	Victor "	3 50 "		8 18	11 27
6 52	11 15		3 02 "	129	Anaconda "	3 36 "		8 04	11 10
7 [illegible]	11 20		3 10 P.M.	131	arr. Cripple Creek " lve.	*[illegible] P.M.		*[illegible]	*11 00
A.M.	A.M.	11 30 P.M.	1 20 P.M.	102	lve. Divide arr.	5 10 P.M.	6 25 A.M.	A.M.	P.M.
		11 55 P.M.	..	111	Florissant	4 42 "	5 32 "		
		12 45 N'HT	2 40 "	133	Spinney	3 55 "	5 07 "		
		1 02 A.M.	3 00 "	144	Hartsel	3 35 "	4 50 "		
		2 17 "	4 15 "	176	+ Buena Vista	2 27 "	3 40 "		
		3 00 "	4 55 "	194	Granite	1 47 "	3 00 "		
		3 32 "	5 25 "	209	arr. Arkansas Junction lve.	1 22 "	2 30 "		
		4 00 "	5 45 "	213	arr. + Leadville lve.	1 05 P.M.	2 00 "		
		3 20 "	6 05 "	213	lve. + Leadville arr.	12 55 NO'N	2 45 "		
		3 48 "	6 15 "	209	lve. Arkansas Junction arr.	..	2 15 "		
		4 20 "	6 48 "	222	Busk	12 21 NO'N	1 55 "		
		5 00 "	7 27 "	224	Ivanhoe	11 45 A.M.	1 18 A.M.		
		5 28 "	7 55 "	234	Sellar	11 05 "	12 37 N'HT		
79	73	6 00 "	8 30 "	245	Thomasville	10 20 "	11 55 P.M.	78	74
P.M.	A.M.	6 50 A.M.	9 20 P.M.	265	arr. Basalt lve.	9 30 A.M.	11 05 P.M.	A.M.	P.M.
*11 10	*9 40	*7 20 A.M.	*9 25 P.M.	265	lve. Basalt arr.	9 25 A.M.	11 00 P.M.	7 05	9 05
11 55	10 30	8 10 A.M.	10 05 P.M.	284	arr. + Aspen lve.	*8 40 A.M.	*10 15 P.M.	*6 25	*8 20
P.M.	A.M.	7 10 A.M.	9 30 P.M.	265	lve. Basalt arr.	9 10 A.M.	10 58 P.M.	A.M.	P.M.
		7 33 "	9 55 "	275	Carbondale	8 45 "	10 35 "		
		7 50 "	10 18 "	286	+ Cardiff	8 30 "	10 18 "		
		8 00 "	10 28 "	289	+ Glenwood	8 20 "	10 08 "		
		8 40 "	10 55 "	301	+ New Castle	7 57 "	9 45 "		
		9 07 "	11 23 "	315	Rifle	7 28 "	9 18 "		
		9 34 "	11 50 P.M.	332	Parachute	7 01 "	8 51 "		
		9 53 "	12 11 N'HT	345	De Beque	6 40 "	8 30 "		
		10 50 A.M.	1 08 A.M.	378	+ Grand Junction lve.	*5 45 A.M.	*7 35 P.M.		
					ARRIVE] [LEAVE				
		9 05 P.M.	12 20 NO'N	669	arr. Salt Lake	7 40 P.M.	9 30 A.M.		
		10 00 P.M.	1 30 P.M.	705	arr. Ogden lve.	*6 35 P.M.	*8 30 A.M.		

JEROME PARK BRANCH.—Train leaves Cardiff †7 00 a.m., arriving Spring Gulch (15 miles) 11 00 a.m. Returning, leaves Spring Gulch †10 30 a.m., arriving Cardiff 1 30 p.m.

The photograph on the top of the next page was taken in 1949, yet the scene is unchanged from the days when CM trains struggled westward toward the Continental Divide along the grade visible on the mountainside. Today, this is a county road. The doubleheader has paused after emerging from the Busk-Ivanhoe Tunnel through the Divide. (both, Denver Public Library Western History Dept.)

The November 1st timetable, the first issued under the name of Colorado Midland Railway, listed George W. Ristine as President and Manager, and, incidentally, the name of W. R. Freeman appeared for the first time as Cashier and Tax Commissioner. After his stint with the CM, this gentleman's name would later loom large in the Colorado railroad picture as the head of the Denver & Salt Lake.

The new timetable took into account the route over Hagerman Pass, and it is interesting to compare the running times for the passenger trains between Busk and Ivanhoe via the two different routes. It will be remembered that the distance over Hagerman Pass was 9.5 miles, as opposed to the 2.1 miles through the tunnel, and involved an additional rise and fall of 1307 ft.

The comparative running times are shown below:

Train No.	Via Busk Tunnel 7/25/97	Via Hagerman Pass 11/1/97
7	10 mins.	40 mins.
5	10 mins.	39 mins.
8	10 mins.*	37 mins.
6	10 mins.*	36 mins.

(*The time is not shown as of 7/25/97 in the Guide listing, but in the last schedule showing the time for eastbound trains, it was ten minutes for each train.)

Thus it can be seen that an allowance had to be made in the overall schedule to compensate for the additional running time over the pass. While this was true as a rule of thumb, it did not always apply. Here is the comparison of the through running times for all four mainline trains between Colorado Springs and Grand Junction, for 7/25/97 and 11/1/97:

Train No.	7/25/97	11/1/97
7	12 hrs. 40 mins.	13 hrs. 5 mins.
5	12 hrs. 28 mins.	13 hrs. 58 mins.
8	11 hrs. 35 mins.	12 hrs. 25 mins.
6	12 hrs. 55 mins.	13 hrs. 0 mins.

This shows that additional time was allowed for all of the trains, with No. 6, at only five minutes more, having the least amount added.

It should be noted that both of the "night" trains, Nos. 7 and 8, were now scheduled to by-pass Leadville as far as the through consist was concerned. This, of course, required the use of stub trains between Arkansas Junction and Leadville, as previously described. Nos. 5 and 6, the "day" trains, still ran to Arkansas Junction, thence to Leadville and return.

No. 8 now left Grand Junction at 7:35 PM, 45 minutes later than under the summer schedule and arrived Colorado Springs at 8 AM. Because of this change, it was now necessary to run four round trips on the Aspen Branch, with each round trip making connection with just one mainline train in order to provide a convenient service for patrons.

There was no change in the equipment handled by Nos. 5 and 6 on their journeys over the CM, but there was a change in the consist of No. 7 and 8. In addition to the two sleepers between Denver, Leadville and Ogden (note that No. 7 once again showed the Leadville sleeper), there is a new and unusual entry in that this train now carried a sleeper from Denver en route to Portland, Oregon, running through in connection with the Oregon Short Line and the Oregon – Washington RR & Navigation Company, both of which are now parts of the Union Pacific. In view of the fact that the consist for No. 8 does not show the Ogden – Denver sleeper, it is possible that the Ogden sleeper shown under No. 7 was actually the Portland sleeper, instead of a car that terminated at Ogden. Whether or not there was another mix-up in the equipment listing, the fact that the CM was handling a sleeping car between Denver and Portland is unusual enough, and although the CM would later participate in a number of tourist car routings, it was not often that the road handled regular sleeping cars over such an unusual route.

During the year, three more of the second class coaches were converted to chair cars, which meant that all ten of these cars had been rebuilt. The cars involved this year were numbered 258-260 (Nos. 251-257 had been converted in 1895). The road's shops also rebuilt first class coach No. 102, which had been wrecked in 1893.

As far as the motive power was concerned, five class 136 2-8-0s, numbered 49-53, were received, which were then the most powerful locomotives that the road owned. They were assigned for the most part to freight helper service on the heavy grades out of Colorado Springs and Basalt and were seldom used in passenger service except in cases of extreme motive power shortage.

1898

This year proved to be relatively quiet on the Colorado Midland, and the road needed a respite after all the activity of the past few years. During this entire year, the CM's trains continued to battle their way up the loops above Busk, tread over the giant wooden trestle and plunge into the darkness of Hagerman Tunnel. Then, with smoking brakeshoes, they moved gingerly down the grade to Ivanhoe. After this stop, they still had the long downhill stretch to Basalt before the gradients and curvature again gained respectability. The schedule for March 30th was essentially the same as the summer before, although No. 8 was advertised to leave Grand Junction about one hour earlier than it had in 1897. This put the train into Colorado Springs at 6:40 AM and Denver at 9:15 AM. Both Nos. 7 and 8 continued to by-pass Leadville with stub runs into and out of that city, while No. 5 and 6 made the trek into the Cloud City from Arkansas Junction.

The Cripple Creek service consisted of three trains each way daily, with two of them through trains between Colorado Springs and Cripple Creek—the other operated as a connection with both Nos. 5 and 6 at Divide. The Portland sleeper, formerly handled on Nos. 7 and 8, now terminated at Huntington, Oregon, where connection was made with other through cars to and from Portland. No. 7 handled a sleeper to Ogden from Denver, as well as the Leadville and Huntington cars, but No. 8 included only the Leadville and Huntington cars eastbound. Nos. 5 and 6 still had their Denver – Ogden sleepers and also advertised a through coach between Denver and Cripple Creek. Nos. 9 and 10 continued to handle the Denver – Cripple Creek sleeper, and the Colorado Springs – Cripple Creek sleeper.

The Aspen Branch was cut back to three round trips; two trips were made in the morning in order to make close connections with Nos. 7 and 6. Since No. 8 was now operating about an hour earlier, it was possible to make connections with both Nos. 5 and 8 with just one evening round trip. these trains were still being numbered in the 70 series. No change was noted for the Jerome Park Branch.

The summer schedule for July 17th continued in much the same manner as the spring schedule above, although No. 8 was put on a new, fast schedule. This eastbound evening train now left Grand Junction at 6:23 PM and arrived in Colorado Springs at 5:50 AM, for an 11 hour 27 minute running time over the CM. This was made possible, in part, by the fact that the train by-passed Leadville, as did No. 7 in the opposite direction. No times were shown for station stops between Buena Vista and Woodland Park. At any rate, this train was certainly the pacesetter for the railroad, as no other made the run in less than 12 hours.

Once again, during the summer, four services were operated to and from Cripple Creek. Passengers leaving Colorado Springs had their choice of departures on through trains at 3:10 AM,. 7:30 AM and 5:50 PM, with an additional service on No. 5 leaving at 11:25 AM. Eastbound passengers could leave Cripple Creek at 7:10 AM, 6 PM, and 11 PM on through trains. The afternoon connection for No. 6 left Cripple Creek at 3:15 PM.

Nos. 9 and 10 still had the two through sleepers, one Denver car and one Colorado Springs car, to and from the gold camp. Nos. 7 and 8 continued to show the Denver – Huntington sleeper (although a public timetable reproduced in *The Timetable Collector* for October 1972 showed the sleeper operating between Denver and Boise, Idaho, on the same July 17th schedule). It still showed the Denver – Ogden sleeper on No. 7 only. Both Nos. 7 and 8 continued with the Leadville sleeper, which was still being handled by the stub run from Arkansas Junction. Nos. 5 and 6, in addition to the Denver – Ogden sleeper, also included a through coach between Denver and Cripple Creek.

The Aspen Branch continued to operate three round trips on the same basis as during the spring timetable, and there was no change on the Jerome Park Branch. The Ute Pass Sunday only trains returned to this schedule, with departures from Colorado Springs for Woodland Park at 9:30 AM and 1:45 PM. Returning, these Sunday trains left at 12:01 PM and 5:07 PM.

This July 17th schedule now showed the additional distance over Hagerman Pass; the mileage was listed at Ivanhoe as nine miles from Busk, and all stations west of that point have seven miles added. The final mileage at Grand Junction was 310 from Colorado Springs. However, this was still not correct, since the 1895 error in mileage between Arkansas Junction and Busk had not been changed.

The only addition to the passenger car fleet was the acquisition of officers car 100, named *Cascade*, built by Pullman in that year. This brought the passenger car fleet up to forty. There was no change in motive power during the year.

GLENWOOD SPRINGS, COLO.

THE KISSINGEN OF AMERICA

STOP-OVER WILL BE ALLOWED AT THIS POINT ON ALL THROUGH TICKETS, INCLUDING PULLMAN.

Stop at Thomasville

on the Frying Pan River for the finest Trout Fishing in the State.

GATHERING WILD FLOWERS IN UTE PASS

These views are from a publication titled Scenic Colorado via the Colorado Midland Railway *and depict crowds of train riders devouring the mountain scenery. Sphinx Rock is near Wild Horse, north of Buena Vista. (Museum collection)*

SPHINX ROCK

1899

The winter schedule effective on January 15, 1899, made changes in westbound schedules only, with the exception of the Cripple Creek trains. No. 5 left Colorado Springs earlier at 11 AM and ran via Arkansas Junction direct, with stub service to and from Leadville. Arrival at Grand Junction was listed for 11:28 PM, one hour 40 minutes earlier than during the previous summer. No. 7 left Colorado Springs at 9:45 PM, running via Leadville and arriving in Grand Junction at 11:44 AM, one hour 4 minutes later than formerly, due mostly to making the side trip into Leadville. No. 9 now left Colorado Springs at 2:40 AM, 30 minutes earlier than in the summer, but did not arrive at Cripple Creek until 6:35, only ten minutes earlier. Colorado Springs – Cripple Creek through trains Nos. 1, 3, 2 and 4 were discontinued for the winter, but connections with CM mainline trains Nos. 5 and 6 were maintained at Divide, so that a double-daily service was still available for the winter months.

Adjustments were also made for trains on the Aspen Branch, and three round trips were offered to make the mainline connections. There was no change on the Jerome Park Branch. The equipment arrangement was identical with that of the previous summer, and the Denver – Huntington sleeper continued in the consists of Nos. 7 and 8.

No. 9	No. 7	No. 5	Mls	*January* 15, 1899.	No. 6	No. 8	No. 10
P. M.				LEAVE] [ARRIVE			A. M.
*11 30	*7 00 P.M.	*8 30 A.M.	0	+ ...... Denver........♁	9 15 P.M.	8 30 A.M.	7 00
□		9 15 A.M.		+.........Pueblo........♁	11 00 P.M.	7 10 A.M.	□
A. M.				LEAVE] [ARRIVE			A. M.
*2 40	*9 45 P.M.	*11 00 A.M.	74	+ ..Colorado Springs..♁	6 40 P.M.	5 50 A.M.	2 20
....	10 02 »	....	78	+......Colorado City......♁	6 28 »	....	....
3 02	10 12 »	11 23 »	81	+.......Manitou........♁	6 15 »	5 30 »	1 57
....	..	11 25 A.M.	82	....Manitou Iron Springs....	6 13 »	....	....
3 32	10 37 »	12 05 NO'N	86	.....‡ Cascade Cañon.....♁	5 58 »	5 13 »	1 40
3 45	10 50 »	12 17 »	90	......Green Mt. Falls...♁	5 31 »	....	1 27
4 05	11 07 P.M	12 33 »	95	.......Woodland Park....♁	5 20 »	4 51 A.M.	1 16
4 35	....	12 53 NO'N	102	arr....... Divide ♁ ... lve.	5 03 P.M.	....	*1 00
4 45		1 10 P.M	102	lve. Divide (Mid. Term. Ry.). arr.	4 45 P.M.		12 50
5 03		1 23 »	108	arr. Midland.. » lve.	4 25 »		12 26
5 33		1 56 »	115	.Gillett...... »	3 59 »		11 56
5 50		2 10 »	121	.Grassy...... »	3 44 »		11 39
6 11		2 31 »	125	.Victor...... »	3 23 »		11 17
6 27		2 48 »	129	.Anaconda.. »	3 06 »		10 58
6 35		2 55 P.M.	131	arr. Cripple Creek » lve.	*3 00 P.M.		*10 50
A. M.	....	1 08 P.M.	102	lve........Divide ♁.....arr.	4 53 P.M.	....	P. M.
	....	1 25 »	111	........Florissant........♁	....	....	
	12 52 N'HT	2 12 »	133	...........Spinney..........♁	3 27 »	3 12 A.M	
	1 14 A.M.	2 33 »	144	...........Hartsel ....♁	3 03 »	....	
	2 42 »	3 45 »	176	+.....Buena Vista.....♁	1 49 »	1 43 A.M.	
	3 28 »	4 22 »	194	.. .. .Granite. ....♁	1 12 P.M.	1 07 A.M.	
	4 10 »	4 52 »	209	arr. Arkansas Junction. ♁ .lve.	12 46 NO'N	12 43 N'HT	
	4 32 »	5 15 »	213	arr... + ‡ Leadville ♁ ...lve.	12 30 »	12 20 N'HT	
	4 42 »	4 35 »	213	lve.... + Leadville ♁ ...arr.	12 20 NO'N	1 00 A.M.	
	....	5 02 »	209	lve.. Arkansas Junction ♁ arr.	...	12 38 N'HT	
	....	5 29 »	222	...............Busk..........♁	11 46 A.M.	....	
	....	5 57 »	231	...........Ivanhoe.........♁	11 18 »	....	
	6 27 »	6 24 »	241	...........Sellar..........♁	10 50 »	11 15 P.M.	
79	7 02 »	6 54 »	252	.......Thomasville.......♁	10 14 »	10 35 »	74
P. M.	7 52 A.M.	7 40 P.M.	272	arr..... ‡ Basalt ♁ lve.	9 22 A.M.	9 50 P.M.	P. M.
*9 55	*9 10 A.M.	*8 05 P.M.	272	lve.......Basalt.......arr.	8 05 A.M.	9 40 P.M.	7 50
10 40	9 55 A.M.	8 50 P.M.	291	arr......+ Aspen ♁.....lve.	*7 20 A.M.	*9 00 P.M.	*7 10
P. M.	8 10 A.M.	8 00 P.M.	272	lve.......Basalt ♁ ....arr.	9 02 A.M.	9 45 P.M.	P. M.
	8 32 »	8 22 »	284	.........Carbondale.........	8 40 »	9 24 »	
	....	....	293	+........Cardiff.........♁	....	....	
	9 05 »	8 51 »	296	+........Glenwood.........♁	8 15 »	8 59 »	
	9 34 »	9 18 »	308	+.......New Castle..... .♁	7 52 »	8 33 »	
	10 01 »	9 45 »	322	..............Rifle..........♁	7 23 »	8 06 »	
	10 28 »	10 12 »	339	.. ..Parachute........♁	6 56 »	7 39 »	
	10 47 »	10 31 »	352	.... De Beque........♁	6 35 »	7 18 »	
	11 44 A.M.	11 28 P.M.	384	+..Grand Junction ♁ lve.	*5 40 A.M.	*6 23 P.M.	
				ARRIVE] [LEAVE			
	10 40 P.M.	9 35 A.M.	676	arr.....Salt Lake......♁	7 40 P.M.	8 30 A.M.	
	11 45 P.M.	10 45 A.M.	712	arr....t..Ogden ♁ ... lve.	*6 35 P.M.	*7 30 A.M.	

JEROME PARK BRANCH.— Train leaves Cardiff †7 00 a.m., arriving Spring Gulch (15 miles) 11 00 a.m. Returning, leaves Spring Gulch †9 30 a.m., arriving Cardiff 1 30 p m.

The ink was hardly dry on the January 15th timetable when the Colorado Midland was beset by its greatest natural disaster. On January 24th it started snowing, and it kept snowing for days on end, until the railroad was completely tied up west of Leadville, over Hagerman Pass and down the Frying Pan toward Basalt. Trains were blockaded, snow plows were stalled in the drifts and could not get through to relieve the beleaguered trains. Things came to a complete standstill, particularly on the west end of the railroad. Many stories have come from the road's epic struggle against the elements during this winter, and the CM did not get dug out of the snow and restore normal operations until April 14th, almost three full months after the snowstorm had first started. Thus it did not make any difference what the schedules were at this time, as the trains were not running anyhow.

With all the difficulties of operating over Hagerman Pass during this winter storm, along with the expense involved in just maintaining the High Line for normal service, let alone during the winter months, the management decided it was time to re-open negotiations with the Busk Tunnel Railway. The owners of the tunnel were equally ripe for discussions, as their expensive bore was sitting there unused and not bringing in any income. Negotiations were completed in June, and the CM returned to the tunnel during the latter part of the month.

The schedule for June 1st was the last to show trains over Hagerman Pass. Nos. 5 and 6, the only ones that listed time at Busk and Ivanhoe, showed that the running time had been reduced to 28 minutes in each direction, as compared to almost 40 minutes when trains had first resumed using Hagerman Pass in 1897. But this was really a minor consideration in discontinuing the High Line.

Under the June 1st schedule, No. 5 was speeded up to the point where it now took only 12 hours nine minutes for the run over the road to Grand Junction. This was done by avoiding the side trip into Leadville by running directly through Arkansas Junction. No. 6 also by-passed Leadville, which was served by stub runs from Arkansas Junction. Although the night westbound train had previously by-passed Leadville, it was now the only one that called there, from 3:40 to 3:50 AM.

Four trains again operated into and out of Cripple Creek this summer season, although there was another unusual operation with these runs. A train still left Cripple Creek shortly after 3 PM to connect at Divide with No. 6, but there was no corresponding return connection off No. 5. There were three through trains from Cripple Creek to Colorado Springs, but there were four trains from Colorado Springs to Cripple Creek. A side note showed an additional train to the three shown in the schedule columns as leaving Colorado Springs at 7:40 AM, Divide at 9:08 AM and arriving Cripple Creek at 11 AM. This was probably train No. 1, as it was on the approximate schedule in 1898, as well as later on in 1899.

Because of No. 5's faster schedule, it was once again necessary to operate four round trips on the Aspen

Branch; the two morning trips were still being operated out of Aspen, and now it required two evening trips in order to maintain close connections with the mainline trains. The Jerome Park schedule remained unchanged.

The equipment listing now showed names for the major trains on the road, as follows:

No. 5 – *Solid Express*
No. 7 – *The Ute*
No. 9 – *11 Come 7*
No. 6 – *Solid Express*
No. 8 – *The Coyote*
No. 10 – *11 Come 7*

With the location of gold being such a great gamble, the reference to the dice game for the Cripple Creek night trains was probably quite appropriate. Both the names *The Ute* and *The Coyote* would be used for a number of years by the road for its premier services to and from the west.

It should be noted that No. 11, a Colorado Springs – Cripple Creek through train, and No. 5, the mainline day train, left the Springs within ten minutes of each other; No. 11 at 11 and No. 5 at 11:10 AM. From the scheduling, it appears that both stopped for lunch at Cascade Canon, as they maintained the ten-minute differential leaving that point at 12:05 PM and 12:15 PM, respectively. It is quite probable that both trains spent some time at Cascade Canon together; there are published photos showing two trains at Cascade Canon, taken either in 1899 or 1900, with the first consisting of an engine and three cars and the second with two engines, two baggage cars and a combine showing. These photos are usually captioned to the effect that there were two sections of No. 5 at the Cascade Canon eating house. The schedule indicates, however, that these photos actually depict No. 11 and No. 5 at Cascade Canon at the same time. This would have been well within the range of possibility under the circumstances.

The equipment listing for the mainline trains showed that changes had taken place in the consists, with the chair cars now operated only to Grand Junction, but the sleepers continuing though to Ogden. Also, the Huntington sleeper had been discontinued bringing an end to the through car accommodation to the Northwest.

Nos. 9 and 10 both showed specifically that sleepers were being operated between Colorado Springs and Cripple Creek, in addition to the regular Denver – Cripple Creek sleeper. No. 9 was due in Cripple Creek at 6:35 AM, and No. 10's connection was due in Denver at 7 AM, so passengers had the option of staying in the cars at either end until 8 AM.

In this summer season there was no mention of the Ute Pass locals. With 11 passenger trains scheduled between Colorado Springs and Divide, together with other regular excursions, like the wildflower train, plus all the freight trains, this was a very busy piece of mountain railroad. It is possible that the Sunday short runs were not scheduled for that reason.

The schedule for June 25th marked the return of the Colorado Midland to the Busk Tunnel, heralding the end of the Hagerman Pass route, which was torn up the following year as soon as the Busk Tunnel Railway was purchased by the Midland.

This schedule was almost identical to that for June 1st, and the only change was for No. 8, which cut 15 minutes off its running time. It is possible that the tunnel problem was settled so quickly that the passenger department did not have time to adjust the schedules to reflect the faster times available to them with the return to the Busk Tunnel. Some of the intermediate times were changes slightly, but these had no effect on the overall times for the other three mainline trains. No other changes were made in the Cripple Creek service or the four round trips on the Aspen Branch.

The previous two schedules have been included since they depict the end of operations over Hagerman Pass and the return to the use of the tunnel, which would continue until the end of operation in 1918. The November 5, 1899 schedule is shown because it was in effect at the turn of the century, surely a significant point in the history of the Colorado Midland. The timetable of November 5th was not superseded until February 25, 1900.

The major changes in the November schedule were in connection with trains 7 and 8. No. 7's connection now left Denver an hour later at 8 PM, and the CM train left Colorado Springs at 10:40 PM, or 55 minutes later than formerly. It was due at Grand Junction the same time, however, at 10:44 AM, for an overall CM running time of 12 hours four minutes. This speed-up was due to the fact that No. 7 now by-passed Leadville, as did all other mainline trains. That city was served now only by the stub runs as previously described. No. 8 now left Grand Junction at 4 PM and did not have a western connection from the Rio Grande Western.

Both Nos. 5 and 7 listed a Denver to Ogden sleeper, but only No. 6 showed an Ogden to Denver sleeper, so there is a question again as to how these cars were handled. Nos. 7 and 8 continued carrying the Leadville sleeper, and the chair cars evidently did not go further west than Grand Junction. Nos. 9 and 10 still had two sleepers each, handling the Colorado Springs set-out car as well as the regular Denver sleeper.

Once again, an oddity creeps into the schedules on the Midland Terminal. Before there were four services west and three services east; under this schedule, there were two through trains east, with three through trains west. A connection was still being run out of Cripple Creek to Divide for No. 6, so that there were three eastbound services from Cripple Creek. Although No. 5's schedule showed a connection from Divide, it was actually No. 11's train that was making the connection.

Here is another curious item: No. 11 now left Colorado Springs 30 minutes behind No. 5 instead of ten minutes ahead of it as in the summer arrangement. No. 5 left at 11 AM and No. 11 got out at 11:30 AM. At Cascade Canon, the 30 minute difference remained, with No. 5 showing at 11:45 AM and No. 11 and 12:15 PM. At Green Mountain Falls, however, No. 5 was due at 12:17 PM with No. 11 right behind at 12:27 PM. No. 5 was into Divide at 1 PM and No. 11 pulled in at 1:05 PM. No. 5 was out of there at 1:10 PM, while No. 11 left for Cripple Creek at 1:20 PM, thus making a connection from No. 5. This would lead one to believe that 11:45 AM for No. 5 at Cascade Canon was the arriving time rather than the leaving time, and No. 5's meal stop there allowed No. 11 to catch up, as it no longer stopped for lunch at Cascade Canon.

The Aspen Branch reverted to three round trips, with two morning trips being required to make the proper connections, while one round trip in the evening sufficed for Nos. 5 and 8, since those two trains met at Basalt. There was still no change on the Jerome Park Branch.

In this manner, the Colorado Midland ushered out the old century and greeted the new one. The only change in the car fleet occurred when baggage car No. 313 was wrecked on October 26th, reducing the fleet to 39 units. The motive power did not change.

William Henry Jackson scrambled over the rocks at Hell Gate with his large view camera and glass plates to obtain these images of his special train soon after the railroad was completed. Much of his work was used in advertising matter distributed by the CM, as was that of H.H. Buckwalter, who a few years later recorded these travelers enjoying the view at the same location. Their train consisted of locomotives 49 and 1, baggage car, chair car and five Pullmans. (Colorado Historical Society)

1900

Not only did this year usher in the new century, but it was a significant one in the annals of the Colorado Midland and is perhaps one of the most interesting years in the history of CM's scheduled passenger service. The first change after the New Year took place on February 25th and was the occasion for a major renumbering of mainline trains. The new numbers, which would remain the same for the rest of the railroad's lifetime, are shown below:

Old Train No. and Name November 1899	New Train No. and Name February 1900
No. 5 – *Solid Express*	No. 5 – *Through Express*
No. 7 – *The Ute*	No. 3 – *The Ute*
No. 6 – *Solid Express*	No. 4 – *Express Train*
No. 8 – *The Coyote*	No. 6 – *The Coyote*

There were also some changes in the numbering of the through trains between Colorado Springs and Cripple Creek, but these were not quite as drastic as the changes to the mainline trains, nor were they to be as permanent. Nos. 9, 10 and 11 stayed the same, while old No. 1 became new No. 7, and old No. 2 became new No. 8. There were no changes in connection with the Aspen Branch trains.

The February 25th schedules were still relatively unchanged from the previous November, with the exception of new No. 6, which was set back at Grand Junction to a 5:40 PM departure, thus regaining an RGW connection and arriving at Colorado Springs at 5:40 AM, for a flat 12 hour running time.

In the equipment listing, No. 5 showed handling a Pullman sleeper from Denver to Grand Junction, with connections west, as well as a chair car between those points. This sleeper returned from Grand Junction in No. 6. No. 3 now showed a through sleeper from Denver to San Francisco, via RGW and SP, with the return car being handled over the CM by No. 4. Nos. 3 and 6 still included the Denver – Leadville car, but the new through San Francisco car replaced the former Denver – Ogden sleeper that had been handled; no Ogden car was listed for any of the trains. Nos. 9 and 10 were still handling the two short haul sleepers from Denver and Colorado Springs to the Cripple Creek District, indicating that there was still a demand for the Colorado Springs sleeper even during this winter season.

Schedules on the Aspen Branch were again increased to four round trips, due to the rescheduling of No. 6, so that convenient connections could be maintained with all mainline trains. The Aspen station was a busy location shortly after 8 PM, what with the connection from No. 5 arriving at 8:10 and the connection with No. 6 leaving at 8:20 PM. The two morning trips were also still operated, in order to provide connections with Nos. 3 and 4 at Basalt.

On July 2, 1900, control of the Colorado Midland was acquired jointly by the Colorado & Southern and the Rio Grande Western. Frank Trumbull, who was president of the Colorado & Southern, was also appointed president of the Midland, and Charles H. Schlacks was appointed general manager. George W. Ristine had formerly held both the presidency and the general manager's position during his tenure. The appointment of Frank Trumbull as president ushered in the so-called "Golden Era" of the Colorado Midland, as his reign during the early 1900s was a period of good business and improvements in the railroad's fortunes. The May 13th schedule, which was published in the August 1900 issue of the Official Guide, listed the new management team that would direct the policy of the railroad for the next several years.

The May 13th timetable contained one major change from that of February in that it scheduled the fastest train ever to be programmed over the mainline of the Midland. No. 6 now left Grand Junction at 6:45 PM, one hour five minutes later, but still arrived in Colorado Springs at 5:40 AM, for a running time of ten hours 55 minutes. This would never be equalled. Just how were they able to cut 65 minutes from the previous schedule? Let's take a look at the intermediate timings for this train and compare the February schedule with that for May, as follows:

Stations	2/25/00	5/13/00	Difference
Grand Junction to Basalt	3 hrs. 17 mins.	3 hrs. 15 mins.	2 mins.
At Basalt	10 mins.	5 mins.	5 mins.
Basalt to Arkansas Jct.	2 hrs. 42 mins.	2 hrs. 20 mins.	22 mins.
At Arkansas Junction	10 mins.	10 mins.	—
Arkansas Junction to Divide	4 hrs. 16 mins.	3 hrs. 40 mins.	36 mins.
Divide to Colo. Springs	1 hr. 25 mins.	1 hr. 25 mins.	—
Totals	12 hrs. 0 mins.	10 hrs. 55 mins.	65 mins.

It can be seen that much of the time was taken out between Basalt and Arkansas Junction, which was a pretty difficult thing to do when the terrain that the train had to negotiate is considered. But cutting off 36 minutes over the stretch between Arkansas Junction and Divide was the real factor in reducing the running time. Even with this fast timing, it is interesting to note that not a minute was taken out of the running time from Grand Junction to New Castle over the Rio Grande Junction. Both schedules called for two hours ten minutes, yet one would think that better running was available along that river level grade than over the Continental Divide and Trout Creek Pass. Whether the CM was able to meet this schedule in

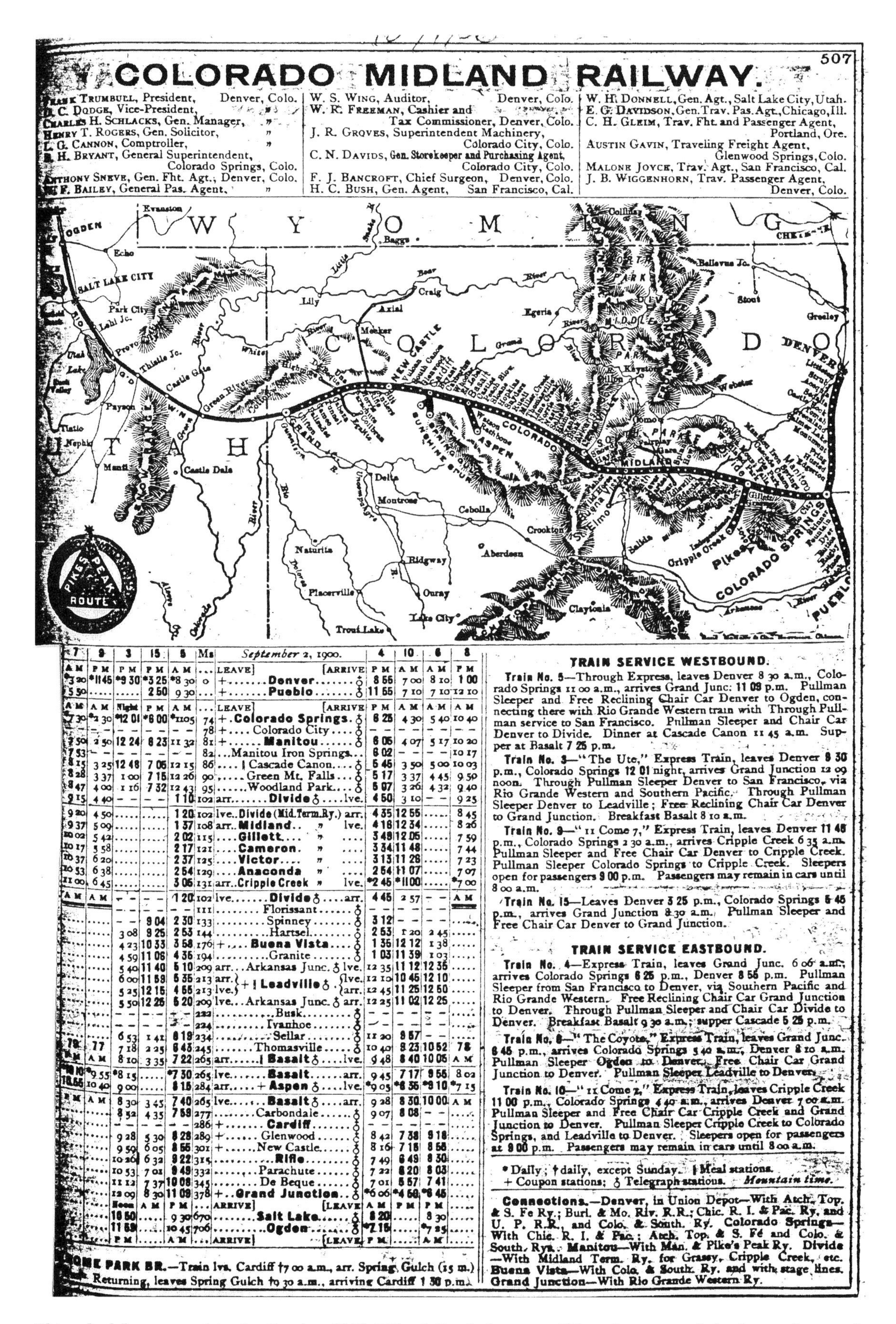

507

COLORADO MIDLAND RAILWAY.

FRANK TRUMBULL, President, Denver, Colo.
D. C. DODGE, Vice-President, "
CHARLES H. SCHLACKS, Gen. Manager, "
HENRY T. ROGERS, Gen. Solicitor, "
L. G. CANNON, Comptroller, "
B. H. BRYANT, General Superintendent, Colorado Springs, Colo.
ANTHONY SNEVE, Gen. Fht. Agt., Denver, Colo.
W. F. BAILEY, General Pas. Agent, "

W. S. WING, Auditor, Denver, Colo.
W. R. FREEMAN, Cashier and Tax Commissioner, Denver, Colo.
J. R. GROVES, Superintendent Machinery, Colorado City, Colo.
C. N. DAVIDS, Gen. Storekeeper and Purchasing Agent, Colorado City, Colo.
F. J. BANCROFT, Chief Surgeon, Denver, Colo.
H. C. BUSH, Gen. Agent, San Francisco, Cal.

W. H. DONNELL, Gen. Agt., Salt Lake City, Utah.
E. G. DAVIDSON, Gen. Trav. Pas. Agt., Chicago, Ill.
C. H. GLEIM, Trav. Fht. and Passenger Agent, Portland, Ore.
AUSTIN GAVIN, Traveling Freight Agent, Glenwood Springs, Colo.
MALONE JOYCE, Trav. Agt., San Francisco, Cal.
J. B. WIGGENHORN, Trav. Passenger Agent, Denver, Colo.

7	9	3	15	5	Ms	*September* 2, 1900.	4	10	6	8
A M	P M	P M	P M	A M	...	LEAVE] [ARRIVE	P M	A M	A M	P M
*3 20	*11 45	*9 30	*3 25	*8 30	0	+.......**Denver**.......♁	8 55	7 00	8 10	1 00
5 50	.....	.....	2 50	9 30	...	+.......**Pueblo**.......♁	11 55	7 10	7 10	12 10
A M	A M	Night	P M	A M	...	LEAVE] [ARRIVE	P M	A M	A M	A M
7 30	*2 30	*12 01	*6 00	*11 05	74	+.**Colorado Springs**.♁	6 25	4 30	5 40	10 40
— —	— —	— —	— —	— —	78	+....Colorado City....♁	— —	— —	— —	— —
7 50	2 50	12 24	6 23	11 32	81	+......**Manitou**......♁	6 05	4 07	5 17	10 20
7 53	— —	— —	— —	— —	82	...Manitou Iron Springs...	6 02	— —	— —	10 17
8 15	3 25	12 48	7 05	12 15	86	....‡ Cascade Canon....♁	5 45	3 50	5 00	10 03
8 28	3 37	1 00	7 15	12 26	90	.....Green Mt. Falls...♁	5 17	3 37	4 45	9 50
8 47	4 00	1 16	7 32	12 43	95	......Woodland Park...♁	5 07	3 26	4 32	9 40
9 15	4 40	— —	— —	1 10	102	arr.......**Divide**♁....lve.	4 50	3 10	— —	9 25
9 20	4 50	.....	.....	1 20	102	lve..**Divide (Mid. Term. Ry.)** arr.	4 35	12 55	.....	8 45
9 37	5 09	.....	.....	1 37	108	arr..**Midland**.. " lve.	4 18	12 34	.....	8 26
10 02	5 42	.....	.....	2 02	115	....**Gillett**.... "	3 49	12 05	.....	7 59
10 17	5 58	.....	.....	2 17	121	....**Cameron**. "	3 34	11 48	.....	7 44
10 37	6 20	.....	.....	2 37	125	....**Victor**.... "	3 13	11 28	.....	7 23
10 53	6 38	.....	.....	2 54	129	....**Anaconda** "	2 54	11 07	.....	7 07
11 00	6 45	.....	.....	3 05	131	arr..**Cripple Creek** " lve.	*2 45	*11 00	.....	*7 00
A M	A M	— —	— —	1 20	102	lve.......**Divide**♁....arr.	4 45	2 57	— —	A M
		— —	— —	— —	111	........Florissant.......♁	— —	— —	— —	
.....	.....	— —	9 04	2 30	133	........Spinney.......♁	3 12	— —	— —	.....
.....	.....	3 08	9 25	2 53	144	..........Hartsel.......♁	2 53	1 20	2 45	.....
.....	.....	4 23	10 33	3 58	176	+....**Buena Vista**....♁	1 35	12 12	1 38	.....
.....	.....	4 59	11 06	4 36	194	..........Granite.......♁	1 03	11 39	1 03	.....
.....	.....	5 40	11 40	5 10	209	arr...Arkansas Junc. ♁ lve.	12 35	11 12	12 35	.....
.....	.....	6 00	11 58	5 35	213	arr. } + ‡ **Leadville** ♁ { lve.	12 10	10 45	12 10	.....
.....	.....	5 25	12 15	4 55	213	lve. } + ‡ **Leadville** ♁ { arr.	12 45	11 25	12 50	.....
.....	.....	5 50	12 25	5 20	209	lve...Arkansas Junc. ♁ arr.	12 25	11 02	12 25	.....
.....	.....	— —	— —	— —	222	..........Busk.........♁	— —	— —	— —	.....
.....	.....	— —	— —	— —	224	..........Ivanhoe.........♁	— —	— —	— —	.....
.....	.....	6 53	1 41	6 19	234	..........Sellar.........♁	11 20	6 57	— —	.....
78	77	7 18	2 25	6 43	245	.......Thomasville.....♁	10 40	8 23	10 52	78
P M	A M	8 10	3 35	7 22	265	arr......‡ **Basalt**♁....lve.	9 48	8 40	10 05	A M
10 10	*9 55	*8 15	.....	*7 30	265	lve.......**Basalt**.......arr.	9 45	7 17	9 55	8 02
10 55	10 40	9 00	.....	8 15	284	arr.....+ **Aspen** ♁....lve.	*9 05	*6 35	*9 10	*7 15
P M	A M	8 30	3 45	7 40	265	lve.......**Basalt**♁....arr.	9 28	8 30	10 00	A M
.....	.....	8 52	4 35	7 59	277	........Carbondale......♁	9 07	8 08	— —	.....
.....	.....	— —	— —	— —	286	+.......**Cardiff**.......♁	— —	— —	— —	.....
.....	.....	9 28	5 30	8 28	289	+......Glenwood......♁	8 42	7 38	9 18	.....
.....	.....	9 59	6 05	8 55	301	+......New Castle......♁	8 16	7 18	8 58	.....
.....	.....	10 26	6 32	9 22	315	..........**Rifle**.........♁	7 49	6 49	8 30	.....
.....	.....	10 53	7 01	9 49	332	........Parachute.......♁	7 22	6 20	8 03	.....
.....	.....	11 12	7 37	10 08	345	.........De Beque.......♁	7 01	5 57	7 41	.....
.....	.....	12 09	8 30	11 08	378	+..**Grand Junction**..♁	*6 06	*4 58	*6 45	.....
.....	.....	Noon	A M	P M	...	ARRIVE] [LEAVE	A M	P M	P M	.....
.....	.....	10 50	.....	9 30	670	..........**Salt Lake**......♁	8 20	.....	8 30	.....
.....	.....	11 59	.....	10 45	706	..........**Ogden**.........♁	*7 15	.....	*7 25	.....
.....	.....	P M	.....	A M	...	ARRIVE] [LEAVE	P M	.....	A M	.....

STONE PARK BR.—Train lvs. Cardiff †7 00 a.m., arr. Spring Gulch (15 m.) Returning, leaves Spring Gulch †9 30 a.m., arriving Cardiff 1 30 p.m.

TRAIN SERVICE WESTBOUND.

Train No. 5—Through Express, leaves Denver 8 30 a.m., Colorado Springs 11 00 a.m., arrives Grand Junc: 11 08 p.m. Pullman Sleeper and Free Reclining Chair Car Denver to Ogden, connecting there with Rio Grande Western train with Through Pullman service to San Francisco. Pullman Sleeper and Chair Car Denver to Divide. Dinner at Cascade Canon 11 45 a.m. Supper at Basalt 7 25 p.m.

Train No. 3—"The Ute," Express Train, leaves Denver 9 30 p.m., Colorado Springs 12 01 night, arrives Grand Junction 12 09 noon. Through Pullman Sleeper Denver to San Francisco, via Rio Grande Western and Southern Pacific. Through Pullman Sleeper Denver to Leadville; Free Reclining Chair Car Denver to Grand Junction. Breakfast Basalt 8 10 a.m.

Train No. 9—"11 Come 7," Express Train, leaves Denver 11 45 p.m., Colorado Springs 2 30 a.m., arrives Cripple Creek 6 35 a.m. Pullman Sleeper and Free Chair Car Denver to Cripple Creek. Pullman Sleeper Colorado Springs to Cripple Creek. Sleepers open for passengers 9 00 p.m. Passengers may remain in cars until 8 00 a.m.

Train No. 15—Leaves Denver 3 25 p.m., Colorado Springs 6 45 p.m., arrives Grand Junction 8 30 a.m. Pullman Sleeper and Free Chair Car Denver to Grand Junction.

TRAIN SERVICE EASTBOUND.

Train No. 4—Express Train, leaves Grand Junc. 6 06 a.m., arrives Colorado Springs 6 25 p.m., Denver 8 55 p.m. Pullman Sleeper from San Francisco to Denver, via Southern Pacific and Rio Grande Western. Free Reclining Chair Car Grand Junction to Denver. Through Pullman Sleeper and Chair Car Divide to Denver. Breakfast Basalt 9 30 a.m.; supper Cascade 5 25 p.m.

Train No. 6—"The Coyote," Express Train, leaves Grand Junc. 6 45 p.m., arrives Colorado Springs 5 40 a.m., Denver 8 10 a.m. Pullman Sleeper Ogden to Denver. Free Chair Car Grand Junction to Denver. Pullman Sleeper Leadville to Denver.

Train No. 10—"11 Come 7," Express Train, leaves Cripple Creek 11 00 p.m., Colorado Springs 4 40 a.m., arrives Denver 7 00 a.m. Pullman Sleeper and Free Chair Car Cripple Creek and Grand Junction to Denver. Pullman Sleeper Cripple Creek to Colorado Springs, and Leadville to Denver. Sleepers open for passengers at 9 00 p.m. Passengers may remain in cars until 8 00 a.m.

* Daily; † daily, except Sunday. ‡ Meal stations.
\+ Coupon stations; ♁ Telegraph stations. *Mountain time.*

Connections.—Denver, in Union Depot—With Atch. Top. & S. Fe Ry.; Burl. & Mo. Riv. R.R.; Chic. R. I. & Pac. Ry. and U. P. R.R., and Colo. & South. Ry. **Colorado Springs**—With Chic. R. I. & Pac.; Atch. Top. & S. Fé and Colo. & South. Rys. **Manitou**—With Man. & Pike's Peak Ry. **Divide**—With Midland Term. Ry. for Grassy, Cripple Creek, etc. **Buena Vista**—With Colo. & South. Ry. and with stage lines. **Grand Junction**—With Rio Grande Western Ry.

This schedule appeared in the October 1900 Official Guide (see page 76) and was one of the first to list Frank Trumbull as president.

actual practice is something that we will probably never know, but the fact that the plan was for No. 6 to run over hill and dale during the night at this rate of speed is something to contemplate. In surveying the schedules of CM trains over the years, the impression is gained that anything under 12 hours between Colorado Springs and Grand Junction was good time. There were many times that 12 hours was more than the road could realistically establish, so this schedule of under 11 hours was downright amazing.

Other changes at this time were of a minor nature, with slight adjustments of a few minutes for the mainline trains as well as the Cripple Creek through trains. This also holds true for the four round trips on the Aspen Branch, although it should be noted that No. 80's departure time from Aspen was 6:35 PM, even though a flaw in the schedule indicates that the train left at 8:35 PM. There was a change on the Jerome Park Branch, which now showed only a Monday, Wednesday and Friday operation, instead of daily except Sunday that had prevailed in the past. No change was made to the mileage to reflect the operation through the Busk Tunnel—and this was nearly a year after trains had resumed using that bore!

During the search through the Official Guides for the various timetables, perhaps the biggest surprise of all was to discover that on August 13, 1900, the CM scheduled a third through train over the length of the railroad. Only a few years previously, the CM was hard pressed to have one through train daily over the road; now there were three trains each way!

The new trains were numbered 15 and 10, with the westbound out of Colorado Springs at 5:45 PM going into Leadville unlike any other through train, tarrying there from 11:55 PM to 12:10 AM, stopping at Basalt from 3:45 to 4:15 AM, New Castle at 6:05 AM, and arriving in Grand Junction at 8:30 AM. Certainly it was not a very fast train, especially since it went into Leadville and stayed at Basalt for 30 minutes. The reason for this stop is puzzling since there was no Aspen connection, and it was rather early for breakfast. The consist listed a Pullman sleeper and a chair car from Denver to Grand Junction, and there was no western connection advertised.

Likewise, No. 10 left Grand Junction at 4:50 PM, New Castle at 7:18 PM and was at Basalt from 8:30 to 8:40 PM, where a connection leaving Aspen at 6:35 PM was advertised. The Arkansas Junction stop was from 11:02 to 11:12 PM, with stub connections for Leadville. The Divide stop was from 2:57 to 3:10 AM, where the sleepers from Cripple Creek were picked up, and arrival at Colorado Springs was set for 4:30 AM. A connection arrived in Denver at 7 AM. No. 10 handled a sleeper and chair car from Grand Junction for Denver, picking up the Leadville sleeper at Arkansas Junction and both sleepers from Cripple Creek at Divide, one of which would be set off at Colorado Springs with the other going through to Denver. If No. 10 did all this, it would mean that it was handling four sleeping cars down the hill from Divide, just about as many cars of this type ever scheduled in one train on the CM. Since No. 6 was still showing as handling a Leadville to Denver sleeper, one again wonders if the equipment listing means what it says. There is no indication that two sleepers operated westbound from Denver to Leadville, so one is led to believe that there was only one eastbound car as well. Handling the Leadville sleeper in No. 10 would provide an earlier arrival at Denver by one hour ten minutes than moving it in No. 6 and would make sense in that respect.

No. 6 still showed the ten hour 55 minutes schedule between Grand Junction and Colorado Springs. The way that No. 10 was scheduled, it appears to have been nothing more than an advanced section of No. 6 and could have been set up to try to assist that train in making time by taking some of the work. Since they were doing that, it could have been figured that No. 10 might as well get the Cripple Creek sleepers as well and thus be able to eliminate the additional through train from the gold camp. No. 15 did not really seem to have a major function, since it had no connections on the west end. It had such a slow schedule that it probably was established to balance the schedule for No. 10's activities. While we know nothing for sure of the background for the establishment of Nos. 15 and 10, it is interesting to speculate on the reasons for these two trains and to contemplate the fact that three trains were scheduled across the railroad at this time.

These three trains on the mainline had an effect on the Cripple Creek service, as there were now three trains westbound between Colorado Springs and Cripple Creek but only one train eastbound. Connections with mainline trains Nos. 4 and 10 were provided from Cripple Creek to Divide, but no westbound connections were shown. The connection listed for No. 5 from Divide was actually No. 11, which still followed No. 5 out of Colorado Springs, as has been noted before. No. 9 handled the sleeping cars from Denver and Colorado Springs to Cripple Creek. The eastbound cars were handled as described above with respect to mainline train No. 10.

The Aspen Branch arrangements were still calling for four round trips daily, and connections were provided for all mainline trains except No. 15. It should also be noted that the mileages west of Busk were now changed to reflect the fact that the trains were passing through the Busk Tunnel, and now totaled 304 miles between Colorado Springs and Grand Junction; the mileage error between Arkansas Junction and Busk still had not been corrected and would remain in error until 1912. The Jerome Park Branch service was restored to a daily except Sunday operation, instead of tri-weekly as listed in May.

A new timetable was issued for September 2nd, which was published in the October 1900 issue of the Guide. The three-train-each-way format was retained, with the major change being that No. 15 now left Colorado Springs 15 minutes later at 6 PM and arrived in Grand Junction at 8:10 AM, the same as formerly. Most of the 15 minutes saved was taken out of the First District schedule

The French actress Anna Held, married to master showman Florenz Ziegfeld, made several American tours. In 1904 she appeared in Colorado Springs and Leadville and poses here on a horse next to her private Pullman in the Midland's Colorado Springs yard. To judge from the style of his holster, the cowboy is probably a member of the troupe and not a western native. (H.H. Buckwalter, Colorado Historical Society)

between Colorado Springs and Arkansas Junction. Another important change was the discontinuance of No. 11, the former 11:30 AM departure from Colorado Springs for the Cripple Creek District, that had followed No. 5 up Ute Pass. A connection off No. 5 at Divide, on the same time as the old No. 11 west of there, was listed to provide passengers with a mid-day service to the gold camp. Cripple Creek through trains still showed an imbalance as there were two westbound and only one eastbound, although connections were still available at Divide with mainline Nos. 4 and 10.

A couple of changes took place in the equipment listing. No. 5 showed a Denver – Ogden sleeper again, returning in No. 6 eastbound. The item for No. 5 goes on to state that "connecting there with Rio Grande Western train with through Pullman service to San Francisco." This is identical to the statement made in the previous schedule when the car ran only to Grand Junction and indicates that it was not removed when the car was extended to Ogden. The Denver – San Francisco car was still being handled in Nos. 3 and 4, and the Leadville sleepers remained the same as before. Nos. 9 and MT/CM 10 still handled the two sleepers from Denver and Colorado Springs to Cripple Creek.

As mentioned, this September 2nd schedule was published in the October 1900 Official Guide, and it should be noted that there was a notice from the Colorado Midland that was too late to be included in the schedule pages:

COLORADO MIDLAND RY., – Page 507.

"Train No. 15 leaving Colorado Springs for Grand Junction formerly 6:00 PM, has been discontinued. Train No. 9 arriving Divide formerly 4:40 AM, now arrives 4:25 AM. Train No. 10 leaving Grand Junction for Colorado Springs formerly 4:50 PM has been discontinued. Train No. 4 leaving Grand Junction formerly 6:06 AM now leaves 6:15 AM, Basalt 10:00 AM, arriving Leadville 1:00 PM. Leaves Leadville 12:15 Noon, Divide 4:50 PM, arriving Colorado Springs as heretofore 6:25 PM. Additional train leaves Divide 2:00 AM, arriving Colorado Springs 3:40 AM."

September 26, 1900

Thus the three-train-each-way schedule of the CM ended on September 26th after 46 days of the experiment, if that is what it was, and the railroad reverted to a double-daily service for the next few years.

Whether the third train was profitable is hard to determine based on the road's passenger revenues. In the fiscal year ending June 30, 1900, the combined revenues for passengers, mail and express totaled about $457,700. The fiscal year ending June 30, 1901, which included all of the time that Nos. 15 and 10 were run, totaled about $475,500. This indicates that Nos. 15 and 10 did not have a significant effect on passenger revenues, since the roughly $18,000 difference could have been chalked up to a number of other factors.

The only change during the year to the motive power and passenger car fleets was that baggage car 313, which had been wrecked the previous year, was rebuilt and restored to service. This brought the car fleet back up to forty.

A three-car passenger train crosses the lofty Maroon Creek bridge into the silver camp of Aspen in the 1890s. (Museum collection)

1901

After all the excitement during 1900, it seems appropriate that 1901 would be a relatively calm year, but this was not to be. Up to this point, the CM/MT combination had shared the Cripple Creek District freight and passenger business with the narrow gauge Florence & Cripple Creek, which had reached the gold camp just months before the Midland Terminal had built into the District. The F&CC connected with the Denver & Rio Grande at Florence and Canon City and provided both day and night service, including sleeping cars between Denver and the District. For Denver passengers, however, this was really the long way around, and the CM/MT route via Colorado Springs furnished a shorter and faster trip than did the F&CC's narrow gauge trains.

Most of the businessmen concerned with the activities in the Cripple Creek District were located in Colorado Springs and were unhappy with the high charges the railroads were making on ore and other freight shipments. Negotiations to have these rates reduced having failed, a group of businessmen had established a new company known as the Colorado Springs & Cripple Creek District Railway in 1899 and started construction from Colorado Springs to the District. This became known and "The Short Line." Previously, these same interests had acquired the Cripple Creek District Railway, which was an electric interurban line between Cripple Creek and Victor, built in 1898, over the mountains between the two terminals. This company also built another line between Cripple Creek and Victor, following much the same route as the Florence & Cripple Creek and the Midland Terminal. The construction of the Short Line had started in 1900, and the road was completed early in 1901. Although the final spike was driven on March 23rd, regular service was not started until April 8th. Passenger operations actually began at 11:45 PM on April 7th, when train No. 16 left Cripple Creek for Colorado Springs, carrying a through sleeping car for Denver via the D&RG.

The initial schedule for the CS&CCD, dated April 8th, called for four round trips between Colorado Springs and Cripple Creek, with trains leaving Colorado Springs at 2:50 AM, 7:30 AM, 10:35 AM and 4:05 PM. The early morning train carried the through sleeper from Denver (leaving that point at 12:01 AM), and the 4:05 PM had a through coach and observation car from Denver. Trains left Cripple Creek at 7:40 AM, 12:40 PM, 4 PM and 11:45 PM. The first train had the through coach and observation car for Denver, while the 11:45 PM train carried the Denver sleeper, due in Colorado Springs at 3:10 AM and arriving Denver at 7 AM via the D&RG. The Short Line did not provide a local sleeper between the District and Colorado Springs as did the CM/MT route, but in frequency of service and accommodations provided, the new route was certainly a stout competitor. The Short Line built a branch from Cameron to Victor, but until this was completed in November 1901, passengers destined to Victor and other points, such as Anaconda and Elkton, were given the option of going into Cripple Creek, and then using the Low Line electric cars to reach their destination. The CM/MT route had the advantage here as its trains ran through Victor and the other two stations prior to their arrival at Cripple Creek, and thus could provide a faster service. After November, when the Short Line branch to Victor was completed, the CM/MT lost some of this advantage, as the Short Line then ran steam powered stub runs between Cameron and Victor as connections with the mainline trains. (A definitive history of The Short Line is Tivis E. Wilkins' *Short Line to Cripple Creek*, published by the Museum as *Colorado Rail Annual No. 16*.)

As a counter to the Short Line's competition, the CM restored four-trains-a-day service between Colorado Springs and Cripple Creek, and continued to maintain both the Denver sleeper and the Colorado Springs sleeper on the night trains. The imbalance in the through train schedules was reversed, for now there were four eastbound from Cripple Creek and only three from Colorado Springs. Mainline No. 5, however, continued to advertise a connection at Divide with Midland Terminal No. 5. One westbound train was added to the schedule, No. 1, leaving Colorado Springs at 6:30 PM. Two new trains were added eastbound: No. 12 leaving Cripple Creek at 2:45 PM and No. 2 leaving at 6:30 PM. It is interesting to note that the times of Nos. 12 and 4 are almost the re-

1	7	9	3	5	Ms	*August* 21, 1901.	4	10	6	8	12	2
P M	A M	P M	P M	A M	...	LEAVE] [ARRIVE	P M	A M	A M	Noon	P M	.....
*3 25	*3 20	*11 45	*9 30	*8 30	0	Denver	8 45	7 00	8 10	12 50	8 45	P M
5 00	5 35	.....	.....	9 00	...	Pueblo	7 35	7 15	7 15	12 10	7 35	11 45
P M	A M	A M	Night	A M	...	LEAVE] [ARRIVE	P M	A M	A M	A M	P M	P M
*6 30	*7 30	*2 30	*12 05	*11 05	74	Colorado Springs	6 15	3 40	5 45	10 30	5 45	9 05
– –	– –	– –	– –	– –	78	Colorado City	– –	– –	– –	– –	– –	– –
6 47	3 07	2 50	12 30	11 32	81	Manitou	5 55	3 22	5 25	10 12	5 24	8 47
– –	– –	– –	– –	– –	82	Manitou Iron Springs	5 53	3 18	– –	– –	– –	– –
7 05	8 25	3 22	12 58	12 25	86	Cascade Canon	5 35	3 00	5 05	9 55	5 06	8 29
7 13	8 33	3 35	1 08	12 32	90	Green Mt. Falls	5 07	2 40	4 50	9 42	4 53	8 17
7 25	8 45	3 55	1 22	12 47	95	Woodland Park	4 57	2 25	4 40	9 32	4 43	8 08
7 45	9 05	4 20	– –	1 10	102	arr. Divide lve.	– –	2 00	– –	9 15	4 30	7 55
7 55	9 15	4 25	....	1 20	102	lve. Divide (Mid. Term. Ry.) arr.	....	1 20	....	9 10	4 20	7 50
– –	9 28	4 39	....	1 37	108	arr. Midland " lve.	....	1 02	....	– –	4 02	– –
8 30	9 50	5 05	....	2 02	116	Gillett "	....	12 36	....	8 33	3 39	7 13
8 42	10 02	5 19	....	2 17	122	Cameron "	....	12 19	....	8 20	3 26	7 00
8 59	10 10	5 38	....	2 39	127	Victor "	....	12 05	....	8 05	3 05	6 45
9 10	10 30	5 55	....	2 55	130	Anaconda "	....	11 50	....	7 55	2 50	6 35
9 15	10 35	6 00	....	3 05	132	arr. Cripple Creek " lve.	....	*11 45	....	*7 50	*2 45	*6 30
P M	A M	A M	– –	1 20	102	lve. Divide arr.	– –	P M	– –	A M	P M	P M
.....	.....		–	– –	111	Florissant	– –		– –	.....	.....	.....
.....	.....		– –	2 30	133	Spinney	3 11	.....	– –	.....	.....	.....
.....	.....		3 27	2 53	144	Hartsel	2 53	.....	– –	.....	.....	.....
.....	.....		4 43	4 00	176	Buena Vista	1 45	.....	1 45	.....	.....	.....
.....	.....		5 20	4 35	194	Granite	1 10	.....	1 12	.....	.....	.....
.....	.....		6 00	5 10	209	arr. Arkansas Junc. lve.	12 45	.....	12 45	.....	.....	.....
.....	.....		6 25	5 35	213	arr. Leadville lve.	12 15	.....	12 15	.....	.....	.....
.....	.....		5 40	4 50	213	lve. Leadville arr.	1 00	.....	1 00	.....	.....	.....
.....	.....		6 10	5 20	209	lve. Arkansas Junc. arr.	12 37	.....	12 35	.....	.....	.....
.....	.....	– –	– –	– –	222	Busk	– –	.....	– –	.....	.....	.....
.....	.....	– –	– –	– –	224	Ivanhoe	– –	.....	– –	.....	.....	.....
.....	.....		7 13	6 19	234	Sellar	11 30	.....	– –	.....	.....	.....
.....	.....	79	7 38	6 42	245	Thomasville	10 47	80	10 54	.....	.....	.....
.....	.....	P M	*8 25	*7 27	265	arr. Basalt lve.	10 00	P M	10 05	.....	.....	.....
.....	.....	*10 10	9 45	7 45	265	lve. Basalt arr.	8 35	7 17	9 55	.....	.....	.....
.....	.....	10 55	10 30	8 30	284	arr. Aspen lve.	*7 50	*6 35	*9 10	.....	.....	.....
.....	.....	P M	8 45	7 45	265	lve. Basalt arr.	9 40	P M	10 00	.....	.....	.....
.....	.....		9 07	8 04	277	Carbondale	9 14	.....	9 41	.....	.....	.....
.....	.....		– –	– –	286	Cardiff	– –		– –	.....	.....	.....
.....	.....		9 28	8 23	299	Glenwood	8 40	.....	9 18	.....	.....	.....
.....	.....		9 59	8 55	301	New Castle	8 25	.....	8 55	.....	.....	.....
.....	.....		10 26	9 22	315	Rifle	7 58	.....	8 30	.....	.....	.....
.....	.....		10 53	9 49	332	Parachute	7 31	.....	8 03	.....	.....	.....
.....	.....		11 12	10 08	345	De Beque	7 10	.....	7 41	.....	.....	.....
.....	.....		12 09	11 09	378	Grand Junction	*6 15	.....	*6 45	.....	.....	.....
.....	.....		Noon	P M	...	ARRIVE] [LEAVE	A M	.....	P M	.....	.....	.....
.....	.....		10 50	9 35	670	Salt Lake	8 20	.....	3 30	.....	.....	.....
.....	.....		11 58	10 45	706	Ogden	*7 15	.....	*7 25	.....	.....	.....
.....	.....		P M	A M	...	ARRIVE] [LEAVE	P M	.....	A M	.....	.....	.....

JEROME PARK BR.—Train leaves Cardiff †7 00 a.m., arriving Spring Gulch 15 miles 9 00 a.m. Returning, lvs. Spring Gulch 10 30 a.m., arr. Cardiff 12 01 noon.

verse of the times of Nos. 5 and 11 a year or so earlier. Now No. 12 left Divide at 4:30 PM with No. 4 right behind at 4:40 PM. As No. 4 made a meal stop at Cascade Canon, No. 12 got to Colorado Springs at 5:45 PM, 25 minutes ahead of No. 4 at 6:10 PM. Both trains made the same connection for Denver, due there at 8:45 PM. It is possible that No. 12 could have been put on to protect the connection for Denver for the Cripple Creek patrons in the event that No. 4 was running late and would have missed that connection.

At this period in the history of the Cripple Creek District, it is interesting to note that there were now ten passenger trains each way in and out of the District. The CM/MT route provided four trains, the Short Line also had four trains and the F&CC had two trains each way. The schedules of the other roads are included as there never would be this density of scheduled passenger trains again.

In addition to the four through trains to and from Divide, the Midland Terminal also listed three daily round trips between Cripple Creek and Cameron on about a 40-minute running time, which provided a service for the miners and later became known as "Hob-Nail Specials." The MT schedule also stated that Nos. 9 and 10 had a Pullman sleeper between Denver and Cripple Creek, but does not mention the Colorado Springs sleeper, which is definitely listed in the Colorado Midland equipment table.

The CS&CCD schedule also made the following statement with respect to the electric lines: "Cars are run on the half hour schedule over the Electric System of the C.S. & C.C.D. Ry. between Cripple Creek and Victor, affording excellent and prompt service to and from the various towns and mines in the Gold District."

The F&CC and its Golden Circle subsidiary were not left out of the District passenger picture either, as they advertised 16 trips from Cripple Creek to Goldfield, with an additional two trips each way between Goldfield and Vista Grande. So it can be seen that the Cripple Creek District in 1901 did not suffer from a dearth of public transportation, as steel rails provided all sorts of service at all hours of the day and night.

Getting back to the Colorado Midland's own passenger operations, the schedule for April 11th showed very little change from that of the previous year's through trains. No. 6's schedule had been lengthened by five minutes so that it now covered the mainline in 11 hours even, while the other three trains were set for approximately 12 hours running time across the railroad. Since all of the through trains now by-passed Leadville, an eating station had been set up at Arkansas Junction for the benefit of the through passengers. The regular meal stations were still shown as Cascade Canon, Leadville and Basalt.

With respect to the consist of the through trains, No. 5 was now called *Pacific Express* and No. 4 was now known as *Eastern Express*. Nos. 3 and 4 were still handling the Denver – San Francisco sleeper, while Nos. 5 and 6 had the Denver – Ogden sleeper. A new item is that No. 5 now had a tourist sleeper on Wednesday, enroute from Chicago to Los Angeles, and another tourist sleeper on Thursday enroute from St. Paul to San Francisco. No. 6 showed the eastbound movement of both of these cars on Thursday but did not show the eastbound Leadville – Denver sleeper. It was traditional for this train to handle this car, and the failure to show it here could be another omission on the part of the railroad. If it did have the Leadville car, as I suspect, then No. 6 on Thursdays must have been a very heavy train, with two sleepers, two tourist cars, a coach, a chair car and head-end cars. This was certainly quite a train to get over the road in 11 hours!

The Aspen Branch service had been cut down to three round trips daily, and it appears that the importance of this mining center was on the wane, based on the timing of the connections with the mainline trains at Basalt. The one morning trip was now designed to make connections with both Nos. 4 and 3 at Basalt. Passengers from Aspen for No. 4 now had to wait at Basalt for one hour 25 minutes before they could leave for the east, while passengers off No. 3 for Aspen had to wait one hour 20 minutes before the branch train left.

It should be noted that the name of C. H. Speers was now shown as the assistant general passenger agent. Mr. Speers became general passenger agent in 1902 and was generally responsible for the railroad's passenger schedule policy from then until the Carlton/Penrose management took over in 1917.

On July 1, 1901, the Denver & Rio Grande acquired control of the Rio Grande Western, thereby also acquiring one-half interest in the Colorado Midland. While the D&RG was the most active competitor of the CM, there was no immediate effect on the Midland's fortunes, since the C&S still had what amounted to a veto power over the D&RG. In addition the Rio Grande had enough problems of its own at that time, so that it did not interfere with the CM.

The schedule dated August 21st had only minor changes in the times of the Colorado Midland trains, and those of the joint CM/MT trains to Cripple Creek. The only change concerned a slight adjustment for No. 4, adding five minutes to the running time. The only other change affected the Jerome Park Branch. This service now left Cardiff at 7 AM daily except Sunday, with arrival at Spring Gulch at 9:30 AM. Returning, the train left at 10:30 AM and arrived back in Cardiff at 12:01 PM. This arrangement now was more reasonable than it had been for the past several years.

The Colorado Midland's shops were busy this year with changes to the passenger equipment. Chair cars 257–259 were converted to combination mail/coach cars, and chair car 260 was converted to a combination baggage/coach, and renumbered 9. Also, gondolas 1501–1506 were rebuilt into suburban coaches and renumbered 1–6. The Midland also purchased five new vestibule chair cars with six-wheel trucks, numbered 246–250, the heaviest such cars on the railroad. The addition of the six suburban coaches, together with the five new large chair cars brought the passenger fleet up to 51 units.

The CM also purchased five new Baldwin 2-8-0 type engines in class 159. These engines were Vauclain compounds, the only such type on the railroad, and came equipped with 60-inch drivers, the highest of any CM engines. Numbered 201-205, they were used a great deal in passenger service, as well as for helpers on the First District from Colorado Springs and Florissant to Divide. It was reported that the 159 class could handle five passenger cars from Colorado Springs to Divide without assistance, whereas the tenwheelers that had been used on the through trains were limited to three cars. Thus it was expected that the new engines would reduce much of the double-heading that had been necessary. The acquisition of the class 159 engines brought the fleet up to 60 locomotives.

1902

The schedule for May 25th had one major change with respect to mainline trains which affected the running time of No. 6, the former "fast" train over the road. This train had 45 minutes added to its schedule, so that its running time was 11 hours 45 minutes. Thirty minutes of this was added between New Castle and Arkansas Junction, with the other 15 minutes added to the First District.

As far as the consists of the trains were concerned, No. 5 now had only the one tourist sleeper, which ran on Wednesdays enroute from Chicago to Los Angeles. This car was handled on No. 6 eastbound on Thursdays, but no mention was made of the former St. Paul – San Francisco tourist sleeper. The Denver – San Francisco Pullmans were still being handled on Nos. 3 and 4. Other equipment remained about the same, although there was still no reference to the eastbound handling of the Leadville – Denver sleeper, which was presumably moved in No. 6.

The main changes in this timetable had to do with the Colorado Springs – Cripple Creek services and included a rather extensive renumbering. No. 9, which had been transporting the Cripple Creek sleepers for years, was now changed to a day train, leaving Colorado Springs at 11:25 AM. No. 1, which had been leaving Colorado Springs around dinner time, was now the night train, with the through Denver – Cripple Creek sleeper. Old No. 1 was replaced by No. 11, which left Colorado Springs at 6:20 PM; No. 7 stayed in its former time slot, providing an 8 AM departure for the gold camp.

Eastbound, Nos. 8 and 10 remained on similar schedules to the previous year, but No. 2 was changed from an evening departure to 1 PM. Because of this new noontime service, No. 12 was set back from 2:45 PM to 3:10 PM, for an afternoon trip to Colorado Springs. The night trains, Nos. 1 and 10, still handled the Denver – Cripple Creek sleeper, but there was no longer any Colorado Springs – Cripple Creek sleeper, nor would there be any future mention of this service which had been a regular operation since 1897.

In 1899 and 1900, the fact that Nos. 5 and 11 were playing tag with their close departures from Colorado Springs was discussed. On this schedule there was a variation on that theme. No. 5 now left Colorado Springs at 11:01 AM, with new No. 9 following at 11:25 AM. While No. 5 was at Cascade Canon for the lunch stop, No. 9 ran around it and went into Divide at 12:50 PM with No. 5 right on its block at 1 PM. In this instance, however, the passenger change had been made at Colorado Springs (both trains working off the same connection which had left Denver at 8:30 AM). No. 9 did not wait at Divide for No. 5 but left right away for Cripple Creek.

Although the CM/MT combination still maintained its four trains a day schedule to Cripple Creek, the Short Line had discontinued its night train with its own Denver sleeper and was now providing a three-train schedule each way, all on daylight timings. By this time, the Victor Branch had been completed, and the Short Line now furnished stub connections between Cameron and Victor for all mainline trains. The schedules were quite competitive, with both the Short Line and the CM/MT route listing their fastest times at two hours 37 minutes from Cripple Creek to Colorado Springs. The best uphill time was posted by the Short Line with a two-hour 40-minute schedule, while the CM/MT route's best time was just five minutes lower.

The Aspen Branch continued with the three round trips, but the morning connections remained poor. One trip sufficed to make connections with Nos. 3 and 4, causing eastbound passengers from Aspen to wait one hour 25 minutes, while passengers off No. 3 for Aspen had to wait one hour 20 minutes for their connection to leave Basalt. Two round trips were run in the evening because the times of Nos. 5 and 6 were too far apart to make the connection with just one train.

On August 18th, the Colorado Springs, Divide and Cripple Creek RPO was established, which now meant that the Midland was handling two RPO routes, as the Colorado Springs – Aspen trip was still in operation. The schedule for October 15th did not result in any changes other than No. 4's time being lengthened by 15 minutes for a later arrival at Colorado Springs.

Seasonal adjustments were made, however, in the Colorado Springs – Cripple Creek service with two trains in each direction discontinued. Nos. 7 and 12 were cancelled for the winter, while Nos. 1 and 10 were discontinued permanently as night trains. This effectively ended an era between Denver and Cripple Creek; never again would a sleeping car be regularly scheduled between these two terminals. These reductions left the Colorado Springs – Cripple Creek service with two trains each way, with morning and afternoon departures from each city.

On the Aspen Branch, one of the evening connections was cut off, which worked against any eastbound passen-

11	9	3	5	Ms	October 15, 1902.	4	6	8	12
P M	A M	P M	A M	...	LEAVE] [ARRIVE	P M	A M	P M	P M
*3 45	*8 30	*9 30	*8 30	0	+ .... **Denver**	9 00	9 30	1 16	9 00
5 00	9 25	.....	9 25	...	+ .... **Pueblo**	7 50	7 55	12 30	7 50
P M	A M	Night	A M	...	LEAVE] [ARRIVE	P M	A M	A M	P M
*6 30	*11 00	*12 01	*11 03	74	+ . **Colorado Springs** .	6 30	6 30	10 45	6 20
6 41	11 10	— —	— —	78	+ .... Colorado City	— —	— —	10 35	6 10
6 50	11 18	12 11	11 15	81	+ ...... **Manitou**	6 07	— —	10 28	5 57
— —	— —	— —	— —	82	... Manitou Iron Springs ...	— —	— —	— —	— —
7 13	11 40	12 47	12 15	86	...... Cascade Canon ...	5 25	5 50	10 10	5 37
7 20	11 49	12 58	12 23	90	..... Green Mt. Falls	5 15	5 36	9 56	5 25
7 32	12 02	1 13	12 40	95	...... Woodland Park	5 03	— —	9 43	5 13
7 50	12 20	1 43	1 05	101	arr. .... **Divide** .... lve.	4 45	5 05	9 25	4 55
7 50	12 2[illegible]	.....	.....	101	lve.. **Divide** (Mid.Term.Ry.) arr.	.....	.....	9 25	4 55
— —	12 33	.....	.....	108	arr.. **Midland** .. " lve.	.....	.....	— —	4 39
8 28	12 56	.....	.....	116	.... **Gillett** .... "	.....	.....	8 47	4 17
8 38	1 09	.....	.....	122	.... **Cameron** , "	.....	.....	8 33	4 03
8 57	1 27	.....	.....	127	.... **Victor** .... "	.....	.....	8 16	3 43
9 10	1 40	.....	.....	130	.... **Anaconda** "	.....	.....	8 05	3 35
9 15	1 45	.....	.....	132	arr.. **Cripple Creek** " lve.	.....	.....	*8 00	*3 30
P M	P M	1 43	1 05	101	lve. .... **Divide** .... arr.	4 45	5 05	A M	P M
.....	.....	—	— —	111	.... Florissant	— —	— —	.....	.....
.....	.....	— —	2 23	133	.... Spinney	3 23	— —	.....	.....
.....	.....	3 25	2 45	144	.... Hartsel	3 08	— —	.....	.....
.....	.....	4 43	3 50	176	+ .... **Buena Vista**	1 58	2 15	.....	.....
.....	.....	5 20	4 24	194	.... Granite	1 25	1 43	.....	.....
.....	.....	6 0[illegible]	‖5 00	209	arr. .. Arkansas Junc. lve.	‖1 00	1 15	.....	.....
.....	.....	6 25	5 25	213	arr. } .. + **Leadville** .. { lve.	12 35	12 50	.....	.....
.....	.....	5 35	4 35	213	lve. } .. + **Leadville** .. { arr.	1 20	1 35	.....	.....
.....	.....	6 10	5 10	209	lve. .. Arkansas Junc. arr.	‖12 50	1 05	.....	.....
.....	.....	— —	— —	222	.... Busk	— —	— —	.....	.....
.....	.....	— —	— —	224	.... Ivanhoe	— —	— —	.....	.....
.....	.....	7 13	6 10	234	.... Sellar	11 38	— —	.....	.....
.....	.....	7 38	6 37	245	...... Thomasville	11 52	11 05	.....	.....
.....	.....	‖8 25	‖7 25	265	arr. ...... **Basalt** .... lve.	10 00	10 10	.....	.....
.....	.....	*9 45	7 50	265	lve. ...... **Basalt** .... arr.	8 35	7 35	.....	.....
.....	.....	10 3[illegible]	8 55	284	arr. ...... **Aspen** .... lve.	*7 50	*6 35	.....	.....
.....	.....	8 45	7 45	265	lve. ...... **Basalt** .... arr.	‖9 40	10 05	.....	.....
.....	.....	9 07	8 04	277	...... Carbondale	9 14	9 45	.....	.....
.....	.....	— —	— —	286	+ ...... **Cardiff**	— —	— —	.....	.....
.....	.....	9 28	8 23	289	+ ..... Glenwood	8 49	9 22	.....	.....
.....	.....	9 59	8 55	301	+ ..... New Castle	8 25	8 55	.....	.....
.....	.....	10 26	9 21	315	.... **Rifle**	7 58	8 30	.....	.....
.....	.....	10 53	9 48	332	.... Parachute	7 31	8 03	.....	.....
.....	.....	11 12	10 10	345	.... De Beque	7 10	7 42	.....	.....
.....	.....	12 09	11 09	378	+ .. **Grand Junction** ..	*6 15	*8 45	.....	.....
.....	.....	Noon	P M	...	ARRIVE] [LEAVE	A M	P M	.....	.....
.....	.....	10 50	9 35	670	.... **Salt Lake**	8 20	8 30	.....	.....
.....	.....	11 50	10 45	706	.... **Ogden**	*7 15	*7 25	.....	.....
.....	.....	P M	A M	...	ARRIVE] [LEAVE	P M	A M	.....	.....

JEROME PARK BRANCH.—Train leaves Cardiff †7 00 a.m., arriving Spring Gulch (15 m) 9 30 a.m. Returning, leaves Spring Gulch †10 33 a.m., arriving Cardiff 12 01 noon.

gers from Aspen intending to catch No. 6 at Basalt. The one train now left Aspen at 6:35 PM and arrived Basalt at 7:35 PM. The return trip left Basalt at 7:50 PM, which was all right for passengers from No. 5 going to Aspen, as that train had arrived Basalt at 7:25 PM. No. 6, however, did not leave Basalt until 10:10 PM, so eastbound passengers had to wait for two hours 35 minutes before they could get out of Basalt. The morning connections were about the same as they had been in May. These schedules point up the fact that the Aspen business had decreased to such an extent that it was no longer profitable to try to make it attractive to the public.

The December 1902 public timetable showed that the schedules were the same as for October 15th in the Official Guide, but it contains more detailed information with respect to times at the various local stations that are not shown in the Guide. The error is still in the mileage between Arkansas Junction and Busk, which throws off all of the mileages to the west.

This timetable lists several equipment changes in that the Denver – San Francisco sleeper was no longer operated. In lieu of that car, No. 3 now handled a Denver – Grand Junction sleeper, as well as the Leadville sleeper, with No. 6 moving the same equipment eastbound from Grand Junction and Leadville.

No. 5 showed an observation-Pullman-parlor-sleeping car from Denver to Ogden, as well as the Thursday tourist sleeper enroute from Chicago to Los Angeles. No. 4 had the same equipment eastbound, with the tourist sleeper from Los Angeles to Chicago also on Thursdays. The observation-sleeper had probably been running prior to this time, but the Official Guide's listing did not identify the car as such, nor would it for several years. Evidently the *Tryphena* was one of those assigned to this run, as the last page of the timetable contains a picture of this car advertising the Midland's service.

Another peculiarity in the timetable is that the equipment list shows No. 5 as *Pacific Express* and No. 4 as *Eastern Express*, but the schedule columns show No. 5 as *Colorado, Utah Limited*, and No. 4 as *Kansas City, Chicago Limited*. After all, what's in a name?

There were no changes during the year in either the passenger car or motive power rosters.

1903

The biggest change in the August 9th schedule for this season was the fact that, once again, all four of the mainline trains were now running into Leadville, stopping at Arkansas Junction prior to going up the hill to the Cloud City and then again on the return to the mainline. This had the effect of adding a little to the overall running times, but the schedules were essentially the same as in the previous year.

The Denver – San Francisco sleeper was restored for this summer's service, being handled in Nos. 3 and 4 over the CM. No. 5 had its Denver – Ogden sleeper, which was presumably an observation car, and also had the Chicago to Los Angeles tourist sleeper on Wednesdays. Eastbound, the Ogden – Denver car was carried in No. 6. We can also assume that the Leadville sleeper was in No. 6, but no mention of this car is made in the consists, although it was moved, as usual, in No. 3 westbound. No. 6 carried the Los Angeles – Chicago tourist sleeper on Thursdays again.

The summer service to Cripple Creek was augmented by the restoration of Nos. 7 and 12 on similar schedules as in 1902, and this provided a three train service between Colorado Springs and Cripple Creek.

Two round trips on the Aspen Branch continued to suffice for all four mainline connections. This service appeared to favor westbound passengers going to Aspen, rather than eastbound passengers from Aspen intending to catch Nos. 4 or 6. Long layovers at Basalt were still required in the eastbound direction, while the longest wait westbound was only 25 minutes—just long enough to get a bite to eat at the eating house.

It should be noted that the name of W. R. Freeman was no longer appearing in the list of officials; his name would turn up as the guiding light for the Denver & Salt Lake in later years. The only change in the equipment roster of the CM was that suburban coach 113 was converted to a baggage-coach and renumbered 10.

W. IRA RUDY,

Scenic Photographer,

CASCADE, COLO.

VIEWS ALONG THE

COLORADO MIDLAND

A SPECIALTY.

Reproduced here in actual size is what was called a "photoplaster." These card-mounted photographs, with the photographer's name and address printed on the reverse, were popular souvenirs in the days before picture postcards. Depicted is a view of one of the CM's light 2-8-0s and a group of loungers at the Cardiff depot. (Charles Albi collection)

1904

The summer season schedule issued July 3rd contained a number of changes from the previous year's timetable; in some cases, these entailed the lengthening of schedules. No. 5 still left Colorado Springs at 11:05 AM but did not arrive in Grand Junction until 11:59 PM, or 44 minutes later than formerly. No. 3 was a little bit faster than it had been. It still left Colorado Springs at 12:01 AM but arrived Grand Junction at 12:30 PM, 15 minutes earlier. Eastbound, No. 4 took the most severe beating on its timing, as it now left Grand Junction at 6:25 AM, ten minutes earlier, and arrived Colorado Springs at 7:15 PM, 45 minutes later. No. 6 left Grand Junction at 7 PM, 25 minutes later but still arrived in Colorado Springs at 6:30 AM. The reason for this was that No. 6 was the only train to by-pass Leadville this season; all the others operated in the same fashion as they had the previous year.

The equipment listing made no mention of the Denver – San Francisco sleeper this year, and No. 3 was shown as having the Leadville and Grand Junction cars from Denver. No. 5 now showed the Denver – Ogden car as an "Observation-Pullman-Parlor-Sleeper," and it carried tourist sleepers enroute from Chicago to Los Angeles on Thursdays and Fridays. No. 4 eastbound had the identical consist, with the tourist sleepers from Los Angeles to Chicago being handled on Fridays and Saturdays. No. 6's consist was the came as no. 3's in the eastbound direction.

The Cripple Creek service remained unchanged this summer with the three train schedule, all on daylight timings. The former No. 7, leaving at 8 AM from Colorado Springs was changed to No. 1, leaving at the same time. The other trains remained unchanged, and No. 9 still left Colorado Springs 20 minutes ahead of No. 5, arriving in Divide 54 minutes ahead of No. 5, due to that train stopping at Cascade Canon for lunch. Speaking of eating stations, it appears that the one at Arkansas Junction had now been discontinued; Leadville was still shown as an eating station but there was no symbol indicating one at Arkansas Junction. No. 4 had been shown as stopping there for meals in 1903, the last year it was shown. Basalt continued as the main eating station on the west end of the railroad.

The schedules on the Aspen Branch were adjusted with the morning trip now leaving Aspen 20 minutes earlier at 7:40 AM, but leaving Basalt 35 minutes later in order to make connections with Nos. 3 and 4. Eastbound passengers still had to wait one hour 30 minutes for No. 4, while westbound passengers from No. 3 had to wait one hour 18 minutes. The evening train out of Aspen now left at 7:20 PM, 55 minutes later than formerly, but did not return from Basalt until 10:35 PM, or two hours 45 minutes later than it had. Thus, eastbound passengers still had to wait at Basalt for two hours 10 minutes for No. 6, while westbound passengers from No. 5 had to wait two hours five minutes. The previous year, westbound passengers had a maximum wait of 25 minutes, while eastbound passengers had to cool their heels at Basalt. With these changes, all had to wait a minimum of one hour 18 minutes for their connecting trains. One wonders at this policy of downgrading the Aspen Branch service to such an extent. Possibly the change of the RPO on April 13th would have had something to do with this. The former Colorado Springs – Aspen RPO was changed on that date to a Colorado Springs – Glenwood Springs RPO, so perhaps there was not enough business at Aspen anymore to justify any kind of decent service.

The only change in the passenger equipment was that chair car 256 was rebuilt to a baggage-coach and renumbered 8. The locomotive fleet continued at the same level as before.

There was a change in the official family sometime prior to the summer schedule of 1904. G. W. Kramer, vice-president, was no longer in that position, and he was replaced by General Manager C. H. Schlacks. The general manager's position was awarded to George W. Vallery, who would remain with the Midland in an executive capacity until the Carlton regime acquired control of the road in 1917.

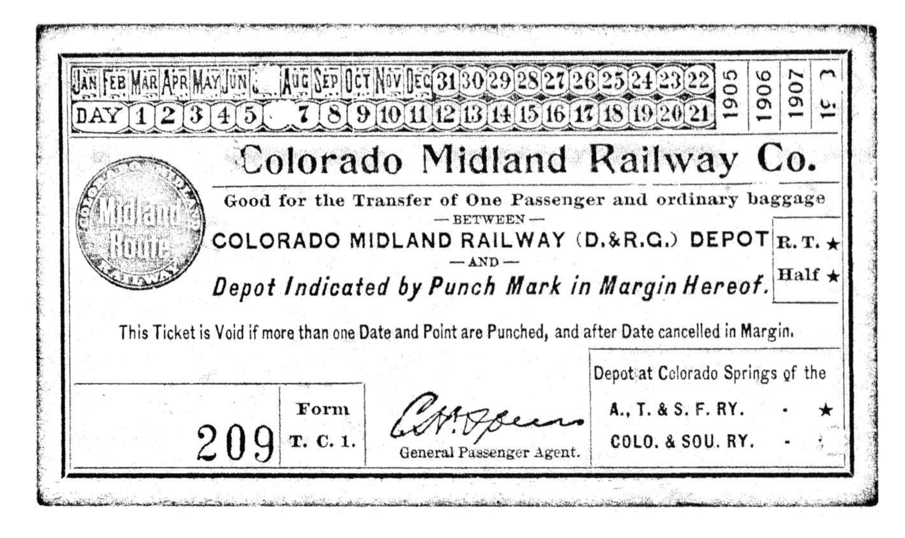

JAN FEB MAR APR MAY JUN AUG SEP OCT NOV DEC 31 30 29 28 27 26 25 24 23 22 1905 1906 1907
DAY 1 2 3 4 5 7 8 9 10 11 12 13 14 15 16 17 18 19 20 21

Colorado Midland Railway Co.

Good for the Transfer of One Passenger and ordinary baggage
— BETWEEN —
COLORADO MIDLAND RAILWAY (D.&R.G.) DEPOT
— AND —
Depot Indicated by Punch Mark in Margin Hereof.

R. T. ★
Half ★

This Ticket is Void if more than one Date and Point are Punched, and after Date cancelled in Margin.

209 Form T. C. 1.

General Passenger Agent.

Depot at Colorado Springs of the
A., T. & S. F. RY. ★
COLO. & SOU. RY.

1905

In January an event took place that had at least an indirect effect on the Colorado Midland. The Colorado & Southern gained control of the Colorado Springs & Cripple Creek District (the Short Line), which now put the C&S in a peculiar position as it controlled two competing railroads serving the same region. The Short Line had been stiff competition for the CM/MT route to Cripple Creek since 1901, but now Frank Trumbull was president of both routes. Continued unbridled competition between the two roads was senseless, so the managements set out to establish an operating agreement that would include the Short Line within the framework of the Cripple Creek Central, which had been set up to operate both the Florence & Cripple Creek and the Midland Terminal.

Before this agreement was signed on July 1st, however, a switch was made in the stations at Colorado Springs. Prior to the C&S control of the Short Line, the latter had worked in conjunction with the D&RG at Colorado Springs; through cars between Cripple Creek and Denver had been handled by the Rio Grande. The Colorado Midland's Cripple Creek trains had used the AT&SF station at Colorado Springs in the same manner as the through trains to and from Grand Junction. With the change in control of the Short Line, the Short Line's trains began using the AT&SF (C&S) station at Colorado Springs. Not wanting to be left out of the Cripple Creek passenger picture, the Rio Grande then made arrangements with the Midland for the CM/MT route trains to use the D&RG station, with the Rio Grande handling the cars to and from Denver. This switch was made effective on March 1st, and as far as the CM/MT route was concerned, lasted until the railroad ceased operation of the Cripple Creek trains. Colorado Midland timetables hereafter would carry a symbol denoting that the Cripple Creek through trains used the D&RG station at Colorado Springs.

The March 1st schedule showed that a few changes had been made since July 1904, but, as far as the mainline trains were concerned, they were insignificant ones of a few minutes either way. On the Cripple Creek trains, the changes were also of small moment, although both Nos. 1 and 2 had been taken off for the winter. There was also very little change in the Aspen Branch schedules, and the Jerome Park trains remained the same as in the previous summer. Even the equipment was the same as in the previous year, with the exception that now the through Denver – Cripple Creek cars were handled by the Rio Grande as mentioned above. It should be noted that, even with the change in management, the Short Line's trains operated at about the same times as the CM/MT trains to and from Cripple Creek, so that the two roads were still competing.

The summer schedule for July 2nd brought about a change in train No. 5, as it now left Colorado Springs one

1	3	11	9	5	Ms	*July* 3, 1904.	4	8	12	6	2	.....
A M	P M	P M	A M	A M	...	LEAVE] [ARRIVE	P M	P M	P M	A M	P M	.....
*3 50	*9 30	*3 45	*8 30	*8 30	0	+.......**Denver**.......♁	10 00	1 15	8 45	9 30	6 00	.....
.....	– –	5 40	9 25	9 25	...	+.......**Pueblo**.......♁	11 40	11 40	7 50	7 55	.....	.....
A M	Night	P M	A M	A M	...	LEAVE] [ARRIVE	P M	A M	P M	A M	P M	.....
*3 00	*12 01	*6 45	*10 45	*11 05	74	+ **Colorado Springs**. ♁	7 15	10 35	6 40	6 30	3 25	.....
3 10	12 11	7 00	10 55	11 15	78	+.... Colorado City....♁	7 00	10 20	6 25	6 17	3 10	.....
3 18	12 21	7 08	11 03	11 25	81	+...... **Manitou**......♁	6 48	10 13	6 18	– –	3 03	.....
– –	– –	7 10	11 05	– –	82	...Manitou Iron Springs...	6 45	10 11	6 16	– –	– –	.....
3 40	12 47	7 30	11 25	12 08	86	.....Cascade Canon....♁	6 30	9 55	6 00	5 52	2 45	.....
3 47	12 58	7 36	11 30	12 15	90	.....Green Mt. Falls.....	6 02	9 42	5 47	5 40	2 32	.....
3 57	1 13	7 47	11 42	12 31	95	......Woodland Park....♁	5 52	9 32	5 37	5 30	2 22	.....
9 15	1 40	8 05	12 01	12 55	102	arr.......**Divide** ♁....lve.	5 35	9 15	5 20	5 10	*2 05	.....
9 15	.....	8 05	12 01	.....	102	lve..**Divide** (Mid.Term.Ry.) arr.	.....	9 15	5 20	.....	2 05	.....
9 30	.....	– –	12 14	.....	108	arr..**Midland**.. " lve.	.....	9 02	5 05	.....	1 50	.....
9 53	.....	8 39	12 36	.....	116	....**Gillett**.... "	.....	8 42	4 43	.....	1 28	.....
10 05	.....	8 51	12 48	.....	122	....**Cameron**. "	.....	8 31	4 31	.....	1 18	.....
10 27	.....	9 07	1 08	.....	127	....**Victor**.... "	.....	8 15	4 16	.....	1 00	.....
10 35	.....	9 20	1 20	.....	130	....**Anaconda** "	.....	8 05	4 06	.....	12 50	.....
10 40	.....	9 25	1 25	.....	132	arr..**Cripple Creek** " lve.	.....	*8 00	*4 00	.....	*12 45	.....
A M	1 40	P M	P M	12 55	102	lve.......**Divide** ♁....arr.	5 35	A M	P M	5 10	Noon	.....
.....	2 06	.....	.....	1 20	111	........Florissant.......♁	5 10	.....	.....	4 42	.....	.....
.....	2 53	.....	.....	– –	133	.........Spinney.......♁	4 25	.....	.....	3 57	.....	.....
.....	3 12	.....	.....	2 30	144	.........Hartsel.......♁	4 07	.....	.....	3 37	.....	.....
.....	4 23	.....	.....	3 50	170	+....**Buena Vista**....♁	2 50	.....	.....	2 20	.....	.....
.....	5 02	.....	.....	4 30	194	..........Granite.......♁	2 18	.....	.....	1 46	.....	.....
.....	5 38	.....	.....	5 08	209	arr...Arkansas Junc. ♁ lve.	1 50	.....	.....	1 20	.....	.....
.....	6 00	.....	.....	5 30	213	arr. + **Leadville** ♁.. lve.	1 40	.....	.....	12 55	.....	.....
.....	6 10	.....	.....	5 50	213	lve. + **Leadville** ♁.. arr.	1 30	.....	.....	1 35	.....	.....
.....	6 18	.....	.....	5 58	209	lve...Arkansas Junc. ♁ arr.	1 10	.....	.....	1 20	.....	.....
.....	6 47	.....	.....	– –	222	...........Busk.........♁	– –	.....	.....	– –	.....	.....
.....	6 57	.....	.....	8 40	224	.........Ivanhoe.......♁	12 40	.....	.....	12 42	.....	.....
.....	7 20	.....	.....	7 03	234	..........Sellar.........♁	11 55	.....	.....	12 02	.....	.....
.....	7 48	.....	.....	7 32	245	.......Thomasville.....♁	11 06	.....	.....	11 20	.....	.....
.....	8 37	.....	.....	8 30	265	arr......**Basalt** ♁....lve.	10 10	.....	.....	10 30	.....	.....
.....	*9 55	.....	.....	*10 35	265	lve.......**Basalt**.......arr.	8 40	.....	.....	8 20	.....	.....
.....	10 55	.....	.....	11 20	284	arr..... + **Aspen** ♁....lve.	*7 40	.....	.....	*7 20	.....	.....
.....	8 57	.....	.....	8 38	265	lve.......**Basalt** ♁.....arr.	9 50	.....	.....	10 26	.....	.....
.....	9 20	.....	.....	8 54	277	........Carbondale.......♁	9 27	.....	.....	10 03	.....	.....
.....	9 40	.....	.....	9 10	286	+.......**Cardiff**........♁	9 12	.....	.....	9 47	.....	.....
.....	9 45	.....	.....	9 18	289	+...... Glenwood.......♁	9 05	.....	.....	9 40	.....	.....
.....	10 13	.....	.....	9 45	301	+......New Castle......♁	8 40	.....	.....	9 16	.....	.....
.....	10 41	.....	.....	10 11	315	..........**Rifle**..........♁	8 13	.....	.....	8 50	.....	.....
.....	11 09	.....	.....	10 42	332	.........Parachute.......♁	7 45	.....	.....	8 22	.....	.....
.....	11 30	.....	.....	11 03	345	.........De Beque.......♁	7 22	.....	.....	8 00	.....	.....
.....	12 30	.....	.....	11 59	378	+..**Grand Junction**..♁	*6 25	.....	.....	*7 00	.....	.....
.....	P M	.....	.....	A M	...	ARRIVE] [LEAVE	A M	.....	.....	P M	.....	.....
.....	11 46	.....	.....	10 40	670	........**Salt Lake**......♁	8 05	.....	.....	8 50	.....	.....
.....	12 55	.....	.....	11 45	706	..........**Ogden**.......♁	*7 00	.....	.....	*7 45	.....	.....
.....	Night	.....	.....	A M	...	ARRIVE] [LEAVE	P M	.....	.....	A M	.....	.....

[JE]ROME PARK BRANCH.—Train leaves Cardiff †7 00 a.m., arriving Spring Gulch (15 ... 9 30 a.m. Returning, leaves Spring Gulch †10 30 a.m., arriving Cardiff 12 01 noon.

hour later than before, at 12:05 PM, with arrival at Grand Junction 35 minutes later at 12:40 AM. No. 3 was speeded up by ten minutes, leaving Colorado Springs the same as formerly, but arriving Grand Junction at 12:20 PM. Eastbound No. 4 now left Grand Junction 24 minutes earlier at 6:01 AM and arrived in Colorado Springs by 6:40 PM, 30 minutes earlier than in the past. No. 6 was changed by less than five minutes at both ends of the railroad. For the Cripple Creek service, the early morning departure at 8 AM was restored, but this year the train was numbered 7 instead of No. 1 as in 1904. Nos. 9 and 11 had minor changes in the arrival times at Cripple Creek. There were more important changes for the eastbound service, as No. 2's departure at 12:45 PM the previous year was not restored. Instead, a new No. 10 was established to leave Cripple Creek at 3:50 PM, and No. 12 was set back to a 5 PM departure.

There were minor changes to the Aspen Branch trains, in order to coincide with the changes on the mainline and while they did not provide close connections, at least they were considerably improved over those of 1904. Now the shortest wait was for one hour three minutes, while the longest was one hour 20 minutes. On the Jerome Park Branch, the return trip from Spring Gulch now left at 9:45 AM, 45 minutes earlier, but the arrival at Cardiff was still listed for 12:01 PM.

The equipment listing again showed no change from the summer season of 1904. It was unusual for the road to maintain the same equipment in its passenger trains for two seasons in a row.

Returning to the Cripple Creek situation for a moment, the Short Line schedule for July 1st, the date of the agreement, showed the management as under the C&S regime. The Cripple Creek Central officers did not take charge until July 4th, when Jesse H. Waters was elected to the position of general manager. It was the intention of the Allied Lines, as the combination was known, to run most of the passenger service between Colorado Springs and Cripple Creek via the Short Line, with just one train via the CM/MT route. Just before the new schedule was to take effect, the CM reminded all that its contract to operate trains over the MT required a six-month notice of cancellation, and that the CM was not going to change its operation. Thus, the CM/MT route continued to operate its three trains each way to and from the gold camp. The Short Line's July 1st schedule showed three trains between the two terminals on similar schedules as the CM/MT trains, except that the Short Line retained the 12:30 PM departure from Cripple Creek, which had been discontinued by the CM/MT. That line, on the other hand, had the last departure from Cripple Creek with No. 12 at 5 PM. It is interesting to note that under both of these July 1st schedules, Frank Trumbull is listed as president of both the Short Line and the CM.

Later in 1905, and under the auspices of the Allied Lines, the Short Line's trains were rerouted via Victor, using MT tracks from there to Cripple Creek and also using the MT depot at that point. This eliminated the operation of passenger trains over Hoosier Pass, between Cameron and Cripple-Creek, and allowed the Short Line to eliminate the stub runs between Cameron and Victor.

Taking another look at the July 1st schedule of the Short Line, it is interesting to note that the CM was not the only one to have an error in its Official Guide listing. It can be seen that the westbound trains in the schedule column had even numbers, and that the eastbound trains had odd numbers—just the reverse of the way that they should have been shown. The equipment list had the proper numbers for west and eastbound trains, although none is listed for Nos. 15 and 14, the summer-only trains at that time.

It should also be noted that after years of serving meals at Cascade Canon, this was no longer listed as a meal station, and had been replaced by Colorado Springs. No longer would westbound trains pause at the top of the four percent grade of Ute Pass while the passengers enjoyed their noon meal. From now on, they would catch their lunch at the Colorado Springs station while waiting for their train to be made up after the arrival of the Denver connection. This lasted until the era of dining cars on the CM.

The October 1st schedule as published in the Travelers Railway Guide, Western Section, for December 1905, contains only one real change in the times of the four mainline trains. No. 6, which by-passed Leadville in the July schedule, now ran into Leadville along with the other three trains. This diversion caused a 30-minute later arrival at Colorado Springs. The other trains had similar schedules to the ones in July.

Unlike former years, when two trains were operated each way between Colorado Springs and Cripple Creek, this year's winter schedule called for just one train, Nos. 11 and 8. The Short Line also operated just one train each way over its line. Just four years earlier, the District had enjoyed the services of ten trains daily in and out of the region! Aspen Branch passengers still had to wait for their connections, but all such waits were now in the neighborhood of one hour 20 minutes.

The interesting facet about this schedule is the fact that it is probably the most detailed listing that appeared in a Guide of that era as far as the stations shown and times of trains. Another interesting fact is that the population of the towns along the railroad is shown, which gives an idea as to the importance of each station for potential passenger travel. The CM served a rather large tributary area, but it can be seen that the country traversed was far from being overcrowded.

During this year, first class coach No. 111 was converted to an observation-chair car. This car is probably the single most famous unit of the CM's car fleet, as it was built in 1887 when the railroad itself was new, and served on the CM for the road's entire existence. It was then sold to the Midland Terminal and served that line right up to its abandonment in 1949. The car was even used on the last passenger train to run between Colorado Springs and Cripple Creek on February 6, 1949. Today the 111 is preserved at the Colorado Railroad Museum.

1906

The June 17th schedule differed little from the previous summer timetable as far as the mainline trains were concerned, with Nos. 5 and 6 running on the same schedule. No. 3 was speeded up and arrived in Grand Junction 25 minutes earlier, and No. 4 was slowed by 16 minutes, leaving Grand Junction that much sooner but arriving Colorado Springs at the same time as before. The consist of these trains was the same as in the previous summer, with the tourist sleepers running on the same two days per week as they had been in 1905.

The primary change was in the Colorado Springs – Cripple Creek service, as there was now only one through train in each direction over the CM/MT route. No. 8 left Cripple Creek at 7:20 AM, and No. 11 left Colorado Springs at 7:10 PM, with other service provided by the Short Line. Nos. 9 and 10 now operated only between Divide and Colorado Springs, furnishing commuter service, with No. 10 leaving Divide at 6:40 AM and No. 9 out of Colorado Springs at 5:20 PM. Nos. 7 and 12 also provided service to Ute Pass points, leaving Colorado Springs at 8:30 AM, and returning from Woodland Park at 3:30 PM.

THE COLORADO & SOUTHERN SYSTEM.

THE COLORADO & SOUTHERN RAILWAY COMPANY.
THE FORT WORTH & DENVER CITY RAILWAY COMPANY.
THE COLORADO SPRINGS & CRIPPLE CREEK DISTRICT RAILWAY COMPANY.
THE TRINITY & BRAZOS VALLEY RAILWAY COMPANY.

THE COLORADO SPRINGS & CRIPPLE CREEK DISTRICT RAILWAY CO.

THE CRIPPLE CREEK SHORT LINE.

For list of officers, see page 557.
For map, see page 556.

No. 4	No. 16	Mls	*June 24, 1906.*	Altitude.	No. 3	....
....	....	....	LEAVE] [ARRIVE	....	....	....
[illegible] A M	....	....	.... **Denver** (*C.& S.*)	5,197	8 00 P M	....
[illegible] A M	....	....	lve.. **Pueblo** (*C.& S.*) arr.	4,668	8 10 P M	....
[illegible] A M	*8 15 A M	....	lve.. **Colorado Springs**..arr.	5,992	6 00 P M	....
– –	– –	0	..**Colorado Springs Yard.** ♁	5,992	– –	....
– –	– –	2.2	..Colorado City Junction..	6,323	– –	....
[illegible] "	8 44 "	6.6	........Sublime........	7,159	5 30 "	....
[illegible] "	8 57 "	10.7	........Fairview....... ♁	7,926	5 16 "	....
[illegible] "	9 10 "	14.9	........St. Peter's........	8,715	5 05 "	....
[illegible] "	9 21 "	18.1	........Duffields........	9,304	4 52 "	....
[illegible] "	9 45 "	21.4	........Summit....... ♁	9,918	4 40 "	....
[illegible] "	9 48 "	22.8	........Rosemont........	9,821	4 26 "	....
[illegible] A M	9 52 "	24.2	........Saderlind........	9,956	4 25 "	....
[illegible] Noon	10 11 "	30.1	..........Clyde........ ♁	9,440	4 05 "	....
[illegible] "	10 22 "	34.2	..........Love..........	9,706	3 54 "	....
– –	– –	38.8	..........Grassy..........	9,077	– –	....
[illegible] Noon	10 38 A M	39.8	+ **Cameron Junction** ♁	10,040	3 40 P M	....
[illegible]	[illegible]	39.5	..**Cameron Junction**..	10,040	Via M. T. Ry.	....
		41.0	.......Hoosier Pass.......	10,360		....
[illegible] P M	11 15 A M	45.8	+...**Cripple Creek**...♁	9,505	*3 00 P M	....
[illegible]	Via M. T. Ry.	39.5	..**Cameron Junction**..	10,040	Via M. T. Ry.	....
		41.1	..Cripple Creek Sampler..	....		....
		41.5	..**Vindicator Junction.**	9,800		....
		42.9	+.......Goldfield........	9,995		....
[illegible] Noon	10 54 A M	44.6	+.........**Victor**.........	9,734	*3 21 P M	....
....	....	....	ARRIVE] [LEAVE	....	....	....

EXPLANATION OF SIGNS.

Trains marked * run daily.
+ Coupon stations; ♁ Telegraph stations.
STANDARD—*Mountain time.*

TRINITY & BRAZOS VALLEY RAILWAY CO.

For list of officers, see page 557.

....	No. 1	Mls	*April, 1906.*	Mls	No. 2	....
....	....	....	LEAVE] [ARRIVE	....	....	....
....	*7 30 A M	0	+.....**Cleburne**.......	78.3	6 00 P M	....
....	8 05 "	10.2	.........Parker.........	68.1	4 20 "	....
....	8 25 "	14.0	+......Covington.......	63.3	4 00 "	....
....	8 40 "	18.7	.........Osceola.........	59.4	3 45 "	....
....	9 15 "	29.7	arr...+**Hillsboro**[1]..lve.	48.6	3 05 "	....
....	9 30 "	29.7	lve.....**Hillsboro**...arr.	48.6	2 50 "	....
....	9 55 "	39.1	.........Bynum.........	39.1	2 23 "	....
....	10 15 "	46.6	+.......Malone.........	31.5	2 03 "	....
....	10 40 "	55.3	+..**Hubbard City**[2]....	23.1	1 38 "	....
....	10 58 "	62.0	.........Munger.........	16.7	1 20 "	....
....	11 10 "	66.4	+......Coolidge.........	12.2	1 07 P M	....
....	11 20 "	69.5	.........Datura.........	9.0	12 53 Noon	....
....	11 33 "	74.1	.......Tehucana.......	4.3	12 44 "	....
....	11 47 A M	78.3	+.....**Mexia**[3]......	0	*12 30 Noon	....
....	....	....	ARRIVE] [LEAVE	....	....	....

EXPLANATION OF SIGNS.

Trains marked * run daily. + Coupon stations. *Central time.*

CONNECTIONS.

[1] Hillsboro—With Missouri, Kansas & Texas Ry. and St. Louis Southwestern Ry.
[2] Hubbard City—With St. Louis Southwestern Ry.
[3] Mexia—With Houston & Texas Central R.R.

THE CRIPPLE CREEK CENTRAL RAILWAY COMPANY

OWNERS AND OPERATORS OF THE FOLLOWING LINES:

THE FLORENCE & CRIPPLE CREEK R.R.	40.30	Miles.
THE GOLDEN CIRCLE RAILROAD	6.00	"
THE CANON CITY & CRIPPLE CREEK R.R.	7.50	"
THE MIDLAND TERMINAL RAILWAY	29.40	"
SPURS AND BRANCHES TO MINES	47.42	"
Total Mileage, 130.62 Miles.		

H. M. BLACKMER, President, New York. | R. E. F. FLINSCH, Vice-President, New York. | JOHN GORLOW, Secretary and Treasurer, New York. | General Offices—54 Wall Street, New York.

FLORENCE & CRIPPLE CREEK, GOLDEN CIRCLE, AND CANON CITY & CRIPPLE CREEK RAILROADS.

HENRY M. BLACKMER, Chmn. of Board, N.Y. City.
J. H. WATERS, President and General Manager, Colorado Springs, Colo.
K. C. SCHUYLER, Vice-Prest. and Gen. Counsel, Colorado Springs, Colo.
J. J. COGAN, Sec'y, Treas. and Asst. to Gen. Mgr., Colorado Springs, Colo.
L. F. LINNEY, Auditor, "
J. R. FUSSELMAN, Cashier, "
W. A. MATLOCK, Traffic Mgr., "
D. C. MACWATTERS, Gen. Pas. Agent, Colorado Springs, Colo.
A. L. BOYD, Purch. Agt., Canon City, Colo.
M. J. BURGDORF, Chief Engineer, Cripple Creek, Colo.
J. B. FLAHERTY, Superintendent, "
A. D. MCCARTHY, Supt. Telegraph & Chief Disp., Cripple Creek, Colo.
FRANK SINGER, Master Mechanic, Colorado Springs, Colo.
General Offices—Mining Exchange Building, Colorado Springs, Colo.

No. 1	Mls.	*February, 1906.*	No. 2	....
....	....	(*Mountain time.*)	....	....
*8 30 P M	0	lve. **Denver** (D.&R.G.) .arr.	....	....
12 15 Night	75.2	lve..Colorado Springs..arr.	....	....
1 35 A M	119.6	lve..... **Pueblo**.....arr.	....	....
*7 00 A M	0	lve. +**Canon City** ♁.arr.	7 30 P M	....
*7 00 A M	....	lve.. +**Florence** ♁..arr.	7 30 P M	....
8 00 A M	17.1	........Adelaide...... ♁	6 31 P M	....
9 24 "	35.0	+.......**Victor**...... ♁	5 23 "	....
9 45 A M	40.7	arr. +**Cripple Creek** ♁ .lve.	*5 00 P M	....

MIDLAND TERMINAL RAILWAY—"THE CRIPPLE CREEK ROAD."

HENRY M. BLACKMER, Chmn. of Board, New York City.
J. H. WATERS, Prest. & G. M., Colorado Spgs, Colo.
K. C. SCHUYLER, Vice-Prest. and Gen. Counsel, Colorado Springs, Colo.
J. J. COGAN, Sec'y, Treas. and Asst. to Gen. Mgr., Colorado Springs, Colo.
L. F. LINNEY, Auditor, "
J. R. FUSSELMAN, Cashier, "
W. A. MATLOCK, Traffic Mgr., "
D. C. MACWATTERS, Gen. Pas. Agt., "
A. L. BOYD, Purchasing Agt., Canon City, Colo.
M. J. BURGDORF, Chief Eng'r, Cripple Creek, Colo.
J. B. FLAHERTY, Superintendent, "
A. D. MCCARTHY, Supt. Telegraph & Chief Disp., Cripple Creek, Colo.
FRANK SINGER, Master Mech., Colorado Spgs, Colo.

....	No. 11	No. 3	No. 15	Mls	*June 24, 1906.*	No. 8	No. 4	No. 14	....
....	....	□	....	....	(*Mountain time.*)	....	□	....	....
....	*5 00 P M	*8 00 A M	....	....	lv. **Denver** (D.& R.G.R.R.) ar.	12 30 Noon	8 00 P M	9 20 P M	....
....	5 00 "	9 00 "	....	....	" **Pueblo**.... " "	12 25 Noon	8 10 "	8 15 "	....
....	7 10 "	10 20 A M	*8 15 A M	....	" ColoradoSpgs(Col.Mid.) "	10 10 A M	6 00 P M	7 00 "	....
....	7 30 "	Via C. S. & C. C. D. Ry.	Via C. S. & C. C. D. Ry.	....	" **Manitou**.... " "	10 03 "	Via C. S. & C. C. D. Ry.	6 20 "	....
....	8 40 "			0	lve......**Divide** ♁...arr.	8 50 "		5 35 "	....
....	8 54 "			6	.........Midland.........	8 36 "		5 20 "	....
....	9 18 "			14	.........Gillett......... ♁	8 10 "		4 54 "	....
....	9 30 "	12 40 Noon	10 35 A M	20	...Cameron Junction . ♁	7 56 "	3 40 P M	4 40 "	....
....	9 35 "	12 44 "	10 39 "	21	.........Bull Hill.........	7 52 "	3 35 "	4 35 "	....
....	9 39 "	12 47 "	10 42 "	22	+....Independence.... ♁	7 49 "	3 32 "	4 32 "	....
....	9 51 "	12 59 Noon	10 54 "	25	+.........**Victor**......... ♁	7 38 "	3 21 "	4 21 "	....
....	9 59 "	1 08 P M	11 03 "	27	+.........Elkton......... ♁	7 29 "	3 12 "	4 12 "	....
....	10 04 "	1 14 "	11 09 "	28	+.....**Anaconda**...... ♁	7 25 "	3 06 "	4 06 "	....
....	10 10 P M	1 20 P M	11 15 A M	30	+...**Cripple Creek**... ♁	*7 20 A M	*3 00 P M	*4 00 P M	....
....	....	....	....	....	ARRIVE] [LEAVE	....	....	....	....

Connection.—At Divide—With Colorado Midland Ry.

THROUGH CARS.

No. 23—Solid Train, Colorado Springs to Cripple Creek. Carries Dining Car Denver to Colorado Springs and Through Observation Car Denver to Cripple Creek. **No. 11**—Solid Train, Colorado Springs to Cripple Creek. Carries Dining Car Denver to Colorado Springs and Through Coach Denver to Cripple Creek. **No. 8**—Solid Train, Cripple Creek to Colorado Springs. Carries Through Coach Cripple Creek to Denver. **No. 24**—Solid Train, Cripple Creek to Colorado Springs. Dining Car Colorado Springs to Denver. Through Observation Car Cripple Creek to Denver.

*Daily; †daily, except Sunday; ¶daily, except Monday. Trains marked □ run via Colorado & Southern Ry. between Denver and Colorado Springs. + Coupon stations; ♁ Telegraph stations.

This was the first Ute Pass service listed in the Official Guide since the summer of 1898. Since then, with up to 12 passenger trains a day between Colorado Springs and Divide plus the freight traffic, there was no necessity for local service. The railroad probably had all the trains that it could handle with any degree of efficiency. Now that the Cripple Creek business was past its prime, local trains were restored in order to meet the requirements of the Ute Pass passengers.

It will be noted that all four mainline trains were running into Leadville after stopping at Arkansas Junction. This was the last timetable that would show such an operation. Also during the year, the original mainline between Snowden and Leadville was abandoned, except for about one mile at the Leadville end which was used as a switching lead to get to the Moyer Mine Branch up California Gulch. Practically all trains had been operating over the line between Arkansas Junction and Leadville for a number of years, and the original mainline from Snowden to just east of Leadville was no longer needed.

The Aspen Branch still had its two round trips, but the positions of Aspen and Basalt in the schedule columns had been reversed. Now excellent connections were made at Basalt with trains to and from the west. The morning eastbound connections still required a wait of about one hour 20 minutes at Basalt, and westbound connections from mainline trains to Aspen required a wait of up to one hour 30 minutes. It seems logical that most of the travel to Aspen would be from the east, but the schedule favored travel the other way around. Perhaps the change in the positions of the stations was a little sleight of hand on the part of the railroad to make the connections look better than they actually were.

Although issued less than a month later, the July 11th schedule contains several important changes. The time of No. 5 was adjusted slightly, while the schedules of Nos. 3 and 4 remained the same. The major change on the mainline was for No. 6. This train now left Grand Junction at 4 PM, almost three hours earlier than in June, and arrived Colorado Springs at a rather early 4:30 AM, with connection arriving in Denver at 7 AM. There was no western connection at Grand Junction for this train, and the 4 PM departure of No. 6 would be a tradition for the next ten years with the exception of the 1912-1913 winter season.

While previously all of the mainline trains had gone into Leadville, now none went there and only the stub runs served that station. Even though the trains bypassed Leadville, running times were not reduced as they still held to the old schedules. Perhaps there was trouble in keeping on time, and this device was used to give the trains some help. The stub run operation is described in the section on the Leadville problem, and this practice was consistently followed from July 11, 1906 until the railroad ceased operations in 1918.

Although the equipment listing remained the same as in June, a new note was added in a separate box stating "Dining Car service now in operation on Midland daylight trains Nos. 4 and 5." During the early part of the year, the Colorado City shops had been busy converting two of the six-wheel truck chair cars into what the Midland called "cafe cars." The pair had been numbered 248 and 249, retaining the same numbers under the new configuration. These cars, which would probably be known as diner-lounge cars today, had a kitchen at one end, with the dining section consisting of six tables seating four each and a parlor section containing eight individual parlor-type chairs that could revolve in place. With the addition of these two cars, which evidently operated through between Colorado Springs and Grand Junction, the Colorado Midland could now boast that it provided all the amenities that any mainline railroad furnished, and the Rocky Mountain scenery was free of charge. the eating station arrangement along the CM had become an anachronism that hurt its competitive position. Other roads had long before gone to dining cars, and the Midland practice of stopping trains while the passengers dashed in, bolted down a hot meal, and then ran back to the train was just too old fashioned for the modern era of 1906. When the CM did go into the dining car business, let it be said that it was done right, as the Midland diners enjoyed an excellent reputation for the quality of their meals and service.

At the outset, the cafe cars were assigned to Nos. 4 and 5. The passengers on Nos. 3 and 6 had to utilize the eating stations, until 1907, when the other two diners went into service.

Since the Cripple Creek roads were now all under the aegis of the Cripple Creek Central management, a new tourist-oriented service was established that gave passengers a chance to make the round trip between Colorado Springs and Cripple Creek via different routes so that the scenery on both lines could be enjoyed. This entailed the operation of train No. 15 from Colorado Springs to Cripple Creek via the Short Line, leaving Colorado Springs at 8:15 AM and arriving at the gold camp at 11:15 AM. The return trip, as No. 14, left Cripple Creek at 4 PM via the Midland Terminal, Divide at 5:35 PM and arrived in Colorado Springs at 7 PM via the Colorado Midland.

Due to the major change in the operation of No. 6, the Aspen Branch trains were adjusted, especially in the evening service connecting with both Nos. 5 and 6. The branch train now left Aspen at 6:30 PM, arriving at Basalt at 7:30 PM, the same time as No. 6. The train laid over at Basalt for the arrival of No. 5 at 9:05 PM and left for Aspen at 9:15 PM, arriving at that mining center by 10:15 PM, if all went well. The morning trains on the branch continued to provide a poor connection with Nos. 3 and 4 at Basalt.

COLORADO MIDLAND RAILWAY.

FRANK TRUMBULL, President, Denver, Colo.
C. H. SCHLACKS, Vice-President, "
GEO. W. VALLERY, General Manager, "
HENRY T. ROGERS, General Solicitor, "
JAMES S. MACKIE, Secretary, 71 Broadway, New York.
H. B. HENSON, Treasurer, 195 Broadway, New York.
LEWIS B. JOHNSON, Assistant Secretary, Denver, Colo.
H. C. BUSH, Traffic Manager, "
C. H. SPEERS, General Passenger Agent, "
W. S. WING, Auditor, "
ROB'T LAW, Jr., Cashier, "
J. C. VINING, General Superintendent, Colorado City, Colo.
W. J. SCHLACKS, Superintendent Machinery, "
C. N. DAVIDS, Gen. Storekeeper and Purchasing Agt., "
F. H. McNAUGHT, Chief Surgeon, Denver, Colo.
W. H. DAVENPORT, General Agent, San Francisco, Cal.

L. H. HARDING, General Agent, Salt Lake City, Utah.
W. B. THROCKMORTON, Trav. Freight and Passenger Agt., Salt Lake City, Utah.
H. W. JACKSON, General Agent, Chicago, Ill.
A. E. BROWN, Trav. Freight and Passenger Agent, "
J. H. HARPER, Trav. Freight and Passenger Agent, "
CHAS. D. SIMONSON, General Eastern Agent, 425 Broadway, New York.
HERBERT BONSOR, Trav. Freight and Passenger Agent, 425 Broadway, New York.
MALONE JOYCE, Dist. Freight and Pas. Agt., Los Angeles, Cal.
MORELL LAW, General Agent, 566 Shiedley Building, Kansas City, Mo.
J. H. DAVIS, City Passenger Agent, Denver, Colo.
F. L. FEAKINS, General Agent, Omaha, Neb.
M. R. SUTTON, Trav. Freight and Passenger Agent, "

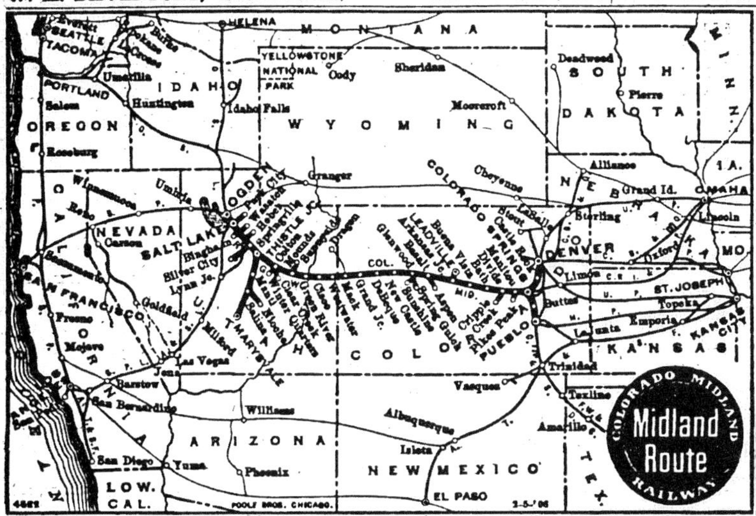

	▲7	▲9	3	▲11	5	Ms	*July 11, 1906.*	4	▲8	6	▲10	▲12	14
....	....	....	P M	P M	A M	...	LEAVE] [ARRIVE	P M	Noon	A M	A M	P M	P M
....	....	....	*9 00	*5 00	*9 30	0	+........**Denver**........♁	9 20	12 30	7 00	11 05	8 20	9 20
....	....	....	8 00	5 00	10 15	...	+........**Pueblo**........♁	8 15	12 25	7 55	....	....	8 15
....	A M	P M	P M	P M	A M	...	LEAVE] [ARRIVE	P M	A M	A M	A M	P M	P M
....	*8 30	*5 40	*11 30	*7 10	*11 55	74	+ | **Colorado Springs**..♁	6 40	10 12	4 30	8 00	4 30	7 00
....	8 40	5 50	11 40	7 20	12 08	78	+.....Colorado City.....♁	6 28	10 03	4 20	7 50	4 20	6 50
....	8 50	8 00	11 50	7 30	12 18	81	+.......**Manitou**.......♁	6 20	9 53	4 12	7 41	4 11	6 42
....	8 52	6 02	- -	7 32	- -	82	...,Manitou Iron Springs....	- -	9 50	- -	7 39	4 09	6 40
....	9 08	6 20	12 18	7 50	12 45	86	.......Cascade Canon.....♁	6 00	9 34	3 54	7 23	3 55	6 24
....	9 20	6 28	12 28	8 00	12 57	90	......Green Mt. Falls....♁	5 45	9 20	- -	7 10	3 40	6 10
....	9 35	6 42	12 43	8 15	1 13	95	.......Woodland Park.....♁	5 33	9 08	3 31	7 00	*3 30	5 56
....	A M	7 00	1 05	8 40	1 40	102	arr.........**Divide**♁......lve.	5 15	8 50	3 15	*6 40	P M	5 35
....	....	P M	....	8 40	....	102	lve..**Divide** (Mid. Term. Ry.) arr.	....	8 50	....	A M	....	5 35
....	....	....	....	8 54	....	108	arr..**Midland**.... " lve.	....	8 36	....	....	....	5 20
....	....	....	....	9 18	....	116	....**Gillett**...... "	....	8 10	....	....	....	4 54
....	....	....	....	9 30	....	122	....**Cameron Jn**.. "	....	7 56	....	....	....	4 40
....	....	....	....	9 51	....	127	....**Victor**...... "	....	7 38	....	....	....	4 21
....	....	....	....	10 04	....	130	....**Anaconda**.. "	....	7 25	....	....	....	4 06
....	....	....	....	10 10	....	132	arr..**Cripple Creek**. " lve.	....	*7 20	....	....	....	*4 00
....	....	....	1 05	P M	1 40	102	lve.........**Divide**♁....arr.	5 15	A M	3 15	....	....	P M
....	....	....	1 32	....	2 08	111	..........Florissant.......♁	4 45		2 43	....	....	....
....	....	....	2 27	....	3 05	133	..........Spinney.........♁	3 51	....	1 52	....	....	....
....	....	....	2 48	....	3 24	144	............Hartsel.........♁	3 30	....	1 31	....	....	....
....	....	....	4 00	....	4 45	176	+.....**Buena Vista**.....♁	2 07	....	12 08	....	....	....
....	....	....	4 43	....	5 27	194	............Granite..........♁	1 28	....	11 32	....	....	....
....	....	....	5 20	....	6 05	209	arr....Arkansas Junc..♁lve.	1 00	....	11 05	....	....	....
....	....	....	5 45	....	6 30	213	arr. } + | **Leadville**♁... { lve.	12 35	....	10 40	....	....	....
....	....	....	5 05	....	6 50	213	lve. } { arr.	1 15	....	11 20	....	....	....
....	....	....	5 30	....	6 15	209	lve....Arkansas Junc..♁arr.	12 50	....	10 55	....	....	....
....	....	....	6 10	....	7 00	222	..............Busk............♁	12 25	....	10 35	....	....	....
....	....	....	6 20	....	7 10	224	...........Ivanhoe..........♁	12 15	....	10 25	....	....	....
....	....	....	6 47	....	7 37	234	............Sellar............♁	11 25	....	9 38	....	....	....
....	....	....	7 19	....	8 08	245	.........Thomasville.......♁	10 30	75	8 44	....	....	....
....	....	....	8 10	....	9 05	265	arr.......| **Basalt**♁.....lve.	9 35	A M	7 50	....	....	....
....	....	....	*6 30	....	*6 30	0	lve......+ **Aspen**♁......arr.	....	10 00	10 15	....	....	....
....	....	....	7 50	....	7 30	18	arr.........**Basalt**.........lve.	....	*8 50	9 15	....	....	....
....	....	....	8 30	....	9 15	265	lve.........**Basalt**♁......arr.	9 25	A M	7 30	....	....	....
....	....	....	8 52	....	9 35	277	.........Carbondale.......♁	8 59	....	7 07	....	....	....
....	....	....	9 10	....	9 50	286	+........**Cardiff**.........♁	8 40	....	6 50	....	....	....
....	....	....	9 20	....	10 00	289	+... Glenwood Springs...♁	8 30	....	6 40	....	....	....
....	....	....	9 50	....	10 30	301	+........New Castle........♁	8 00	....	6 10	....	....	....
....	....	....	10 17	....	10 56	315	..............**Rifle**...........♁	7 27	....	5 44	....	....	....
....	....	....	10 46	....	11 24	332	........Grand Valley......♁	7 00	....	5 16	....	....	....
....	....	....	11 07	....	11 44	345	..........De Beque.........♁	6 40	....	4 56	....	....	....
....	....	....	12 05	....	12 35	378	+...**Grand Junction**...♁	*5 45	....	*4 00	....	....	....
....	....	....	Noon	....	Night	...	ARRIVE] [LEAVE	A M	....	P M	....	....	....
....	....	....	11 10	....	10 25	670	..........**Salt Lake**........♁	8 00	....	....	....	....	....
....	....	....	12 05	....	11 30	706	...........**Ogden**..........♁	*7 00	....	....	....	....	....
....	....	....	Night	....	A M	...	ARRIVE] [LEAVE	P M	....	....	....	....	....

JEROME PARK BRANCH.—Train leaves Cardiff †7 00 a.m., arriving Spring Gulch (15 miles) 9 30 a.m. Returning, leaves Spring Gulch †9 45 a.m., arriving Cardiff 12 01 noon.

TRAIN SERVICE AND EQUIPMENT.

WESTBOUND.

No. 3—"The Ute."

Solid Through Train Denver to Grand Junction. Carries Chair Car and Pullman Sleeping Car. Also Pullman Sleeping Car Denver to Leadville.

No. 5—Pacific Express.

Solid Through Train Denver to Grand Junction. Carries Observation Pullman Parlor Sleeper Denver to Ogden, via Salt Lake. Chair Car and Coach Denver to Grand Junction. Tourist Sleeper each Thursday and Friday en route Chicago to Los Angeles.

No. 11—Cripple Creek Express.

Solid Through Train Colorado Springs to Cripple Creek.

EASTBOUND.

No. 4—Eastern Express.

Solid Through Train between Grand Junction and Denver. Carries Observation Pullman Parlor Sleeping Car, en route Ogden to Denver, Coach and Chair Car. Tourist Sleeper each Friday and Saturday en route Los Angeles to Chicago.

No. 6—"The Coyote."

Solid Through Train Grand Junction to Denver. Carries Chair Car and Coach Grand Junction to Denver. Pullman Sleeper Grand Junction to Denver and Pullman Sleeper Leadville to Denver.

No. 8—Colorado Springs Accommodation.

Local Accommodation Train between Cripple Creek and Colorado Springs. Carries Through Chair Car Cripple Creek to Denver.

Dining Car Service now in operation on Midland Daylight Trains Nos. 4 and 5.

EXPLANATION OF SIGNS.

Trains marked * run daily.

▲ Trains Nos. 8, 10, 11 and 12 connect from Denver, via D. & R. G. R.R., and Trains Nos. 7, 8, 9, 10, 11 and 12 use D. & R. G. depot at Colorado Springs.

| Meal stations.

+ Coupon stations.

♁ Telegraph stations.

STANDARD—*Mountain time.*

CONNECTIONS.

Denver, in Union Depot—With Atchison, Topeka & Santa Fe Ry., Chicago, Burlington & Quincy Ry., Chicago, Rock Island & Pacific Ry. and Union Pacific R.R. and Colorado & Southern Ry

Colorado Springs—With Chicago, Rock Island & Pacific, Atchison, Topeka & Santa Fe and Colorado Southern Rys.

Manitou—With Manitou & Pike's Ry.

Divide—With Midland Terminal Ry. for Grassy, Cripple Creek, etc.

Buena Vista—With Colorado & Southern Ry. and with stage lines.

Grand Junction—With Rio Grande Western Ry.

INTERIOR OBSERVATION CAR

EXTERIOR OBSERVATION CAR

EQUIPMENT on the Colorado Midland consists of solid through vestibuled trains of coaches, observation cars and Pullman sleepers, Denver to Grand Junction; standard and Tourist Pullmans to all Utah, Nevada and California points. Our dining car service is unexcelled. "Meals on Wheels, Serves You Right." Only line operating daily Pullman observation cars on its daylight trains across the Rockies between Denver and Salt Lake City.

DENVER OFFICE
17TH AND CALIFORNIA STS.

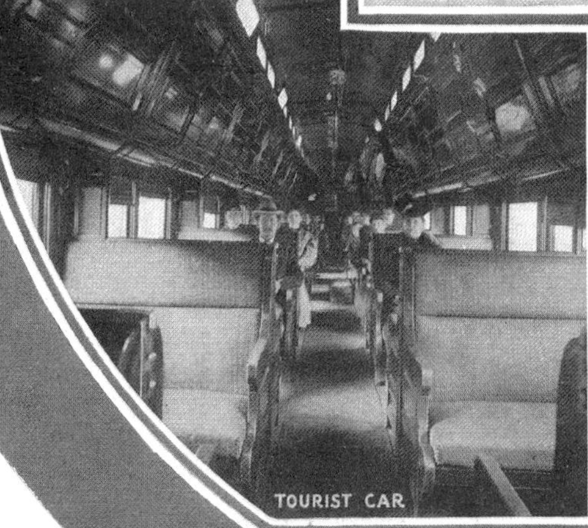
TOURIST CAR

DINING CAR

The Midland's advertising staff created some unusual items, including the circular booklet, reproduced here in part, titled "The Bull's-eye of the Rockies." This dates from about 1907. (Museum collection)

1907

The spring and summer schedules of the Colorado Midland contained some changes from the previous year as far as the through train service was concerned. The big item of interest was that the note now read "Dining Car Service, meals a la carte on trains Nos. 3, 4, 5 and 6." This indicated that the conversion of vestibule chair cars 247 and 250 into diners *Idlewild* and *Ivanhoe* had been completed, and that the cars were in service as of June 16th. The new dining cars seated no more than the cafe cars that had been placed in service in 1906, since the configuration was tables for four on one side of the aisle and for two on the other side. Thus, all of the cars accommodated 24 passengers at one seating, but the new ones allowed for more room for both passengers, waiters and cooks.

With the four cars now in service, the Colorado Midland was in a position to furnish service for all meals on all four of the through passenger trains, thus eliminating the need for the meal stations enroute. However, meal stations would return, as will be seen later on, when the fortunes of the railroad went into decline. With the new arrangement, it was the practice to operate diners on trains Nos. 5 and 4 between Colorado Springs and Grand Junction. Another diner was operated out of Grand Junction on No. 6 to Thomasville, serving dinner enroute, and returning the next morning on No. 3 from Thomasville to Grand Junction, serving breakfast and, if the train was late prior to arrival at the western terminal, lunch as well. This operation required three cars with one held in reserve, to be used when one of the regular cars was in the shop, or for use on a special train.

As far as the mainline trains were concerned, the June 16th schedule had No. 5 leaving Colorado Springs 20 minutes late at 12:15 PM, with arrival at Grand Junction one hour 10 minutes later at 1:45 AM. No. 3 now left Colorado Springs one hour 30 minutes earlier than in 1906, at 10 PM, but its arrival at Grand Junction was just 15 minutes earlier at 11:50 AM. So both of the westbound trains were considerably slowed in their running times. Eastbound, No. 4 left Grand Junction 45 minutes later at 6:30 AM, but only lost five minutes enroute, being due in Colorado Springs 50 minutes later at 7:30 PM. No. 6 still left at 4 PM, but lost a full hour of its running time, being due at Colorado Springs at 5:30 AM, instead of 4:30 AM as in 1906.

For the summer season, Nos. 7 and 12, which had operated during the summer of 1906 between Colorado Springs and Woodland Park, did not reappear on the schedule, thus reducing the Ute Pass service by one train

7	3	▲11	5	Ms	*June 16, 1907.*	4	▲8	6	10	14
	P M	P M	A M		LEAVE] [ARRIVE	P M	Noon	A M	P M	P M
	*7 30	*4 00	*9 30	0	+........**Denver**........♁	10 05	12 35	8 00	8 30	10 05
		5 00	10 15		+........**Pueblo**........♁		11 30	7 50	7 55	
A M	P M	P M	Noon		LEAVE] [ARRIVE	P M	A M	A M	P M	P M
*9 00	*10 00	*6 45	*12 15	74	+..**Colorado Springs**..♁	7 30	10 05	5 30	3 35	7 10
9 12	10 15	6 58	12 28	78	+.....Colorado City.....♁	7 18	9 55	– –	3 25	6 58
9 23	10 26	7 11	12 40	81	+.......**Manitou**.......♁	7 11	9 45	5 10	3 16	6 48
9 25	– –	7 18	– –	82	....Manitou Iron Springs....	– –	9 43	– –	3 13	6 47
9 44	10 55	7 30	1 10	86	.......Cascade Canon.....♁	6 53	9 27	4 52	2 57	6 31
9 54	11 08	7 38	1 23	90	......Green Mt. Falls....♁	6 40	9 13	4 38	2 42	6 17
10 10	11 26	7 52	1 42	95	.......Woodland Park.....♁	6 30	9 02	4 28	2 32	6 07
10 30	11 55	8 15	2 10	102	arr........**Divide**♁.....lve.	6 15	8 45	4 12	*2 15	*5 50
A M		8 15		102	lve..**Divide** (Mid.Term.Ry.) arr.		8 45		P M	5 50
		8 29		108	arr..**Midland**.... " lve.		8 31			5 37
		8 53		116	....**Gillett**..... "		8 05			5 12
		9 05		122	....**Cameron Jn.**.. "		7 51			5 00
		9 26		127	....**Victor**...... "		7 33			4 41
		9 38		130	....**Anaconda**.. "		7 20			4 26
		9 45		132	arr..**Cripple Creek**. " lve.		*7 15			*4 20
	11 55	P M	2 10	102	lve........**Divide**♁....arr.	6 15	A M	4 12		P M
	12 25		2 40	111	..........Florissant........♁	5 40		3 37		
	1 25		3 40	133	..........Spinney..........♁	4 48		2 45		
	1 49		4 03	144	..........Hartsel..........♁	4 27		2 25		
	3 15		5 28	176	+.....**Buena Vista**.....♁	3 02		12 52		
	4 02		6 17	194	..........Granite..........♁	2 23		12 15		
	4 45		7 00	209	arr....Arkansas Junc..♁ lve.	1 55		11 45		
	5 15		7 26	213	arr. } ..+ **Leadville**♁... { lve.	1 30		11 20		
	4 30		6 45	213	lve. } ..+ **Leadville**♁... { arr.	2 10		11 58		
	5 00		7 10	209	lve....Arkansas Junc..♁ arr.	1 45		11 35		
	5 50		7 55	222	..........Busk..........♁	1 20		11 15		
	6 00		8 05	224	..........Ivanhoe..........♁	1 10		11 05		
	6 27		8 30	234	..........Sellar..........♁	12 17		10 07		
	7 00		9 00	245	........Thomasville........♁	11 20		9 00		
	7 55		8 55	265	arr........| **Basalt**♁.....lve.	10 20		8 00		
	10 00		11 05	283	arr......+ **Aspen**♁.....lve.	*6 30		*5 50		
	*6 30		*8 50	283	lve.........**Aspen**.......arr.			11 05		
	8 05		10 05	265	lve........**Basalt**♁.....arr.	10 10		7 50		
	8 28		10 28	277	..........Carbondale........♁	9 44		7 23		
	8 45		10 45	286	+.........**Cardiff**.........♁	9 25		7 05		
	8 55		10 55	289	+...Glenwood Springs...♁	9 15		6 53		
	9 35		11 35	301	+.......New Castle.......♁	8 45		6 20		
	10 02		12 03	315	..........**Rifle**..........♁	8 19		5 50		
	10 30		12 30	332	........Grand Valley......♁	7 49		5 19		
	10 51		12 50	345	..........De Beque..........♁	7 28		4 58		
	11 50		1 45	378	+...**Grand Junction**...♁	*6 30		*4 00		
	A M		A M		ARRIVE] [LEAVE	A M		P M		
	11 30		12 50	670	..........**Salt Lake**.........♁	6 50				
	12 30		2 00	706	..........**Ogden**..........♁	*5 45				
	Night		P M		ARRIVE] [LEAVE	P M				

JEROME PARK BRANCH.—Train leaves **Cardiff** †7 00 a.m., arriving Spring Gulch (15 miles) 9 30 a.m. Returning, leaves Spring Gulch †9 45 a.m., arriving Cardiff 12 01 noon.

7	3	▲11	5	Ms	*August 4, 1907.*	4	▲8	6	10	14
	P M	P M	A M		LEAVE] [ARRIVE	P M	Noon	A M	P M	P M
	*7 30	*4 00	*9 30	0	+........**Denver**........♁	10 05	12 35	8 00	8 30	10 0
		5 00	10 15		+........**Pueblo**........♁		11 30	7 50	7 55	
A M	P M	P M	Noon		LEAVE] [ARRIVE	P M	A M	A M	P M	P M
*9 00	*10 00	*6 45	*12 15	74	+..**Colorado Springs**..♁	7 30	10 05	5 30	3 35	7 1
9 12	10 15	6 58	12 28	78	+.....Colorado City.....♁	7 18	9 55	– –	3 25	6 5
9 23	10 26	7 11	12 40	81	+.......**Manitou**.......♁	7 11	9 45	5 10	3 16	6 4
9 25	– –	7 18	– –	82	....Manitou Iron Springs....	– –	9 43	– –	3 13	6 4
9 44	10 55	7 30	1 10	86	.......Cascade Canon.....♁	6 53	9 27	4 52	2 57	6 3
9 54	11 08	7 38	1 23	90	......Green Mt. Falls....♁	6 40	9 13	4 38	2 42	6 1
10 10	11 26	7 52	1 42	95	.......Woodland Park.....♁	6 30	9 02	4 28	2 32	6 0
10 30	11 55	8 15	2 10	102	arr........**Divide**♁.....lve.	6 15	8 45	4 12	*2 15	*5 5
A M		8 15		102	lve..**Divide** (Mid.Term.Ry.) arr.		8 30		P M	5 5
		8 29		108	arr..**Midland**.... " lve.		8 17			5 3
		8 53		116	....**Gillett**..... "		7 51			5 1
		9 05		122	....**Cameron Jn.**.. "		7 38			5 0
		9 26		127	....**Victor**...... "		7 18			4
		9 38		130	....**Anaconda**.. "		7 05			4
		9 45		132	arr..**Cripple Creek**. " lve.		*7 00			*4 2
	11 55	P M	2 10	102	lve........**Divide**♁....arr.	6 15	A M	4 12		P M
	12 25		2 40	111	..........Florissant........♁	5 40		3 37		
	1 25		3 40	133	..........Spinney..........♁	4 48		2 45		
	1 49		4 03	144	..........Hartsel..........♁	4 27		2 25		
	3 15		5 28	176	+.....**Buena Vista**.....♁	3 02		12 52		
	4 02		6 17	194	..........Granite..........♁	2 23		12 15		
	4 45		7 00	209	arr....Arkansas Junc..♁ lve.	1 55		11 45		
	5 15		7 26	213	arr. } ..+ **Leadville**♁... { lve.	1 30		11 20		
	4 30		6 45	213	lve. } ..+ **Leadville**♁... { arr.	2 10		11 59		
	5 00		7 10	209	lve....Arkansas Junc..♁ arr.	1 45		11 35		
	5 50		7 55	222	..........Busk..........♁	1 20		11 15		
	6 00		8 05	224	..........Ivanhoe..........♁	1 10		11 05		
	6 27		8 30	234	..........Sellar..........♁	12 17		10 07		
	7 00		9 00	245	........Thomasville........♁	11 20		9 00		
	7 55		9 55	265	arr........| **Basalt**♁.....lve.	10 20		8 00		
	10 00		11 05	283	arr......+ **Aspen**♁.....lve.	*6 30		*8 50		
	*6 30		*8 50	283	lve.........**Aspen**.......arr.			11 05		
	8 05		10 05	265	lve........**Basalt**♁.....arr.	10 10		7 50		
	8 28		10 28	277	..........Carbondale........♁	9 44		7 23		
	8 45		10 45	286	+.........**Cardiff**.........♁	9 25		7 05		
	8 55		10 55	289	+...Glenwood Springs...♁	9 15		6 53		
	9 35		11 35	301	+.......New Castle.......♁	8 45		6 20		
	10 05		12 03	315	..........**Rifle**..........♁	8 19		5 50		
	10 37		12 30	332	........Grand Valley......♁	7 49		5 19		
	11 00		12 50	345	..........De Beque..........♁	7 28		4 58		
	11 59		1 45	378	+...**Grand Junction**...♁	*6 30		*4 00		
	A M		A M		ARRIVE] [LEAVE	A M		P M		
	11 30		12 50	670	..........**Salt Lake**.........♁	6 50				
	12 30		2 00	706	..........**Ogden**..........♁	*5 45				
	Night		P M		ARRIVE] [LEAVE	P M				

JEROME PARK BRANCH.—Train leaves **Cardiff** †7 00 a.m., arriving Spring Gul
miles) 9 30 a.m. Returning, leaves Spring Gulch †9 45 a.m., arriving Cardiff 12 01 noo

The timetables below and at right are the last issued before and the first issued after the change of division point from Basalt to Cardiff.

3	▲11	5	Ms	*October 1, 1907.*	4	▲8	6
P M	P M	A M	...	LEAVE] [ARRIVE	P M	Noon	A M
*7 30	*4 00	*9 30	0	+........**Denver**........	10 05	12 15	8 00
.....	5 00	10 15	...	+........**Pueblo**........	.....	11 30	7 50
P M	P M	Noon	...	LEAVE] [ARRIVE	P M	A M	A M
*1000	*6 45	*12 15	74	+..**Colorado Springs**..	7 30	9 50	5 30
10 15	6 58	12 28	78	+.....Colorado City.....	7 19	9 38	– –
10 26	7 11	12 40	81	+........**Manitou**.......	7 11	9 28	5 10
– –	7 18	– –	82	....Manitou Iron Springs....	– –	9 26	– –
10 55	7 30	1 10	86	.......Cascade Canon.......	6 53	9 10	4 52
11 08	7 38	1 23	90	......Green Mt. Falls.....	6 40	8 56	4 38
11 26	7 52	1 42	95	.......Woodland Park......	6 30	8 46	4 28
11 55	8 15	2 10	102	arr.........**Divide**.....lve.	6 15	8 30	4 12
.....	8 15	.....	102	lve..**Divide** (Mid.Term.Ry.) arr.	.....	8 30	.....
.....	8 29	.....	108	arr..**Midland**.... " lve.	.....	8 17	.....
.....	8 53	.....	116	....**Gillett**...... "	.....	7 51	.....
.....	9 05	.....	122	....**Cameron Jn**.. "	.....	7 38	.....
.....	9 26	.....	127	....**Victor**...... "	.....	7 18	.....
.....	9 39	.....	130	....**Anaconda**.. "	.....	7 05	.....
.....	9 45	.....	132	arr..**Cripple Creek**. " lve.	.....	*7 00	.....
11 55	P M	2 10	102	lve.........**Divide**.....arr.	6 15	A M	4 12
12 25	.....	2 49	111	..........Florissant........	5 40	.....	3 37
1 25	.....	3 40	133	..........Spinney........	4 48	.....	2 45
1 49	.....	4 03	144	..........Hartsel........	4 27	.....	2 25
3 15	.....	5 28	176	+.....**Buena Vista**.....	3 02	.....	12 52
4 02	.....	6 17	194	..........Granite........	2 23	.....	12 15
4 45	.....	7 00	209	arr....Arkansas Junc...lve.	1 55	.....	11 45
5 15	.....	7 25	213	arr. } ..+**Leadville**... { lve.	1 30	.....	11 20
4 30	.....	6 45	213	lve. } { arr.	2 10	.....	11 59
5 00	.....	7 10	209	lve....Arkansas Junc...arr.	1 45	.....	11 35
5 50	.....	7 55	222	..........Busk........	1 20	.....	11 15
6 00	.....	8 05	224	..........Ivanhoe........	1 10	.....	11 05
6 27	.....	8 30	234	..........Sellar........	12 17	.....	10 07
7 00	.....	9 00	245	........Thomasville........	11 20	.....	9 00
7 55	.....	9 55	265	arr.......**Basalt**.....lve.	10 20	.....	8 00
10 00	.....	11 05	283	arr......+**Aspen**.....lve.	*6 30	.....	*6 50
*6 30	.....	*6 50	283	lve.......**Aspen**.......arr.	.....	.....	11 05
8 05	.....	10 05	265	lve.......**Basalt**.....arr.	10 10	.....	7 50
8 28	.....	10 28	277	.........Carbondale........	9 44	.....	7 23
8 45	.....	10 45	286	+........**Cardiff**........	9 25	.....	7 05
8 55	.....	10 55	289	+...Glenwood Springs...	9 15	.....	6 53
9 35	.....	11 35	301	+.......New Castle.......	8 45	.....	6 20
10 05	.....	12 03	315	............**Rifle**........	8 19	.....	5 50
10 37	.....	12 30	332	........Grand Valley.....	7 49	.....	5 19
11 00	.....	12 50	345	..........De Beque.......	7 28	.....	4 58
11 50	.....	1 45	378	+...**Grand Junction**...	*6 30	.....	*4 00
A M	.....	A M	...	ARRIVE] [LEAVE	A M	.....	P M
11 30	.....	12 50	670	..........**Salt Lake**.......	6 50	.....	.....
12 30	.....	2 00	706	..........**Ogden**........	*5 45	.....	.....
Night	.....	P M	...	ARRIVE] [LEAVE	P M	.....	.....

JEROME PARK BRANCH.—Train leaves Cardiff †7 00 a.m., arriving Spring Gulch (15 miles) 9 30 a.m. Returning, leaves Spring Gulch †9 45 a.m., arriving Cardiff 12 01 noon.

each way. Old No. 9 was also discontinued to Divide, and these trains were replaced by new Nos. 7 and 10 between Colorado Springs and Divide, providing a morning service from Colorado Springs westbound and an afternoon service eastbound. These changes resulted in almost no commuter service from Ute Pass points to Colorado Springs in the morning, and none in the late afternoon in the reverse direction. Cripple Creek trains Nos. 11 and 8 really did not meet the needs of Ute Pass commuters.

It is curious to note that No. 7 was due to leave Colorado Springs at 9 AM, to arrive at Divide at 10:30 AM. These times correspond closely to the traditional times of the wildflower special, and it is possible that the Colorado Midland was using this train to kill two birds with one stone. It provided a local service between Colorado Springs and Divide, as well as handling the sightseers, operating as an extra west of Divide. Under this reasoning, it is doubtful that the train ran as far west as Spinney, since it would be unlikely to return to Divide in time to operate as No. 10 from there to Colorado Springs. No. 10 left at 2:15 PM for a 3:35 PM arrival in Colorado Springs. The traditional arrival of the wildflower train was at 5 PM. Based on the running times of the through trains between Divide and Spinney of about one hour 30 minutes, it was

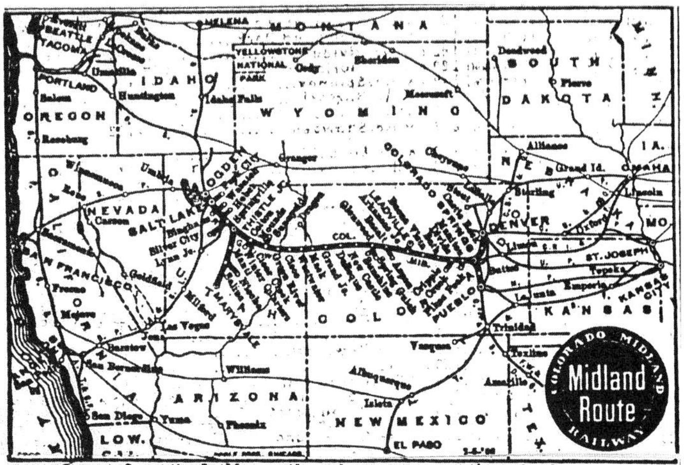

3	▲11	5	Ms	*November 10, 1907.*	4	▲8	6
P M	P M	A M	...	LEAVE] [ARRIVE	P M	P M	A M
*7 30	*4 00	*9 30	0	+........**Denver**........	8 45	1 00	8 00
.....	5 00	10 15	...	+........**Pueblo**........	.....	11 30	7 50
P M	P M	Noon	...	LEAVE] [ARRIVE	P M	A M	A M
*1000	*6 45	*12 01	74	+..**Colorado Springs**..	7 00	10 20	5 30
10 15	6 58	12 13	78	+.....Colorado City.....	6 45	10 08	– –
10 26	7 11	12 25	81	+........**Manitou**.......	6 35	9 58	5 10
– –	7 18	– –	82	....Manitou Iron Springs....	– –	9 56	– –
10 55	7 30	12 55	86	.......Cascade Canon.......	6 17	9 40	4 52
11 08	7 38	1 08	90	......Green Mt. Falls.....	6 05	9 26	4 38
11 26	7 52	1 25	95	.......Woodland Park......	5 55	9 16	4 28
11 55	8 15	1 52	102	arr.........**Divide**.....lve.	5 40	9 00	4 10
.....	8 15	.....	102	lve..**Divide** (Mid.Term.Ry.) arr.	.....	9 00	.....
.....	8 29	.....	108	arr..**Midland**.... " lve.	.....	8 47	.....
.....	8 53	.....	116	....**Gillett**...... "	.....	8 21	.....
.....	9 05	.....	122	....**Cameron Jn**.. "	.....	8 08	.....
.....	9 26	.....	127	....**Victor**...... "	.....	7 48	.....
.....	9 39	.....	130	....**Anaconda**.. "	.....	7 35	.....
.....	9 45	.....	132	arr..**Cripple Creek**. " lve.	.....	*7 30	.....
11 55	P M	1 52	102	lve.........**Divide**.....arr.	5 40	A M	4 10
12 25	.....	2 20	111	..........Florissant........	5 05	.....	3 32
1 25	.....	3 19	133	..........Spinney........	4 15	.....	2 45
1 49	.....	3 45	144	..........Hartsel........	3 52	.....	2 25
3 15	.....	5 08	176	+.....**Buena Vista**.....	2 27	.....	12 52
4 02	.....	5 55	194	..........Granite........	1 48	.....	12 15
4 45	.....	6 35	209	arr....Arkansas Junc...lve.	1 20	.....	11 45
5 15	.....	7 00	213	arr. } ..+**Leadville**... { lve.	12 55	.....	11 20
4 30	.....	6 20	213	lve. } { arr.	1 35	.....	11 59
5 00	.....	6 45	209	lve....Arkansas Junc...arr.	1 10	.....	11 35
5 50	.....	7 30	222	..........Busk........	12 45	.....	11 15
6 00	.....	7 40	224	..........Ivanhoe........	– –	.....	11 05
6 27	.....	8 05	234	..........Sellar........	11 50	.....	10 10
7 00	.....	8 35	245	........Thomasville........	10 55	.....	9 12
7 55	.....	9 30	265	arr.......**Basalt**.....lve.	9 50	.....	8 05
10 00	.....	10 30	283	arr......+**Aspen**.....lve.	*6 30	.....	*6 50
*6 30	.....	*6 50	283	lve.......**Aspen**.......arr.	.....	.....	10 30
7 55	.....	9 30	265	lve.......**Basalt**.....arr.	9 50	.....	8 05
8 18	.....	9 54	277	.........Carbondale........	9 23	.....	7 36
8 50	.....	10 27	286	+........**Cardiff**........	9 00	.....	7 15
9 00	.....	10 38	289	+...Glenwood Springs...	8 35	.....	6 53
9 35	.....	11 10	301	+.......New Castle.......	8 05	.....	6 20
10 05	.....	11 38	315	............**Rifle**........	7 36	.....	5 50
10 37	.....	12 05	332	........Grand Valley.....	7 04	.....	5 19
11 00	.....	12 27	345	..........De Beque.......	6 43	.....	4 58
11 50	.....	1 30	378	+...**Grand Junction**...	*5 45	.....	*4 00
A M	.....	A M	...	ARRIVE] [LEAVE	A M	.....	P M
11 50	.....	12 50	670	..........**Salt Lake**.......	6 50	.....	.....
1 05	.....	2 00	706	..........**Ogden**........	*5 45	.....	.....
A M	.....	P M	...	ARRIVE] [LEAVE	P M	.....	.....

JEROME PARK BRANCH.—Train leaves Cardiff †7 00 a.m., arriving Spring Gulch (15 miles) 9 30 a.m. Returning, leaves Spring Gulch †9 45 a.m., arriving Cardiff 12 01 noon.

possible to make that round trip in three hours 45 minutes, allowing 15 minutes to turn and service the engine at Spinney, but this would have precluded any stops to pick flowers or to hunt for fossils in the Pisgah area. So here again, we are faced with a dilemma with respect to the Colorado Midland's schedules, leading to considerable conjecture as to the railroad's policies and motives as to its scheduling practices.

Returning to the schedules of June 16th and August 4th of this year, there were no changes in the equipment handled in the through trains, other than already mentioned concerning the operation of the new dining cars. The sleepers, as well as the tourist cars, were the same as in 1906, and the Cripple Creek trains carried through chair cars between Denver and Cripple Creek.

With minor changes in the schedules, the through Cripple Creek service remained the same as in the previous year, with just the one train coach way providing the

COLORADO MIDLAND RAILWAY CO.
Rate of Pay for Engineers, April 1, 1907.

RUNS BETWEEN	TRIPS	IF MADE WITHIN		PAY OF ENGINEERS	
		PSGR	FRT	PSGR	FRT
		Hours/Minutes			
Colorado City – Leadville	Single	8 00	11 15	$6.35	$7.40
Colo. City/Colo. Sprgs. – Woodland Park/Divide	Double	6 00	6 00	4.10	4.10
Colo. City/Colo. Sprgs. – East of Woodland Park	Double	3 00	3 00	2.05	2.05
Colo. City/Colo. Sprgs. – Florissant	Double	7 00	7 00	4.60	4.60
Colo. City/Colo. Sprgs. – Cripple Creek	Double	11 30	11 30	7.40	7.40
Colo. City/Colo. Sprgs. – Midland	Double	7 30	7 30	4.60	4.60
Buena Vista/Wild Horse – Bath	Double	3 05	3 05	2.05	2.05
Florissant – Divide	Double	3 00	3 00	2.05	2.05
Leadville – Busk	Double	3 00	3 00	2.05	2.05
Leadville – Ivanhoe	Double	3 45	3 45	2.55	2.55
Leadville – Sellar	Double	5 17	5 17	4.25	4.25
Leadville – Thomasville	Double	7 50	7 50	6.40	6.40
Leadville – Basalt	Single	6 10	6 10	4.10	4.10
Leadville – Aspen	Single	7 40	7 40	4.95	4.95
Basalt – Thomasville	Double	3 00	3 00	2.05	2.05
Basalt – Ivanhoe – Thomasville	Single	7 00	7 00	4.80	4.90
Basalt – Ivanhoe	Double	9 13	9 13	5.80	5.95
Thomasville – Ivanhoe	Double	4 47	4 47	3.80	3.90
Basalt – New Castle	Double	6 00	6 00	4.10	4.10
Basalt – Grand Junction	Single	—	8 45	4.60	5.45
Wild Horse – Arkansas Jct.	Double	5 03	5 03	2.77	2.77
Wild Horse – Ivanhoe	Double	7 36	7 36	4.66	4.66
Wild Horse – Ivanhoe – Leadville	Single	5 12	5 12	3.60	3.60
Wild Horse – Ivanhoe – Leadville – Wild Horse	Double	8 48	8 48	5.15	5.57
Leadville – Bath	Double	8 45	8 45	4.81	5.51
Leadville – Wild Horse (Minimum)	Double	6 00	6 00	4.10	4.10
Leadville – Wild Horse	Double	5 40	5 40	3.12	3.12
Florissant – Leadville	Single	6 00	8 28	4.63	5.31
Florissant – Bath	Double	8 10	8 10	4.47	5.12
Leadville – Cardiff	Single	7 52	7 52	5.26	5.26
Cardiff – Ivanhoe	Double	12 36	12 36	8.10	8.25
Cardiff – Ivanhoe – Basalt	Single	10 55	10 55	6.95	7.09
Cardiff – South Canon	Double	1 12	1 12	0.82	0.82
Cardiff – New Castle	Double	2 35	2 35	1.78	1.78
Cardiff – Rifle	Double	4 55	4 55	2.41	2.84
Cardiff – Grand Valley	Double	7 58	7 58	3.83	4.51
Cardiff – DeBeque	Double	9 55	9 55	4.87	5.73
Cardiff – Grand Junction	Single	7 42	7 42	3.78	4.45
Cardiff – Sellar	Double	10 27	10 27	6.43	6.43
Aspen – Glenwood	Double	7 00	7 00	3.67	4.01
Basalt – Sellar	Double	7 00	7 00	4.13	4.13
Basalt – Arkansas Jct.	Double	11 29	11 29	7.89	7.89
Cardiff – Arkansas Jct.	Double	14 52	14 52	10.19	10.19
Leadville – Bath – Wild Horse	Single	5 55	5 55	3 25	3 72
Basalt – Aspen	Double	3 00	3 00	2.05	2.05

Other rates of pay

Yard Engineers	– $3.75 for 10-hour day, except at Leadville. $4.00 for 10-hour day at Leadville.
Work Trains	– $4.40 for 12 hours or less, overtime at 0.44 per hour.
Cardiff Coal Branch	– $6.00 for 12 hours or less, regular assigned crew. $3.00 per round trip for extra crews, overtime after six hours.
Rotary Snow Plow	– $5.00 for 12 hours or less, overtime at 0.40 per hour.
Overtime	– $0.47 per hour for road freight crews $0.44 per hour for road passenger crews. 1/10 of one day's pay per hour for yard crews.

Continued on next page

Miscellaneous rules and regulations.

Engineer's pay increased 5% additional when handling engines with over 150,000 lbs. weight on drivers.
Time computed for each run will begin at time designated in the caller's book for the train to leave. Arrival time of engines at terminal stations to be taken from the Round House register and engineer's slips.
D&RG rate of pay will apply to trips between Grand Junction and Bovina when handling stock.
In the event of suburban service between Colorado Springs and Divide, where more than one double trip is made within 12 hours, mileage rate of 6.15¢ per mile with minimum of $4.00 will apply. Regular overtime rates in effect.

Districts – 1st – Colorado Springs to Leadville, including Midland Terminal.
2nd – Leadville to Grand Junction, including Aspen and Cardiff Coal Branches.
Crews have rights only over their own District.

(Association of American Railroads)

basic service: No. 8 from Cripple Creek in the morning and No. 11 westbound in the early evening. The circle trip, via the Short Line's No. 15 in the morning to Cripple Creek and the combined MT/CM No. 14 in the afternoon, was operated again this season.

The method of showing Aspen Branch trains was changed again, and now only the arriving and leaving times at Aspen were shown. The schedules themselves were much the same as in 1906, with a long wait for eastbound passengers out of Aspen at Basalt to get No. 4. Passengers desiring to catch No. 6 had a much better time of it, as the connections were quite close, mostly due to the earlier operation of No. 6, as instituted in July 1906. No changes were made in the caboose accommodations as furnished on the Jerome Park Branch.

In anticipation of the change of the west end division point from Basalt to Cardiff later in the year, the railroad negotiated a new agreement with the unions. Fortunately, the agreement with the locomotive engineers has been preserved at the Association of American Railroads Library in Washington, DC. The new rates of pay for engineers are tabulated showing the runs, whether they were straightaway or round trips, the time allowed on straight time for both passenger and freight service, and the rates of pay for both classes of service. Additional rates of pay were established for such services as yard switchers, work trains, snowplows, with flat rates for certain branch lines. While the actual rates did not differ materially from those under the 1897 agreement, the list of runs was significantly more sophisticated than it had been in the earlier agreement. Incidentally, the mention of Bovina refers to the first station west of Grand Junction on the RGW (now called Durham) and CM crews evidently had the right to go to Bovina for stock shipments.

It is interesting to note what were considered to be "good" jobs as far as pay was concerned, especially in light of present-day standards. Many of the daily rates in those days would not qualify for a minimum hourly wage today. Since it was such a difficult railroad to operate, the Midland paid "mountain" rates to its operating employees, which were higher than operating over more level roads. In spite of the CM's financial problems over the years, its transportation employees were in a higher echelon compared with those who worked for other railroads that were much better off.

The change in the division point evidently took place on or about November 10, 1907; the last Official Guide schedule showing Basalt as the division point was dated October 1st and appeared in the November Guide. The schedule in the December Guide was dated November 10th, and there were adjustments in the timings between Basalt and Cardiff, although the overall times were not materially changed. Under the October 1st schedule, all four trough trains were allowed ten minutes at Basalt for changing engines and crews and servicing the train, with Cardiff shown as just another station stop. Under the November 10th schedule, however, no time was allowed at Basalt, and the time was considerably extended for the stop at Cardiff, although only the leaving time was listed for the new division point. To illustrate how this was done, the running times between the affected points are shown below:

Westbound running times leaving Carbondale to leaving Cardiff,

Train No.	10/1/07	11/10/07
3	17 min.	32 min.
5	17 min.	33 min.

Eastbound running times leaving Glenwood Springs to leaving Cardiff,

Train No.	10/1/07	11/10/07
4	10 min.	25 min.
6	12 min.	22 min.

The additional time, of course, was to allow for the changing of engines and crews and to service the train.

Although the engineers' agreement defined the 2nd District as the territory between Leadville and Grand Junction, including the two branches, the change in the division point meant that passenger and freight crews, instead of operating between Leadville and Basalt and between Basalt and Grand Junction, would now operate between Leadville and Cardiff and between Cardiff and

Grand Junction. It also meant that a number of employees had to be uprooted from their homes in Basalt and transplanted to the new location at Cardiff. This was not a long move in distance, but certainly a traumatic event in their lives, being no different then than it would be today.

The October and November schedules are included primarily to reflect the change in the division point, but they are also representative of the winter schedules on the Colorado Midland at this time. The October schedule is almost a twin of the August listing, with the exception of the Ute Pass summer service being dropped, as well as the afternoon train No. 14 from Cripple Creek. The November schedule showed minor adjustments to both Nos. 5 and 4, as well as a change on the Aspen Branch connection with No. 5. The equipment handled is the same as during the summer, at least on the through trains, including the operation of the tourist sleepers two days a week in each direction.

In addition to the conversion of the diners, which has already been discussed in detail, the Colorado City shops also rebuilt first class coaches 110 and 112 into vestibule chair cars during the year, possibly to make up for the loss of Nos. 247 and 250 as such. The passenger fleet also suffered a loss when baggage car 312 was wrecked on April 8th and removed from the roster.

Although it had little to do with passenger train operation, the CM received its largest locomotives during the year, when the 175 class was delivered. This consisted of six 2-8-0s numbered 301-306, which were normally assigned to freight helper service, with four engines at Basalt and two at Colorado City. Perhaps there were occasions when these were used to assist passenger trains up the grade from Basalt to Ivanhoe, or from Colorado City and Florissant to Divide, but they were usually to be found on freight trains in these territories. The 301 class was to be the last group of locomotives purchased by the Colorado Midland. Although the management hoped, at various times, to buy more modern power, the fading financial fortunes the carrier precluded any such activity, and the 301s were destined to be the biggest and best the Midland would ever own. At an average cost of $17,370.59, the engines proved to be worth every penny, and they all outlasted the railroad itself. When the Midland shut down in 1918, they all ultimately were sold for service in Mexico, with five lasting until 1953 and one remaining in service until 1957.

1908

The schedules for the summer of 1908, as shown in the June 28th timetable, contained only minor changes of five to nine minutes for some of the mainline trains. One change was the elimination of times for No. 6 at the local stations between Grand Junction and New Castle on the Rio Grande Junction. Even if the train did not make these stops, the running time of two hours 20 minutes over the RGJ was not affected. The service to Cripple Creek was similar, with changes of five minutes or so on the regular trains, 11 and 8. This summer, No. 14, the "Circle Trip" train that ran in conjunction with the Short Line, now left Cripple Creek at 4 PM, and arrived at Colorado Springs at 6:55 PM. This was the third and final season for this train. Nos. 7 and 10, the trains scheduled between Colorado Springs and Divide, were on identical schedules with the 1907 season, and one wonders of this arrangement was supposed to take care of the wildflower operation as well as provide a local service to the Ute Pass stations.

The equipment for the through trains was the same as the prior year, except that the tourist sleepers in No. 5 now ran over the Colorado Midland on Monday and Friday, enroute from Chicago to Los Angeles. The eastbound tourist sleepers ran in No. 4 on Friday and Saturday as in the past. Dining cars continued on the same basis as in the previous year. Service on the Aspen Branch changed only to the extent that adjustments had to be made for changes in the mainline trains, and the Jerome Park Branch continued as before.

The schedule above was published in the Official Guide for August 1908, and while that shown in the September Guide was also dated June 28th there were certain changes in the equipment listings. One item concerned the names of the trains that had been carried for several years. Now the names had been dropped, and just the individual train numbers were shown. The other change had to do with the expansion of tourist sleeper operations during the "colonist rate period." This item read as follows:

> During Colonist Rate Period, September 1st to October 31st, the following through Tourist car service from points named to Pacific Coast will be maintained, passing over Colorado Midland Railway on Train No. 5, two days later than shown from starting point. Through Tourist Car service over Colorado Midland Ry., every day except Tuesday.
>
> From Chicago (via CB&Q) Tuesdays.
> From St. Louis (via CB&Q) Wednesdays
> From Chicago (via CRI&P) Mondays, Wednesdays, and Saturdays.
> From St. Louis (via CRI&P) Tuesdays, Thursdays and Fridays.
> From St. Paul and Minneapolis (via CGW) Mondays.

This rather ambitious arrangement of tourist sleepers resulted in two cars each over the CM on Wednesdays, Thursdays and Saturdays, with one each on Saturdays, Sundays and Mondays. These cars were evidently in addition to the regular tourist sleepers that were handled westbound in No. 5 on Thursdays and Mondays and eastbound in No. 4 on Fridays and Saturdays. No mention is made of the eastbound movement of the additional tourist cars, so it is presumed that they were deadheaded back to their origins. Whether or not they traveled over the CM in this fashion is not known, but it was the usual practice to deadhead cars over the same route as the revenue movement had taken place.

The November 1908 public timetable lists schedules that were identical to those shown as of June 28th, with the exception that the summer trains (Nos. 7, 10 and 14) were discontinued for the season. This timetable shows that tourist cars were operated westbound in No. 5 on Thursdays and Mondays, with an eastbound tourist sleeper in No. 4 on Tuesdays. It was evidently in effect from November 1st to the 21st, when a new employee timetable was issued containing some changes.

This timetable, No. 60, effective November 22, 1908, contains no changes in the westbound through trains, but eastbound No. 4 left Grand Junction 35 minutes later than before at 6:20 AM, with arrival at Colorado Springs now set for 7:50 PM, 45 minutes later. No. 11 had its arrival time at Cripple Creek changed from 9:50 PM to 10 PM, and No. 8 left Cripple Creek 15 minutes earlier at 7 AM, arriving Colorado Springs 20 minutes sooner at 9:50 AM. This schedule also restored the times of No. 6 at the local stations on the Rio Grande Junction, but with the same running time of two hours 20 minutes from Grand Junction to New Castle.

The equipment for the individual trains still showed tourist sleepers in No. 5 on Thursday and Monday and the eastbound tourist cars in No. 4 on Friday and Saturday. The special note on tourist cars, however, states that the eastbound cars were handled only on Saturday. Once again, the CM's listing is contradictory.

A supplement to the employee timetable of November 22nd was issued on December 20th, which changed the time of No. 3 over the Second District between Leadville and Grand Junction. Twenty-nine minutes were taken out of the schedule, with the arrival at Grand Junction changed from 11:59 AM to 11:30 AM. there were no other changes in either schedules or equipment, as shown by the Official Guide for the same dates.

As a sidelight to the scheduled passenger trains during the year, it is interesting to note the records of E. W. Hartzog when he first started to run passenger trains after his promotion to engineer on November 20, 1906. He evidently filled a vacancy for several days in March 1908 and between Florissant and Leadville. For five trips he had engine 17, and the assignment appears to have covered No. 3 west one day and back on No. 4. The following day he would go west on No. 5 and return that same evening on No. 6. This sequence did not always work out. One day he went west on No. 3 but came back the same day on No. 42, a freight train, with engine 39. His next trip west was on No. 5 with engine 38, and he again returned from Leadville with No. 42 the same evening with engine 39. From the times shown on his reports, the passenger trains were running fairly close to schedule.

In July he was back working out of Colorado City, and caught two trips on passenger trains from Colorado Springs to Florissant and return. On July 23rd he had engine 306, on duty at 9:20 PM for No. 3 (this allowed for the backover movement of the engine from Colorado City to the passenger station at Colorado Springs to get the train, due to leave at 10 PM). He returned from Florissant to Colorado Springs with No. 6, and marked off duty at 8:20 AM at Colorado City. As No. 6 was due at 5:25 AM, it appears that it was running late that morning. On July 24th he had the 305, again called on duty at 9:20 PM for No. 3. Returning from Florissant with No. 6, he tied up at Colorado City at 5:55 AM, which would make them just about on time at Colorado Springs.

There were times when two sets of engines and crews were needed to get the passenger trains over the First District, as described in Cafky's *Colorado Midland* on page 223 by former engineer Jack Hickman. A large engine was used between Colorado Springs and Florissant in order to avoid the use of a helper, and a smaller engine was used on to Leadville. The crew out of Colorado Springs returned from Florissant on the next eastbound train, and the crew out of Florissant returned from Leadville on a later passenger (or freight) train. This evidently was the reason why Ed Hartzog worked the above assignments in the manner that he did. Later in the year he worked through from Colorado Springs to Leadville and return, but split crews probably were used during periods of heavy traffic.

Late in October and November, Hartzog again worked on passenger trains, going west on No. 3 and returning the next day on No. 6. The next trip from Colorado Springs would be on No. 5 to Leadville, returning the following day with No. 4. For most of these trips, he had engines 202, 203 and 205. Early in December, when on the same runs, he used smaller tenwheelers such as Nos. 11, 19, 21 and 22. Checking his times on and off duty, it appears that the trains were fairly close to being on time, with the exception of No. 4. This train was due in Colorado Springs at 7:50 PM, but the earliest he tied up at Colorado City after handling No. 4 was 10:05 PM. This might make the Colorado Midland look bad, but as No. 4 received a connection from the Rio Grande Western at Grand Junction, the late operation could have been due to a late connection at that point.

During 1908, the shops at Colorado City were busy. First class coach 109 was rebuilt into a vestibule chair car, but the big assignment was to convert the 200 class engines from compound to simple. These had not been a howling success since they had come on the property in 1901, due to the high maintenance expense, so it was decided to make them into simple engines. The work could have been the reason why engineer Hartzog used the 300 class in July, as the 300s were normally used in freight helper service. It developed that the rebuilding was not a great success either, as the engines had larger cylinders than they were able to keep supplied with steam. However, at least one in this class was in service on the Louisiana & Arkansas into the late 1940s.

One item of importance concerning corporate structure of the Colorado Midland occurred on August 1, 1908, when all of the subsidiaries of the D&RG were merged into the Denver & Rio Grande Railroad. This included the Rio Grande Western which owned 50 percent of the Midland, with the result that instead of indirect ownership through the RGW, the D&RG now had a direct half interest in the Colorado Midland. With the Colorado & Southern still having the other half interest, this development had little effect.

This pair of images of the staff and interior of the Colorado Midland station at Glenwood Springs presents a fascinating array of framed lithographs, wall maps, posters, ticket and timetable cases. Native artifacts and game specimens are displayed on the wall and marble-top counter, beneath a huge overhead light bulb. It is regrettable that names of these proud railroad employees are lost to history. (H.H. Buckwalter, Colorado Historical Society)

1909

The year 1908 was the last for President Frank Trumbull on the Colorado Midland. The Chicago Burlington & Quincy acquired control of the Colorado & Southern, of which Trumbull was also president, late in 1908. In the house cleaning that followed, Trumbull was out, and a young vice president of the CB&Q, Daniel Willard, was appointed president of the C&S and the CM.

Trumbull was appointed president of the Chesapeake & Ohio and went on to a long and distinguished career on that road, both as president and as chairman of the board. He was one of the best railroad men of his time; during his CM tenure the railroad reached its zenith, and he would be greatly missed in the years to come by the Midland family. Now with half ownership of the road in the hands of an indifferent carrier and the other half in the hands of a deadly competitor, the railroad was in for some hard times.

Willard retained his vice presidency of the CB&Q during his short stint as president of the CM and was not able to devote as much time to the problems of the mountain road as would otherwise be expected. He went on to become the most famous of all presidents of the Baltimore & Ohio. It could never be said that the Midland did not have some superb executives associated with it over the years.

The summer schedule effective May 23, 1909 had some significant changes from the previous year, especially in connection with day trains 4 and 5. Although still leaving at one minute after noon from Colorado Springs, the schedule was lengthened by a full hour and 15 minutes, so that No. 5 did not arrive in Grand Junction until 2:45 AM. This additional time was split almost evenly between the First and Second Districts, with 40 minutes added between Colorado Springs and Arkansas Junction and 35 minutes from there to Grand Junction. With a 2:45 AM arrival at Grand Junction, this was hardly a "day" train.

No. 4 was also slowed by 20 minutes, as it now left Grand Junction ten minutes earlier, and arrived in Colorado Springs ten minutes later. No. 3 left Colorado Springs 45 minutes earlier than it had in December, at 9:15 PM but it also arrived Grand Junction 45 minutes earlier at 10:45 AM with no change in running time. The only change to No. 6 was that it was due in Colorado Springs ten minutes later at 5:35 AM, but still held to its 4 PM departure from Grand Junction.

There was no change at all in consists of the through trains, and the contradictory note continued in connection with the eastbound operation of the tourist sleepers. The equipment list for No. 4 showed tourist cars handled on Friday and Saturday, while the item under tourist cars service showed that the eastbound car departed Los Angeles on Saturday. This indicates movement over the Colorado Midland on Monday.

The Cripple Creek service continued with just Nos. 11 and 8 providing one train each way, as the operation of No. 14 in the afternoon was discontinued via the MT/CM route. The sightseers now traveled both ways over the Short Line between Colorado Springs and Cripple Creek. As mentioned, 1908 was the last summer season that No. 14 ran over the MT/CM route.

The two round trips on the Aspen Branch were continued but now had a connection only with Nos. 3 and 6. If a passenger from Aspen desired to travel toward Colorado Springs in the daytime, he or she would have to leave Aspen at 5:30 AM and wait at Basalt almost four hours before the arrival of No. 4. On the other hand, a westbound passenger on No. 5 for Aspen would have to stay all night at Basalt, as the branch connection from No. 6 had already been gone for almost two hours. This circumstance pretty much limited westbound passengers for Aspen to riding No. 3. The branch connections for Nos. 3 and 6 were quite convenient, so in this respect the service was better than it had been, but it still points up the fact that Aspen was no longer the passenger market that it had been a few years before.

A major change was made on the Jerome Park Branch in that an additional round trip was added between Cardiff and Gulch. Nos. 61 and 62 remained the same on a morning schedule between the two points, but No. 63 was added to leave Cardiff at 1 PM except Sundays and was due at Gulch at 3:15 PM. The return trip, as No. 64, was scheduled at 3:30 PM with arrival in Cardiff at 5:45 PM. The second trip was not put on due to any dramatic increase in passenger traffic, but was established because of increased coal loadings, as passengers were still being handled in the caboose. The train had probably been running extra for some time and had become such a regular operation that it was added to the timetable. The miners and their families now could count on the afternoon service. The only change during the year on the passenger car roster was the conversion of first class coach 108 into a vestibule chair car.

1910

The schedule for June 19, 1910 showed that A. D. Parker was now president of the Colorado Midland, revealing how short was the reign of Daniel Willard. Parker, at one time, had been auditor of the C&S so was well qualified to handle the finances of the Midland. The Guide also had a tremendously expanded list of traffic officials, as compared with previous years. It is presumed that many of these individuals shared duties with the CB&Q and C&S in an effort to increase the CM's handling of both passenger and freight traffic.

The schedule showed no additional summer service in line with the policy inaugurated in 1909. No doubt the wildflower special was run during the summer months as an extra train.

No. 5 now left Colorado Springs 16 minutes earlier than in 1909, at 11:45 AM, and arrived in Grand Junction 20 minutes earlier at 2:25 AM, a grand speed-up of four minutes. No. 3 had considerable time added to its schedule, as it now left Colorado Springs at 8:45 PM, 30 minutes earlier, but did not arrive at Grand Junction until 11:20 AM, 35 minutes later, for an overall slow-down of one hour five minutes. No. 11 still provided the same evening run from Colorado Springs to Cripple Creek.

Eastbound service was almost the same as in 1909, with the exception that No. 4 was due to arrive in Colorado Springs 15 minutes later. It was now slowed to an overall running time of 14 hours five minutes. No. 8 also ran on the same schedule in the morning out of Cripple Creek.

The equipment list now showed that the diner on No. 3 ran from Thomasville to Grand Junction, with the return of the car in No. 6. This was the first listing in the Guide of the actual terminals of the dining cars. Of course, it was the same arrangement as when the car was originally established in 1907.

No. 5's equipment was the same, with two exceptions. The Chicago – Los Angeles tourist sleeper operated over the CM only on Thursdays, with no car eastbound at all in No. 4. The eastbound train also carried an Ogden – Denver first class coach, which was the first time since 1898 that the road provided a through coach or chair car service between those cities. No corresponding westbound car was advertised.

No. 11 also showed a through coach from Denver to Cripple Creek. While a through coach had been shown in No. 8 from Cripple Creek to Denver, the listing for the past few years had not included a through westbound car, indicating that passengers had to change at Colorado Springs. Now there were through cars in both directions.

The morning trip on the Aspen Branch was adjusted to make the proper connection with No. 3 at Basalt, but the evening run remained the same. Again, there was no advertised connection for mainline trains 5 and 4 to and from Aspen. There was no change on the Jerome Park Branch. It might be noted that the schedule for June 19, 1910 remained in effect until May 1, 1911, certainly one of the longest schedules to be maintained during the history of the railroad.

The only change to the rolling stock during the year was the loss of two baggage cars; No. 309 was destroyed on August 16th, while No. 308 was destroyed on November 5th. This reduced the passenger car fleet to 48 units.

After his brief flurry of passenger activity in 1908, Ed Hartzog spent most of 1909 and 1910 handling engines in freight and helper service. He did handle a few passenger runs on the Second District early in the year. The Tennessee Pass tunnel of the Rio Grande caved in sometime during the year, and whether his trips were caused by that situation is not known. With the regular enginemen being assigned as pilots for the detouring Rio Grande trains, First District enginemen could have been borrowed to work in these unfamiliar surroundings.

Regardless of the reason, Hartzog had engine 10, on duty at 7:35 PM January 2nd, for No. 5 at Leadville, enroute to Cardiff where he signed off at 12:25 AM. On January 3rd, he had the same engine and handled No. 4 from Cardiff to Leadville, on duty at 12:20 PM and off at 5:45 PM. On January 4th he was called for No. 5 again, this time with engine 5 and on duty at 7:35 PM. He did not complete this trip until 6:35 AM at Cardiff, indicating that there had been some difficulty enroute. He went right back on duty at 10:32 AM and handled No. 4 with engine 5, signing off at Leadville at 4:45 PM. As the schedules for 1909 and 1910 were quite similar for Nos. 5 and 4, a comparison of those with the times shown, indicates that these trains were running somewhat off the schedule. As this was during the winter, there could have been good and sufficient reason for a tardy operation.

Later in the year, Hartzog was back in Colorado City, and in September he handled passenger trains between Colorado Springs and Leadville. On the 16th he had engine 16 with train No. 3, on duty at Colorado City at 8 PM and off duty in Leadville at 5:10 AM. On the 17th, he returned with engine 21 on No. 6, reporting at 11:25 PM and tying up at Colorado City at 6:10 AM. On the 18th he went out again on No. 3 with engine 21, on duty at 8 PM as usual, and tied up at Leadville at 4:30 AM. On the 19th, he had engine 15, on duty at 11:30 PM for No. 6, and off at 6:10 AM at Colorado City. On the 20th, he was called at 9 PM to help No. 3 to Leadville, with engine 15, and tied up there at 4:35 AM. Back again on No. 6 on the 21st, he had engine 16, on duty at 11:25 PM and, after dropping the train at Colorado Springs, he marked off at Colorado City at 6:10 AM.

Because of the Christmas holidays, the regular engineer evidently marked off the board, as Hartzog was called for 9 PM to help No. 3 with engine 14 on December 24th to Leadville, where he was off at 4:25 AM Christmas Day. That same day, he was on duty at 11:35 PM with engine 17 and handled No. 6 from Leadville to Colorado Springs, where he signed off at 6:10 AM the 26th.

1911

As mentioned for the previous year, the schedule that was in effect on June 19, 1910 remained in effect until May 1, 1911, so there was no change during the first four months of this year.

It is of interest to note that engineer Hartzog was assigned to the Colorado Springs – Cripple Creek trains 11 and 8 from March 7th to March 31st. Typically, he was on duty at Colorado City at 5:45 PM, or one hour prior to the leaving time of No. 11 from Colorado Springs. This allowed time for the three-mile backover movement of the light engine from the enginehouse to the station. He was released at 10 PM or on arrival at the train at Cripple Creek. The next morning, he would go on duty at 7 AM, the advertised departure time of No. 8. This indicates that there was a hostler on duty at Cripple Creek who took care of the incoming engine in the evening and prepared it for the outbound trip the following morning. The arrival of No. 8 was listed for 9:50 AM at Colorado Springs, and the engineer was released at Colorado City at 10:30

3	▲11	Ms	October 29, 1911.	▲8	6
P M	P M	...	LEAVE] [ARRIVE	Noon	A M
*8 20	*4 00	0	+........Denver........ δ	12 35	8 20
5 00	4 35	...	+........Pueblo........ δ	11 50	8 00
P M	P M	...	LEAVE] [ARRIVE	A M	A M
*11 00	*6 45	74	+..Colorado Springs.. δ	9 50	5 35
11 10	6 55	78	+.....Colorado City..... δ	9 40	5 23
11 20	7 05	81	+.......Manitou....... δ	9 31	5 14
– –	–	82	....Manitou Iron Springs....	– –	– –
12 02	7 30	86	..........Cascade......... δ	9 15	4 55
12 13	7 38	90	......Green Mt. Falls......	9 00	4 42
12 33	7 55	95	.........Woodland......... δ	8 50	4 30
1 05	8 20	100	arr.........Divide δ.....lve.	8 35	4 15
...	*8 20	100	lve..Divide (Mid.Term.Ry.) arr.	8 35	.....
...	9 40	127	....Victor......	7 20	.....
	10 00	132	arr..Cripple Creek. lve.	*7 00	.....
1 05	P M	102	lve.........Divide δ.. ..arr.	A M	4 15
1 35	...	111	.........Florissant......... δ	.....	3 30
2 41	.....	133	.........Spinney.........	.....	2 41
3 08	.....	144	.........Hartsel......... δ	.....	2 20
4 07	.....	165	.........Newett......... δ	.....	1 33
4 33	.....	176	+.....Buena Vista..... δ	.....	12 57
5 20	.....	194	.........Granite......... δ	.....	12 29
6 05	.....	209	arr....Arkansas Junc.. δ lve.	.....	11 59
6 35	.....	213	arr. } ..+Leadville δ... { lve.	.....	11 25
5 50	.....	213	lve. } { arr.	.....	12 05
6 20	.....	209	lve....Arkansas Junc.. δ arr.	.....	11 48
7 00	.....	222	.............Busk......... δ	.....	11 16
7 10	.....	224	...........Ivanhoe...........	.....	11 05
7 37	.....	234	...........Sellar.......... δ	.....	10 15
8 05	.....	245	........Thomasville....... δ	.....	9 20
9 00	.....	265	arr..........Basalt δ......lve.	.....	8 13
10 10	.....	283	arr.......+ Aspen δ......lve.		*6 20
A M	.....	283	lve.........Aspen........arr.	.....	P M
9 00	.....	265	lve.........Basalt δ......arr.	.....	8 13
9 27	.....	277	........Carbondale........ δ	.....	7 43
10 00	.....	286	+.........Cardiff......... δ	.....	7 22
10 15	.....	289	+...Glenwood Springs... δ	.....	7 02
10 50	.....	301	+.......New Castle......... δ	.....	6 38
11 18	.....	315	.............Rifle.......... δ	.....	6 00
11 50	.....	334	........Grand Valley........ δ	.....	5 29
12 12	.....	345	..........De Beque......... δ	.....	5 03
12 54	.....	365	..........Palisade..........	.....	4 22
1 20	.....	378	+...Grand Junction... δ	.....	*4 00
2 10	...	389	............Fruita............	.....	P M
2 18	...	394	............Loma.............	.....	.....
5 11	.....	483	.........Green River.........	.....	.....
7 45	...	555	...........Helper............	.....	.....
11 30	.....	625	...........Provo.............	.....	.....
12 50	.....	670	..........Salt Lake........ δ	.....	.....
2 00	.....	706	...........Ogden......... δ	.....	.....
A M		...	ARRIVE] [LEAVE	.....	.....

* Daily; †daily, except Sunday. ▲Trains Nos. 8 and 11 connect from Denver, via Denver & Rio Grande R.R. ‡ Meal stations. + Coupon stations; δ Telegraph stations. STANDARD—*Mountain time.*

Connections.—Denver, in Union Depot—With Atchison, Topeka & Santa Fe Ry., Chicago, Burlington & Quincy Ry., Chicago, Rock Island & Pacific Ry. and Union Pacific R.R. and Colorado & Southern Ry. Colorado Springs—With Chicago, Rock Island & Pacific, Atchison, Topeka & Santa Fe and Colorado Southern Rys. Manitou—With Manitou & Pike's Peak Ry. Divide—With Midland Terminal Ry. for Victor, Cripple Creek, etc. Buena Vista—With Colorado & Southern Ry. and with stage lines. Grand Junction—With Rio Grande Western Ry.

JEROME PARK BRANCH.—Trains leave Cardiff *7 00 a.m., †1 00 p.m., arriving Gulch (15 miles) 9 30 a.m., 3 15 p.m. Returning, leave Gulch *9 45 a.m., †3 30 p.m., arriving Cardiff 12 01 noon, 5 45 p.m.

TRAIN SERVICE AND EQUIPMENT.

No. 3—Solid Through Train Denver to Grand Junction. Carries Chair Car, also Drawing-room Pullman Sleeping Car Denver to Grand Junction and Denver to Leadville. Dining Car service Thomasville to Grand Junction. Meals a la carte.

No. 11—Solid Through Train Colorado Springs to Cripple Creek. Through Coach Denver to Cripple Creek.

No. 6—Solid Through Train Grand Junction to Denver. Carries Chair Car and Coach Grand Junction to Denver. Pullman Sleeper Grand Junction to Denver and Leadville to Denver. Dining Car service Grand Junction to Thomasville. Meals a la carte.

No. 8—Local Accommodation Train between Cripple Creek and Colorado Springs. Carries Through Chair Car Cripple Creek to Denver.

Dining Car Service, meals a la carte on Trains Nos. 3 and 6.

AM, allowing time for the backover of the light engine to the roundhouse. The only exception to this was on March 11th, when he did not get off until 11:30 AM, or one hour later than usual. During the entire period, engine 22, once the "hoodoo" engine of the CM, was assigned to the run and apparently was on good behavior during the time that Ed Hartzog was assigned to it. During this assignment, he made the round trip every day.

The May 1st timetable made only a slight change in the time of No. 4, in that it left Grand Junction ten minutes later at 6:20 AM, but still arrived Colorado Springs at 8:15 PM. The other mainline trains, as well as the Cripple Creek trains, remained on the same schedule as previously. The principal change was with the connections at Grand Junction for Nos. 5 and 4. Under train service and equipment is stated:

> Note – West of Grand Junction, Standard Through Pullman Sleeper handled on Trains Nos. 5 and 4, and Through Day Coach and Through Tourist Sleeper handled on Trains Nos. 7 and 8.

The connecting schedules of D&RG train Nos. 5, 4, 7 and 8 were shown in the condensed schedules following the Grand Junction listing of the Colorado Midland trains. D&RG train Nos. 7 and 8 were usually summer-only Grand Junction – Ogden trains put on during the tourist season. The tourist sleeper in No. 5 operated over the CM on Thursdays only, and there is no mention of any eastbound tourist car again this year. A through coach was now operating between Denver and Ogden both ways in trains Nos. 5 and 4.

The dining car service on Nos. 3 and 6 was changed. No. 3's diner was now attached at Arkansas Junction and was in service to Grand Junction for breakfast and lunch too, if the train were late. Eastbound, the diner on No. 6 was in service from Grand Junction to Cardiff, and presumably it deadheaded from there to Arkansas Junction in order to protect the movement in No. 3 the following morning. From this, it is apparent that passengers from Aspen who boarded at Basalt had no chance to avail themselves of the diner's evening meal service.

There were still two round trips on the Aspen Branch, but these made connections with Nos. 3 and 6 only, and there was still no attempt to provide any decent connections with Nos. 5 and 4 at Basalt. The two round trips were also continued on the Jerome Park Branch on the same schedules as before.

The Official Guide listing is also notable in that it was now illustrated with a cut of Hell Gate, one of the major scenic attractions on the Colorado Midland. In order to make room for this on the page, the list of traffic representatives was considerably reduced. A perusal of the lists of 1910 and 1911 indicates that the off-line sales people were now strictly Colorado Midland representatives, as all the names and addresses are different for the 1911 listing than they had been in 1910. Perhaps the joint sales efforts of the CB&Q and C&S did not work for the benefit of the CM, and it re-established its own offices. A month and a half later, on June 18th, a new schedule was published, which showed that A.D. Parker was no longer president of the Colorado Midland. George W. Vallery had been appointed to that position. Vallery had been general manager of the road since 1904, and evidently the powers-that-be felt that he was deserving of the position after the many years in that office.

The June 18th schedule made only one important change in the time of trains, that of No. 3. This train now left Colorado Springs two hours 15 minutes later than formerly, at 11 PM, and arrived Grand Junction at 1:20 PM. This later timing assured the need for the diner to serve lunch enroute. Under the train service and equipment item, the note about handling of the cars for Nos. 5 and 4 west of Grand Junction was still shown, but the connecting schedule for Nos. 7 and 8 was not shown, nor was the tourist car listed under the equipment for No. 5. It was still listed, in the special tourist car service footnote. Once again, the reader has a choice of what to believe as to the equipment actually assigned to this train.

Over several years, Colorado Midland passenger trains were taking an increasingly longer time to get over the road, and this summer's schedules are an indication of what had ben happening to running times. here is the way they stacked up.

Train No. 5	–	14 hours 40 minutes
Train No. 3	–	14 hours 20 minutes
Train No. 4	–	13 hours 55 minutes
Train No. 6	–	13 hours 35 minutes

Just a few years preciously it had been the rule-of-thumb that trains took about 12 hours to make the run between Colorado Springs and Grand Junction. Now, due to heavier trains, poor track and light locomotives, the schedules were flirting with a 15-hour running time. No. 6 was still listed as the fastest train over the road, but that was a far cry from the ten hour 55 minute schedule of 1900 and points up how badly things had deteriorated. It should be noted that the station name of Cascade Canon, was now Cascade.

Since No. 3 was running so much later, it was now possible for the Aspen Branch morning train to make a connection with No. 4 at Basalt, and an adjustment was made in the schedule so that both connections could be made. Westbound passengers on No. 3 had to wait one hour 45 minutes for No. 4 to arrive at Basalt before the branch train left, and arrival at Aspen was set back to 11:55 AM. The connection was made, but at the cost of further delay for these passengers, if there were many by this time.

The schedules of June 18th remained in effect until October 28th, and then something took place that had not happened on the CM since 1896. There was only one passenger train each way over the length of the railroad. The schedule of October 29th eliminated Nos. 5 and 4, leav-

MIDLAND ALPHABET.

A for the Antelope coursing the plains,
Seen by the tourists from platforms of trains.

B for the Burro, with resonant bray,
That carried all loads ere the road built its way.

C for the Cañons,—vast, gloomy and deep,—
Where the train winds along by the perilous steep.

D for the Dividends, sure not to fail;
Thus to gold turning the steel of the rail.

E for the Engines, as proudly they ride
On the crest of the great Continental Divide.

F for the Fruits which the rich valleys give,
Enabling the owners to live aud let live.

(5)

Here are five of 40 pages in a little illustrated pamphlet, the title page of which reads, "The Midland Primer for Old and Young - A Hand-book of Information of THE GREAT STATE OF COLORADO and the TERRITORY OF UTAH compiled for the Passenger Department of the Colorado Midland Railway Company by Isidore Wise, Denver, Colorado, 1892." (Museum collection)

G for the Gold of the mountains and streams,
the nuggets of which the emigrant dreams.

H for the "Horseshoe," there in the green,
Its pattern in silver, deep-printed, is seen.

I for the Invalids whom the train brings
To the sunshine, the ozone, the clear mineral springs.

J for the Journey by cañon, cascade,—
By Green Mountain Falls in the deep forest glade.

K for the lord Ethiopian, "King Koal,"—
The miners have found him a "jolly old soul."

L for Loch Ivanhoe—never a Scot
Has found 'mid his heather a lovelier spot.

M Manitou Springs, the Great Spirit's will
Gave waters of health to the weak and the ill.

N for No Nothings, at home, in the East,
Who come not to taste where the West spreads its feast.

(6)

O for the Owl with his friend, rattlesnake,
A home in the prairie dog burrow they make.

P for Pike's Peak, whose snow-bastions still shine,
As when miners first hailed them in old '59.

Q for the Quantity, as yet unknown,
When our Colorado's vast output is shown.

R for the Road, in the passes it lies
Like a ribbon uniting the earth with the skies.

S Salt Lake of Utah—mid-continent sea!
A sapphire expanse, where the breezes blow free!

T for the Tunnel that Hagerman made;
Thro' the heart of Saguache, you may ride undismayed.

U the Ute Indians, who once ruled the land,
Whose remnant survives as a wandering band.

V for the silver Veins, glimmering bright,
In the deep hearts of mountains, away from the light.

(7)

W is for Water, in Glenwood's great pool—
In winter, a warm bath; in summer, a cool.

X for the Xcellence of our train men;
They are "A No. Ones"—hurrah once again!

Y tall, stately Yucca, the pride of the plain.
Gleaming cups, thorny spears, the bayonet of Spain.

Z the road's Zigzags o'er mountain and plain;
Just ride on it once, and you'll try it again.

—*Virginia Donaghe McClurg.*

CARRIAGE ROAD UP PIKE'S PEAK.

MIDLAND PRIMER.

Where Is Colorado?

Look at the map of the United States, and you will see that Colorado is bounded on the north by Wyoming and Nebraska, on the east by Nebraska and Kansas, on the south by Indian Territory and New Mexico, and on the west by Utah.

How Large Is the State?

It has an area of 104,500 square miles, with an average length, east and west, of 380 miles, and an average breadth, north and south, of 280 miles. It is larger than all of the New England states combined, with Ohio thrown in. It is larger than England, Scotland and Wales combined. It is, indeed, a *very* large state.

What Are the Physical Features?

Mountains and Plains. Among the mountains and foothills are the wonderful Parks, which have made the State so famous. These parks are large areas of rolling land, green, beautiful and fertile, sometimes covered with rich forests and watered by innumerable little creeks and rivers. These parks are four in number in the State, but we have to deal only with the most renowned one—the South Park. You will see, by and by, that we select this park because the great Midland Railway passes through it.

Why Is Colorado a Great and Wonderful State?

Because it is located in the center of the great Rocky Mountain region and is the natural highway from the Atlantic to the Pacific and from Canada to the Gulf. The State is 16 years old, the leading mining state in the Union, a great [illegible] the West. Its climate is the finest on the Continent. It is a vast health-resort, very beneficial to invalids, especially those suffering with lung and throat diseases. The soil is rich, there is an abundance of timber, and there

(9)

ing Nos. 3 and 6 as the sole providers of passenger service west of Divide. The reasons for this drastic action are easy to understand. The railroad had been accumulating increasing deficits over the past few years, and President Vallery was looking for anything that would assist in cutting costs. Nos. 5 and 4 were more tourist-oriented that Nos. 3 and 6, and they were expensive to operate, with through cars to and from Ogden, as well as the two diners that had to be run over the length of the railroad, with their costly crews and food expense. Thus, with the tourist season over, it was decided to eliminate these trains for the winter. Nos. 3 and 6 handled the bulk of the mail and express business, as well as providing overnight sleeping car accommodations between Denver, Leadville and Grand Junction for the benefit of businessmen. They were more useful to the local passengers along the line.

The elimination of Nos. 5 and 4 was the important change made with the mainline trains. There was no change in the timings of Nos. 3 and 6 nor the Cripple Creek trains Nos. 11 and 8. As far as the equipment was concerned, the dining car for Nos. 3 and 6 was switched back to Thomasville as the overnight stop. The other principal change occurred on the Aspen Branch. Up to this point, there had been two trips a day, running as mixed trains at least since 1908, with both originating in Aspen, running to Basalt to make connection with the mainline and then returning. With this schedule, the home terminal was changed to Basalt. The crew made only one trip each day, still as a mixed train, leaving Basalt after the arrival of No. 3, going to Aspen, switching at that point and then returning in the early evening to Basalt to connect with No. 6. No change was made to the mixed service on the Jerome Park Branch.

Evidently, the schedule for No. 3 out of Colorado Springs at 11 PM, did not work out too well. On November 12th, this was changed to a departure at 8:45 PM, with arrival at 11:10 AM at Grand Junction. No other mainline trains were changed, and the Aspen Branch mixed operated an hour earlier in both directions, in order to make the proper connection with Nos. 3 and 6.

There had not been a change in the mail handling operations over the CM for some years, as far as the RPO cars were concerned, but a definitive mail-handling procedure as of January 1911 is explained on pages 389-391 of Cafky's *Colorado Midland*. This is summarized as follows:

RPO in Nos. 5 and 4 between Colorado Springs and Glenwood Springs, with the car through to Grand Junction with closed pouches.

RPO in Nos. 11 and 8 between Colorado Springs and Cripple Creek.

Closed pouches were also handled:

Nos. 3 and 6 between Colorado Springs and Glenwood Springs.

Nos. 21, 22, 23, and 24, between Arkansas Junction and Leadville.

Nos. 75 and 78, between Basalt and Aspen.

Nos. 61 and 62, between Cardiff and Spring Gulch

Presumably, the RPO car from Colorado Springs to Glenwood Springs was handled in Nos. 3 and 6 after Nos. 5 and 4 were withdrawn during the winter of 1911-1912.

There were no changes in the passenger car fleet during the year. Tenwheeler 14 was changed to 60-inch drivers, making it into a class 104 locomotive. It was then primarily used in passenger service.

1912

After the winter hiatus, the schedule of April 28th restored train Nos. 5 and 4 for the summer tourist season. Departure of No. 5 from Colorado Springs was the same as in 1911, at 11:45 AM, but the arrival at Grand Junction was now set back to 3 AM—a whopping 15 hours and 15 minutes to get over the road. No. 3 was also 25 minutes longer making the trip than in November 1911, now being due at Grand Junction at 11:35 AM. No. 4 ran on the same schedule as in the summer of 1911, but No. 6 had 30 minutes added to its running time, and was now scheduled into Colorado Springs at 6:05 AM. The Cripple Creek service changed only slightly with No. 8 still on the same schedule, but No. 11 left Colorado Springs 30 minutes earlier at 6:15 PM and was due in Cripple Creek 20 minutes earlier at 9:40 PM. The Aspen Branch mixed train remained on the same schedule as previously and provided connections with No. 3 in the morning and No. 6 in the evening at Basalt. There was no connection with Nos. 5 and 4 at Basalt for Aspen. The Jerome Park schedule also changed; the second trip in the afternoon now ran only to Sunlight, leaving Cardiff at 1 PM, with returning departure at 3 PM, except Sundays. No arrival times were shown at either terminal.

Under the equipment listing in the Guide, train names were restored as follows:

No. 3 – *Western Express*
No. 5 – *Pacific Express*
No. 11 – *Denver-Cripple Creek Express*
No. 4 – *Eastern Express*
No. 6 – *Denver Express*
No. 8 – *Cripple Creek-Denver Express*

In view of the slow running times, the use of the word "express" seemed inappropriate, as well as being inaccurate with respect to the Cripple Creek trains. The through Denver coach was no longer listed, and the equipment shown indicates that these trains were strictly Colorado Springs-Cripple Creek locals.

Other equipment changes show that the Denver-Ogden first class coach no longer ran through in Nos. 5 and 4 but was terminated at Grand Junction, requiring any through passengers to change cars at 3 AM! The dining car operation was changed only slightly from the previous year. Nos. 4 and 5 included diners all the way between Colorado Springs and Grand Junction. No. 3's diner was added at Leadville, rather than Arkansas Junction, and No. 6's diner was in service from Grand Junction to Cardiff, thus requiring a deadhead move from there to Leadville.

The equipment listing showed that the observation pullman sleeping car in No. 5 and No. 4 between Denver and Ogden was the only one, other than possibly some head end cars, that traveled beyond the railroad's west end at Grand Junction. This indicated that the railroad was more and more becoming just a local carrier between its two terminals.

As a matter of information, the schedules of the Florence & Cripple Creek and leased lines and Midland Terminal are shown. The Short Line continued to provide a single round trip between Colorado Springs and Cripple Creek, westbound in the morning and eastbound in the afternoon, just the opposite of the CM/MT route. The F&CC's Canon City – Cripple Creek route showed just one train, a mixed, between those two terminals. This schedule of January 1, 1912, which was still being shown in the Official Guide for October 1912, was destined to the the last one for the original mainline of the F&CC, as a cloudburst and flood on July 21st wiped out much of the track between Cramer and McCourt, and the damage was never repaired. This schedule also showed just one morning train eastbound from Cripple Creek to Vista Grande on the Golden Circle without a corresponding return trip.

The local schedules of the Midland Terminal showed the full operation of the Colorado Springs trains over the MT, as well as the "hob-nail" miners trains, Nos. 20 and 21 between Cripple Creek and Victor. The officers were the same for both the F&CC and leased lines and the Midland Terminal, and the paucity of passenger service points up how far the great gold camp had fallen since the heyday of service in 1901.

Service for the winter of 1912-1913 was again reduced to one train each way across the mainline of the CM, but this season Nos. 3 and 4 were discontinued. No. 5, the only westbound train, now left Colorado Springs at 12:05 PM and was carded for a 3 AM arrival in Grand Junction. Eastbound, No. 6 had its traditional departure of 4 PM changed to 2 PM from Grand Junction, with arrival set for the ungodly hour of 4:20 AM at Colorado Springs and a 7 AM arrival at Denver. No. 5 had a drawing-room sleeper from Denver to Ogden (not an observation sleeper as during the summer), and a first-class coach to Grand Junction. The diner was in service from Wild Horse to Arkansas Junction only. No. 6's equipment was the same with the exception of the diner, which is shown from Cardiff to Thomasville. Just how the diners were scheduled is a good question, since both trains were serving the evening meal making it impossible for one car to cover. Another problem with this arrangement was that No. 6 advertised a connection from D&RG No. 4. That train was due in Grand Junction from the west at 5:40 AM. As CM No. 6 did not leave until 2 PM, it meant a layover of over eight hours at Grand Junction for the car and any through passengers. This schedule did not provide nearly as much convenience for patrons in either direction as the operation of Nos. 3 and 6 the previous winter.

The Aspen Branch mixed, which left Basalt sometime after 7 AM, did not provide any connection for No. 5, but the return trip in the afternoon did furnish a fairly decent connection with No. 6.

This schedule dated October 21, 1912, was published in the February 1913 Guide, which is why George W. Vallery is listed as receiver, as will be discussed later. It should be noted that the mileages were now shown in miles and tenths from Colorado Springs, thus ending the mileage error that had been in public schedules since 1895. The mileages listed now corresponded to those shown in the employee timetables, as well as the company's profile and track chart.

Checking engineer Hartzog's records for 1912, it is found that he did not handle too many passenger trains during the year, still being mostly in freight and helper service, but the few that he did run are of interest. For some reason, he handled a round trip on the Second District, which was unusual since he was assigned as a First District engineer. A run of this type was done only in emergencies. On May 19th he had engine 10, one of the "little hogs," and ran No. 3 from Leadville to Cardiff, reporting at 3:45 AM and marking off at 7:45 AM. This was right on time, according to the schedule. Returning the same day, he had engine 10 again and was on duty for No. 6 at Cardiff at 7:45 PM, going off duty at Leadville at 12:30 AM, again right on time.

His only other runs during the year were on the wildflower special from Colorado Springs to Spinney and return. This train was advertised to leave Colorado Springs at 9 AM and to return by 5 PM. It is interesting that Engineer Hartzog showed these trains as Nos. 7 and 10, which leads us to believe that they must have been in the employee timetable as scheduled trains, although unlisted in the Guide's schedules. The April 28th schedule was still being used in the October 1912 Guide. It is quite possible that the CM showed the wildflower trains in the operating timetable (as will be shown later), but as the trains were for the benefit of sightseers, they were not advertised to serve the local stations between Colorado Springs and Spinney. Hartzog made five trips on the wildflower specials: July 8th with engine 11, July 30th with engine 40, and August 20th through 22nd with engine 17. He was on duty at 8 AM for each of the trips and reported off duty between 5:45 PM and 6:15 PM.

In an effort to get much-needed cash, the management of the Colorado Midland sold its 50 percent interest in the Rio Grande Junction to the D&RG on November 13th. This action, of course, gave the Rio Grande complete ownership of the RGJ, but the CM retained the right to operate between Rifle and Grand Junction and to have access to the industries on that railroad as heretofore. As far as passenger and freight operations were concerned, the sale had little effect on the CM's operations. The money realized from the sale of the RGJ did not stem the flow of red ink on the company's ledgers, and the Midland was forced to declare bankruptcy on December 13th, with George W. Vallery appointed receiver by the court.

Even though the railroad's fortunes were on the decline, the Colorado City shops were able to convert chair cars 253, 254, and 255 to vestibule chair cars. Vestibules were also added to coaches 106 and 107 during the year.

1913

After the elimination of Nos. 3 and 4 during the winter season of 1912-1913, these trains were restored in the spring. On June 7th, the Colorado Springs & Glenwood Springs RPO was extended and now was known as the Colorado Springs & Grand Junction RPO. The summer schedule was issued on June 29th, and now included trains Nos. 7 and 10, the wildflower special, between Colorado Springs and Spinney. No. 7 was due to leave Colorado Springs at 9 AM daily, and to arrive at Spinney at 12:35 PM. Returning as No. 10, it was due to leave at 12:45 PM with an arrival at Colorado Springs at 5:15 PM. Local stops were made enroute, so, for this year at least, these trains were also available to and from Ute Pass stations and were not strictly excursions.

As far as the through mainline trains were concerned, both Nos. 3 and 5 were speeded up by 25 minutes. although leaving Colorado Springs at the same time as in 1912, the arrival at Grand Junction was that much earlier. Eastbound No. 6 reverted to the 4 PM departure from the western terminal and was on the same schedule as the summer of 1912. No. 5 was advanced considerably, now leaving Grand Junction at 4 AM, two hours 20 minutes earlier than in the previous season. Arrival in Colorado Springs was two hours 45 minutes earlier at 5:30 PM with the connection due in Denver at 8:20 PM. While the early departure from Grand Junction may have been inconvenient for passengers, the earlier arrival at Denver was much better than the previous 11 PM. The D&RG arrival at Grand Junction was also that much earlier, and the through passengers in the Ogden-Denver sleeper were not inconvenienced at all by the earlier departure from Grand Junction.

The coach and sleeping car arrangements remained the same as in 1912, but there was a change in the dining car operation. A car would now start form Leadville at 3:45 AM in No. 3 enroute to Grand Junction. It would then depart Grand Junction the same afternoon in No. 6 at 4 PM to Cardiff, arriving at 7:45 PM. The car sat there overnight and was picked up by No. 4 leaving at 7:25 AM. No. 4 set the diner off at Hartsel at 2:29 PM, where it was picked up by No. 5 at 3:40 PM and taken to Leadville for a 7:25 PM arrival. It was ready to start the cycle over again on No. 3 the next morning. This arrangement required only two cars to complete the cycles of two days each and still protected all meals except one for the four trains involved. The exception was lunch for No. 5's passengers who were invited to use the Fred Harvey restaurant at Colorado Springs station.

The schedules of the Colorado Springs – Cripple Creek trains were changed this season, with No. 11 operating 20 minutes later than in 1912, and No. 8 running 40 minutes earlier out of Cripple Creek. On the Aspen Branch, even though No. 3 now reached Basalt the same as before, arrival of the mixed train at Aspen was set back to 9:45 AM, 35 minutes later. The afternoon departure from Aspen was also set back by 20 minutes, which helped to cut down on the lengthy wait at Basalt, since No. 6 was not due there until 8:35 PM. There was no change to the two trains on the Jerome Park Branch. The schedule for September 1st eliminated the wildflower specials, Nos. 7 and 10. No. 8 was now carded out of Cripple Creek at 7:45 AM, one hour 25 minutes later and was due in Colorado Springs at 10:40 AM.

After reducing the service during the winter months for the previous two years, the Midland maintained all four trains during the 1913-14 winter season. The changes in the schedule were more cosmetic than anything else, but there were a few. No. 5 left Colorado Springs 35 minutes earlier at 11:45 AM and was due in Grand Junction at the same time as before, 2:35 AM. No. 3's schedule was not changed, nor was that of No. 6 eastbound. No. 4 left Grand Junction at 3:30 AM, off a D&RG connection and was due in Colorado Springs at 5:30 PM. The two Cripple Creek trains, Nos. 11 and 8, were kept on the same schedule, as were the Aspen branch mixed and the Jerome Park trains.

The equipment listed was identical to that of the previous schedules, and the observation-sleeping car continued to operate in Nos. 5 and 4, enroute to and from Ogden. The diners also continued on their route as before, parked overnight at Cardiff and Leadville and turning at Hartsel and Grand Junction.

During the year, the Colorado City shops converted suburban coach No . 6 into an open observation car, and combined coach-baggage No. 8 was converted into a "coach-lunch" car; both of these were then assigned to the wildflower special. Suburban coaches 1-3 were converted to stock drovers cars with the same numbers. This reduced the actual passenger fleet to 45 units. Between 1913 and 1915, coaches 101 through 104 were rebuilt with vestibules, but the actual dates of these conversions are not definitely known for each. There was no change in the motive power fleet during the year.

1914

The summer schedule for this year called for the same trains as the previous season with the exception of the wildflower special, which will be discussed later. No. 5 was now due to leave Colorado Springs at 12:20 PM, 35 minutes later, but still managed to arrive in Grand Junction at 2:35 AM. No. 3 also left Colorado Springs 45 minutes later at 9:30 PM, with Grand Junction arrival unchanged at 11:10 AM. No. 4 was getting out of Grand Junction during the wee hours at 3:30 AM, with arrival at Colorado Springs set for the same time, 5:30 PM. There was no change in the schedule of No. 6, nor was there any change in the timings of Nos. 11 and 8 to and from Cripple Creek.

The most noticeable change in the equipment listing was the elimination of the Denver-Leadville sleeper, long a tradition on the Colorado Midland. The Denver-Grand Junction sleeper continued to operate, but any Leadville passengers in that car had to rouse themselves to get off at Arkansas Junction at 3:50 AM. Eastbound passengers could get on the sleeper in No. 6 at 12:05 AM, if it was on time at Arkansas Junction, which was not quite as inconvenient as the westbound arrangement. It should be noted that the Denver-Leadville sleeper would not return until the spring of 1916.

The dining car situation also continued its slow decline, with No. 5 now advertising the car only between Wild Horse and Leadville. This gave passengers less than two hours for dinner, if they were going to Leadville. They had only one hour 25 minutes if they were destined to points west of Arkansas Junction. Nos. 3 and 6 still had their diners between Cardiff and Grand Junction, but the notice for No. 4 is rather ambiguous, stating only "dinner and supper in the dining car." This evidently meant that the Midland diner operated only from Leadville at 11:20 AM to Wild Horse, due about 12:40 PM. Supper was very likely obtained in the diner on the Colorado Springs-Denver connection. Incidentally, it was still shown that lunch for No. 5's passengers was to be obtained in the Fred Harvey dining room in the Colorado Springs station.

There was no change in the schedules for the Aspen Branch or the Jerome Park Branch for this season. Instead of being shown in the timetable, the wildflower special was operated on a train-order schedule, giving it right over all except first class trains. These orders were mimeographed in advance with blank spaces for the engine number, day and date. These orders could be amended, of course, by specific meet orders or run late orders, but at least they showed all concerned the times that the trains were expected to run. An example of a 1914 order is below:

Order No. 12 of August 30, 1914 at Divide, Colo.

Engine _17_ will run special, Colorado Springs to Spinney and return to Colorado Springs, leaving Colorado Springs _Sunday, Aug. 30th_ as follows with right over all except first-class trains:

Leave	Colorado Springs	9:00 AM	Leave	Spinney	12:40 PM
"	Colorado City	9:15 AM	"	Howbert	12:52 PM
"	Manitou	9:25 AM	"	Idlewild	1:00 PM
"	Crags	9:40 AM	"	Springer	1:10 PM
"	Cascade	9:58 AM	"	Lidderdale	1:25 PM
"	Culver	10:03 AM	"	Lake George	1:33 PM
"	Green Mtn. Falls	10:15 AM	"	Metcalf	1:40 PM
"	Bison	12:25 AM	"	Florissant	1:45 PM
"	Woodland	10:35 AM	"	Pisgah	2:33 PM
"	Edlowe	10:47 AM	"	Bellevue	2:50 PM
"	Divide	11:00 AM	"	Divide	3:05 PM
"	Bellevue	11:05 AM	"	Edlowe	3:15 PM
"	Pisgah	11:15 AM	"	Woodland	3:55 PM
"	Florissant	11:25 AM	"	Bison	4:00 PM
"	Metcalf	11:30 AM	"	Green Mtn. Falls	4:05 PM
"	Lake George	11:34 AM	"	Culver	4:10 PM
"	Lidderdale	11:40 AM	"	Cascade	4:18 PM
"	Springer	11:50 AM	"	Crags	4:25 PM
"	Idlewild	12:01 AM	"	Manitou	4:36 PM
"	Howbert	12:10 PM	"	Colorado City	4:45 PM
Arrive	Spinney	12:20 PM	Arrive	Colorado Springs	5:00 PM

It will be noted that the westbound schedule was three hours 20 minutes and the eastbound schedule was an hour longer. It appears that sightseeing stops were made on the eastbound trip at Lidderdale, Pisgah and Woodland; and that the train ran through on the westbound run, except for the necessary service stops to supply the engine and check the train.

The experiment of the winter of 1913-14, if that is what it was, was not repeated during the winter of 1914-15, and trains Nos. 3 and 4 were discontinued. The schedule showing this reduced service is dated January 10, 1915, and is discussed in the section for that year.

During 1914, cafe car No. 248 was retired to storage. Since the dining car operation only required two cars under the current schedules, it was decided to retire one car, leaving car No. 249 as a spare, for relief at Idlewild and Ivanhoe or to handle any special movements that might require a diner. During the year, the shops equipped the passenger end of combine No. 10 with a vestibule.

3	▲11	No. 5	Mls.	*April* 20, 1914.	4	No. 8	▲8
P M	P M	.....	.....	LEAVE / ARRIVE	P M	....	P M
*6 45	*3 40	*9 30 A M	.....	+ Denver	8 20	8 50 A M	1 35
4 30	4 30	9 50 A M	.....	+ Pueblo	7 50	7 45 A M	1 00
P M	P M	....	.....	LEAVE / ARRIVE	P M	....	A M
*9 30	*6 35	*12 20 Noon	0	+ Colorado Springs	5 30	6 05 A M	10 40
9 45	6 45	12 35 "	3.0	+ Colorado City	5 15	5 52 "	10 30
9 55	6 55	12 45 Noon	6.1	+ Manitou	5 06	5 43 "	10 21
10 25	7 25	1 20 P M	11.5	Cascade	4 48	5 25 "	10 03
10 40	7 40	1 32 "	14.9	Green Mt. Falls	4 35	5 11 "	9 50
10 58	7 57	1 50 "	20.0	Woodland	4 25	5 00 "	9 40
11 20	8 20	2 15 P M	26.9	arr. Divide lve.	4 10	4 45 A M	9 25
.....	8 20	....	26.9	lve. Divide (Mid. Term. Ry.) arr.	...	....	9 25
.....	9 40	....	51.6	Victor " ...	....	....	8 08
.....	10 00	....	56.9	arr. Cripple Creek " lve.	....	....	*7 45
11 20	P M	2 15 P M	26.9	lve. Divide arr.	4 10	4 45 A M	A M
11 45	...	2 45 "	35.8	Florissant	3 20	4 00 "	.....
11 54	....	2 55 "	40.3	Lake George	3 08	3 48 "	.....
12 40	..	3 47 "	57.7	Spinney	2 30	3 12 "	.....
1 04	....	4 14 "	68.9	Hartsel	2 11	2 52 "	.....
2 05	...	5 07 "	90.3	Newett	1 25	2 05 "	.....
2 30	...	5 30 "	100.9	+ Buena Vista	12 50	1 27 A M	.....
3 08	....	6 20 "	118.2	Granite	12 15	12 47 Night	.....
3 50	....	7 05 "	133.5	arr. Arkansas Junc. lve.	11 45	12 15 Night	.....
4 15	....	7 35 "	137.3	arr. + Leadville lve.	11 20	11 50 P M	.....
3 35	....	6 50 "	137.3	lve. + Leadville arr.	11 59	12 30 Night	.....
4 00	....	7 15 "	133.5	lve. Arkansas Junc. arr.	11 35	12 05 Night	.....
4 45	...	8 00 "	141.7	Busk	11 10	11 40 P M	.....
4 55	...	8 10 "	143.7	Ivanhoe	11 00	11 30 "	.....
5 21	....	8 38 "	153.7	Sellar	10 10	10 38 "	.....
5 50	....	9 08 "	165.2	Thomasville	9 13	9 42 "	.....
6 45	....	10 07 P M	185.3	arr. Basalt lve.	8 05	8 35 P M	.....
9 45	...	....	203.7	arr. + Aspen lve.	A M	*5 30 P M	.....
A M	...	*5 30 P M	203.7	lve. Aspen arr.	9 45	....	.....
6 45	....	10 07 P M	185.3	lve. Basalt arr.	7 45	8 35 P M	.....
7 10	....	10 32 "	196.7	Carbondale	7 18	8 05 "	.....
7 40	....	11 05 "	205.6	+ Cardiff	7 00	7 45 "	.....
8 00	....	11 20 P M	209.0	+ Glenwood Springs	6 35	7 20 "	.....
8 40	....	12 01 Night	221.1	+ New Castle	6 00	6 45 "	.....
9 08	....	12 28 Night	235.1	Rifle	5 30	6 05 "	.....
9 41	....	1 01 A M	252.4	Grand Valley	4 57	5 31 "	.....
10 03	....	1 23 "	265.1	De Beque	4 33	5 05 "	.....
10 46	....	2 09 "	285.0	Palisade	3 52	4 22 "	.....
11 10	....	2 35 "	298.0	ar. + Grand Junction lv.	3 30	*4 00 P M	.....
12 55	....	3 27 "	308.9	Fruita	2 47	....	.....
12 04	....	3 34 "	314.1	Loma	2 27	....	.....
3 05	...	6 35 "	403.6	Green River	11 30	....	.....
5 46	....	9 20 A M	474.9	Helper	9 30	....	.....
8 30	....	1 02 P M	545.0	Provo	6 05	....	.....
10 55	...	2 30 "	589.5	Salt Lake	4 50	....	.....
12 10	....	3 45 P M	626.4	Ogden	*3 30	....	.....
Night	....	....	.....	ARRIVE / LEAVE	P M	....	.....

It was also decided to retire the small class 93 ten-wheelers 23, 24, and 25, as they could no longer handle the heavier passenger trains of the era. These three engines had generally been assigned to the "alkali district" between Cardiff and Grand Junction, which had the easiest grades on the railroad and the lightest trains under normal conditions. With the exception of engine No. 35, which had been destroyed when it blew up at Basalt in 1896, these were the first motive power retirements since the railroad's inception.

1915

As mentioned above, the Midland again took off Nos. 3 and 4 during the winter of 1914–15. The schedule dated January 10th showed that No. 5 left Colorado Springs at 12:20 PM, the same as it had during the summer of 1914, and arrived in Grand Junction at the same time of 2:35 AM. Eastbound No. 6 stayed on the 4 PM departure time from Grand Junction but was 45 minutes longer reaching Colorado Springs at 6:50 AM. The sleeper on Nos. 5 and 6 was changed to a standard 12-section car form the observation sleeper that they carried during the summer months. This was the only sleeper mentioned, as the Denver-Leadville car was not carried on "daylight" train No. 5 from Denver to the cloud city. The diners again were handled westbound in No. 5 from Wild Horse to Arkansas Junction and eastbound in No. 6 from Grand Junction to Cardiff, so the quandary remains as to how these cars were actually moved.

The CM/MT route dropped the Colorado Springs-Cripple Creek through train for the winter; at least it was discontinued in the schedule but was still shown in the equipment listing. This was the first time since the Midland Terminal was built in 1896 that through service had been discontinued over the CM/MT route between the two cities, but there was evidently not enough passenger traffic in the winter to support two trains each way daily. The business that was available was left to the Short Line, as that road continued one train each way daily. A note in the schedule columns said that Nos. 3 and 4 would be reinstated about April 1st, but there was no such note with respect to Nos. 11 and 8. They did reappear during the summer, however, but were destined to be discontinued each winter until the CM ceased operation.

The April 11th schedule restored Nos. 3, 4, 8 and 11 for the summer season. No. 5 was on almost the same schedule as the previous year, but No. 4 was set back to a 5 AM departure,, although D&RG No. 2 arrived Grand Junction at 3:20 AM which resulted in a layover of one hour 40 minutes. Arrival of No. 4 was now 6:45 PM at Colorado Springs, with an eventual arrival in Denver at 9:30 PM. No. 3 was also set back, to a 10:45 PM departure from Colorado Springs, and did not arrive in Grand Junction until 12:30 PM. No. 6 still left at the traditional 4 PM, and for the first time in several years, listed a D&RG connection from the west. This was off D&RG No. 16, which arrived in Grand Junction at 12:01 PM, so the connection was not a close one. No. 6 also lost another 45 minutes on its run, and did not arrive in Colorado Springs until 6:50 AM. The running time of 14 hours 50 minutes was almost four hours longer than it had taken in 1900!

The Colorado Springs-Cripple Creek service also received minor adjustments, with No. 11 leaving 25 minutes later at 7 PM and No. 8 leaving Cripple Creek 15 minutes later at 8 AM. With No. 3 now running over an hour later than it had in the previous year, the Aspen Branch mixed train was correspondingly later, with arrival at Aspen listed for 10:40 AM. The return left that mountain community at 6:30 PM one hour later than in the summer of 1914. There was no change on the Jerome Park Branch.

The equipment assigned to the trains was similar to the previous year, although No. 4's listing showed "Breakfast, luncheon and supper in the Dining Car," which is curious, since westbound No. 5 still had the diner operating only between Wild Horse and Leadville. Just how the railroad was able to protect all three meals in No. 4 is a question that has yet to be answered.

For the first time in the Official Guide, there was a listing and mileage shown for Hell Gate, and this schedule is the only one where time there was shown for all four mainline trains. Some of the questions raised in this context are discussed in the section on Colorado Midland mileages.

The wildflower special was operated during the summer season on a train order schedule which was identical in timing as the one listed for 1914. An example is train order No. 11, of July 8th, 1915, at Colorado City, addressed to C & E Engine 39. Evidently, engine 39 was more or less assigned to the special that season, as it is mentioned several times in engineer Hartzog's records. While 1915 was not a good year for him as an engineer (he spent a great deal of time in the Colorado City yards, running switch engines 100 and 102), he did catch several trips on the helper for the wildflower train, and engine 39 was the road engine in all cases.

On August 6th, he had engine 27 and helped special 39 to Divide, returning light to Colorado City. On the 15th, he had engine 14, and helped the wildflower train all the way from Colorado City to Spinney and return. The next day, August 16th, he drew engine 27 and again went as far as Divide as the helper for the special. He tied up at Colorado City at 12:35 PM, but went back to work that evening at 7 PM with engine 102. He switched in the yards until 6 AM, August 17th. He was called right out at 9:15 AM, with engine 27 to help the wildflower train to Divide and finally tied up for that day at 12:45 PM at Colorado City. On the 18th, he made a turn to Wild Horse, with D&RG 754 as a helper on first No. 5. On the 20th, he started out again on another cycle, with the helper on the wildflower train to Divide with No. 27, then spent 11 hours that evening on engine 100 in the Colorado City yards. On the 21st, he again had engine 14 and helped the special 39 to Divide.

The helper trip on the 21st was the last where he assisted engine 39, for, on the 27th, special 39 east, returning from Spinney, had a head-on collision with No. 43, a freight train with engines 36 and 32, near Idlewild. According to accident report No. 291, the only one dealing with the CM in the ICC files, the collision was caused by the crew of special 39 east overlooking a train order directing them to wait at Idlewild. They mistook it to read "Lidderdale" and passed the siding where they should have waited for No. 43. Due to this accident, engineer Hartzog was called for 3:25 PM on the 27th with engine 202 and handled the wrecker from Colorado City to MP 48. They worked through the night clearing up the wreckage and then tied up at Florissant at 7:05 AM on the 28th.

The schedule issued December 12th again discontinued the operation of Nos. 3, 4, 8 and 11, leaving Nos. 5 and 6 as the only passenger trains on the railroad. Once again a note in the schedule columns stated that the trains would be reinstated about April 1916, which they were. No. 5, the lone westbound passenger train, now left Colorado Springs at 12:20 PM, the same as under the prior schedule and was due in Grand Junction at 2:30 AM, ten minutes earlier than in the past. There was no change in the time of No. 6. No. 5 now carried a through 12-section, one-drawing-room standard sleeper from Denver to Salt Lake City, instead of the observation sleeping car that had previously gone through to Ogden. This car returned in No. 6, again with the four-hour layover in Grand Junction.

The operation of the dining cars continued to be an enigma under this schedule, as No. 5 still had a diner from Wild Horse to Leadville, and No. 6 from Grand Junction to Cardiff. It seems that it would have been uneconomic to operate two cars, requiring deadhead movements, no matter how the arrangement was worked out. Both trains advertised serving the evening meal in the diner. As they met east of Thomasville, this would preclude the transfer of cars between trains. If the equipment listing means what it says, it appears that No. 6 would move a deadhead car off No. 5 from Arkansas Junction to Wild Horse to position it for the next day, and that No. 5 would have to deadhead No. 6's car from Cardiff to Grand Junction for the same purpose. Of course, it would be possible to deadhead the diners back to their originating stations in freight trains..

Since there was no longer a morning connection from Basalt to Aspen, off the discontinued No. 3, the mixed train was given its own listing as No. 75, leaving Basalt at 8:25 AM, and arriving in Apsen at 9:40 AM. Eastbound, No. 78 was shown out of Aspen at 5:30 PM, with the estimated arrival at Basalt about 6:40 PM for the connection with No. 6.

One wonders why the Colorado Midland continued to schedule No. 5 as the only westbound train during the winter months. The normal pairings of trains for many years had been Nos. 5 and 4, and Nos. 3 and 6, yet for several winters the CM ran Nos. 5 and 6 for some unknown reason. If it was desired to maintain the through sleeping car to Utah, No. 5 provided that service with its close connections at Grand Junction. But this arrangement was not as convenient in the eastbound direction, with the four-hour layover at Grand Junction in order for the car to connect with No. 6. Whatever the reasons for this peculiar operation were, they are lost in the passage of time and perhaps will never be explained.

As far as the equipment roster was concerned, the Colorado City shops rebuilt chair cars 251 and 252 into day coaches. This was the only major work undertaken during the year.

1916

The schedule for May 7th restored Nos. 3 and 4, with the former on the same schedule as during the summer of 1915. No. 5, also maintained the same timings as it had during the winter. There was a significant change, however, in the eastbound schedules for both trains. No. 4 now left Grand Junction at 1:55 AM, or three hours 15 minutes earlier and was due in Colorado Springs at 3 PM, with a correspondingly earlier arrival at Denver of 5:50 PM. After a traditional departure of 4 PM for the prior ten years (except for the winter of 1912–13), No. 6 now left Grand Junction at 2:15 PM and advertised a western connection from the D&RG, although there was still a layover of two hours 15 minutes. The CM night train now was due in Colorado Springs at 3:50 AM, with a Denver connection due there at 7 AM. This was an awkward arrival at Colorado Springs, but it was evident that the train was scheduled for the Denver trade.

The through Colorado Springs-Cripple Creek service was also restored with this timetable, and both Nos. 11 and 8 operated on the same schedule as during the summer of 1915. The single round trip mixed train continued to suffice for the Aspen business; No. 3's connection now arrived there at 9:40 AM, one hour earlier, and No. 6's connection left at 5 PM, one hour 30 minutes earlier. There was no change on the Jerome Park Branch with the usual morning trip to Gulch and the afternoon trip to Sunlight.

The equipment listing showed that the Denver-Leadville sleeper was restored and handled in Nos. 3 and 6 as in the past. These trains still handled the Denver-Grand Junction sleeper as well. Nos. 5 and 4 again carried the observation sleeper between Denver and Ogden, which was directed at attracting the tourist business. The dining car service now required two cars, each one staying overnight at Leadville and Ruedi, and operating as follows:

No. 3 - Leadville to Cardiff, serving breakfast.
No. 6 - Cardiff to Ruedi, serving supper.
No. 4 - Ruedi to Florissant, serving breakfast and lunch.
No. 5 - Florissant to Leadville, serving supper.

No. 5's passengers were still advised to secure lunch at the Fred Harvey restaurant in the Colorado Springs station.

The wildflower special continued to operate on a train order schedule during the summer, and the timings in the order were identical with those during 1914 and 1915. This was exemplified in train order No. 13, July 6, 1916, at Colorado Springs, Colo., to C & E Engine 27. The only trip Ed Hartzog worked this season was on August 8th, when he had engine 202 and assisted special 27 from Colorado City all the way to Spinney and return. He was on duty at 9:15 AM and tied up at 6 PM. The use of a 200-class engine would indicate that this was a particularly heavy day for the wildflower train.

A new schedule, dated August 10th, was published in the October Guide, and the only change was the elimination of the afternoon trip form Cardiff to Sunlight on the Jerome Park Branch. On November 19th, the winter schedule took effect. Nos. 5 and 4 were discontinued, as well as Nos. 11 and 8 to and from Cripple Creek. No. 3 continued to leave Colorado Springs at 10:45 PM but took a half-hour longer to reach Grand Junction, being due there at 1 PM. No. 6 also took 30 minutes longer, still leaving Grand Junction at 2:15 PM and due in Colorado Springs at 4:20 AM. The Denver arrival was still 7 AM.

The note concerning train Nos. 5 and 4 stated: "Trains

COLORADO MIDLAND RAILROAD
FORM OF TRAIN ORDER COVERING WILDFLOWER SPECIAL TRAIN

Order No. 13, July 6, 1916, at Colorado Springs, Colo.

To C&E *Eng. 27*

Engine *27* will run special, Colorado Springs to Spinney and return to Colorado Springs, leaving Colorado Springs *July 6, 1916* as follows, with right over all except First-class trains:

Leave	Colorado Springs	900 AM	Leave	Spinney	1240 PM
"	Colorado City	915 AM	"	Howbert	1252 PM
"	Manitou	925 AM	"	Idlewild	100 PM
"	Crags	940 AM	"	Springer	110 PM
"	Cascade	958 AM	"	Lidderdale	125 PM
"	Culver	1003 AM	"	Lake George	133 PM
"	Green Mtn. Falls	1015 AM	"	Metcalf	140 PM
"	Bison	1025 AM	"	Florissant	145 PM
"	Woodland	1035 AM	"	Pisgah	233 PM
"	Edlowe	1047 AM	"	Bellevue	250 PM
"	Divide	1100 AM	"	Divide	305 PM
"	Bellevue	1105 AM	"	Edlowe	315 PM
"	Pisgah	1115 AM	"	Woodland	355 PM
"	Florissant	1125 AM	"	Bison	400 PM
"	Metcalf	1130 AM	"	Green Mtn. Falls	405 PM
"	Lake George	1134 AM	"	Culver	410 PM
"	Lidderdale	1140 AM	"	Cascade	418 PM
"	Springer	1150 AM	"	Crags	425 PM
"	Idlewild	1201PM	"	Manitou	436 PM
"	Howbert	1210 PM	"	Colorado City	445 PM
Arrive	Spinney	1220 PM	Arrive	Colorado Springs	500 PM

AFH

(This schedule indicates that only service stops were made on the westbound trip, while sightseeing stops were made at Lidderdale, Pisgah and Woodland on the eastbound trip.)

THE COLORADO MIDLAND RAILWAY.

GEO. W. VALLERY, Receiver, Denver, Colo.
HENRY T. ROGERS, General Solicitor, "
H. L. HOBBS, Treasurer, "
L. A. RAFERT, General Freight Agent, "
C. H. SPEERS, General Passenger Agent, "
W. S. WING, Auditor, "
GEO. L. LINNEY, Car Accountant, "
M. L. PHELPS, Superintendent, Colorado City, Colo.
J. R. GROVES, Superintendent of Machinery, "
V. B. WAGNER, Chief Engineer, "
C. N. DAVIDS, Gen. Storekeeper and Purchasing Agt., "
F. H. McNAUGHT, Chief Surgeon, Denver, Colo.

Aspen, Colo.—W. L. GRAVES, Agent.
Buena Vista, Colo.—H. KIRKPATRICK, Agent.
Chicago, Ill.—350 Marquette Building—H. W. JACKSON, Gen. Agent.
C. E. WEBB, Traveling Freight and Passenger Agent.
N. B. WOOD, Soliciting Freight and Passenger Agent.
Colorado Springs, Colo.—121 East Pikes Peak Avenue—
H. E. GARDNER, General Agent.
Denver, Colo.—714 Seventeenth Street—
C. D. PEIRCE, City Passenger Agt. E. D. WHITLEY, City Ticket Agt.
Glenwood Springs, Colo.—C. M. KECK, General Agent.
S. J. LOWE, Depot Agent.
Grand Jn., Colo.—R. E. VICKERY, Gen. Agt. B. E. GREGORY, Depot Agt.
Kansas City, Mo.—566 Sheidley Bldg—M. R. SUTTON, General Agent.
Leadville, Colo.—C. B. CARTER, Agent.
Los Angeles, Cal.—Room 216, 702 South Spring Street—
MALONE JOYCE, General Agent.
New York, N.Y.—Room 1322, Woolworth Building, 233 Broadway—
F. N. DOWLER, General Eastern Agent.
Omaha, Neb.—411 First National Bank Bldg, 13th and Farnham Sts.—
P. J. MURPHY, General Agent.
Pittsburg, Pa.—838 Oliver Building—C. A. CREITZ, General Agent.
Salt Lake City, Utah—523 Judge Bldg—J. H. DAVIS, General Agent.
San Francisco, Cal.—291 Monadnock Bldg—C. L. BROWN, Gen. Agt.
F. C. THOMPSON, Traveling Freight and Passenger Agent.

3	▲11	No. 5	Mls.	*May 7, 1916.*	4	No. 6	▲8
P M	P M	....	.....	LEAVE] [ARRIVE	P M	....	P M
*7 45	*3 30	*9 00 A M	.....	+ .... **Denver** .... ♂	6 50	7 00 A M	2 15
6 40	6 40	9 45 A M	.....	+ .... **Pueblo** .... ♂	4 05	1 00 P M	1 00
P M	P M	....	.....	LEAVE] [ARRIVE	P M	....	A M
*10 45	*7 00	*12 20 Noon	.0	+ ‖ **Colorado Springs** .. ♂	3 00	3 50 A M	11 05
[illegible]	[illegible]	[illegible]	[illegible]	...... Colorado City ...... ♂	[illegible]	[illegible]	[illegible]
11 07	7 20	12 45 Noon	6.1	+ .... **Manitou** .... ♂	2 41	3 31 "	10 41
11 40	7 45	1 15 P M	11.5	.... Cascade .... ♂	2 23	3 13 "	10 23
11 50	7 57	1 30 "	14.9	...... Green Mt. Falls	2 10	3 00 "	10 10
12 07	8 10	2 00 "	20.0	.... Woodland .... ♂	2 00	2 50 "	10 00
12 30	8 30	2 30 P M	26.9	arr. ...... **Divide** ♂ ..... lve.	1 45	2 35 A M	9 45
.....	8 30	....	26.9	lve. **Divide** (Mid. Term. Ry.) arr.	.....	....	9 45
.....	8 50	....	51.6	.... **Victor** ...... "	.....	....	8 23
.....	10 10	....	56.9	arr. **Cripple Creek.** " lve.	.....	....	*8 00
12 30	P M	2 30 P M	26.9	lve. ...... **Divide** ♂ ..... arr.	1 45	2 35 A M	A M
12 55	....	2 55 "	35.8	.... Florissant .... ♂	1 05	2 00 "	.....
1 05	....	3 10 "	40.3	.... Lake George	12 55	1 50 "	
1 50		3 53 "	57.7	.... Spinney	12 20	1 10 A M	
2 17		4 18 "	68.9	.... Hartsel .... ♂	12 01	12 50 Night	
3 13		5 15 "	90.3	.... Newett .... ♂	11 10	12 03 Night	
3 45		5 40 "	100.9	+ ..... **Buena Vista** ..... ♂	10 31	11 21 P M	
4 35		6 21 "	118.2	.... Granite .... ♂	9 51	10 41 "	
5 15		7 05 "	133.5	arr. Arkansas Junction ♂ lve.	9 20	10 10 "	
5 40		7 30 "	137.3	arr. .... + **Leadville** ♂ ... lve.	8 55	9 45 "	
5 00		6 50 "	137.3	lve. ...... **Leadville** ..... arr.	9 35	10 25 "	
5 25		7 15 "	133.5	lve. Arkansas Junction ♂ arr.	9 10	10 00 "	
6 05		7 55 "	141.7	.... Busk .... ♂	8 45	8 35 "	
6 15		8 05 "	143.7	.... Ivanhoe .... ♂	8 35	8 25 "	
- -		- -	149.7	.... Hell Gate	- -	- -	
7 12		9 06 "	165.2	.... Thomasville ..... ♂	6 45	7 30 "	
8 10		10 05 P M	185.3	arr. ...... **Basalt** ♂ ..... lve.	5 45	6 20 P M	
9 40		....	203.7	arr. .... + **Aspen** ♂ ..... lve.	A M	*6 00 P M	
A M		*5 00 P M	203.7	lve. ...... **Aspen** ...... arr.	9 40	....	
8 10		10 05 P M	185.3	lve. ...... **Basalt** ♂ ..... arr.	5 45	6 20 P M	
8 36		10 33 "	196.7	.... Carbondale ...... ♂	5 22	5 57 "	
9 10		11 05 "	205.6	+ .... **Cardiff** .... ♂	5 05	5 40 "	
9 25		11 20 "	209.0	+ ... Glenwood Springs ... ♂	4 45	5 15 "	
9 37		11 32 "	213.3	.... South Canon	4 34	5 03 "	
9 55		11 50 "	219.4	.... Vulcan	4 20	4 50 "	
10 00		11 55 P M	221.1	+ ..... New Castle ...... ♂	4 15	4 45 "	
10 13		12 09 Night	227.9	.... Silt	4 01	4 30 "	
[illegible]		12 22 "	[illegible]	.... **Rifle** .... ♂	3 48	4 16 "	
11 00		12 51 Night	252.4	...... Grand Valley ...... ♂	[illegible]	[illegible]	
11 24		1 13 A M	265.1	.... De Beque ...... ♂	2 50	3 18 "	
12 04		1 59 "	285.9	.... Palisade	2 19	2 38 "	
12 30		2 30 "	298.0	arr. + **Grand Junction** ♂ lve.	1 55	2 15 P M	
- -		3 28 "	308.9	.... Fruita	12 52	11 33 A M	
- -		3 34 "	314.1	.... Loma	12 42	11 24 "	
4 40		6 30 "	403.6	...... Green River	9 55	7 55 "	
6 37		9 25 A M	474.9	.... Helper	7 35	5 35 "	
8 54		12 48 Noon	545.0	.... **Provo**	4 04	1 53 A M	
8 55		2 10 P M	589.5	...... **Salt Lake** ...... ♂	2 45	12 30 Night	
11 00	....	3 25 P M	626.4	.... **Ogden** .... ♂	*1 25	*11 00 P M	
P M	....	....	.....	ARRIVE] [LEAVE	P M	....	.....

• Daily; † daily, except Sunday. ‖ Meal stations. + Coupon stations; ♂ Telegraph stations. STANDARD—*Mountain time.*

▲ Trains Nos. 8 and 11 connect from Denver and Pueblo via Atch. Top. & Santa Fe Ry., Colo. & So. Ry. and Denver & Rio Grande R.R.

HELL GATE—CROSSING THE CONTINENTAL DIVIDE.
THE BACKBONE OF THE AMERICAN CONTINENT.

Jerome Park Branch.—Train leaves Cardiff †7 00 a.m., arriving Gulch (15 miles) 9 30 a.m. Returning, leaves Gulch †10 00 a.m., arriving Cardiff 11 30 a.m. Leaves Cardiff for Sunlight (7 miles) †1 00 p.m. Returning, leaves Sunlight †3 00 p.m.

TRAIN SERVICE AND EQUIPMENT.

WESTBOUND.

No. 3—Western Express.—Solid Through Train Denver to Grand Junction. Carries First-class Chair Car and Modern Electric-lighted, Steam-heated, 12-Section Drawing-room Pullman Sleeping Car Denver to Grand Junction. Modern Electric-lighted, Steam-heated, 12-Section Pullman Sleeping Car Denver to Leadville. Dining Car Leadville to Cardiff, serving breakfast (meals a la carte). Connects at Grand Junction with D. & R. G. train No. 15 for all points west thereof to and including Salt Lake City, Ogden and beyond.

No. 5—Pacific Express.—Solid Through Train Denver to Grand Junction. Carries Modern Electric-lighted, Steam-heated, Observation Parlor Pullman Sleeping Car Denver to Ogden, via Salt Lake City. First-class Chair Car Denver to Grand Junction. Luncheon at Fred Harvey Eating House, Colorado Springs. Dining Car Florissant to Leadville, serving supper (meals a la carte). Connects at Grand Junction with D. & R. G. train No. 5 for all points west thereof to and including Salt Lake City, Ogden and beyond.

No. 11—Denver-Cripple Creek Express.—Solid Through Train Colorado Springs to Cripple Creek, connecting with all lines at Colorado Springs from Denver, Pueblo and all Eastern and Western points.

EASTBOUND.

No. 4—Eastern Express.—Solid Through Train Grand Junction to Denver. Carries Modern Electric-lighted, Steam-heated, Observation Pullman Parlor Sleeping Car Ogden to Denver, via Salt Lake City, connecting with D. & R. G. train No. 4, leaving Ogden 1 25 p.m. First-class Chair Car Grand Junction to Denver. Dining Car Ruedi to Florissant, serving breakfast and luncheon (meals a la carte).

No. 6—Denver Express.—Solid Through Train Grand Junction to Denver. Connects at Grand Junction with D. & R. G. train No. 16 from the West. Carries First-class Chair Car and Modern Electric-lighted, Steam-heated, 12-Section Drawing-room Pullman Sleeping Car Grand Junction to Denver. Modern Electric-lighted, Steam-heated, 12-Section Drawing-room Pullman Sleeping Car Leadville to Denver. Dining Car Cardiff to Ruedi, serving supper (meals a la carte).

No. 8—Cripple Creek-Denver Express.—Solid Through Train Cripple Creek to Colorado Springs, connecting with all lines at Colorado Springs for Denver, Pueblo and all Eastern and Western points.

STOP-OVER PRIVILEGES.—Stop-over privileges will be allowed at all points on the Colorado Midland Ry. on passes and on all through tickets the limit of which will permit, regardless of the conditions of the ticket, whether stamped "Continuous Passage," "No Stop-overs Allowed," etc., or not, provided there is a final limit on one-way tickets or a transit limit on round-trip tickets of sufficient length to enable the passenger to make the stop-over desired, resume the journey and reach destination within said final or transit limit; on condition, however, that the passenger assumes all risk of ticket expiring in his hands beyond our own lines.

CONNECTIONS.—Denver, in Union Depot—With Atch. Top. & S. Fe Ry., Chic. Burl. & Quincy Ry., Chic. Rk. Isl. & Pac. Ry., Union Pac. R.R. and Colo. & So. Ry. **Colorado Springs**—With Chic. Rk. Isl. & Pac. Ry., Atch. Top. & S. Fe Ry. and Colo. & So. Ry. **Manitou**—With Manitou & Pike's Peak Ry. **Divide**—With Mid. Term. Ry. for Victor, Cripple Creek, etc. **Buena Vista**—With Colo. & So. Ry. and with stage lines. **Grand Junction**—With Denver & Rio Grande R.R. and Grand Junction and Grand River Valley Ry.

5 and 6 (sic), service discontinued during Winter months—will be reinstated during Summer, 1917". Unfortunately, this was a false promise, as Nos. 5 and 4 would never again reappear. Thus, after 21 years (except for a few winter schedules of the recent past, when one train each way had been sufficient), the double-daily train service of the CM had come to a close. The era of the tourist-oriented "day" trains was over. Under the current operation, a westbound train arriving Grand Junction at 2:30 AM and an eastbound train departing at 1:55 AM could hardly be called "day" trains when a great portion of their trips were conducted during darkness.

The connection for the Aspen Branch from No. 3 now arrived in Aspen at 10:10 AM with the 5 PM departure remaining for the connection with No. 6 at Basalt. Curiously, the Jerome Park Branch witnessed a significant speed-up in its schedule, with the morning run form Cardiff to Gulch now taking only one hour 30 minutes, a full hour faster than the traditional schedules. The return run was also faster by 15 minutes, indicating that the coal business on this branch had declined to the point where these mixed trains were handling negligible traffic as compared to previous years. The round trip was now scheduled for less than four hours, leaving Cardiff at 7:30 AM and being due back in town by 11:15 AM.

The equipment on Nos. 3 and 6 continued as it had during the summer season, with the exception of the diner. Now one car sufficed being in the trains only between Ruedi and Cardiff to protect breakfast for No. 3 and supper for No. 6. This arrangement allowed only about an hour and a half for the meals to be served in each direction. It should also be noted that under this schedule, there were no advertised connections west of Grand Junction. In effect, Nos. 3 and 6 were now strictly local Colorado Midland schedules and no longer catered to any through passengers.

During the year, in spite of continued financial problems, the shops at Colorado City managed to build three new combined RPO-coaches with steel underframes—the only passenger cars so equipped on the CM. These were numbered 260 through 262 and effectively replaced the all-wood RPO cars that had been used in this service. This was done upon the instructions of the Post Office which the railroad to provide this type of car or lose the mail business. Most roads were already furnishing all-steel RPO cars. Perhaps the Midland was able to compromise the situation by building steel underframe cars due to the condition of its finances, and the state of the roadbed, although all-steel baggage and express cars of other roads had been routinely handled over the line for several years. There was no change in motive power during the year.

1917

The schedule for November 19, 1916 remained in effect until June 24, 1917, as it was still being listed in the Official Guide for June. In the meantime, certain events occurred that would have a significant effect on the Colorado Midland. On January 20th, the Colorado Springs, Divide and Cripple Creek RPO was discontinued, which was a delayed action since the train had not run since the middle of the previous November. Now the RPO was handled only by the Short Line between Colorado Springs and Cripple Creek. On February 4th, the Colorado Springs and Grand Junction RPO was again cut back to the Colorado Springs and Glenwood Springs RPO. It is assumed that the car handled closed pouches west of Glenwood Springs to Grand Junction as it had in 1911.

The main event affecting the Colorado Midland occurred on April 21st when the road was sold at foreclosure. A.E. Carlton and associates were the successful bidders. The name of the railroad was changed to Colorado Midland *Railroad*, and Spencer Penrose was named chairman of the board, with Carlton as president. The new management immediately started a program of rehabilitation, primarily involving the roadbed which was rapidly reaching an advanced state of decay. The Carlton management also had plans for the extension of the line to Salt Lake City, as well as for improved motive power and rolling stock. The full story has been well documented elsewhere.

The new company issued its timetable No. 1, on June 24th, which has been reproduced in *The Timetable Collector* for October 1972. This schedule called for a single through train in each direction, Nos. 3 and 6, as had been the practice of the former management. No. 3 was due to leave Colorado Springs at 10:55 PM and, if all went well, was to arrive Grand Junction by 12:30 PM. No. 6 left Grand Junction at 1:45 PM and, 14 hours 25 minutes later, was due in Colorado Springs at 4:10 AM, with the connecting train due in Denver at 7:30 AM. The through Colorado Springs-Cripple Creek service was restored for the summer, with No. 11 leaving Colorado Springs at 7 PM and reaching Cripple Creek at 10:10 PM. No. 8 left Cripple Creek at 8 AM and was due in Colorado Springs at 11:05 AM.

One interesting aspect was that the wildflower special was put in the timetable as trains 9 and 10. Westbound, No. 9 left Colorado Springs at the traditional 9 AM and, after making six regular stops and 4 flag stops, was due in Spinney at 12:20 PM. After turning No. 10 was out of there at 12:40 PM, scheduled for seven regular and five flag stops, with arrival in Colorado Springs at 5 PM. The westbound schedule was almost identical to the train order that had been in effect the previous three years, but there were some changes eastbound for No. 10. The main item was that 50 minutes were allowed from leaving Edlowe at 2:55 PM to leaving Woodland at 3:45 PM, a distance of 3.3 miles. This indicates a rather lengthy stop at Woodland.

On the Aspen Branch, mixed No. 75 left Basalt at 8:30 AM and was due in Aspen at 9:45 AM. After spending the day performing whatever switching chores were required, the crew returned as mixed train No. 78, leaving at 4:50 PM and due in Basalt at 6 PM to connect with No. 6 at 6:15 PM. There were no scheduled trains listed for the Jerome Park Branch, but the round trip from Cardiff to Gulch in the morning and the afternoon trip to and from Sunlight were operating as extras. The public schedule showed the train leaving Cardiff at 7 AM, except Sunday, and arriving at Gulch at 9:30 AM. The return trip left at 10 AM and was due in Cardiff at 11:30 AM. The afternoon trip was listed from Cardiff at 1 PM, except Sunday, and turned at Sunlight leaving at 3 PM.

The September 1917 Guide showed a timetable dated August 12th, but there were no changes in either schedules or equipment form that of June 24th. Nos. 3 and 6 were still handling both the Leadville and Grand Junction sleepers, and the diner was still operating between Ruedi and Cardiff. Also, no connection was advertised west of Grand Junction for either train during this summer.

Back in 1915, the Carlton interests, in the name of the Cripple Creek & Colorado Springs Railroad, had taken over the remaining lines of the Florence & Cripple Creek and the Golden Circle, and on May 1, 1915, had leased the Colorado Springs & Cripple Creek District Railway (The Short Line). With all of the Cripple Creek roads except the Midland Terminal under one management, and in control of the Colorado Midland as of 1917, it was only natural that the MT should be included within the Carlton empire. Accordingly, on July 22, 1917, the Cripple Creek & Colorado Springs Railroad leased the Midland Terminal and, on the same date, acquired trackage rights over the Colorado Midland between Colorado Springs and Divide. This was like granting yourself the right to operate over your own railroad, but it did have some ramifications.

Ever since the Midland Terminal had been constructed, the agreement with the Colorado Midland called for the CM to operate through passenger trains with its own equipment, crews and motive power, and this contract had remained in effect up into 1917. The freight operation had been a horse of a different color, as this traffic had traditionally been interchanged at Divide. MT trains would come out of the District to Divide where outgoing cars would be dropped and incoming ones for the District would be picked up. The Colorado Midland, on the other hand, had trains from Colorado City make Divide turnarounds to handle the MT traffic, and, frequently, Florissant turns would also handle this business. Engineer Hartzog's records contain many instances where he ran extra from Colorado City to Divide and return, as well as from Colorado City to Florissant and return, and it is presumed that much of the traffic handled by these extras was in connection with the Midland Terminal.

No. 3	Mls.	*November 18, 1917.*	No. 6
		LEAVE] [ARRIVE	
*7 45 P M		+ ....**Denver**........ ♁	7 00 A M
5 40 P M		+ ....**Pueblo**........ ♁	1 00 P M
		LEAVE] [ARRIVE	
*10 55 P M	0	+ ..**Colorado Springs**.. ♁	4 00 A M
11 10 »	3.0	+ .....Colorado City..... ♁	3 48 »
11 21 »	6.1	+ ....**Manitou**........ ♁	3 38 »
11 58 P M	11.5	..........Cascade.......... ♁	3 20 »
12 12 Night	14.9	......Green Mt. Falls......	3 10 »
12 32 »	20.0	.........Woodland......... ♁	3 00 »
12 57 Night	26.9	arr.........**Divide** ♁ ....lve.	2 45 A M
	26.9	lve. **Divide** (C. C. & C. S. R.R.) arr.	
	51.6	....**Victor**...... »	
	56.9	arr. **Cripple Creek.** » lve.	
12 57 Night	26.9	lve.........**Divide** ♁.....arr.	2 45 A M
1 25 A M	35.8	.........Florissant........ ♁	2 05 »
1 34 »	40.3	.......Lake George.......	1 45 »
2 25 »	57.7	..........Spinney..........	1 04 A M
2 52 »	68.9	..........Hartsel.......... ♁	12 43 Night
3 47 »	90.3	..........Newett.......... ♁	11 49 P M
4 17 »	100.9	+ .....**Buena Vista**..... ♁	11 01 »
5 07 »	118.2	..........Granite.......... ♁	10 23 »
5 48 »	133.5	arr. Arkansas Junction ♁ lve.	9 50 »
6 05 »	137.3	arr....+ **Leadville** ♁ ...lve.	9 25 »
5 25 »	137.3	lve......**Leadville**.....arr.	10 05 »
5 58 »	133.5	lve. Arkansas Junction ♁ arr.	9 40 »
6 40 »	141.7	............Busk............ ♁	9 15 »
6 50 »	143.7	..........Ivanhoe.......... ♁	9 05 »
7 20 »	153.7	...........Sellar...........	8 06 »
7 28 »	157.7	............Nast............	7 38 »
7 45 »	165.2	........Thomasville........ ♁	7 04 »
8 02 »	170.2	...........Ruedi...........	6 40 »
8 45 A M	185.3	arr.........**Basalt** ♁ .....lve.	5 50 P M
10 10 A M	203.7	arr......+ **Aspen** ♁ .....lve.	*4 30 P M
8 45 A M	185.3	lve.........**Basalt** ♁ .....arr.	5 50 P M
9 10 »	196.7	........Carbondale........ ♁	5 20 »
9 45 »	205.6	+ ....**Cardiff**......... ♁	5 00 »
10 00 »	209.0	+ ...Glenwood Springs... ♁	4 39 »
10 11 »	213.3	.......South Canon.......	4 24 »
10 30 »	221.1	+ ......New Castle...... ♁	4 05 »
10 43 »	227.9	............Silt............	3 48 »
10 58 »	235.1	...........**Rifle**........... ♁	3 29 »
11 30 »	252.4	.......Grand Valley....... ♁	2 55 »
11 54 A M	265.1	.........De Beque......... ♁	2 30 »
12 34 Noon	285.9	..........Palisade..........	1 48 »
1 00 P M	298.0	+ ...**Grand Junction**... ♁	*1 25 P M
		ARRIVE] [LEAVE	

EXPLANATION OF SIGNS.

Trains marked * run daily. ‖ Meal stations.
+ Coupon stations; ♁ Telegraph stations.
STANDARD—*Mountain time.*

Thus, the granting of trackage rights by the Colorado Midland to the Midland Terminal, through the CC&CS, now permitted Midland Terminal crews to operate to and from Colorado Springs (Colorado City in the case of freight trains). They could pass right through Divide as though it were all one railroad, except for the requirement to pick up orders and a clearance at that station. The contract with respect to the passenger trains was still in effect, as far as can be determined, but it is quite possible that the new agreement also made this service available to Midland Terminal employees.

Returning to the 1917 schedules, timetable No. 2 of the Colorado Midland Railroad went into effect on November 18th. No. 3 now left Colorado Springs at 10:55 PM, the same as before, but took a half-hour longer to reach Grand Junction, being due that point at 1 PM. No. 6 now left Grand Junction at 1:25 PM, 20 minutes earlier than in the summer, and arrived Colorado Springs at 4 AM, ten minutes earlier. These were the only passenger trains on the mainline, as No. 11 and 8 to and from Cripple Creek were discontinued for the winter. This had been the practice since late in 1915. The wildflower trains, Nos. 9 and 10, had also been discontinued with the end of the tourist season.

No. 75 on the Aspen Branch now left Basalt at 9 AM for a 10:10 AM arrival, at Aspen, while No. 78 returned at

4:30 PM with a 5:40 PM arrival at Basalt. For the first time since 1895, neither the operating nor the public timetables listed any service on the Jerome Park Branch, and the trackage was shown as cut back to Sunlight, 9.8 miles from Cardiff. The only other trains scheduled, other than through freight trains Nos. 41 and 42, were Nos. 31 and 32, through freights between Colorado Springs and Cripple Creek, evidently established because of the new trackage rights agreement between the MT and CM.

The equipment of the two through passenger trains was still the same as it had been during the summer months, with the sleepers for Leadville and Grand Junction and the diner between Ruedi and Cardiff. There were no connections listed west of Grand Junction, so the CM trains remained strictly a local operation between Denver and Colorado Midland stations.

As a result of the construction of the new steel underframe mail-RPO-coaches 260 through 262, the older cars were retired during the year. Thus cars 11, 257, 258 and 259 were all retired, bringing the car fleet down to 43 units. There was no change in motive power, and it remained at 63 locomotives.

Engineer Hartzog spent most of the year running helper engines out of Florissant. Later in the year he was transferred to Wild Horse, where he ran helpers up to Bath in one direction and to Arkansas Junction or Leadville in the other. As a result, he had no opportunity to run any passenger trains as a road engineer this year.

The joint use of the Allied Lines motive power during the last months of the Colorado Midland is illustrated by train 6 passing Bison (near Woodland Park) in 1918 behind Midland Terminal 2-8-0 No. 56. (Otto Perry, Denver Public Library Western History Dept.)

1918

This was destined to be the last year of Colorado Midland operations, and as previous histories have discussed the events leading up to the railroad's closure they will not be covered here. The schedule of November 18, 1917 was continued in effect until the road ceased operations, with the last No. 6 scheduled from Grand Junction on August 4th. In the index of the August 1918 Guide opposite the CM listing, was the terse statement "service discontinued" and no page number given. However, the November 18, 1917 schedule was still published on page 567. This indicates that information was received too late by the publishers to remove the schedules from the body of the Guide. They were effective for four days that month, so in context there was nothing wrong with the listing. Coincident with the cessation of passenger service on August 4th, the RPO operating between Colorado Springs and Glenwood Springs was cancelled and was replaced by a Colorado Springs-Cripple Creek RPO, which was handled by the Midland Terminal, as will be explained later.

Prior to the August demise of the Colorado Midland there were some matters of interest. The Cripple Creek & Colorado Springs Railroad and Midland Terminal Railway Consolidated issued timetable No. 1 on February 24, 1918. J.J. Cogan was listed as vice president; he was also the general manager of the Colorado Midland under the Carlton regime. Other joint officers included B. Johnson, trainmaster on the CM (later superintendent transportation, car service & telegraph) and superintendent of the Cripple Creek roads. Several members of the dispatching crew performed services for the consolidated operation.

The joint timetable No. 1 contained the schedules of the Midland Terminal but other than Nos. 20 and 21, the "hob-nail special" between Cripple Creek and Independence, listed only the new through freight trains. There were Nos. 31 and 32 between Divide and Cripple Creek which operated over the Colorado Midland. The Colorado Springs-Cripple Creek passenger service was provided by the Short Line Nos. 3 and 4, with the former leaving Colorado Springs at 11:50 AM and due in Cripple Creek at 2:55 PM. No. 4 left Cripple Creek at 3:50 PM, and was due in Colorado Springs by 6:35 PM. The bulk of the schedules shown in this timetable were for the high line and low line electric districts, which continued to provide a comprehensive service between Cripple Creek and Victor. Under the Carlton management it was the policy to have most of the freight traffic between Colorado Springs and Cripple Creek move over the CM/MT route, in order to provide as much revenue as possible for the Midland. The passenger trains were to be run via the more scenic Short Line and timetable No. 1 reflects this policy.

This situation changed when, on May 15, 1918, Short Line bridge No. 3-A over Bear Creek burned completely. This effectively cut the Short Line in two, and the one passenger train a day each way had to be diverted to the CM/MT route via Divide. As far as can be determined, this detour operation was not advertised in Colorado Midland schedules, and the operating timetable was not changed to reflect this additional passenger train between Colorado Springs and Divide. Perhaps it was felt at the time that the detour would be a temporary affair and that the bridge would be repaired shortly. The change could have been covered by a train order schedule, as had been used for the wildflower specials in 1914–1916 or a bulletin could have been issued covering this train as a special. The bridge, however, was not repaired promptly, and the trains continued to use the route via Divide until the middle of 1919, long after the Colorado Midland had ceased operation. Thus, during the last few months that the Midland operated, there was a through Colorado Springs-Cripple Creek passenger train run each way every day, but it was not shown on the schedule. Here again, the trackage rights agreement between the CM and MT could have come into play, and these trains could have been operated by MT crews. On the other hand, it is possible that the Short Line trains were handled in a regular detour manner, using Short Line crews with Midland Terminal pilots. The Short Line might have furnished motive power and equipment, with the trains handled by Midland Terminal crews. Morris Cafky, in *Rails Around Gold Hill*, published an Otto Perry photo on page 411, showing Short Line engine No. 8 being prepared for a run at the Colorado City enginehouse of the CM. It is possible that this was in preparation for a passenger trip to Cripple Creek. At any rate, it certainly appears that the Colorado Springs-Cripple Creek passenger service was operated over the CM/MT route during the period that the Short Line was out of service between May 15, 1918 and July 15, 1919. If for no other reason, this protected the mail contract.

This situation brings up another curiosity with respect to the schedules of the Colorado Springs-Cripple Creek trains and how they were published during this period. The Official Guides for June through September 1918 still showed the schedules via the Short Line under date of February 24th in consolidated timetable No. 1. In that same period, no schedule was shown for through trains over the Midland Terminal other than the "hob-nail special". This action, or lack of it, lends credence to the proposition that management felt the disruption to the Short Line's service on account of the bridge fire was a temporary matter and that there was no need to advertise the detour via Divide. The October 1918 Guide, however, did have the schedule of trains 3 and 4 between Colorado Springs and Cripple Creek via Divide. The times at the terminals were identical to those shown in the February 24th schedule, and it was dated simply "September 1918". This schedule was published under the name of "Cripple Creek & Colorado Springs RR and Leased Lines" and showed the Colorado Midland line between

Colorado Springs and Divide as though it were all one railroad. Nothing was listed for the Short Line route.

As all of the Pikes Peak region roads were being operated by the Carlton management, it was an easy matter to switch motive power of each to locations on any of the others where the engines would be most useful. Accordingly, MT and CS&CCD locomotives began showing up on the Colorado Midland and there are recorded instances when Colorado Midland engines were utilized by the Cripple Creek roads. According to Hartzog's records, Midland Terminal engines had started to be used by the CM as early as September 1917, as he used No. 13 to help extra MT 58 east from Wild Horse to Bath on September 19th. Both MT engines 55 and 58 showed up several times during the remainder of 1917 on his reports.

Since the Short Line's power was generally superior to many of the CM's own engines, it was used to supplement CM power. The first time that a CS&CCD engine showed up on Hartzog's records is on February 7th when he used CS&CCD engine No. 4 to help extra 53 east from Wild Horse to Bath. From that time until the railroad stopped operating in August, he ran every CS&CCD engine of the 2-8-0 group except No. 1. The last CS&CCD engine that he used was on July 10th, when he had No. 7 in helper service from Wild Horse to Ivanhoe. Midland Terminal engines started to show up in greater numbers in April 1918, and on successive trips between April 20th and 22nd, he had engines 56, 57, and 55 out of Wild Horse and Colorado City.

With the continued use of Short Line engines, it was decided to renumber the CM 1–10 series locomotives to avoid confusion and having to show "CS&CCD" Eng. __" in train orders, when such power was used. The first record of the renumbered engines in Hartzog's reports is on May 10th when he had both 67 and 68 (former 7 and 8) on a round trip helper job from Wild Horse to Arkansas Junction. Thereafter, it appears that engines 69 and 70 stayed pretty close to Wild Horse, as he caught them fairly regularly.

Hartzog continued to work out of Wild Horse, which had been established as the new division point for freight crews early in 1918 in order to equalize the mileage between the first and second districts. He worked both ways: eastbound to Bath regularly but sometimes all the way to Colorado City on helper jobs. Westbound, he was used on helper engines to Arkansas Junction, Leadville and Ivanhoe on a regular basis and, infrequently, went even farther west. This helper work, however, was always in connection with freight trains, and his last passenger run (or at least on a first class schedule) was when he had engine 10 on March 27th on second No. 6 from Wild Horse to Colorado City. His last run of all was with engine 53 as a helper for extra 303 east from Wild Horse to Bath, on duty at 7:15 PM August 8th. He tied up at Wild

No. 3	Mls.	November 1[illegible], 1917.	No. 8
		LEAVE] [ARRIVE	
*7 45 P M		+ .... Denver .... ♁	7 00 A M
4 55 P M		+ .... Pueblo .... ♁	12 30 Noon
		LEAVE] [ARRIVE	
*10 55 P M	0	+ ... Colorado Springs .. ♁	4 00 A M
11 10 "	3.0	+ ..... Colorado City ..... ♁	3 43 "
11 21 "	6.1	+ .... Manitou .... ♁	3 33 "
11 39 P M	11.5	.... Cascade .... ♁	3 20 "
12 12 Night	14.9	..... Green Mt. Falls	3 10 "
12 32 "	20.0	.... Woodland .... ♁	3 00 "
12 57 Night	26.9	arr. .... Divide ♁ ..... lve.	2 45 A M
	26.9	lve. Divide (C. C. & C. S. R.R.) arr.	
	51.5	.... Victor ...... "	
	56.9	arr. Cripple Creek. " lve.	
12 57 Night	26.9	lve. .... Divide ♁ ..... arr.	2 15 A M
1 25 A M	35.8	.... Florissant .... ♁	2 05 "
1 34 "	40.3	...... Lake George	1 45 "
2 25 "	57.7	.... Spinney	1 04 A M
2 52 "	68.9	.... Hartsel .... ♁	12 43 Night
3 47 "	90.3	.... Newett .... ♁	11 49 P M
4 17 "	100.9	+ ..... Buena Vista ..... ♁	11 01 "
5 07 "	118.2	.... Granite .... ♁	10 23 "
5 43 "	133.5	arr. Arkansas Junction ♁ lve.	9 50 "
6 05 "	137.3	arr. .... Leadville ♁ ... lve.	9 25 "
5 25 "	137.3	lve. ..... Leadville ..... arr.	10 05 "
5 58 "	133.5	lve. Arkansas Junction ♁ arr.	9 40 "
6 40 "	141.7	.... Busk .... ♁	9 15 "
6 50 "	143.7	.... Ivanhoe ...... (♁	9 05 "
7 20 "	153.7	.... Selfar	8 05 "
7 28 "	157.7	.... Nast	7 58 "
7 45 "	165.2	.... Thomasville ...... ♁	7 04 "
8 02 "	170.2	.... Ruedi	6 40 "
8 45 A M	185.3	arr. .... Basalt ♁ ..... lve.	5 50 P M
10 10 A M	203.7	arr. ...... + Aspen ♁ ..... lve.	*4 30 P M
8 45 A M	185.3	lve. .... Basalt ♁ ..... arr.	5 50 P M
9 10 "	196.7	.... Carbondale ...... ♁	5 20 "
9 45 "	205.6	+ .... Cardiff .... ♁	5 00 "
10 00 "	209.0	+ ... Glenwood Springs ... ♁	4 39 "
10 11 "	213.3	...... South Canon	4 24 "
10 30 "	221.1	+ ..... New Castle ...... ♁	4 05 "
10 43 "	227.9	.... Silt	3 48 "
10 58 "	235.1	.... Rifle .... ♁	3 28 "
11 30 "	252.4	...... Grand Valley ..... ♁	2 55 "
11 54 A M	265.1	.... De Beque .... ♁	2 30 "
12 34 Noon	285.9	.... Palisade	1 48 "
1 00 P M	298.0	+ ... Grand Junction ... ♁	*1 25 P M
		ARRIVE] [LEAVE	

Only one coupon necessary, which should read via the Colorado Midland Railroad between Denver, Colorado Springs or Pueblo and any point on Colorado Midland Railroad west of Colorado Springs up to and including Grand Junction.

TRAIN SERVICE AND EQUIPMENT.

WESTBOUND.

No. 3—Western Express.—Solid Through Train Denver to Grand Junction. Carries First-class Chair Car and Modern Electric-lighted, Steam-heated, 12-Section Drawing-room Pullman Sleeping Car Denver to Grand Junction. Modern Electric-lighted, Steam-heated, 12-Section Pullman Sleeping Car Denver to Leadville. Dining Car Ruedi to Cardiff, serving breakfast (meals a la carte).

EASTBOUND.

No. 6—Denver Express.—Solid Through Train Grand Junction to Denver. Carries First-class Chair Car and Modern Electric-lighted, Steam-heated, 12-Section Drawing-room Pullman Sleeping Car Grand Junction to Denver. Modern Electric-lighted, Steam-heated, 12-Section Drawing-room Pullman Sleeping Car Leadville to Denver. Dining Car Cardiff to Ruedi, serving supper (meals a la carte).

STOP-OVER PRIVILEGES.—Stop-over privileges will be allowed at all points on the Colorado Midland R.R. on passes and on all through tickets the limit of which will permit, regardless of the conditions of the ticket, whether stamped "Continuous Passage," "No Stop-overs Allowed," etc., or not, provided there is a final limit on one-way tickets or a transit limit on round-trip tickets of sufficient length to enable the passenger to make the stop-over desired, resume the journey and reach destination within said final or transit limit; on condition, however, that the passenger assumes all risk of ticket expiring in his hands beyond our own lines.

EXPLANATION OF SIGNS.

Trains marked * run daily. (Meal stations.
+ Coupon stations; ♁ Telegraph stations.
STANDARD—*Mountain time.*

CONNECTIONS.—Denver, in Union Depot—With Atch. Top. & S. Fe Ry., Chic. Burl. & Quincy R.R., Chic. Rk. Isl. & Pac. Ry., Union Pac. R.R. and Colo. & So. Ry. Colorado Springs—With Chic. Rk. Isl. & Pac. Ry., Atch. Top. & S. Fe Ry., Colo. & So. Ry. and Cripple Creek and Colo. Spgs. R.R. Manitou—With Manitou & Pike's Peak Ry. Divide—With Cripple Creek and Colo. Spgs. R.R. for Victor, Cripple Creek, etc. Buena Vista—With Colo. & So. Ry. and with stage lines. Grand Junction—With Denver & Rio Grande R.R. and Grand River Valley Ry.

Horse for the last time at 3:05 AM on August 9th. It might be noted that the 200s and 300s were often used on freight trains during the dying days of the railroad, as they were working their way back to Colorado City for the final time.

Due to the sudden decline in business, the Colorado Midland Railroad was forced into bankruptcy on June 30th, 1918, and A.E. Carlton was appointed receiver on July 1st. At first the court demanded that the railroad be abandoned, torn up and disposed of as promptly as possible, but the Carlton group argued that it could be operated profitably once the war was over. Thus, the railroad was left intact and remained in a state of limbo for a couple of years. The Midland Terminal leased the trackage between Colorado Springs and Divide, as well as the terminal tracks as Colorado City. The MT even used some CM engines for a while, as the valuation engineering survey stated that the MT was using, but did not own, CM 49, 50, 52, 53, 63, 70, 301 and 303 as of June 30, 1919. The MT later purchased CM engines 50 and 53 and several passenger cars.

The Rio Grande Junction was evidently of the opinion that CM trains would again return over its line between New Castle and Grand Junction, as its timetable No. 106, July 20, 1919, continued to show Nos. 103, 106, 141 and 142 (RGJ numbers for CM trains).

But the hopes of all were not to be, as far as the resurrection of the Midland was concerned, and, after several years, the Colorado Midland Railroad of 1917 was dissolved on May 21, 1922.

When the Midland ceased operations, it apparently had the following passenger train equipment on the roster:

Type of Car	Numbers	Total
Baggage	301, 303-306, 310, 311, 313, 314-316	11
Coach-Lunch	8	1
Coach-Baggage	9, 10	2
Mail-Coach	12, 260-262	4
First Class Coach	101, 102, 103, 104, 106, 107, 251, 252	8
Vestibule Chair Cars	108-112, 253-255, 246	8
Observation Chair Car	111	1
Dining Cars	*Idlewild, Ivanhoe*	2
Cafe Cars	249	1
Officers Cars	99 *Manitou*, 100 *Cascade*	2
Suburban Coaches	4-5	2
Open Observation	6	1
Total Equipment		43

A number of the above were subsequently purchased by the Midland Terminal and were used for many years for passenger trains between Colorado Springs and Cripple Creek. These cars included Nos. 8, 107, 109, 110, 111, 251–254, 304, 316 and business car 100 *Cascade*. Also purchased was an open observation car, presumably CM No. 6, for a total of 13 cars taken over by the Midland Terminal.

EPILOGUE

Part of the fascination of the Colorado Midland is to wonder what might have occurred had the railroad resumed operations after the end of World War I, with the Carlton interests still in control. This management had already begun the rehabilitation of the property with the installation of heavier rail and new ties, and it is certain that this program would have been expanded. It is also probable that new, larger motive power would have been secured in order to cope with the heavier trains of the period and to be able to initiate all-steel equipment over the road. Just what kind of power would have been acquired is hard to say, but there were certainly a large number of wheel arrangements to choose from at that time, to augment the road's aging fleet of Tenwheelers and Consolidations.

It has been reported that the Carlton management wanted to extend the Midland to Utah via the routes of the Grand River Valley RR, an interurban electric line running from Grand Junction to Fruita, Colorado, as well as the Uintah Railway, a narrow gauge line from Mack, Colorado, to Watson, Utah. The latter had some horrendous grades and curves over Baxter Pass. New construction would have been necessary to fill in the gap between these lines in Colorado and to reach Salt Lake City or Ogden. It was also planned to bore a tunnel under Baxter Pass in order to relieve the heaviest of the grades over that part of the Uintah. Whether or not the Carlton interests could have raised the capital necessary to implement such grandiose plans of expansion is problematical. It is logical to suppose that cooler heads would have prevailed, and that the expansion of the Colorado Midland, at this late date, would have been suspended for all time.

It is also reasonable to assume that, even if the Colorado Midland and the Midland Terminal would have been merged, the combined operations would not have had the stamina to survive the depression of the 1930s. The Rio Grande, with a much stronger traffic base than the Midland, was hard put to survive the 1920s, let alone the severe problems of the 1930s, without the competition from a revitalized Midland. Had both railroads been operating through these years, it is a certainty that both would have had even more difficulty in remaining afloat than did the Rio Grande as the surviving railroad in the region.

Looking at the situation through the years that have elapsed since the Colorado Midland ceased operations, it is apparent to this observer that the railroad had outlived its usefulness to the Rocky Mountain region that it served, and the court order that required it to close was delivered with more insight than most people gave credit for at the time. Had Carlton's plan for the resurrection of the Midland taken place, more good money would have been wasted, as the railroad certainly would not have survived beyond the Depression years. It may well have dragged the Rio Grande down with it.

As Morris Cafky has so eloquently put it: "And it is here that we have the Colorado Midland's ultimate triumph—in dying it achieved immortality". To this end, while the physical property has been long gone, the legends live on and seem to gather strength as the years pass by. It is hoped that this study of the passenger service scheduled during the life of the Midland will end some of the myths that have grown during the years and will contribute to the legends that properly belong to the memory of the famous old mountain railroad—The Colorado Midland!

BIBLIOGRAPHY

American Railway Guide Co., Chicago, Ill., *Travelers Railway Guide, Western Section*, December 1905.

Blair, Edward, *Leadville, Colorado's Magic City*, Pruett Publishing Co., Boulder, Colo., 1980.

Cafky, Morris, *Rails Around Gold Hill*, Rocky Mountain Railroad Club, Denver, Colo., 1955.

———, *Colorado Midland*, Rocky Mountain Railroad Club, Denver, Colo., 1965.

———, "4'-8½" To the Narrow Gauge Country, The Colorado Midland Story – I", *Trains*, Vol. 17 No. 10, August 1957.

———, "The Railroad That Became a Legend, The Colorado Midland Story – II," *Trains*, Vol. 17, No. 11, September 1957.

Colorado Railroad Museum, Golden, Colo., Colorado Midland timetable reprints:

ATSF-CM Division, Timetable No. 66, January 1, 1895.

CM Public timetable, December 1902.

CM Public timetable, 1908.

CM Operating Timetable No. 60, November 22, 1908.

CM Operating Timetable No. 2, November 18, 1917.

RGJ Operating Timetable No. 106, July 20, 1919.

Graves, Carl, "The Colorado Midland", Bulletin No. 36, *Railway & Locomotive Historical Society*, Boston, Mass., 1936.

Interstate Commerce Commission, Valuation Docket No. 673, Midland Terminal Railway et al., 1926, 110 ICC 451. Colorado Midland material found in Appendix 2, pp 483-509. (Includes Valuation Engineering Survey as June 30, 1919.)

Le Massena, Robert A., *Rio Grande—To The Pacific!*, Sundance Limited , Denver, Colo., 1974.

———, *Colorado's Mountain Railroads*, Sundance Publications, Limited, Denver, Colo., Revised Edition, 1984.

Lipsey, John J. *The Lives of James John Hagerman*, Golden Bell Press, Denver, Colo., 1968.

McFarland, E.M., *Midland Route, A Colorado Midland Guide and Data Book*, Pruett Publishing Co., Boulder, Colo., 1980.

———, *The Cripple Creek Road, A Midland Terminal Guide and Data Book*, Pruett Publishing Co., Boulder, Colo., 1984.

National Association of Timetable Collectors, *The Timetable Collector*, October 1972.

National Railway Publication Co., New York, N.Y., various issues of *The Official Guide*, 1888–1918.

Shoemaker, Len, *Roaring Fork Valley*, Sundance Limited, Denver, Colo., Revised Edition, 1973.

Sprague, Marshall, *Money Mountain*, Little Brown & Co., 1953.

———, *Newport in the Rockies*, Sage/Swallow Press, Chicago, Ill., Revised Softbound Edition, 1980.

Thode, Jackson C., "A Century of Passenger Trains. A study of 100 years of Passenger Service on the Denver & Rio Grande Railway, Its Heirs, Successors and Assigns." *The 1970 Denver Westerners Brand Book*, The Denver Westerners, Inc., Denver, Colo., 1972.

Wagner, F. Hol, Jr., *The Colorado Road*, Intermountain Chapter, National Railway Historical Society, Denver, Colo., 1970.

Wentworth, Frank L., *Aspen on the Roaring Fork*, Sundance Limited, Denver, Colo., Revised Edition, 1976.

Wilkins, Tivis E., *Florence & Cripple Creek RR*, Colorado Rail Annual No. 13, Colorado Railroad Museum, Golden, Colo., 1976.

———, *Short Line to Cripple Creek*, Colorado Rail Annual No. 16, Colorado Railroad Museum, Golden, Colo., 1983.

THE COLORADO MIDLAND RAILWAY

THAT COMPANY INAUGURATING

DOUBLE DAILY TRAIN SERVICE

WESTBOUND ON APRIL 12

Train__________ **Leaves**__________________________

Train__________ **Leaves**__________________________

EASTBOUND ON APRIL 13

Train__________ **Lea**

Train__________ **L**

Please note the co ... e. The Day train to see the scenery. The Night tr...

SA ... S DAY

Chair Cars, Pulln... rs.

We will be glad to ... for your trip, quote fares and explain this splendid train se... ation to

COLORADO MIDLAND RY. CO. AUG 1 1918 BUENA VISTA C.

The ticket dater used by the agent at Buena Vista is preserved at the Colorado Railroad Museum and was used to produce this impression of the date of the final train.

A pair of horse-drawn cars has just emerged from the Denver City Railway carhouse and barn at 17th and Wynkoop streets across from Union Station, about 1888. A large wall sign advertised the company's service to arriving train passengers, while along the sidewalk a real estate firm promoted property in "More's Park Heights, Bellemont and Park Hill." Over a century later, this imposing brick structure stands in the heart of the lower downtown business revival. (Denver Public Library Western History Dept.)

STREETCARS & SUBURBS:
The Impact of Denver's First Light Rail Network

by Thomas J. Noel

Almost 200 books track Colorado railroads, but street railways have captured far less fanfare. Yet these contraptions, inspired by and named for steam railroads, are more than historical relics. They may well become state-of-the-art transportation once again.

Talk of light rail for metro Denver in the 1990s has focused on electric mass transit operating on existing railroad track and/or right-of-ways. Revival of the Fort Collins Municipal Railway in 1985 and the 1989 opening of the Platte Valley Trolley by the Denver Rail Heritage Society sparked dreams of a streetcar renaissance. Indeed, the Denver Regional Transportation District's planning for the 21st century revolves around restoring a light rail system not unlike the streetcar spiderweb that the pioneers began spinning in the 1870s.

Then as now street railways appeared to be a solution to urban transportation problems. As Denver grew from a town of 4,749 in 1870 to a city of 106,713 in 1890, it faced problems of density and congestion which plagued cities such as Boston, New York and Philadelphia where many residents squeezed into boarding and tenement houses. Mushrooming metropolises could not grow up and had to grow out. Although Elisha G. Otis had invented the elevator in 1872, steel-frame skyscrapers were not developed until later. As streetcar technology was in place, it enabled cities to grow horizontally; verticalism came with the 20th century development of skyscrapers. In 1832, New York City began using horse drawn street railways and other cities soon followed suit. By 1880 practically every major American city boasted horsecar lines.

By 1900, not only Denver but Aspen, Boulder, Colorado Springs, Cripple Creek, Durango, Fort Collins, Grand Junction, Leadville, Pueblo, Trinidad and Victor boasted streetcars. It is difficult to overstate the impact of streetcars on urban life. In Denver, for instance, streetcars help to explain why the city never had congested tenement districts comparable to those in Eastern centers. Streetcars, introduced in 1871 at the beginning of Denver's 1870–1893 boom, enabled the Mile High City to grow outward. Promoters even built lines in advance of settlement hoping to cash in on rising real estate prices. As no large body of water blocked Denver's expansion, streetcar lines could easily be built in every direction, creating a spacious—some would say sprawling—city of single family homes with generous yards.

By following streetcars out onto the prairies, Denver began a pattern of settlement later accelerated by the automobile. The Mile High City prided itself, as the journalist Richard Harding Davis reported in 1892, on having "mile after mile of separate houses . . . with a little green breathing space between."[1]

The first streetcar line, the Denver Horse Railroad Company, was constructed in 1871 by a Chicago financier, Lewis C. Ellsworth.[2] That line originated between 6th and 7th on Larimer Street, running northeast to 16th Street. There it turned on 16th, next turning onto Champa and trotting out to the end of the line a half block beyond 27th Street. There, out in open country, Denverites built homes in the city's first streetcar suburb, Curtis Park.[3]

At each end of the line, drivers used a turntable to redirect the cars, simple omnibuses on cast iron wheels. Some streetcars had bicycle racks mounted on the rear and also carried mail, newspapers and express items. Cable cars once sported different colors to indicate the street they served—red for Broadway, white for Colfax. Many of the streetcars were built in Denver by the Woeber Brothers Carriage Company on 11th Street between Market and Larimer.

The Denver Horse Railroad Company in 1872 changed its name to the Denver City Railway Company but continued to use horsepower, which consisted of, according to a company roster, bays, whites, grays, browns, blacks, chestnuts, sorrels and one "mud colored" horse. The firm's second line, constructed in 1873, started at Larimer and ran northwest down 15th across the railroad tracks and over the South Platte River. In North Denver it stopped at a turntable on a dirt path (the future Federal Boulevard) in largely vacant Highland, which William Larimer had staked out in 1858. Only after the horsecar provided quick and easy transit to the jobs, markets and amusements of Denver did Highland thrive.

The third line, installed by the Denver City Railway Company in 1874, extended the 16th Street tracks to Broadway and then on Broadway to Cherry Creek. This service fostered growth along Broadway and in Capitol Hill, the most elegant of Denver's streetcar suburbs. The Park Avenue line, also established in 1874, took a diagonal route (23rd Street and Park Avenue) from Champa to Downing, spurring development in the North Capitol Hill

The Cherrelyn horsecar line was the last to operate, surviving until 1910. Sometime during the 1890s it is seen southbound from its terminal at Broadway and Hampden, an area now in the center of suburban Englewood. The car was still lettered "West Denver-Union Depot Car 55," its old route on the Denver City Railway. (Denver Public Library Western History Dept.)

and City Park neighborhoods. By 1884 the Denver City Railway boasted 15.5 miles of track, 45 cars, 200 horses, 100 employees, and a new carbarn on 17th Street opposite Union Station.[4] Disembarking railroad passengers could walk across Wynkoop Street and board five-cent-fare horsecars to many parts of the city.

Commercial and residential real estate flourished along the streetcar tracks, particularly on 16th Street which emerged as Denver's retail shopping spine. Fifteenth Street property owners founded their own transit company to build along that thoroughfare. In 1886, John Evans, his son William Gray Evans, *Rocky Mountain News* editor William Byers, Henry C. Brown and others formed the Denver Tramway Company (DTC). Although this merger of two previously existing streetcar firms never succeeded in making 15th as important as 16th Street, it eventually dominated Denver's public transit.[5]

The Denver Tramway Company secured the right to build cable or electric lines, thereby circumventing the horsecar franchise of the Denver City Railway Company. Tramway officials had faith in electric lines since in 1885 a University of Denver physics professor, Sidney H. Short, had developed a vehicle powered by current picked up from a slot between the rails. By July 1886, these electric cars were rolling along 15th, giving the Mile High City the second electric street railway in the United States. Short's contraption proved shocking to animals and pedestrians who stepped on the slot during wet weather. Water would cause a short between the wire and the metal lips of the pickup slot, causing the slot to become "hot."

Within a year, the DTC scrapped this $200,000 mistake and switched to cable lines. In 1890 it introduced the safer overhead trolley system that would not be abandoned until 1950.[6] Small wheels called trolleys, which rolled along the electrified lines overhead, were mounted on metal poles atop the roofs of the streetcars. The switch to electric and cable lines was spurred by the epizotic plague of 1872, which killed many horses, by complaints about horse pollution and by objections from animal rights societies.

By 1889 the Denver City Railway Company was controlled by New York investors and renamed the Denver City Cable Railway Company. This outfit installed underground cables similar to those still used in San Francisco and built a large, elegant brick powerplant, carbarn and corporate office at 18th and Lawrence streets. The Denver City Cable Railway constructed the city's first viaduct, Larimer Street, and next built the 16th Street Viaduct. The city contributed 15 percent of the cost of the latter to add access for pedestrians and horse-drawn vehicles. By 1890, Denver had one of America's more extensive cable car networks. The Welton Street cable, according to Jerome Smiley's *History of Denver*, was the world's longest. Smiley also claimed that the still-standing powerplant at 18th and Lawrence was the world's largest.[7]

Another technology used briefly in Denver was the steam dummy, a steam powered streetcar disguised to look like a horsecar or small electric trolley in order not to frighten horses. Steam dummys operated on the Denver & Berkeley Park Rapid Transit Company routes to northwest Denver, the Denver & Park Hill Railroad Company, the Denver Circle Railway to South Denver and University Park, and the Fairmount Railway Company.[8]

The Denver City Cable and the Denver Tramway, the two giants among at least a dozen Denver street railway companies, competed mightily to reach new developments. These firms lobbied and bribed City Council members for the municipal street railway franchises and sometimes construction crews fought over thoroughfares. On a December weekend in 1889, the chief of police arrested part of the Denver Tramway's 1,600-man construction army in order to stop them from laying track illegally.

This Denver City Railway car has just turned east on Colfax from Pearl Street, circa 1888. It is usually assumed that the second horse helped the car up the 17th Avenue hill, but this location is several blocks beyond that point. (Denver Public Library Western History Dept.) About the same year Larimer, looking northeast from 16th, was the main business and retail street. Horse cars were at their peak. (William Henry Jackson photo, E.J. Haley collection)

Streetcar-mania also afflicted smaller, independent operators. If a land developer could not coax existing transit companies to build to his tract, he might construct his own line to assure potential customers of access to public transportation. John J. Cook, for instance, built a horsecar line from the DTC line on Williams Street out East 34th Avenue to Colorado Boulevard to help promote Cook's Addition. Although a busy real estate developer and city councilman, Cook personally ran the horsecar line, hoping to coax more lot buyers and home builders to his neighborhood. As most Denverites could not afford a horse and buggy, such public transit was essential to those moving out of the heart of the city to new residential sections.

To persuade the Denver Tramway Company to lay track out East Colfax Avenue to York Street and south on Broadway to Alameda Avenue, property owners paid $200,000 to the transit titans. The investment paid off; the value of land bordering East Colfax between Broadway and Milwaukee Street alone more than doubled between 1887 and 1891—rising to over $13 million.[9]

During the flush times, homes and stores popped up like dandelions along the newly laid tracks. Then the Crash of 1893 smashed subdividers' schemes: more than 2,000 homes were constructed in Denver in 1890 but only 124 in 1894.[10] Unfinished basement excavations pockmarked the city's outskirts, where abandoned subdivisions were repossessed by prairie dogs.

The Depression of 1893 weakened rivals, enabling the Denver Tramway Company by 1900 to monopolize 150 miles of streetcar lines.[11] These included the routes of the Denver City Cable Railway Company, which had collapsed under a $4.3 million debt in 1898. The Tramway Company abandoned the cable network in favor of the more reliable and flexible trolley system. Only a handful of independents survived, notably the Denver Lakewood & Golden Railroad and a few small horsecar outfits, such as Englewood's celebrated Cherrelyn Horsecar.

Between 1870 and 1893, Denver had developed an outer ring of streetcar suburbs. Initially, homebuilders and buyers were impressed with the area around Curtis

By 1890 cable cars had almost entirely replaced the horses. A two-car train of open grip-car and closed trailer is outbound to Sloan's Lake and Elitch's Garden in this superb cityscape by Jackson. On the next page another car and open trailer head up 16th Street past the Masonic and Kittredge buildings in 1893. One hundred years later, both structures have been restored to their former grandeur as centerpieces of the 16th Street Mall. (both, E.J. Haley collection)

Park, Denver's first city owned park. Families took streetcars out Larimer, Curtis, Champa, Stout and Welton to look at new brick homes dressed in the fashionable Italianate style, characterized by flat roofs, wide and bracketed eaves, elongated windows, and elegantly framed front porches. Real estate agents pointed out that area residents included Mayor Wolfe Londoner, dry goods merchant J. Jay Joslin and former governor William Gilpin.

As Curtis Park blossomed with homes, streetcar lines shot beyond northeast Denver to industrial suburbs named for the smelters they served—Argo, Swansea and Globeville. Immigrants swarmed into these districts, finding work at the fiery ore furnaces that became the city's leading industry during the 1880s. Within the shadows of smelter smokestacks, blue collar families found company housing and cheap rental units while others built their own shanties.[12]

The noisy, smelly, industrial areas north and west of Curtis Park prompted the status-sensitive to seek homes east and south of downtown. There streetcar lines traveling out East 34th, 31st, 28th, 22nd, 19th, 17th, Colfax, 13th, 6th and 4th avenues facilitated settlement of the City Park, Park Hill, Montclair and Harman neighborhoods. Promoters offered 50 x 125-foot lots rather than the standard 25 x 125-foot city lots. Spacious yards pleased suburbanites fancying expansive lawns, flower beds and vegetable patches.

Park Hill, a haven for the upper crust on the high ground east of City Park, was platted in 1887 by an eccentric German, the Baron Eugene A. Von Winkler. This character came to Denver after being discharged from the Prussian Army, reportedly for falling off his horse. The baron purchased a large tract east of Colorado Boulevard to build a race track surrounded by a posh residential subdivision. These exotic plans died with the Baron, who committed suicide.

Saner developers, such as Denver Park Commissioner Warwick Downing, picked up the pieces of Baron Von Winkler's dream and platted the finest of Park Hill's subdivisions, Downington. This suburban oasis bounded by Forest Street and Monaco Street parkways between East Colfax Avenue and Montview Boulevard claimed its residential parkways rivaled the "Auteil or Passy in Paris, Mayfair in London, the Ring Strasse in Vienna, Thiergarten in Berlin, Riverside Drive in New York [and] the broad avenues and 'circles' for which Washington is famous."[13]

Downington's lavish promotional brochure proclaimed that Capitol Hill had been spoiled as a residential area by the intrusion of multiple family housing and commercial buildings. That error would not be repeated in Downington, "Denver's Largest Restricted Residence District". Amid Park Hill's parkways and croquet wickets, the children of Downington would "be free from the contaminating influence of down-town city streets" where "their delicate moral fibers are tarnished by evil associations."

Southeast of Park Hill lay Montclair, platted by the Baron Walter von Richthofen shortly before his friend Baron von Winkler laid out Park Hill. Richthofen, uncle of Manfred von Richthofen, the Red Baron of World War I aviation fame, had come to Denver in the 1870s. In 1885 he announced the grand opening of Montclair, "The Beautiful Suburban Town of Denver". At 12th and Olive, Richthofen built his own castle as a show home. Not only Richthofen's castle guarded Montclair; a town ordinance forbade the use of "common, vulgar, indecent, abusive or improper language". Despite the castle, the moral atmosphere and Montclair's trolley connections, the Baron found it difficult to lure buyers to his paradise on the prairie.[14]

Park Hill and Montclair both relied on the East Colfax Avenue horsecar line of the Denver City Railway, which was later replaced by the DTC's cable line. Additional routes ran out East 23rd, 17th and 8th avenues. After its

Here are two views of Denver Tramway's white painted Colfax cable cars: above, looking west from Lafayette Street when the area was almost rural; below, outbound on 15th at Lawrence. The low-slung front outside seats were a unique feature. (both, Denver Public Library Western History Dept.)

1890 founding, Fairmount Cemetery ultimately became Colorado's largest city of the dead. Many of the early residents arrived via the Fairmount Railway Company, which ran from the end of the 8th Avenue line south along Quebec Street to the cemetery park.

A livelier streetcar suburb was parented by Edwin and Louise Harman who made a townsite out of their 320-acre farm on the north bank of Cherry Creek between University and Colorado boulevards. Harman boasted a streetcar line, a town hall at East 4th Avenue and St. Paul Street, a sandstone school house, and $75 lots. Reflecting the haphazard, spotty development of Denver's suburban fringe, Harman, like Montclair, did not fully blossom until the coming of the automobile and the post World War II boom. Then Harman became better known as the Cherry Creek neighborhood, which boasted Denver's first major shopping center.

South Denver, stretching from Alameda to Yale avenues and from Colorado Boulevard on the east to Pecos Street on the west, embraced nearly 12 square miles, making it Denver's largest streetcar suburb. In 1890 most of its 1,491 residents lived close to the streetcar lines extending south from Denver. Town father James A. Fleming donated his mansion as a town hall after he was elected mayor. His brothers opened a lumber yard and built whole blocks of homes at a time. "It seems no more trouble for them to build a house," noted South Denver's newspaper, the *Denver Eye*, "than it is for a shoemaker to half sole a pair of shoes."[15]

Disturbed by the saloons, dance halls, and gambling

UNITED STATES OF AMERICA.

Incorporated under the Laws of the State of Colorado.

THE DENVER CIRCLE

REAL ESTATE FULL PAID AND NON-ASSESSABLE. COMPANY

CAPITAL STOCK $ 300.000

3000 SHARES $100 EACH

No. 290 OF THE STATE OF COLORADO. Shares.

This is to Certify that ______ is the owner of ______ Shares of the Capital Stock of THE DENVER CIRCLE REAL ESTATE COMPANY, transferable only on the books of the Company in person, or by Attorney, on the surrender of this Certificate.

In Witness whereof the President and Secretary have hereunto set their hands and affixed the Seal of said Company this ____ day of ______ A.D. 188_

Secretary. President.

KENDALL BANK NOTE CO. NEW YORK.

Countersigned and Registered this ____ day of ____ 188_ the Farmers Loan and Trust Co.

Pioneer capitalist W.A. H. Loveland incorporated the Denver Circle Real Estate Company in 1882 in conjunction with his Denver Circle Railroad. Neither venture was financially successful, except perhaps in running circles around the stockholders, and Loveland happily sold out in 1887 to the Santa Fe Railway, which needed the right-of-way for access to Denver. (Museum collection)

joints clustered around Overland Park race track, South Denver's residents incorporated in 1886 in order to crack down on vice. After the town banished liquor by imposing an annual $3,500 saloon license fee, the *Denver Eye* rejoiced that "roadhouses and saloons were all cleaned out" and predicted that South Denver was "destined to be filled with the homes of our best and most prominent citizens".[16]

University Park—the home of the University of Denver after 1890—was among many communities that never became incorporated towns. The Evans family, principal founders of both the University of Denver and the DTC, saw to it that the campus had early and adequate streetcar service. So many DU students were given DTC jobs that the school was dubbed "Tramway Tech".

Broadway streetcar tracks reached Orchard Place (Englewood) and pushed on to the country town of Littleton, which had grown up around Richard Little's Rough and Ready Flour Mill in the 1860s. Englewood and Littleton, together with Aurora, Lakewood, Arvada and Golden, formed an outer ring of suburbs tied to Denver by railroad as well as streetcar passenger service.

Areas east of the South Platte River were initially more accessible to the city center than those west of the rail yards and the river. Then viaducts and bridges gradually opened up southwest and northwest Denver. By 1888 the streetcar suburbs of Sheridan Heights, Valverde and Barnum had sprouted in southwest Denver. They grew slowly, despite the promotion of circus king Phineas T. Barnum, who allegedly crowed that the Barnum area had the finest climate in the world.

North of Barnum, Villa Park with its twisting lanes gave Denverites a chance to escape from the city's monotonous street grid. Another unusual development pattern was the alley homes in the Snell Addition to Capitol Hill. This experiment in more densely constructed single family housing, commemorated today by its designation as a Denver Landmark Preservation Commission Historic District, did

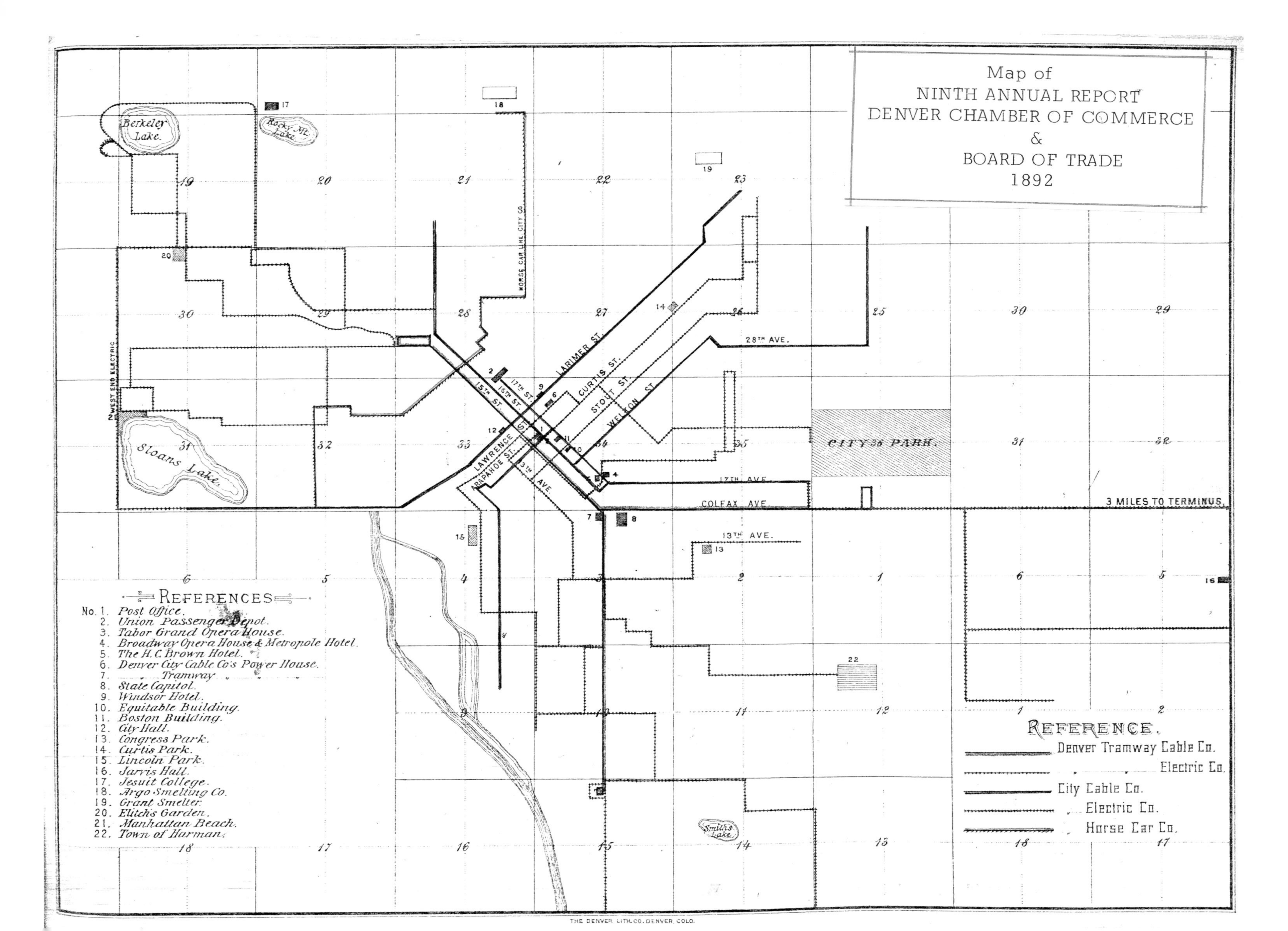
Map of
NINTH ANNUAL REPORT
DENVER CHAMBER OF COMMERCE
&
BOARD OF TRADE
1892
LARIMER ST.
CURTIS ST.
STOUT ST.
WELTON ST.
LAWRENCE ST.
ARAPAHOE ST.
15TH ST.
16TH ST.
17TH ST.
13TH AVE.
17TH AVE.
28TH AVE.
COLFAX AVE.
13TH AVE.
3 MILES TO TERMINUS.
CITY PARK.
HORSE CAR LINE CITY CO.
WEST END ELECTRIC
Berkeley Lake.
Rocky Mt. Lake.
Sloans Lake.
Smith's Lake.
REFERENCES
No. 1. Post Office.
2. Union Passenger Depot.
3. Tabor Grand Opera House.
4. Broadway Opera House & Metropole Hotel.
5. The H. C. Brown Hotel.
6. Denver City Cable Co's Power House.
7. Tramway
8. State Capitol.
9. Windsor Hotel.
10. Equitable Building.
11. Boston Building.
12. City Hall.
13. Congress Park.
14. Curtis Park.
15. Lincoln Park.
16. Jarvis Hall.
17. Jesuit College.
18. Argo Smelting Co.
19. Grant Smelter.
20. Elitch's Garden.
21. Manhattan Beach.
22. Town of Harman.
REFERENCE.
Denver Tramway Cable Co.
Electric Co.
City Cable Co.
Electric Co.
Horse Car Co.
THE DENVER LITH. CO. DENVER, COLO.

Denver & Berkeley Park Rapid Transit "dummy" No. 9 is at West 30th Avenue and Zuni Street in 1900 after being acquired by the Denver Tramway. It had Baldwin construction No. 10909 (1890). The enclosed cab was supposed to make the locomotive more acceptable in an urban environment. (Denver Public Library Western History Dept.) The Fairmount line connected Colfax with Fairmount Cemetery, using a different arrangement of 0-4-0T locomotive with two four-wheel trailers. It is easy to see that the electric trolley car was a vast improvement over the steam railways. The 1892 map on the opposite page includes three of the transit modes in operation at the time: horse, cable and electric. (below and map, E.J. Haley collection)

not catch on in Denver, where homebuilders demanded larger single family lots. As if reacting to crowded cities elsewhere, Denverites preferred large lots with plenty of elbow room.[17]

The West Side blossomed after streetcar lines crossed the river via the 15th Street Bridge and the 16th Street Viaduct. Colfax, a community settled by Jewish immigrants from Eastern Europe, emerged in 1891 as an incorporated town served by the Denver City Cable Railway Company's West Colfax line and later by the Denver Lakewood & Golden. Construction of Fort Logan and of the Fort Logan Street Railway promoted growth in College View (home of Loretto Heights College), Petersburg, Sheridan and Fort Logan.

Temperance advocate Horatio B. Pearce had platted the town of Highlands on his ranch northwest of Denver in 1871. After petitioning the territorial legislature to incorporate his town and getting himself elected mayor, Pearce inexplicably moved to sinful Denver. His town, however, persevered. It grew to over 5,000 people in 1890, when it ranked as Colorado's sixth largest city.

Besides seven streetcar lines, there were other "secrets of Highlands' success" according to the town's report for 1891:

> True to her name and nature, she stands high and sightly, where the pure air from the mountains—that God-given slayer of disease—is used first-hand by her people and swells their lungs with strength and healthfulness. With no smelters, factories or emitters of smoke within her borders.[18]

Northwest of Highlands, John Brisbane Walker and the British investor, Dr. William Bell, grew alfalfa at Berkeley Farm until the late 1880s. Then they parlayed their $1,000 investment into $325,000 by selling the acreage to a Kansas City syndicate which developed the town of Berkeley. With a lake, a large park and a fledgling Jesuit High School and College (Regis), Berkeley had much to offer prospective residents. Like Highlands it puffed its pure air and pure morals.

Denver's suburban ring included both unincorporated

Danver Tramway 333, a former West End Electric car, heads down 16th Street at Arapahoe in 1902, operating on the 17th Avenue line. (Denver Public Library Western History Dept.) Below, car 236, built in 1891 by J.G. Brill of Philadelphia, turns west on the Evans Avenue wye from the private right-of-way along the east side of South University Boulevard, in 1905. This line had been built as the University Park Electric Railway, the first in Denver to operate with an overhead trolley. (H.H. Buckwalter photo, R.A. Ronzio collection) On the previous page, a Park Hill car passes the Colorado Midland city ticket office at 17th and California one morning about 1907. Union Station is visible at the foot of the street. (H.H. Buckwalter photo, R.H. Kindig collection)

One day in 1910, L.C. McClure opened an upper floor window in the Metropolitan Building and made this fine photograph of a placid 16th Street, its entire length occupied by two Tramway cars and eight automobiles. Sharp-eyed Denver history students will be able to spot six major downtown buildings still in existence today. (Denver Public Library Western History Dept.)

"additions" to the city and a dozen incorporated towns with their own officials and services. Many of these towns became financially strapped during the 1893 Depression and accepted annexation to Denver as the solution. Such was the case with South Denver, Highlands, Harman, Colfax and Barnum. Creation of the City and County of Denver in 1902 brought into the city limits the towns of Berkeley, Elyria, Globeville, Montclair and Valverde. Beyond the city's western limits lay Arvada, Edgewater, Lakewood, Mountain View and Wheat Ridge—suburbs which remain separate, incorporated towns to this day.

Although Americans of the automobile age came to think of rumbling, creaking, screeching streetcars as slow, uncomfortable and noisy, they were a marvelous convenience to 19th century city dwellers. Of course, a few saw streetcars as the devil's work. Jim Baker, the old mountain man, warily boarded an electric car which he described as "the stage like thing".[19] When it moved without the help of horses or other visible power he panicked and jumped off, falling in the street.

Most Denverites gratefully accepted the Tramway's Venetian red and carbody yellow trolleys with gold leaf striping and numerals as a fact of life—and even of death.[20] The Tramway served Denver's suburban cemeteries—Fairmount, Crown Hill, Riverside, and Mount Olivet—with Funeral Car A. This closed car, black with elegant gold trim and window curtains, was specially constructed to hold the casket and the bereaved. For large funerals extra cars were added, but if the mourners grieved excessively they had to pay four dollars an hour for overtime.[21] On livelier occasions charter cars were rented for excursions, "Seeing Denver" tours, and even honeymoons.

Streetcars reshaped the city and the lives of its citizens. To this day some routes are identifiable by extra wide streets, rounded street corners, neighborhood shopping areas, and old tracks, now buried under asphalt, that sometimes resurface. By enabling people to live miles from their workplaces, streetcars revolutionized urban life. In traditional cities, homes, shops, amusements and jobs had all been within easy walking distance. Streetcars permitted some city dwellers to move out to the country, knowing that a five-cent ride would whisk them back into town.

One of the more subtle impacts of streetcars was promoting a greater sense of community. Transportation became a collective effort, rather than an individual matter. Whereas Denverites once were able to go whenever and wherever their legs or their horses could take them, streetcars tied them to a community network. The streetcar tentacles of urban, industrial society had a great, if un-

A newel post of the wrought iron fence around the State Capitol grounds frames Woeber-built car 54 and trailer 502 inbound on Broadway with a rush hour crowd from University Park about 1901. Below, on a warm February 1906 afternoon, 19th Avenue car 237 rolls south on Broadway between Trinity Methodist Church and the Brown Palace Hotel, which nine decades later remain Denver landmarks. (both, E.J. Haley collection)

These three scenes looking down 15th Street from Champa in 1896, 1907 and 1911 reveal a gradual evolution of buildings, vehicles and women's fashions. Of the structures in the 1911 view on the next page, only the white terra cotta Gas & Electric Building and the Granite Block, just visible on the right margin, remain today. (below and opposite, L.C. McClure; all, Denver Public Library Western History Dept.)

measured, psychological and symbolic impact on city folks. For the masses of Denverites, work, play and shopping began to revolve around the routes, fares and schedules of the Denver Tramway Company, which also served as one of the city's largest employers.

Yet streetcars also had negative impacts. Like later automobile suburbs, streetcar suburbs were sprawling and not always well planned. Lines ran helter-skelter to where people were, or where developers hoped they would be. Property near the tracks was built up first. Lots a few blocks away developed more slowly. Real estate parcels without connections remained empty, creating a checkered cityscape.

Streetcars also permitted those who could afford suburban homes the chance to escape from the saloons, brothels, crime, congestion, disease and other pitfalls of city life. Business and professional men might tolerate and even patronize downtown bars, bordellos and gambling halls. But they did not want their wives and children exposed to them and thus fancied wholesome communities such as Berkeley, Highlands, Montclair, Park Hill, South Denver and University Park, which used restrictive covenants to keep out undesirable usages and people.[22]

Although streetcar suburbanization enhanced the quality of life for the middle and upper classes, it left others behind in older, crowded, less desirable neighborhoods. Thus Denver's first light rail scheme allowed many Denverites to pursue suburban dreams instead of tackling urban problems, launching a pattern of urban blight and suburban flight.

Notes:

1. Richard Harding Davis, "The Heart of the Great Divide," *Harper's Weekly*, June 11, 1892, p. 571.
2. Smiley, Denver, p. 854; Vickers, Denver, p. 267. Ellsworth Avenue, the dividing line between north and south street addresses in Denver, is named for Ellsworth, a state senator active in railroad as well as streetcar promotion.
3. Much of Curtis Park survives today as a colorful, Victorian residential neighborhood protected by National Register and Denver Landmark Preservation historic districts.
4. Jones, *Mile High Trolleys*, p. 8.
5. Smiley, *Denver*, p. 856.
6. Breck, *William Gray Evans*, p. 111. Rubber tired

Sometime between 1899 and 1908 two Tramway seven-window "spliced" cars (so called because each was rebuilt from two smaller cars) running on the Union Depot-City Park route meet on Colfax at Grant. Visible at the lower right is a raised sandstone stoop which provided easier access to high mounted carriages of the era. (E.J. Haley collection) At the top of the next page, car 332 waits at the end of route 8-University Park, East Evans and Milwaukee, about the time of World War I. The two-story building is still there in 1991. (Denver Public Library Western History Dept.) A few years earlier, at the opposite end of the system, Berkeley-Elitch's car 63 turns off West 46th Avenue into Yates Street. The track in the foreground is the Denver & Northwestern line to Arvada and Golden. (H.H. Buckwalter, Colorado Historical Society)

electric buses, known as "trolley coaches," operated from 1940 to 1955.

7. Smiley, *Denver*, pp. 865–868.
8. Morris Cafky, "Steam Tramways of Denver," Denver: Rocky Mountain Railroad Club, II (1950; revised and reprinted 1982), pp. 5–22.
9. Smiley, *Denver*, p. 860.
10. Smiley, *Denver*, p. 918.
11. King, *History of Government of Denver*, p. 196.
12. Larry Betz, *Globeville: Part of Colorado's History* (Denver: The Author, 1972).
13. This and other quotations on Park Hill are from *The Road to Downington: Denver's Most Beautiful Residence Section* (Denver; n.p., ca. 1907), pp. 5, 6, 13.
14. Noel, *Richthofen's Montclair*, pp. 8, 7, 19. The heart of the old Montclair neighborhood is now a Denver Historic District.
15. J. O. Patterson, "History of South Denver, in the *Denver Eye*, c. 1900.
16. *Denver Eye*, January 1, 1890.
17. Denver's propensity for sprawling, Los Angeles-style suburbs of detached single family homes with large lots is explored in Thomas J. Noel and Barbara S. Norgren, *Denver: The City Beautiful and Its Architects*. (Denver: Historic Denver, Inc., 1987). For a brief, crackerjack history of the Snell Addition see the Denver historic district nomination by a resident, the late Louisa Arps, in the Denver Planning Office landmark files.
18. *Town of Highlands: Its Progress, Prospects and Financial Condition: First Annual Report*. Highlands: Highlands Chief Press, 1891, p. 10. Potter-Highlands, bounded roughly by West 32nd and 38th between Zuni and Federal is now the largest Denver Historic District.
19. William C. Ferril Scrapbook (Scrapbook in Denver Public Library, Western History Division), Vol. I, p. 139.
20. Denver Tramway Company, *1923 Chart of Standard Colors*, in possession of E. J. Haley, Denver.
21. David F. Halaas, *Fairmount and Historic Colorado* (Denver: The Fairmount Cemetery Association, 1976), pp. 47–66 and Cafky, op. cit., "Steam Tramways of Denver," pp. 18–22.
22. See the chapter on "moral geography" in Thomas J. Noel, *The City and the Saloon: Denver, 1858–1916* (Lincoln: University of Nebraska Press, 1982), pp. 67–78.

8
332

BERKELEY
ELITCH'S
33

Sources:

I am deeply indebted to E. J. Haley for two intensive reviews of this manuscript in which he found errors, made many helpful suggestions and provided additional material for this overview of Denver's streetcar suburbanization. Professor Steve Leonard of Metropolitan State College of Denver also reviewed this several times, making many improvements.

The best brief account of Denver's streetcars is in Jerome Smiley, *History of the City of Denver* (Denver: Times-Sun Pub. Co., 1901). See also Clyde L. King, *The History of the Government of Denver with Special Reference to Its Relations with Public Service Corporations* (Denver: Fisher Book Co., 1911). King, a reform-minded professor of political science, offers a critical account of the rise of the Denver Tramway Company "monopoly," as does Judge Ben Lindsey in his muckraking classic, *The Beast* (Garden City, N.Y.: Doubleday, Page & Company, 1910). Less critical are Allen D. Breck, who devotes a chapter to the Denver Tramway Company in *William Gray Evans* (Denver: University of Denver History Department, 1964), and Sam Lusky, *101 Years Young: The Tramway Saga* (Denver: A.B. Hirschfield Press, 1968). William C. Jones, F. Hol Wagner, et. al. produced a handsome pictorial history, *Mile High Trolleys* (Boulder: Pruett Publishing Co., 1975). Morris Cafky gives a good review of the steam "dummy" lines in *Steam Tramways of Denver* (Denver: Rocky Mountain Railroad Club, 1950 – reprinted 1982). For the history of one of the most popular streetcar and bus lines see Kenton Forrest, *Route 3, Englewood: The Broadway Line. . . .* (Denver: Tramway Press, 1990).

For helpful reminiscences, consult Henry Goeddertz, "Early Public Transportation in Denver," *Colorado Magazine*, XXVI (April 1949), pp. 125–27; Carl F. Williams, "Desire for College Education Motivated 'Trailer Hound' Williams to Work on Streetcar," in *The University of Denver News*, October 1980, p. 6; and C. Arthur Hochmuth, "Denver's Student Conductors," *Colorado Magazine*, XL (October 1940), pp. 271–77.

The keen interest in neighborhood history since the 1970s has led to several studies of streetcar suburbs. See Don D. Etter, *Denver University Park: Four Walking Tours, 1886–1910* (Denver: Graphic Impressions, Inc., 1974); Etter's *Auraria: Where Denver Began* (Boulder: Colorado Associated University Press, 1972); William A. West and Don D. Etter, *Curtis Park: A Denver Neighborhood* (Boulder: Colorado Associated University Press, 1980); Phil Goodstein, *Denver's Capitol Hill* (Denver: Life Publications, 1988); and Thomas J. Noel, *Richthofen's Montclair: A Pioneer Denver Suburb* (Boulder: Pruett Pub. Co., 1978). Ruth E. Wiberg, *Rediscovering Northwest Denver* (Boulder: Pruett Publishing Co., 1978) offers 212 pages on the various towns and neighborhoods now comprising Northwest Denver.

Shortly after it was built in the Tramway's own shops in 1923, car 802's shiny red and yellow paint reflects the morning sun at the end of route 40-Park Hill, East 23rd Avenue and Hudson Street. The motorman at his controller and the conductor with his regulation coin changer reflect the pride that transit employees of that time had in their work. This two-unit car is identical in concept to light rail vehicles in use today in cities around the world with modern transit systems. (Denver Public Library Western History Dept.)

The dash sign on this Englewood car, northbound on flag-decorated Broadway at 13th Avenue, advertises the Arvada Harvest Festival. The year is 1932, and the products of automobile dealers such as the one seen here are taking away a big share of the street railway's former patrons. (Harry Rhoads photo, Denver Public Library Western History Dept.) In the late 1930s the paint scheme of Denver's trolleys was changed to solid yellow, and by June 1, 1950, route 14-Aurora cars 815 and 816 rounding the Poplar Street loop were less than 60 hours from their demise. Dual-wire overhead was ready for replacement trolley buses, which would continue the electric transit era in Denver another five years. The crackerbox Ford gas bus provided connecting service to Lowry Field. (Erwin Krebs)

Durango, June 6, 1949. Note the structures and K-series 2-8-2 at left behind the water tank. (Robert W. Richardson)

PREFACE

Much has been written about *The Silverton*, some general in nature, other of a more specific character. Various incidents in the history of the line have been discussed, a fragment here, a fragment there. Missing, however, has been a definition of the fabric of *The Silverton*, a communication to the reader of the almost undefinable "glue" that takes the sensory pieces of the experience and ties the whole thing together.

With "A Silverton Trilogy" we examine the line from three distinct yet interconnected points of view. First, Bob Richardson looks at the line before it was discovered by the tourists, the era between 1940 and 1962. Bob was there; he saw the moves toward abandonment and worked to save the line against odds that even today seem quite formidable. The second part finds John S. Walker Jr. describing the line from a corporate point-of-view during the period 1963 through 1966, when Rio Grande appointed Alexis McKinney to run the show and turn a profit. In the third section R.C. Farewell ties *The Silverton* to the big picture of Rio Grande's declining narrow gauge empire and its final days. He then chronicles the transition of a soon-isolated Silverton Branch under Rio Grande ownership in 1967 to sale and subsequent operation by Charles E. Bradshaw, Jr. R.C. finishes by looking at the train of today, the Durango & Silverton Narrow Gauge Railroad and its mainline operation.

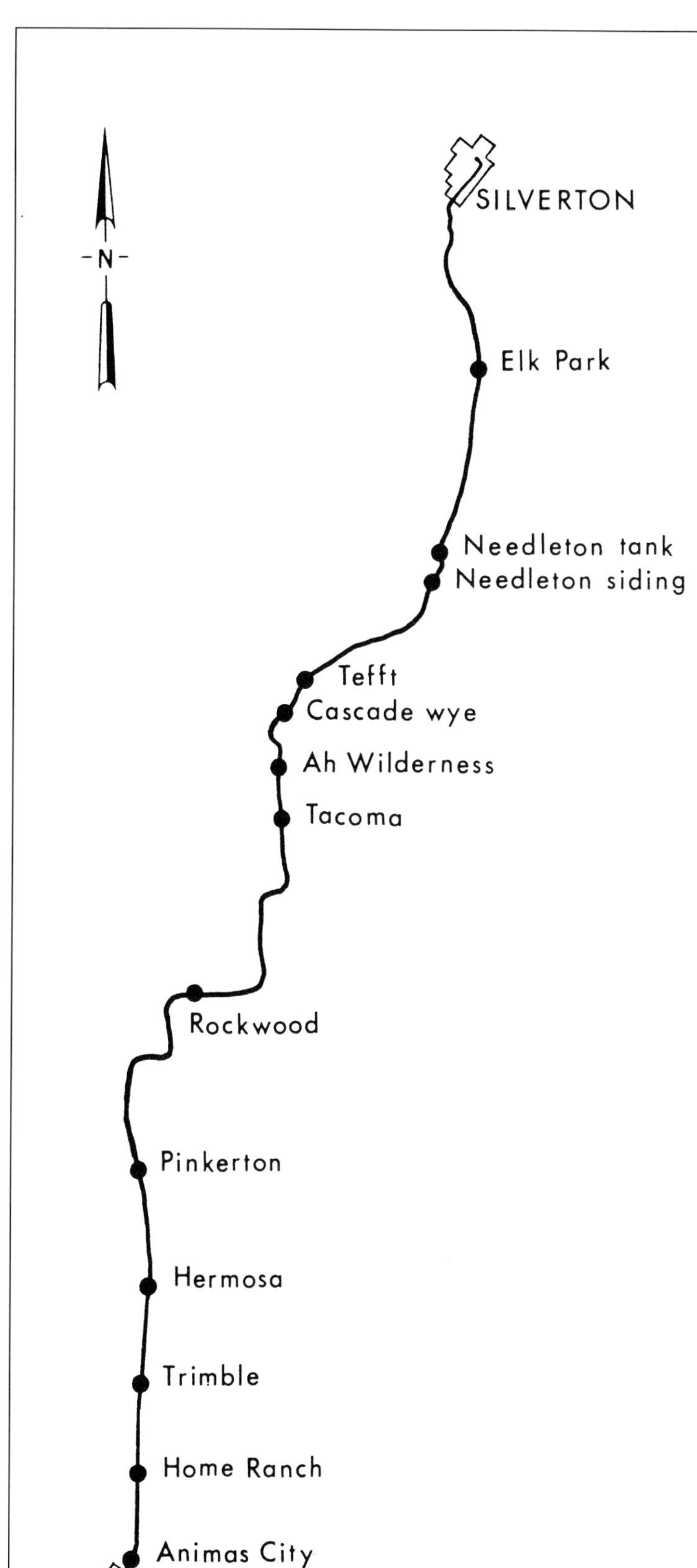

Westward ↓					↑ Eastward	
SECOND CLASS					SECOND CLASS	
463 Mixed	**461** Mixed	Mile Post	**COLORADO DIVISION** Silverton Branch Subdivision 12 **Stations**	Capacity of Siding	**462** Mixed	**464** Mixed
Lv. Daily	Lv. Daily				Ar. Daily	Ar. Daily
0930	0830	451.5	DURANGO . . . . DBJK	Yard	1730	1830
			11.0			
1015	0915	462.5	HERMOSA . . . . W	13	1642	1742
			6.6			
1044	0944	469.1	ROCKWOOD . . . . Y	24	1615	1715
			3.2			
f1105	f1005	472.3	TACOMA	18	f1554	f1654
			1.7			
f1114	f1014	474.0	AH WILDERNESS	. . . . . .	f1545	f1645
			4.0			
f1135	f1035	478.0	TEFT	. . . . . .	f1529	f1629
			6.0			
f1201	f1101	484.0	NEEDLETON . . . . W	13	f1505	f1605
			6.5			
f1232	f1132	490.5	ELK PARK . . . . Y	14	f1435	f1535
			6.2			
1300	1200	496.7	SILVERTON . . . . Y	Yard	1405	1505
Ar. Daily	Ar. Daily		(45.2)		Lv. Daily	Lv. Daily

No. 461 and No. 463 are superior to No. 462 and No. 464

	MPH
Zone Speeds	15
Exceptions -- Loop Track Durango	5
Rockwood MP 469.1-Bridge 471.23	8
Bridge 471.23	5
Bridges 495.64 and 496.12	10
K-36, K-37 types over Bridge 452.42	10
All turnout speeds	10
Sidings	10

A Silverton Trilogy

Map by R.C. Farewell

Durango, Colorado is pictured before the tourists found The Silverton. *Narrow gauge railroading was at its finest, a gemstone which could have been lost to history years, perhaps decades ago. Luckily, the insulating mechanism of the San Juan Mountains kept modernazation and an evolving world at bay for a very long time. Seen in the image above is simply routine switching being accomplished, a string of narrow gauge passenger cars being moved into position for forthcoming departures from the Durango depot. Coupled onto D&RGW C-19 345's pilot is the consist for the eastbound departure of the* San Juan, *dressed in green with gold lettering and accents. Following the* San Juan's *mandatory parlor car, in its standard fifth consist position, is a string of yellow-gold freshly painted coaches assigned to Silverton Branch mixed-train service. Both strings of passenger cars will depart from the Durango depot; the* San Juan *heading southward before turning east at Carbon Junction, the Silverton Branch mixed leaving northbound for Hermosa, Rockwood, Elk Park and finally, Silverton.*

From Mixed Trains to Tourists

by Robert W. Richardson

Saturday morning, July 5, 1941, was a scene of extra activity in the railroad yard at Durango. The Silverton mixed was being prepared for its first run in six weeks. It had been a tough winter with lots of snow in the mountains, and the spring flow of the Animas River had been dangerously high. At dawn that morning the roadmaster and sectionmen left Rockwood on motor cars to check the track. By 5 AM the high water crest had passed Tacoma power plant, and the workers headed for Hunt's to finish a shoofly at a washout.

The two of us, myself and Dave Davis, with military service imminent, had come to Colorado to make a circle tour of the narrow gauge. Leaving our car at Pueblo we had endured a chilly Pullman to Alamosa, taken the two-day round trip on the Chili Line to Santa Fe, then continued by the parlor-dinette equipped *San Juan* on the 4th to Durango. Now, after a largely sleepless night in hotel rooms above a noisy bar we found our arrival well timed to travel to Silverton by rail.

From a little roster given to us by a crew member we learned the little 2-8-0 switching the train to be a relic of 1881. I hardly expected that number "346" to ever again have any meaning to my life. Much later, I was involved in the acquisition of the 346, which would form the cornerstone of a collection of narrow gauge equipment. Ultimately this would become part of the Colorado Railroad Museum.

A two-engine train was to run that day. No. 478, a K-28 2-8-2 still with original spelled-out "Denver & Rio Grande Western" lettering on its tender side, backed down to a short train of several boxcars, combine 210 and caboose. Ahead, "mudhen" 459 picked up 15 cars of sheep and filled out the train's tonnage with more boxcars. We swung aboard the combine to find ourselves the sole passengers. Later a couple of Hispanic sheepherders would climb aboard. After leaving Durango the train moved cautiously as it reached the meadows north of town; the backwaters of the Animas were over the rails as much as six inches in places.

The conductor suggested the best place to see the scenery was from atop the caboose cupola, and he was correct. That was to be my perch for the next three hours. The wind blew steadily from the north, so the drawbacks of the rooftop perch were generous volumes of smoke and plenty of cinders—some rather hot. Just above the Hermosa road crossing the train stalled; brakes were sticking somewhere among the weary wooden cars. Eventually after the crew examined all cars, and with tall columns of smoke and sometimes slipping drivers, the journey resumed. At Rockwood the train stopped again for checking.

Snaking around the high line, my perch upon the cupola provided a splendid overview as the train negotiated the sharp curves far above the muddy Animas. The next three hours were a never-tiring mixture of snowy peaks ahead, a

D&RGW "mudhen" 459, long a Silverton Branch fixture, pulls north with its cut of stock cars through the damp early-morning rain. At left is K-28 478 which will be cut in toward the rear of the train as the helper locomotive. Trailing No. 478's tender are three boxcars for concentrate loading, mixed-train combine 210 and caboose 0540. (all, Robert W. Richardson)

river literally lapping at times at the ends of the ties, cinders (some of which required a lot of practice to flick from my eyes), smoke and a chilly wind.

At Hunt's, a recurring snow slide spot named for an 1880s vice-president, the roadmaster and his minions were putting the finishing touches to a new shoofly. Here the original alignment was close to the slope. After repeated slides, the alignment was relocated nearer the river. The newest version of the shoofly in service that morning was a reverse curve that dipped somewhat in the middle. To the obvious relief of the railroaders, the train safely negotiated this questionable spot.

Silverton early that afternoon did not look prosperous, for junk and decrepit sheds were everywhere. Judging by the smoke rising from buildings the town was but half occupied. No. 459 backed onto the wye with the stock cars to unload the rather sooty sheep. No. 478 pulled the combine and caboose to the station where, to our surprise, an agent was on duty. Late in the afternoon we heard the departing train whistle off, with the helper running ahead light, returning the empty stock cars to Durango. It was a rather typical trip on the branch, the fascinating scenery making the train seem somewhat puny.

Silverton was quiet, water trickled down the side streets from melting snows. Tourist accommodations were meager. The hotel was heated only to extent of a trickle of heat that came from the owner's kitchen. Removing soot from my tear-streaked face with ice water was unsatisfactory, not to be remedied until 24 hours later. In the meantime I just stayed grimy.

Next morning, a walking tour resulted in noting the Silverton Northern enginehouse being used in part as a stamp mill, the tender of one engine having been moved out. We found SN 3 and 4, both 2-8-0s. In the other direc-

The portion of the trip from Durango through the relatively level Hermosa Valley to the hamlet of Hermosa proper was problem free. However, after leaving Hermosa tank, the combination of a two-and-one-half percent ruling grade, wet rail and dragging brakes became significant; the train stalled.

For a few minutes the clouds parted and the sun could shine through. At left the train stops at Needleton tank to take on water while the surroundings are bathed in full sunshine. It was a brief respite, though. Once No. 459's tender was filled the head-end whistled off and moved forward so that mid-train helper 478 could take a drink. The water stop accomplished, it was off up the line toward Silverton.

tion in town was the locked enginehouse that once served the Silverton Gladstone & Northerly. Outside were a caboose, a flanger and paint-peeling freight cars of the SG&N. We walked briskly to keep warm, for overnight the various streets had frozen solid. The noon Rio Grande Motorway bus for Montrose was warm, and the driver held it long enough for us to snap a short Rio Grande Southern freight at Ridgway.

At that time, I had a feeling that I was seeing the Silverton for the last time. It turned out to be the first of many trips. The next was in October 1945, with a government sponsored around-the-world trip accomplished in the meantime. There were changes since 1941. No. 459 had gone to Mexico along with combine 210. Who would have thought 459 was to be standard-gauged, finally ending up in a storage yard, in far off Pueblo, Mexico? The Silverton Branch combine was now No. 212. Actually the Alamosa shop force had switched bodies with 215, because the original 212 also went to Mexico. But 346 was again the switcher, and again I paid little attention.

Now in 1945, with the war just ended, began an increasing number of Durango visitors, virtually all railfans, of course, if they were riding the train. Sometimes the combine's 24 seats were not enough, and a spare coach would be added. To the enginemen's dismay C-25 No. 375, an outside frame 2-8-0, was often the helper, its rigidity and tendency to derail making for uneasy crews traversing the high line. Nine of the K-27s survived at Durango and Montrose and on the RGS, so motive power was ample. But in 1949 and following years, one by one the engines went to scrap when needing repairs. There were no longer any lines of dead engines. Of the four classes of 2-8-2 "Mikado" type locomotives, only the two older and smaller classes were permitted to operate on the Silverton Branch. Larger K-36 and K-37 engines built in 1925 and 1928–30 were, until the upgrading of the line under the Durango & Silverton Narrow Gauge Railroad in the 1980s, not permitted on the branch north of Rockwood.

Ridership grew from 50 to 75 per train during the summers of 1945–46 to 267 and 275 on the final trips of 1950,

At Silverton, No. 459 went about switching the cut of stock cars into the wye. No. 478 continued on toward the depot with the concentrate-service boxcars, combine and caboose. Seen here, author Bob Richardson is running to catch the caboose while Dave Davis watches from the platform.

K-28 No. 476 was recorded on the Durango turntable on an overcast day in June 1949. The careful observer will note that the roundhouse door frames on stalls one through four have been raised. This was done to allow K-36 and K-37s to be backed all the way into the structure. (all, Robert W. Richardson)

DURANGO

Durango was Mecca to followers of the Silverton Branch. Present there were all the major facets of the narrow gauge operation: shops, engine servicing facilities and yards. Within the roundhouse were operational locomotives whose date with the scrapper's torch was long since due. Indeed, in the image of the Durango roundhouse seen above, in June 1949, are the noses of Rio Grande Southern 20 and 41 along with D&RGW 463, 453, 315 and 319, faintly visible. Below, the Durango roundhouse looks more like it is the permanent residence of Rio Grande Southern than the D&RGW. Seen at left is RGS caboose 0409, while the RGS's work goose and goose No. 2 are seen in the foreground. The date: July 5, 1941. Both the RGS and D&RGW are in full swing.

albeit still only operated on Sunday, Wednesday and Friday. The need for some sort of open sightseeing car became obvious. Management took outfit car 0313, an old coach, and rebuilt it from the floor up with a glass roof and open sides, and named the result *Silver Vista*. The car was poorly designed, though, as it did not facilitate the passengers' desire to stand up and take pictures, since the roof glass extended partly down on each side. The end platforms were very small, intended only for a crew member, and were always jammed with passengers. The designers had wrongly assumed everyone would remain in the reserved seats. Another drawback was that El Rancho Encantada, 13 1/2 miles from Durango, would reserve most seats in advance, so walk-in passengers were lucky to obtain space. When the car was destroyed in the Alamosa car shop fire of 1953 no replacement was built.

The Durango agent-operator used the car's name in a manner that roused my ire and had me intending to enforce some laws and regulations. During the summer of 1949 many potential riders complained they could not get on the train, allegedly sold out, but seen departing the depot with many empty seats. So one morning at 5 AM I walked around the two coaches in the Alamosa car yard, finding no tags indicating repairs needed. Then at Durango, staying out of sight of the agent, I entered the depot via the express room. Two women soon requested "four round trips to Silverton, please", only to receive the gruff reply, "*Silver Vista* all sold out". Following them outside I overheard them telling two other women, "We can't go, the train is sold out". I informed them their question had not really been answered and that *Silver Vista* was merely the name of reserved seat car. I advised them, since obviously the train was not sold out, to go back to the window and insist on their tickets. Having seen me talking to them, the agent stamped the tickets this time without comment.

When the *Silver Vista* was not available for one reason or another, the conductors would couple an ordinary gondola on the rear of the train. Passengers could get in and out of the gondola, of course, only at stops. If a typical shower came along things became rather damp and chilly. Moreover the dried-out car timbers were full of splinters, and passengers had to keep tweaking same from their jackets if not also from fingers.

On June 18, 1950, the "painted train" made its inaugural run composed of engine 473, with cab and tender painted "Grande Gold", and equipped with the first of the "goofy" diamond stacks and box headlights. The headlight and stack were unauthentic reproductions of a type completely out of place on the 1923-vintage locomotives. Combination car 212 and the remaining open platform coaches, Nos. 280, 284, 306 and 320, also had the yellow paint. Harold F. Eno, passenger traffic manager of the Rio Grande, got credited for this being done, having convinced President Wilson McCarthy of the traffic needs. Alfred E. Perlman, vice-president of operations, was in Israel at the time advising that country on its railroads. His advice was to get

Consider the almost timeless image of the Durango coaling dock and San Juan*-assigned K-28 No. 472, below, taken in mid-1941. Change was in the wind. By the end of the following year, No. 472 would be working in Alaska on the White Pass and Yukon Route for the War Department, never to return to its old haunts again.*

The Silverton mixed was still a true mixed-train when recorded by Bob Richardson from the hills above Animas City in August 1949.

rid of them, and as the country's roads soon became gridlocked, they learned that this had been a great mistake. Upon his return, the clerks' gossip was that Eno's painted train caper nearly got him fired. The train received good publicity over the nation, and passenger revenues rose. The immediate future was bright, if not in the long range. The schedule for that summer was again three round-trips a week—Sunday, Wednesday and Friday.

The postwar era was one of filming Westerns. The movie-making impressed management to the extent that attempts were made to capitalize on the films for publicity for the Rio Grande. Railroad officials were dazzled by being on a first-name basis with Hollywood characters. The *Silverton* was involved in several ventures that were box office successes, as well as others that hardly got raves in reviews. Late night television still occasionally sees the comedy *Ticket to Tomahawk* or the definitely Grade B horse opera *Denver & Rio Grande*, which featured the head-on collision of engines 319 and 345 at "Scrap Iron Junction", just above the Ah Wilderness flag stop. Rio Grande Southern 20 was the star of *Ticket to Tomahawk* and lavish cosmetic treatment was given the engine. Two freight cars, combine 212, and RGS caboose 0409 received nice "Tomahawk & Western" paint ensembles.

The paint schemes for *Denver & Rio Grande* were quite the opposite, with peculiar off-shades of green and other colors used. No. 268, the C-16 2-8-0, played a starring role, but C-19 No. 345 was its stand-in for the head on collision. Thus, some scenes show a view of the engineer looking past the round "chocolate drop" domes of the 268. Then as the crash neared, the quite different old-fashioned domes of the 345 suddenly appeared. Rio Grande was not going to bang up the real 268, since it was still needed for the Baldwin Branch. When the movie premiered in Denver, No. 268 steamed back and forth on a short piece of track at the D&RGW freight house in that city.

One result of all the movie making was the loss of the ornate oil coach lamps as, one by one, they were gifts to actors and others. On one occasion the remaining original plush coach seats of the combine were borrowed for Hollywood studio use. It took months of efforts by special agents from California railroads to get them back. A full sized wooden replica of engine 20 was made for *Ticket to Tomahawk* and went on to imitate the real engine in a television series. Some Hollywood Michelangelo painted a full-rigged ship on the tender. The RGS needed the engine for stock season assignment and ran the 20 that way. Undoubtedly it soon had the sootiest painting in the nation on its tender.

Lucius Beebe, now virtually unremembered in Durango, gave that area a million dollars worth of national publicity in the course of promoting his books (and himself). His 1947 rail book classic *Mixed Train Daily* featured the Silverton. *Narrow Gauge in the Rockies* of 1958 became one of the most popular railroad books of all time. Beebe, a professional writer and sometime newspaper columnist, along with his photographer companion Charles Clegg, cut quite a swath in high social circles. He liked to visit the more remote railroads of Colorado and Nevada and also authored a series of photo books entirely devoted to steam in its glory. Whatever Beebe said or did was national news, and so southwest Colorado, and Durango in particular, benefited greatly from his lavish prose.

The first book entirely about the Silverton was titled *The Silverton Train*, by Louie Hunt in 1955. A Fresno, California newspaper photographer, Hunt was inspired by Beebe and made a round trip from Fresno to Durango. He became so enthused by the photos he took there that he wrote the book quickly. Knowing little of the narrow gauge lines, Hunt received our approval to use the *Narrow Gauge News* and incorporated seven years of that into 70 pages of his book. One result was an "author's dinner" in Denver sponsored by bookseller Fred Rosenstock upon

Louie's second visit to Colorado.

Another Californian, John Hungerford of Reseda, had a small publishing plant, and he too became enthused after a visit to Durango, producing *Narrow Gauge to Silverton*, also in 1955. It went through 20 editions before his death years later. Thomas Taber of New Jersey published, on behalf of the Railroadians of America, a silver-jacketed paper-back on *The Silverton* in 1955 or 1956.

Turning back to the railroad, in February 1951 "little mudhen" 361, a class C-21 2-8-0, was trapped in a slush slide on the distant Crested Butte Branch. This event would seem to have nothing to do with *The Silverton*. In September, 361 arrived in Salida to be spotted in the empty old narrow gauge roundhouse. It was not to be overhauled. The purchasing agent was asked in the meantime for a price on it, but time went by with no quote. On a nice fall day I drove to Salida to see what would be involved in moving 361 and found no engine! It had been hurriedly shipped to Pueblo for scrap. On the way home I had time to contemplate a contemptuous railroad officialdom and, thinking of my experience with advertising, by the time Alamosa was reached I had determined on an advertising campaign for *The Silverton*. My goal was to inspire perhaps a ten percent increase in patronage each year. So most of my days off during the next year were spent doing advertising of the line. A color postcard, for example, was still several years in the future, so I made up black and white cards and managed to get a few places to carry them. That was one approach. The owner of Durango's largest drug store, however, declined. "Nobody would buy a postcard of a train." Thousands of pocket folders went everywhere. I wrote what might be termed press releases. So, when in Durango today, does anyone wonder at my good humor when up to 200,000 people a year ride up the canyon? One might say the ghost of the vanished 361 is part of the train's consist.

In the early days tourist riders during the summer enjoyed the unexpected little delays; it gave them something to relate back home. During dry years it seemed impossible to make a trip without stops to put out cinder-induced fires. Those crowding the *Silver Vista's* rear platform would be startled by a mushrooming blaze literally scorching the car. The railroad's fire crew followed all trains with a tank of water on a motor section car and usually could quickly douse a blaze. But once in a while the train crew and some hardy passengers would join the battle. The movie people had problems with fires interrupting their shooting. They wanted smoky, noisy trains which lavished sparks. At times train crew, players and extras all joined in the fire fighting.

At Trimble Hot Springs on August 9, 1949, the Silverton Mixed was rolling through the hardwoods with special passenger equipment on the rear end. (Robert W. Richardson)

K-27 No. 453 and C-25 No. 375 were recorded in September 1948 dragging tonnage up the 2.5% ruling grade between Hermosa and Rockwood. (all, Robert W. Richardson)

When fall comes to the San Juan Mountains, the air turns crisp in the morning and the aspens begin to change color toward their final blast of gold before falling to the ground for winter. Seen below, fall has come to Durango, for it is September 18, 1948, and the chill air condenses the smoke and steam from K-27 453 and C-25 375 almost as soon as it leaves the locomotives' stacks. The pair was building up steam pressure just before departing Durango. Freight traffic to Silverton was still common in those days; indeed, passenger traffic was only of minor importance on the branch, ferried behind the string of revenue freight in D&RGW combine 212.

D&RGW No. 375, a long-term fixture on the Silverton Branch, was recorded in 1948 at Elk Park siding doing a bit of switching, while Mt. Garfield watched over the smoke-filled putterings from the high background.

The train carried a few hikers and fishermen. The Needle Mountains were, and are, a very popular destination. The fishermen were mostly local people, sometimes railroad employees. They would be let off anywhere they wanted, and the returning train's crew would be on the lookout for them for miles, occasionally blowing the whistle, as they did not want to leave a fisherman out in the canyon overnight.

The crew was looked on as a source of all sorts of information. Names of mountains? Bears? Elk? Ghost towns? Why this? Why that? They seemed to enjoy it; none of them could be termed a "grouch". Alva Lyons especially enjoyed talking with small groups of passengers and had an endless supply of stories. Once he played a typical practical joke on me. As I wandered into the gondola, Alva was busy with a quartet of passengers. As I appeared, he broke off with, "Here's Bob. Bob, you take up lying to these people where I left off!" What does one do with that sort of an introduction to a group of strangers? I heard one woman say to her husband, "Do you think he really was lying to us?" Anyway, I lamely excused myself by saying that "I wouldn't even attempt to match Conductor Lyons".

All during the trip a coffee pot simmered on the caboose stove. As the day wore on the liquid became very strong, something even avid coffee drinkers could barely inhale. A cup of the potent brew handed after dark to an occupant of the cupola could be discreetly emptied by dumping it outside, no doubt with fatal results to any bush it may have fallen on. Luckily there was no Environmental Protection Agency then.

The growing loads of passengers elicited no cheers from the mining element in Silverton. Squatting against their favorite corner on the sunny side of the street, these loafers spat as they saw the train's passengers coming toward the main street and commented, "Here come those - - - - tourists, raising prices and cluttering up our town." This seemed to be a general attitude in Colorado's mining towns, as if tourists somehow contributed to the decline in mining.

Management, after the D&RGW came out of trusteeship in 1947, had decided to create a mainline bridge system. A map of the narrow gauge showed that by abandoning a portion here and there, the "narrow gauge circle" could be ended, as each abandonment harmed the remaining mileage. In 1949 the Black Canyon route was abandoned. In 1951 the Valley Line went, as did the Rio Grande Southern. To weaken the Alamosa-Durango line the daily *San Juan* passenger train was discontinued. Although the mail transit contract pay alone would have kept the train in the black, an obedient Colorado Public Utilities Commission ignored that fact. With the loss of the daily train each way in winter, which had kept cuts clear and knocked aside big snow drifts, heavy additional costs in operating flanger trains were incurred as freight trains could not feasibly do what the light passenger trains could. With the *San Juan* gone, cars were sold or scrapped instead of being kept for the growing Silverton traffic.

A southbound train on the Sliverton Branch on August 11, 1951, provided passengers with an extra thrill when engine 473 found a broken rail and ended out on a rock pile, firmly wedged, so it could not be simply rolled back. The superintendent tried pulling it back with a bulldozer and its winch, anchoring the dozer to the track. No. 473 did not budge, but the track did, scaring the wrecking crew, which was then permitted to use jacks and blocks. That day's passengers were rescued by a movie train and brought to Durango. Passenger trains did not run again on the branch until September 7th.

In 1952 things got so gloomy that the year was expected to be *The Silverton's* last. Rio Grande Vice-President Perlman made a state visit to Durango early in 1953 to wine and dine gullible locals and play on their conservative local feelings. They deluded themselves that fishing, hunting and Mesa Verde were all that was attracting visitors. Only "nuts" rode the train, it was often said.

The Silverton line was closed for 89 days during the winter of 1951–52, with the first train operated through to Silverton on March 24, 1952. Silverton had 251 inches of snow that winter. The "painted train" resumed runs on July 27th. Locomotives 476 and 478, now also with goofy stacks, were the motive power. The 473 eventually returned from overhaul at Alamosa with a normal straight stack but repainted black.

On August 25th, just as the sold out, turning them away, train was ready to depart, came orders from Denver to remove coach 280 and send it east in that day's freight. The 44 passengers in the coach had the choice of crowding in elsewhere or taking refunds. From that trip onward, revenues of the train on most trips would be 44 fares fewer. Car 280 had been sold by Perlman for $1400 to go to a park display at Boulder, Colorado. Dr. John B. Schooland had put on a campaign there to buy a coach to go with RGS engine 74 and caboose, claiming the D&RGW was going to sell all the cars to Mexico. Later Schooland complained that Silverton Branch employees had been rude to him. It happened he had, with an air of pride of accomplishment, told a switchman he was the person who had obtained the coach. The switchman declared that, if the good doctor would stand in the track, they would run him down!

As long as Charlie Chase managed the Sunnyside mine at Eureka so efficiently, there were many carloads of con-

High cars and combine 212 are on the high line enroute to Silverton. (Robert W. Richardson)

A few feet farther along the high line than the previous page, K-27 No. 463 has things well under control as it smokes its way west a short distance from Rockwood. It is April 5, 1950. There is no snow to be seen, but up the line significant accumulations of the winter white stuff will be found. Moreover, if any of the many slides along the mountain slopes beyond Elk Park have run, then some of the snow and ice debris will have slid across the track, requiring the efforts of the mega-plow attached to the pilot of No. 463 to open the line into Silverton. (Robert W. Richardson)

The San Juan Mountains rise to the sky, not unlike a mid-Pacific atoll from the sea. As a result they squeeze copious amounts of rain during the summer and snow during the winter from air masses that drift by. The higher into the range that one goes, the higher the amount of precipitation. Silverton, it so happens, is located in a valley in the shadow of the highest of the San Juan peaks. Thus Silverton gets a good deal of moisture, whatever the time of year. The slopes leading down the mountainsides to the course of the Animas River come in one style: vertical. Thus, the heaps of snow that fall during the winter do not drift; they roar down into the river bottom. And, as one might expect, they bury the Silverton Branch trackage in the process. When the snow and ice cascade down, anything and everything loose is picked up enroute to the bottom, including rocks, logs and trees.

At left, K-28 No. 473 was on the high line enroute to Silverton on a snowy February 5, 1951. Below, things came to a halt near the Snowshed slide where the line had to be shoveled open and debris cleared. (all, Robert W. Richardson)

SNOW!

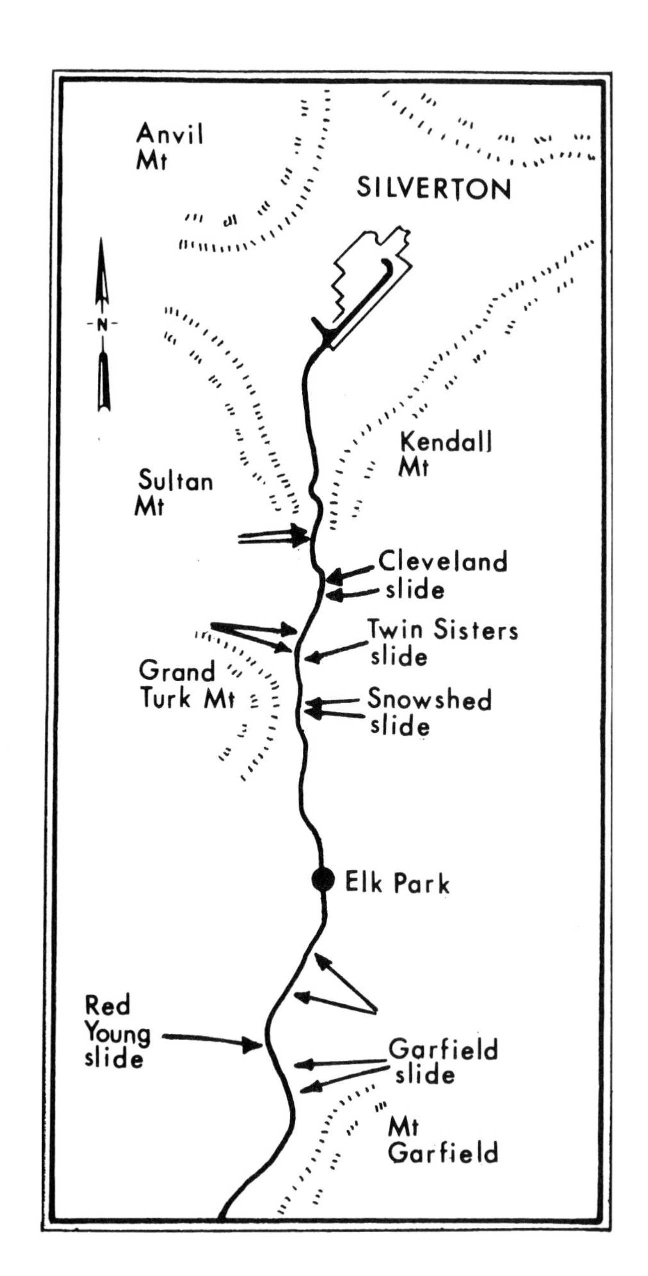

Further on, at the location of the Snowshed slide proper, the chute had run in all its glory, with rocks and tree trunks in its bulk. Thus, the previous hand-shoveling routine was again repeated.

Left, major snowslides along the Silverton route. (Map by R.C. Farewell)

Above, once the line was clear it was back to the train to move ahead to the next mass of white. Below, a quick blast through a minor drift knocked 473's headlight askew; a climb onto the pilot plow, a little work with a pry bar and the headlight was as good as new.

Needleton tank is depicted in the dead of winter; note the huge icicles on the tank sides. (both, Robert W. Richardson)

centrate traffic shipped from Silverton. The D&RGW received a good portion of the long haul revenue, 27 percent mostly, as the stuff went to processors outside Colorado. But finally even Charlie's skills were to no avail and, on February 18, 1953, the mine closed.

That day's Silverton mixed brought up more box cars from Durango so that loading could continue during any snowslide interruptions, even if a train could not make it through for several weeks. We have all read of ghost towns, mine closings and such, but to experience the actual day was something never to be forgotten. As we pulled in, the crew met the agent and several townspeople. It was a gloomy conversation. There were no smiles in the Best Cafe. It was a somber atmosphere in the caboose on the trip back, taking with us all those empty box cars. The darkening winter gloom seemed to match ours. As Conductor Bruce, a very religious man, observed, "Sometimes it seems even the good Lord Himself is against our little train".

The bad news kept coming. On September 30, 1953 the *Silver Vista* was destroyed in the Alamosa car shop fire. Car B-2 of the president's train also caught fire but escaped with severe clerestory damage. This brought on its sale to an Oklahoma man. The car returned a decade later to become the *Cinco Animas* for special group charters. Car B-1, used on the head-end of the president's special, also was sold for $1550 to become a coal yard office at Cañon City. Stripped of trucks, it returned later to its present exhibit spot at Alamosa. The B-3 had several owners at Durango and eventually came into the possession of the *Cinco Animas* group. It was renamed *Nomad* after a car mentioned in Beebe's books which was just a figment of his fertile imagination.

When a budget item came through to allocate funds to repair the snowshed at milepost 492 +, Perlman scratched it and had the snowshed removed, a costly error. Every winter that same slide ran, frequently several times. To buck it clear was not easy, as the slide usually included trees and rocks. Any vibrations could trigger a slide onto the engine. The bulldozer operator risked great danger, and, at least on one occasion an operator was noted fleeing down the track as his machine was hit by a slide.

In the late fall of 1949 and 1950 mudhens 463 and 464 became the exception to the shrinking K-27 class. Each received a major overhaul at Alamosa, including new fireboxes. They were road tested in January for use during the usual February through May snow problems. No. 463 was equipped with huge plow that reached up to its headlight, while 464 had more normal plow up to the middle of the smokebox front. The 464 put in many trips as well on the Rio Grande Southern in that line's final years. On March 31, 1949, the 463 had its first crack at the Snowshed Slide on the Silverton Branch. Uncoupling a train length away from the slide, 463 hit the leading edge of the slide higher than the locomotive itself. It barely broke through but went on a half mile farther to burst through several smaller slides. I learned that day that what looks like snow was really large chunks of frozen ice and snow, as some rained down on my head, and me with no hard hat!

The big wedge plow on the front of 463 had no room for a coupler, so switching at Silverton was time consuming. The engine would plow up to loaded box cars, then had to go to the wye, turn, and back up to the boxcars to couple. The section men had to wearily shovel out the last few feet to the boxcar, and again, as on many such occasions, I realized they were the unacknowledged hardest workers of the railroad.

That particular trip to Silverton included only two through passengers. Because of all the delays, arrival back in Durango was at midnight. Compounding the fatigue was learning that a foot of snow had fallen in Durango as well. One final delay for tired crew and laborers occurred as we neared the Animas bridge. The train came to a sudden stop, as if we had hit a granite wall. The main rod of the locomotive had come loose and plunged into the right of way, luckily missing rocks, or else the engine would have surely been pushed over! Wearily they got the main rod on the deck of the tender, the conductor meanwhile returning from a hike to use someone's phone. With no spare engine available, we would have to make it in, or walk, snow and all. The slight grade beyond Durango's Main Avenue now seemed as formidable as Cumbres' four percent. But, with the skill from years of experience, the engine crew got the engine working on one side rod only, and the train made it through town to the quiet Durango yard.

Another winter trip found 473 still decked out with the box headlight and yellow paint (now rather grimy) and with plow pilot. As usual there was little snow in the Hermosa Valley, but half way up the Animas canyon west of Rockwood the snows began to get deeper, and some small slides were noted as well. This caused more hard work for the section crew, who had to carry some large rocks off the track, but no dynamite was needed. This trip got as far as the Snowshed Slide beyond milepost 492. The slide had run about headlight high. After looking the situation over, there was a crew consultation. The conductor eyed the cliffs above, well aware that as the sun went down the sudden freeze somewhere up there could trigger another slide and maybe bury us all. The engineer settled it by pointing out that the 473 had outside cylinder cocks which would break off if he tried bucking. Moreover, the plow pilot was intended just to plow snow, not to buck whatever a slide might contain. So we backed the 28 miles to Rockwood and wyed rather than choosing to spend an hour wyeing at Elk Park with its dubious tail end stub switch.

Aware that Tacoma's postmaster would likely be on his motorcar from Rockwood to Tacoma, under the assumption that no train was due for hours, a sharp lookout for the motorcar was kept from the caboose cupola. The crew

Returning from a successful bout with the Animas Canyon snowslides, No. 463 was at Rockwood during a very overcast momentary respite.

was ready to set the air at first sight of the speeder. The vigil was to no avail as the postmaster came around a sharp curve on the high line with his head down to avoid the wind and only saw the caboose coupler when it was a few feet from him. The crash sure finished the motor car; the postmaster rolled off in the last several seconds before the crash. The caboose coupler suffered a slight scratch. A large sack of flour had burst and "ghosted" the postmaster and everything else in the vicinity. We picked up the surviving groceries and left the limping mailman at Rockwood, and the conductor made up an accident report.

Blasting rocks off the track was a science of sorts—a guessing based on experience. So during one trip when an unfriendly large rock was discovered in the middle of the track the roadmaster strategically placed several sticks of dynamite, while crew and passenger retreated back to second telegraph pole from the removal project. There the conductor decided we had ample safety from any falling debris. During the blast a one or two-foot oblong portion of the boulder went way above our heads, turning over and over and splashing into the Animas behind us. No one said anything, we just quietly climbed back into the caboose.

Summer operations over the Silverton Branch were much easier than during the winter. Normal weather patterns seemed to include a cloudless sky in the morning, rapidly gathering clouds by noon and scattered showers during mid- to late afternoon. Violent rainstorms, occasionally a cloudburst, would sweep masses of mud and rocks onto the tracks. There were many slide spots, all of which were named. Included were the Red Young Slide, named for an engineer who lost his life there. The McAtee Slide was named for the district general agent early in this century. A cloudburst in 1952 caused a slide which poured an enormous amount of debris down the mountainside at milepost 489 creating a lake. New track about a quarter-mile long was built up against the hillside, leaving the original track in the water. The superintendent of the division would not OK expenditures to bulldoze out the "dams". So passengers that summer were startled to hear the crew passing through the coaches shouting "Coleman Lake!" The submerged track could be seen in the water. Rain and weeds would make it much harder for the engines to keep traction, thus limiting train length to ten passenger cars. Under the best of conditions 11 or even 12 could be handled. It often took a half hour or more extra time for the northbound run, and quite a business developed in Silverton to swiftly feed the delayed but hungry travelers.

Management worried about the lack of communications along the route. The telegraph line was allowed to go out of use, however. In case of trouble the section men riding fire patrol speeders would be the messengers. One time the sole operable engine was dispatched from Durango. When Foreman Leonard Winckel was asked what he would do to rescue a disabled train, he outlined his plan to use a much heavier K-37, the only "hot" engine he had left. He would run it light beyond its restricted limit of Rockwood. He was sure it would carefully negotiate the curves and tight clearances of the high line, but at the light bridge over the Animas River at milepost 471.2 he would try a different strategy. One crewman would walk across the bridge, the other would start the engine and step off. If it made it across the first engineman would climb aboard! The stunt never had to be tried, fortunately.

During those first post-war years the two terminal towns could hardly be described as boosters of the Silverton trains. When a new chamber of commerce manager was

The date is February 18, 1953. Silverton was successfully reached on this particular trip. Mundane switching chores are now in order: moving empty concentrate boxcars into position for loading and staging loads for the run back to Durango. The task is made a bit more difficult by the presence of the pilot plow, an appliance that left no provision for a coupler. (both, Robert W. Richardson)

An excursion is at the Silverton depot, ready to depart down the canyon to Durango. The date: June 6, 1949. Narrow gauge passenger service was still in full swing on the Rio Grande. Note the train's consist, made up of cars from the San Juan *and* Shavano *pools, still in immaculate green with gold lettering and trim.*

hired at Durango in 1953, instead of the usual local retiree, the chamber selected a hot-shot experienced Californian. When he proposed a folder advertising the train, one of the town's prominent businessmen got up and killed the idea. "If the chamber spends one dime advertising the D&RG's trains, I'll have my lawyer put a stop to it!" When apprised of imminent probability of loss of railroad payroll, another Main Avenue merchant replied to the effect that it would be fine to be rid of those overpaid union people. At that time, full-time store employees received 40 or 45 cents per hour.

The situation was hardly different at Silverton. One businessman stated that, with his influence, he would get 15 miles of right of way and control access to cabins, hunting and fishing. The newspaper publisher brushed aside my plea to help prevent an abandonment and stated, "go on back to Alamosa and mind your own business". (Alamosa's railroad payroll depended somewhat on *The Silverton*, thus being very much my business.)

Railroad officials were somewhat ambiguous about the train. General Passenger Agent Eno in the summer of 1949, while standing in one of the vestibuled coaches, referred to it as "this junk". Several years later he was quoted in the press: "We have a little gold mine and don't know what to do with it". Another official, upon seeing a press clipping stating that the train had netted $93,000 the previous year, angrily declared he would not bend over to pick up such small change off the floor. Part of this attitude was that great plans were afoot to upgrade the mainlines from Denver and Pueblo to Salt Lake City and Ogden. Perlman, in 1951, told an analyst that, "Sure they could make something of the narrow gauge, but it would take funds and people that, if invested in the mainlines, would return much greater dividends".

In 1950 General Manager Ed West told banker Gotthelf (in my presence) that the Rio Grande's policy was quite simple. To become a "bridge carrier", it would get rid of all branch lines of whatever gauge, all passenger and local freight trains. Subsidiary Rio Grande Motorway would handle that. "Just change engines and cabooses at Pueblo, Denver and Salt Lake and run through traffic across both states." Gotthelf knew the railroad (his father had been Otto Mears' partner) and its history. His retort was that Colorado had put up with a second-rate railroad for 70 years and deserved a better return on its investment than to be treated like this. On our drive back to the San Luis Valley, he held forth at length, promising to get rid of the Rio Grande securities in his trust department.

Carlton Sills, the D&RGW advertising manager, came in one day to see what of the narrow gauge equipment we had saved at Alamosa he could get for resale to Knott's Berry Farm in California. He spoke while waving his arms around. He also wanted the address of the Rocky Mountain Railroad Club, to obtain the preserved Rio Grande Southern locomotive 20 from them. I am certain that Walter Knott knew nothing of this, nor later when D&RGW promised him the entire "painted train" for his desert ghost town project of Calico. Rio Grande management was certain they would be out of the Silverton train business very soon.

One unusual, but very satisfactory, side result of all this determination was that RGS "Galloping Geese" 6 and 7 survive to this day. The Brinkerhoff brothers of Rico employed the two unique vehicles in dismantling Rio Grande's Gunnison lines in 1955. Management told them to hang on to their equipment, because before long they would have the Silverton Branch to tear up. As years went by Jack and Paul Brinkerhoff would inquire as to status of *The Silverton*. They finally sold the two geese to Bob Shank, Jr. In 1984 the geese came to the Colorado Railroad Museum.

Sills disclosed in his comments that management had the idea that the passengers were all a bunch of "railroad nuts"—i.e., railfans. He did not choose to accept a contrary opinion that fans were a small minority of the passengers, most of whom were just tourists, the same kind of

It is a cold, snowy, bleak day in the winter of 1942. The Silverton Northern has run its last mile and the end has come to another of Otto Mears' dreams. D&RGW 319 is towing SN No. 4 from its Silverton home toward the diminutive locomotive's final meeting with destiny. (Hammond Mathews photo, Richard H. Mathews collection)

SILVERTON

During the depths of winter it may be some time between train arrivals at Silverton. Thus, quite a fleet of empty boxcars are kept on hand at the depot as a buffer to allow the mills to keep running. Such is the case seen here, with 463 doing a little shuffling before leaving town for Durango with loads. (Robert W. Richardson)

Colorado visitors who went to Mesa Verde and Rocky Mountain National Park. Sills was amazed to learn that one midwestern manufacturer, who with his family had unsuccessfully tried to ride the train and "wasted two days" of his vacation, was planning to tell his traffic manager to omit the Rio Grande on 14 cars a month of West Coast-bound freight. Apparently, management never thought such persons during their vacations would wish to ride *The Silverton* if they possibly could. Business people in Durango and Silverton were hardly more observant

Though a bias against railfans was evident, the railroad employees sometimes did things that showed an interest in their jobs beyond the time clock. Lake Trump, a volunteer at the Colorado Railroad Museum, learned all he could from us about operating and maintaining steam locomotives. On his first day on the job at Durango as a hostler helper, he opened the try-cocks on the boiler of a K-28 just being fired up. When both "spit" at him (no water, just steam!) he ran for the foreman who had just arrived for duty. At dawn the sleepy regular hostler had fired up both the K-28 and a K-37, trusting only to the gauge glass readings. As it turned out, these were false due to corrosion in their fittings. Luckily the fires had not yet scorched the crown sheets in either engine. Train 461 departed that morning only a little late.

A grateful Foreman Winckel held out his hand in thanks next time he saw me, wondering how I knew to always check the try-cocks and surprised that a "picture taker" would know this. He handed over a carton of old cab cards of long vanished engines to add to his thanks. "You rail nuts know more about running this railroad than we do," grunted one chief clerk at Alamosa.

Roundhouse Foreman Newt "Knucklejoint" Spearman one day asked me if I could measure a curve. Assured that it could be done with string, he told me to go get a ball of twine. "I'll pay for it," he added. With a hostler helping, we measured the curve of the switch leading to the balloon loop in the Durango yard. Only then did I learn that locomotive 492 had derailed there recently. The roadmaster denied that the track was at fault and insisted something was wrong with the K-37. He lost that one, for we computed about a 40-degree curve! But before Newt took it up with the roadmaster, I retreated to neutrality and allowed Newt to show off his newly learned "engineering" skill. The derailment not only had delayed *The Silverton* but an urgent Farmington freight as well.

There was extra work during the summer at Durango. That time of year being slack on the Delaware & Hudson Railway, where he was a locomotive engineer, Richard "Dick" Cooper would come to Colorado from New York and work summers as a fireman out of Durango. As a "griever" for the Brotherhood of Locomotive Engineers and Firemen he had years of experience with crewmen. He began collecting seniority rosters of the D&RGW, now a useful reference file at the Colorado Railroad Museum. Dick's years of service were mostly during the Rio Grande-land period, 1963 and later.

Except during the gas and oil boom of the 1950s, crews much of the year were all qualified engineers and conductors. The names that became so familiar were, in order of seniority: Lyons, Henry, Bryan, Smith, Blackstone, Murray, Thayne, Schaaf, Shell, Boles and Morgan. Engineers included Dieckman, Johnson, Connor, Dodds and Cummins. Tom Cummins also served as road foreman and assistant to the superintendent. The latter was a job that would have been refused by lesser persons, but Tom was a good all-around competent man for the job. No doubt I have omitted some names. I used to be able to count on Dick Cooper for that data, but he is gone now, too.

Frank Young, a quiet man, took the senior conductor's

Silverton usually gets blasted with all the debris of winter: ice, snow, and anything else the heavens can dish out. Ice between the rails is especially nasty to deal with, hidden by seemingly harmless snow drifts. K-27 459 stumbled on the ice and has managed to make things difficult for its continued progress. Fortunately, as seen in the background, help has arrived. (Hammond Mathews photo, Richard H. Mathews collection)

July 1, 1955. The tourists have begun to discover the Silverton experience. The operation is still a mixed train, but coaches far outnumber freight cars. (Robert W. Richardson) Below, on May 29, 1955, Dick Kindig was on hand just east of Rockwood for this double-headed excursion, recorded at 9:52 AM and powered by K-28s 478 and 476. Opposite, milepost 497, the end of track in Silverton, October 1945. (Robert W. Richardson)

job on *The Silverton* one summer because some other jobs had irritated him, but he did not like the Silverton job either. George Andriko used his seniority to be with the movie trains. George preferred to be a freight conductor, but enjoyed the movie runs and had a great time. When his uniform was given to the Colorado Railroad Museum the pocket still contained the train orders for his last trip on *The Silverton*, as part of a three-day excursion from Alamosa. Conductor Wayland Bruce retired January 1, 1953. He was credited with starting the tradition of coffee being served to chilled passengers, a popular public relations effort by the crews. His flat topped, old-fashioned cap now sits in one of our museum cases.

At the time the *California Zephyr* entered service, management introduced a "bus driver" style of cap and coat, abandoning the traditional dark-blue color for gray. The Durango crews were actually measuring themselves for the new outfits, when they realized bus uniforms would never do for *The Silverton* and stayed with overalls and occasionally a blue serge uniform like George's.

On March 29, 1954, the Wednesday-only off-season mixed was canceled, hereafter to operate only if there was a minimum of ten cars of freight to be delivered to or picked up from Silverton. The branch had now become the nation's first "tourist train" operation. Denver officials frowned and declared that this was hardly "public convenience and necessity", and the assistant superintendent insisted mother nature would end it all by either a cloudburst or a wall of water during the spring thaw following several warm cloudless days in the mountains.

However, 1954 saw some improvements, not the least being Al Perlman's departure to the ill-starred New York Central. The layover at Silverton was increased to two hours. No. 476, after its stack was removed for a movie role, kept the fake box headlight. This so impressed a post-

card producer that he used it as a subject of a giant color card that became immediately popular. So many riders showed up that, in mid-July, service was increased to five days a week, excepting only Tuesday and Saturday. The total for the year came to 15,068 passengers.

All of the passenger cars were turned out for the 1955 season in "Grande Gold" with an antique style lettering gracing the letter boards above the coach windows. A track extension at Silverton came into use on July 30th, allowing trains to pass by the depot and turn up 12th Street to Greene, just one block from the main street of town. That year, 81 trips carried 20,352 patrons.

Upon Perlman's departure from the Rio Grande, President McCarthy had called the department heads together. "We are no longer a one man railroad, and I expect each of you to manage your own departments." Long in poor health, McCarthy passed away February 12, 1956. Fifteen days later a new era was ushered in by election of the experienced and personable Gus Aydelott as president.

In 1956, 23,981 rode the train to Silverton and thousands more were turned away. Even though the train was not in the timetable, every trip was "sold out". Next year the *Alamosa*, the last parlor car on the narrow gauge, had its ten seats removed and was converted into a regular coach. Former Denver Tramway trolley bus seats were installed in other cars to bring the total train capacity to four hundred. The first run in 1957 was on June 14th, delayed by as much as two feet of water over the tracks in the Animas Valley meadows. The 476 and 478 also now had the fake diamond stacks installed. From then on to the advent of Rio Grande-land in 1963, things were much the same.

Even though 12 trips were canceled in the 1957 season, 24,868 patrons rode the 80 trips which did run and the parlor car *Nomad* began being added to trains on occasion. Finally, in 1958, the train was scheduled daily during in the peak portion of the summer, with tri-weekly trips in early June and September. It was now designated as train 461 westbound and 462 eastbound. White flags (which designated "extra" trains) were abolished in 1957.

In 1960 the Pueblo, Colorado, banking interests of Thatcher and White tried to acquire *The Silverton* but had to withdraw. Another group was formed to acquire the branch but it did not include anyone with railroad expertise. Finally, in 1959, management moved to file to abandon the branch. Eventually the Interstate Commerce Commission turned them down, despite the best efforts of the railroad's sarcastic Attorney Porter. On Wednesday, December 13, 1961, at an ICC hearing in Washington, DC, Porter tried hard to press the fact that the road should not have to run a tourist train. Early in 1962, the railroad was denied its application by the ICC and after deciding not to appeal, prepared to do an about face and see what could be done by operating the Silverton Branch in a positive manner.

It its decision of August 16, 1968, the Interstate Commerce Commission gave its approval to the abandonment of Rio Grande's narrow gauge mainline form Antonito to Farmington but stated:

> The passenger excursion business has in the past sustained and appears to continue to sustain the Silverton Branch, and the evidence shows a strong public desire and need for the benefits of tourism which flow therefrom. Abandonment of that branch is not proposed, but the abandonment of the issue lines would sever its only rail connection. Applicant intends therefore upon such abandonment to improve or enlarge the Durango roundhouse and move thereto all machinery necessary to maintain the motive power for the Silverton branch.

Case closed; *The Silverton* had survived.

Highball in Rio Grande-land! Changes to the Silverton mixed became highly obvious during the McKinney era. The incongruous "diamond" stack which had first appeared in 1950 on No. 473, seen here blasting through Animas City, was resurrected for all three K-28s, but fortunately the "box" headlight was not. (Robert W. Richardson)

Alexis McKinney and Rio Grande-land

by John S. Walker, Jr.

In February 1963, President G. B. Aydelott of the Denver & Rio Grande Western Railroad sent Alexis McKinney, former Assistant to the Publisher of the *Denver Post*, to manage *The Silverton* operation. The previous year the Interstate Commerce Commission had denied the company's petition to abandon the branch, and management had decided that it must find a way to improve revenue from operating the train which had become such a "cause celèbre". As soon as McKinney arrived in Durango, and before he had a chance to become well-acquainted with the wonderful world of narrow gauge, he started meeting with individuals who had forgotten more about railroading than he would ever need to know. They were that special combination of evangelist, zealot, statistician, historian, economist and curator for which there is no satisfactory name. They were too dignified to fit the word "buff" or "fan", too serious to be "enthusiasts" and too stable to deserve the descriptives of "bug" or "nut".

The more they talked, the more serious they became about the future of the 80-year-old narrow gauge empire. McKinney soon learned that among those who loved and respected the little railroad, there could be as many divergent opinions as there are among any other given number of people. These veteran devotees of slim gauge rail transportation were eager to tell him how they would run the railroad—an 1882 narrow gauge railroad just recast from the role of an ailing great-grandmother-in-law to that of prima ballerina, with the spotlights beaming and the orchestra playing. With such thoughts and with much fanfare McKinney dubbed his little kingdom "Rio Grande-land".

On a few points there was complete agreement among the "experts". First, the decision of the D&RGW to put money, effort and imagination into the preservation and perpetuation of the narrow gauge Silverton Branch was a great one—historically, philosophically, popularly and, quite likely, financially. Second, the Rio Grande's purchase of old properties in the immediate vicinity of the Durango depot was a remarkable example of farsightedness and common sense. Third, authenticity in the restoration and future planning for the railroad and the properties was essential.

But from there opinions began to vary, particularly as to what was authentic and what was phony. About the only solid point of agreement on this subject was that steam was to be king, and anything that remotely suggested diesels, streamlining or modernization was the depth of abomination. Unfortunately, deep ardor for authenticity can often be unsure in its concepts of what is authentic. It was up to McKinney to decide how far "authenticity" would be permitted to circumscribe the rebuilding of the long-neglected Durango-Silverton operation.

It would, McKinney said, be highly authentic to run up the canyon on 30-pound rail, but neither safe nor practical with the anticipated traffic brought on by the proposed renaissance. And in the restoration of old Durango, if he recreated faithfully the scene depicted in the 1890 photographs, train fans trying to cross Main Avenue would be up to their hips in mud after a rainstorm.

Some of these same disciplines preached that modern automobiles were not nearly as good as those 40 years ago. But McKinney could remember buying a quart of oil with every five gallons of gas and bragging when he had made 100 miles in a day. After he had listened to one particular diehard's diatribe against all things modern, a proverb came to him which he had inscribed on the wall

"Journey to Yesterday." By 1964 Alexis McKinney was advertising The Silverton *full bore. The new direction was a complete turn-about from prior years, when the Rio Grande wanted to abandon the line. Management finally realized that a tidy profit could be turned from hauling tourists between Durango and Silverton. Moreover, expansion of business activities into related areas surrounding the Durango depot opened the possibility for even greater returns. For the tourist, Rio Grande worked to make the trip as easy as possible. After all, if it was possible to make a patron feel that they "roughed-it" even though he or she rode on cushioned seats and enjoyed a gourmet meal in Silverton, then more the better. This WAS still the wild west and the Silverton experience was being described by Rio Grande as "A Matchless Travel Adventure," all the way down to old style lettering on some promotional material. About the only thing missing from Rio Grande's "lusty frontier days" was a staged train robbery or gun fight enroute. (Both, Museum collection)*

"Journey to Yesterday"

A journey on The Silverton is a scenic adventure unparalleled anywhere in the United States. But more than that, it is also a trip backward in time—back to the lusty frontier days of railroading in the Rockies.

The coach you ride in . . . the engine with its smells and sounds of steam, smoke and working steel . . . the syncopated rhythm of wheels on rails . . . the vastness of the mountains and the solemn intimacy of evergreen forests—all these would be familiar to the hardy pioneers who rode the train in 1882.

That was the year the narrow gauge track reached Silverton, fastest-growing mining camp in the scenic San Juans. In an amazing feat of construction, men had laid the rails all the way from Durango in nine months and five days, working through the howling blizzards of winter.

The Silverton line was a branch of the Denver & Rio Grande's pioneer system, built on the 3-foot gauge that had proved uniquely adaptable to steep grades and sharp curves.

By 1890, the Rio Grande had completed a more direct main line west from Denver which was standard gauge (4 feet 8½ inches) all the way to Salt Lake City—a vital link in transcontinental transportation, straight through the towering Rockies.

Thus the narrow gauges were by-passed, but the Silverton Branch served well—carrying most of the $300 million in ore produced in the region over the years.

By the 1950's, abandonments had reduced the little frontier lines to a few freight operations, with only a single passenger train still running on schedule: The Silverton.

Then, when it was the last—and probably because it was the last—The Silverton stirred with new life. First a few, then a few hundred of the new-day railroad devotees and vacationers came to ride the train for the sheer fun and inspiration of the "Journey to Yesterday." Soon the passengers each summer numbered in the thousands. In the 1963 season, there were more than 50,000.

Today, The Silverton can look to years of continued operation over its 45 miles of track through a region of matchless beauty and rugged grandeur. The Rio Grande has provided for its perpetuation as a living memorial to all the railroads and railroaders who helped win the West.

Meet Rio Grande-land

Rio Grande-land is the area of old Durango along Main Avenue in the two blocks adjacent to the depot. Work in progress now is evidence of the Rio Grande Railroad's determination to preserve not only the historic narrow gauge passenger train, but also as much as possible of its old-time surroundings.

Restoration of the turn-of-the-century buildings will include shops, entertainment, places for good eating, the arts, pioneer memorabilia, as well as excellent lodging accommodations as modern as today.

An important part of the development is a readily-accessible and adequate parking area adjacent to the depot.

Plan a little extra time to visit the Rio Grande-land. The attractions already established will make it well worth your while.

Alexis McKinney, *Director, Durango, Colorado*

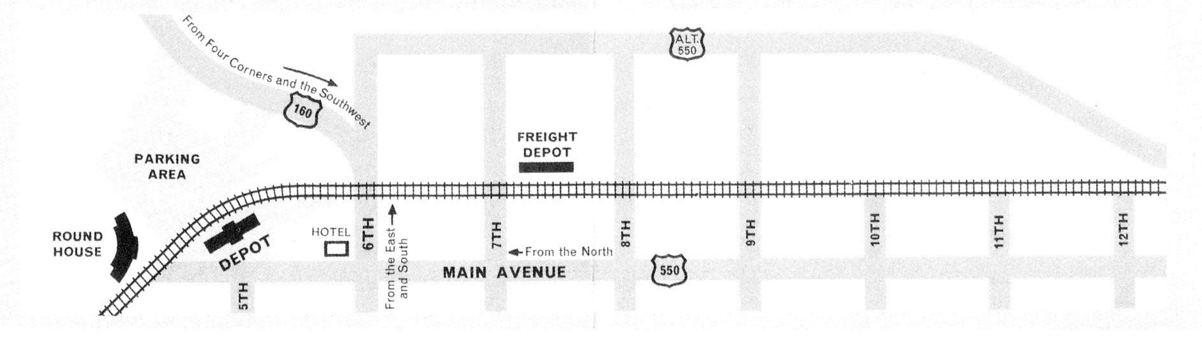

What was missing, however, was the mixed train of years past. When the Sunnyside Mine near Silverton shut down, the need for boxcars evaporated. Freight traffic was reduced to a trickle, an occasional drop-bottom load of coal every now and then. Of course Rio Grande continued to offer freight service over the line, but before long the caboose and passenger-accommodating combine were gone from the train, replaced with strings of "painted train" coaches.

Indeed, that was progress; Rio Grande had created "Rio Grande-land" which not-too-slowly replaced the old ways of the mixed train. In the process of defining its project, Rio Grande had created its own gold mine. The multi-fold increase in patronage over the line during the McKinney era showed that they found a product that they could sell. The question pondered was whether they really wanted to be in the tourist business in the first place.

This is the way it was on the Silverton Branch before tourists discovered the train. D&RGW No. 478 rolled train 462 eastbound across the meadows at Hermosa enroute back to Durango. Ahead of the combine and required caboose were a string of loaded concentrate boxcars and a pair of empty coal gondolas. Opposite, as the tourists found the Silverton, changes began to appear. Seen above is train 461 rolling toward Silverton with No. 473 on the point with a fake diamond stack and pseudo-oil style headlight applied. The changes were for a movie appearance, but were a portent of things to come. (both, Otto Perry, Denver Public Library Western History Dept.)

in his Rio Grande-land headquarters: "Beware, lest love of the antique lead to lamentation over progress."

In 1881, General William Jackson Palmer was building a narrow gauge empire he dreamed of expanding from Denver to Salt Lake City and all the way to Mexico City. In that year the Silverton Branch was started northward from Durango to carry the millions of dollars of ore coming from the mines of the high San Juan Mountains.

The line was built in less than ten months; the track reached Silverton on July 6, 1882. The Silverton train was in business. For decades, it knew no real competition in the southwest corner of Colorado. It could transport more people, more goods, heavier machinery and bigger loads than anything else that moved on land. The little close-together rails and short engines and cars could go where standard gauge trains could not: up steep grades, around sharp curves and along slender ledges hewn out of granite. Then came the competition in the form of paved roads, Model A's and Model T's, trucks and busses. By the 1930s, narrow gauges had had their day.

The Rio Grande had been improving its standard gauge mainline through the Rockies every year since 1890, and goods that once could go only by narrow gauge were being trucked to and from mainline points where they were shipped or arrived cross-country. These were waning years when forlorn little trains continued to struggle across Cumbres, Marshall, Poncha, Lizard Head and other fabled passes, fighting 20-foot snows in winter and hauling scantier loads with every passing month.

Finally, few were riding the narrow gauges to get anywhere, and no one was shipping anything on them if time counted. The age of abandonment began. It was an age of acrimony. Although hardly anyone rode or shipped on the narrow gauge, each community fought to keep its railroad. But in regulatory commissions and courts the railroads succeeded in shucking off one by one the once stalwart branches that had withered and atrophied.

None of those who were among the handful of persons aboard, including McKinney, then editor of the *Alamosa Daily*, could forget the 1941 last trip on the Chili Line, a too-flippant name for a valiant branch of the D&RGW between Antonito, Colorado, and Santa Fe, New Mexico. As the last train paused at Española, Embudo and Tres Piedras, the men and all the Indians stood silent, while the Hispanic and Anglo women broke out their handkerchiefs. Two years later, McKinney rode the last Colorado & Southern narrow gauge train down the mountain from Climax to Leadville, Colorado, the last remnant of the old Denver South Park & Pacific. That line was converted to standard gauge, so the loss was not quite so great.

The last narrow gauge passenger train to go was the spunky *San Juan*, which ran daily between Alamosa and Durango, with as many as six cars behind a flashy K-28. It made the 199.8 miles of winding grades in a flurry that took most of the hours between dawn and dusk. The trouble was that a bus or truck could make the same trip, 149 miles by highway, and back again in far less time. So in 1951, the *San Juan* chugged off into memories and onto the pages of the wonderful books on Colorado's mountain railroads.

Finally there was only one mixed train left. Fortune had ordained that it was to be the Silverton train. Of all the little railroads that might have survived, none could have been more fitting or deserving. Historically, scenically and in the affections of the public, it had much of the best of the others.

The Silverton, as it was now officially designated, had a destiny, but more of the amalgam of history and fate had to be added before that destiny took shape. Top management of the Rio Grande was not too interested at first in a swelling drumbeat that was reverberating across the hills from Durango. Because it was the last, people were beginning to rediscover *The Silverton*. In 1947, the train ran on 50 days, and 3,444 persons paid money to ride it. The conductors, brakemen, engineers, firemen and station agents were conducting their own sales campaign with anyone who would listen, and everyone on the train had to listen.

The campaign did not really take fire until 1953 when, with 48 summer trains, 12,264 passengers tried frontier railroading. Unrecovered from the economic and public relations pummeling it had taken in the declining days of the narrow gauge, the railroad insisted it was not in the sightseeing business. *The Silverton* was not transportation; it was sightseeing.

Some outside interests began to look at the line and offered to buy it if the Rio Grande would abandon the line and sell it at scrap prices. One overture came from William M. White of Pueblo, who paid a big chunk of earnest money to the railroad, expecting to acquire the line and operate it as a non-profit foundation. But his idea of a living museum of pioneer railroading went down the drain under a deluge of protest from Silverton and Durango. Many reasons were given for the opposition, but one underlay them all: the two counties affected would have lost their largest single source of tax revenue. In those days, this amounted to about $187,000 a year from the railroad.

William Kostka of Denver and a group of associates, who revered old railroads but respected legitimate profits, also explored the possibility of buying the Silverton Branch. A group of Durango leaders, all mindful of the railroad's economic importance to the region, formed a corporation, subscribed to stock, completed operational studies and made an offer.

But by 1960, the year the White Foundation withdrew, passengers on *The Silverton* had increased to 35,871. The next year's total was nearly 2000 more, and in 1962, with the train running on a record 100 days, the ridership reached 37,855.

There was a hearing on abandonment. The D&RGW proved, as is true today, that maintenance and operating costs of a Victorian era railroad in the space age are indeed steep. But the word painting of vacationing America clogging the highways to Durango to ride *The Silverton* was too persuasive. On April 16, 1962, the Interstate Commerce Commission decreed a final "No".

Under McKinney's benign direction *The Silverton* became one of the premier railroad attractions in America. This was not, however, because it traversed one of the noblest mountain realms on the continent. It was not because it was narrow gauge. It was not due to the fact that the train was exclusively steam-powered. Other passenger train operations had had all of these elements and died. McKinney discerned that the real reason was the single fact that *The Silverton* was the last.

Steam power, as an attraction in itself, did not draw paying customers in sufficient numbers to survive, or all America would still be riding behind steam. And scenery, in itself, did not draw customers in sufficient numbers to make passenger trains pay. Rio Grande-land's parent, the standard gauge and dynamic Denver & Rio Grande Western, was running two fine trains through some of the most magnificent mountain scenery on the continent. One of them passed through the Moffat Tunnel and amid the towering peaks west of Denver; the other went via Pueblo and up through the most formidable rock cleft ever pierced by rails—the Royal Gorge. The most plentiful thing aboard each was empty seats. People did not buy steam for steam's sake, and they did not buy scenery for scenery's sake.

What was the winning combination of "authenticity" and efficiency? *The Silverton* had just enough equipment to operate until it could get more. It had three steam locomotives and enough of the necessary rare breed of men to keep it running. It had scenery in breathtaking abundance. It was the last of its kind in our country, but could McKinney keep it authentic while making it profitable?

With the existing equipment all of the people who wanted to ride the train could not be carried. That is where simple logistics created a conflict of desires, as well as an inevitable compromise of some ideals. McKinney would have to alloy the pure and mellow gold of authenticity with some of the tougher and baser metals of realism and practicality. He believed the resulting product would still be lustrous and high-karat. After all, authenticity is an exceedingly elusive thing, either to define or to capture. This was true both with the train itself and with that section of Durango he was seeking to develop as a tourist center.

No doubt some of the earliest defenders of steam railroads cried "unauthentic!" when coal began to replace wood in the firebox. Shovels, stokers and oilburners were successively authentic in their days, and each marked a stratum of the steam epoch. So, in the flashback into history that he was trying to mold and perpetuate in southwestern Colorado, which era would McKinney choose?

The answer was no specific stratum, for none would be acceptable, popular, or even possible of re-creation, much less profitable. He could not go back to 30-pound rail, and the little locomotives that first ran up the Rio de las

Animas Perdidas in the 1880s were long gone. But there were enough of the old coaches to make up a beautiful train, and the 470-series locomotives were genuine and old enough to satisfy all who have ridden behind them.

For a while plans were in a state of continual change. The wooden cars were taken to Denver one at a time to be fitted with steel reinforcing sills. The last business car, the B-7, was reworked for use as a charter car for special parties.

The people who came to ride *The Silverton* early that spring of 1963 made it obvious to McKinney that all of the old equipment on the Rio Grande was not going to be enough. Therefore two new coaches were constructed at the railroad's Burnham Shops in Denver. These were the first new passenger cars built for the slim gauge since the parlor car *Alamosa* had been turned out in 1904 and the first ever of steel construction. Steel beam trucks were obtained from two former postal cars, 66 and 122, which had been assigned to outfit service. The new cars matched very closely in external appearance the older wooden ones, with open platforms, truss rods (for looks only), clerestory roofs, coal stoves and kerosene side lamps inside. Window frames were aluminum and the car sides were "scribed" to simulate wood siding.

Next came first one, then a second, covered gondola, equipped with seats running longitudinally. Each was turned out in little more than a week. Numbered 400 and 401, they proved instantly not only acceptable but highly popular. They were made from old standard gauge freight cars that had been converted in the 1950s to narrow gauge gondolas for use on the Alamosa-Durango-Farmington freights during the oil and gas boom in northern New Mexico. The tops were regular metal boxcar roofs painted aluminum. These open sided cars still had freight car trucks, which did not make for the softest ride. However, the pair were not unattractive additions to the train.

Up to the time of delivery of the two gondolas to Durango, each day's train was a worry. Twelve cars with every seat occupied made a maximum load for a 470-class locomotive; on the grades, the little engines were obviously burning their hearts out. On occasions when the business car *General William Jackson Palmer*, the private car *Nomad*, or both, were added the temporary answer was double-heading.

Since engine 476 was undergoing a complete overhaul at Alamosa and had not been available all that year, McKinney had only the 473 and 478 to do the doubling-up. But, while this was as pretty a sight as could be seen, it had its worrisome aspects. There was no other motive power to send up the line if anything stopped the operation with two engines up ahead. There were twelve heavier locomotives, six 480s and six 490s, but they were too big for the Silverton Branch's existing bridges and clearances.

With the arrival of the first gondola, *The Silverton* made history. From that day, July 20, 1963, the daily passenger train on the narrow gauge ran in two sections. It was a big day in Durango, both for the townspeople, who take almost a family pride in the train, and for the railroad employees. Only a rail enthusiast can savor fully the significance of that morning when green flags were mounted up front on engine No. 478; the flags meant "another section following".

Nobody could remember ever hearing of green flags on a narrow gauge engine, and there were none in Durango. So Hubert Meek, the trainmaster, went uptown to the J.C. Penney store and bought the green cloth. Then Mrs. Leonard Winckel, wife of the roundhouse foreman, assumed the role of Betsy Ross and produced as neat and

Opposite, in front of the D&RGW depot, No. 473 simmers while the patrons of an excursion enjoy the thin air of Silverton. Note the presence of both green and gold coaches as well as the caboose behind 473's tender. Above, Needleton tank is a water stop frequented by most northbound trains. Following expectation, No. 476 has paused for a drink. Note the box headlight, but as yet the absence of a "diamond" shaped cover attached to the engine's stack. Change was coming; before long No. 476's stack would resemble that of sibling No. 473. (both, Robert W. Richardson)

symbolic a pair of banners as ever flew athwart a smokestack. Two trains up the Animas! It made front page headlines in Durango and Silverton.

The old 9605 open-top gondola, veteran of many railfan excursions, went into the regular consist as part of the second section so that if any in the overflow ticket line wanted to ride standing up, they could get aboard. The two covered gondolas brought daily seating capacity to 591. Except for a few days, when the Durango Spanish Trails Fiesta and three rainy mornings cut into the business, it was standing room only, with the trains sold out from one to three days ahead of time.

On August 13th, a particularly bright and warm day, 697 persons rode *The Silverton*, then the all-time high and a sobering figure McKinney did not try to equal. That morning Amos Cordova, the Durango agent, tried to close the ticket window when the stand-up gondola was comfortably full. But people in line, including men and women carrying children, demanded to get aboard, even though they knew they would have to stand up for three hours and 25 minutes each way.

Those who remembered when the narrow gauge was running out its days on the Chili line to Santa Fe, over Cumbres Pass from Alamosa to Durango and across Marshall Pass to Gunnison found the Durango depot platform a wondrous place those mornings. In the 1920s and 1930s three or four cars would have a dozen people aboard, on the better days, and sometimes only two or three. That was grimly authentic.

Now there were crowds at the depot. At 4:30 AM a line started forming to get first chance at possible cancellations of reservations or for standing room. When the trains pulled out, there were faces in every window, and the gondolas were fully loaded.

Durango's affection for the narrow gauge was genuinely a remarkable phenomenon. Morning after morning, for both trains, children came out of houses near the track and along the bluffs overlooking the city to wave. They would be back waving when *The Silverton's* two sections came whistling home in the evening. Living near the railroad tracks used to be a social stigma; in Durango, it became a status symbol. At Silverton, a restaurant owner

smelled the train smoke, drew a deep breath, and remarked, "that's the smell of money." This kind of unauthenticity McKinney did not discourage.

If the jammed train was not perfectly authentic, neither was the method the ex-newspaper editor adopted to see that as many as possible got seats. Formerly, it was the practice to get everybody with tickets to board the train half an hour before departure time. The conductor would go through the cars and note by the empty seats how many no-shows there were. He then took this information to the agent in the ticket office, who would sell tickets to those waiting in line.

Now, a few minutes before departure time, McKinney would send the conductor through the train with a walkie-talkie. He spoke into his transmitter, and the agent heard, loud and clear from the receiver on his counter, "four seats in the 327". In a few seconds four people, tickets in hand were starting for car 327. But the walkie-talkies would stay behind in the depot, and once the train started up the line, it was as pleasing a combination of happy, modern America and beautiful old railroad train as anyone could desire.

Even the improvised covered gondolas seemed to fit into the picture. They had a cheerful air about them, but they did not seem out of place, and they filled a desperate need. With eight cars on one train and seven on the other, the 470s took the grades like the high-stepping little thoroughbreds they were.

An interesting occurrence was the operation of the two trial trips to Aztec, New Mexico, on the Farmington Branch. These featured a two-and-one-half hour stopover allowing passengers to visit the Aztec Ruins National Monument and enjoy a chuckwagon lunch put on by the town. The first trip on September 7th had 128 riders and the second a week later drew a few more, both far short of a capacity crowd. The purpose was to determine if such a trip could be an alternate if, as sometimes happened, high water would prevent operation up the Animas Cañon.

But what of next year and the future beyond that? McKinney had no doubt that in the "four-corner" area of southwestern Colorado existed one of the greatest vacation and tourist potentials in the nation. However, Durango was not ready yet and neither was the narrow gauge. During the three and a half months of the greatest tourist activity, the community did not have accommodations for all who did come, and there must have been many who did not come because they knew they would find no rooms available.

The same was true of the train. Those who were hoping for cancellations or who rode standing up were apart from scores who undoubtedly never went near the depot. They either had phoned or learned from motel operators that the train was sold out.

At the end of the 1963 season it was McKinney's conservative estimate that the daily trains would have averaged 725 passengers, instead of the still amazing 512, if there had been cars to carry that many. Although a public relations man by profession, he therefore made little effort to encourage the national publicity that was within easy reach. It might sound strange, but is nevertheless true, that he hoped there would not be a great amount of such publicity that year, and for a valid reason. Until Du-

Opposite, the transition to "Rio Grande-land" occurred over a period of time. At Trimble Hot Springs, 473 sports an altered stack and headlight. Note the train's consist, gold in front, green to the rear. Above, The Silverton mixed in transition, in the dead of winter at Hermosa. (both, Robert W. Richardson)

rango and the railroad could take care of the people who were already coming, it would be foolish to promote any more visitors.

The development of the Rio Grande-land tourist attractions did not gain startling headway in the first few months, but it had a good beginning. An architect started a master plan for the area on South Main Avenue owned by the railroad. Three buildings were remodeled according to concepts brought forth by this architect, Curtis Copeland of Denver.

Here, again, the pace had to be deliberate rather than rapid. If a full blown amusement and entertainment center were created overnight in Durango, the result would be to attract more people than either the town or the Rio Grande could accommodate. Thus the community, the Rio Grande-land project and the train had to grow simultaneously, McKinney decided.

In 1963 visitors to Durango saw what was the beginning of a bold and, in a sense, unprecedented railroad venture. Those who had been there before saw a great deal of change. A large parking lot across the tracks from the depot had replaced a portion of the railroad yard that six months before had been an unsightly expanse of junk heaps, decrepit equipment and weeds. Parking no longer was the major headache it once was for the customers, the railroad and the city. The old daily jumble of parked cars around the depot itself had been an eyesore, inconvenience and hazard in seasons past. The new lot did away with that. Now photographers could get pictures of the trains, the depot and the waiting crowds without obstructions.

The old depot had been spruced up without altering its plan and functional frontier design, and a new shingle roof set it off admirably. New and adequate restrooms had taken the place of a wholly authentic but much criticized old facility. A commodious new waiting room occupied the north end of the building, where the express office once had been. The pop, coffee and donut machines in the corner were neither historic nor authentic, but they were there to serve a need only until the Rio Grande-land facilities took over in more fitting style.

These were only starters in McKinney's "Grande" design. There would be an attractive fence to separate the parking area from the yard tracks. The coming winter would see more restorations in Rio Grande-land and announcements of attractions that would open in the spring of 1964.

In a report on his first few months' progress to the National Railway Historical Society's 1963 convention in Denver, McKinney invited members to visit southwestern Colorado and the Durango-Silverton narrow gauge domain. Early in the 1964 season, a group of 17 travel agents accepted McKinney's invitation. They wanted to see first-hand what they were selling to people who were planning vacations in the West. The group had traveled by jet, by car and by bus; on a bright southwestern Colorado morning they climbed aboard a little yellow-orange railroad car at the Durango depot.

Rio Grande was changing more than just The Silverton *toward the end of its narrow gauge heyday. Consider USA 4700N, leased to examine the possibility of dieselizing the remainder of the narrow gauge empire. Near Bondad, Colorado on the Farmington branch on February 24, 1954, No. 4700N was rolling along with 44 cars in tow. (R. H. Kindig)*

To modernize switching chores at Durango, in 1963 Rio Grande purchased a narrow gauge diesel locomotive from Edward Hines Lumber Company. This mini-monster packed an impressive 20,550 pounds of tractive effort into its diminutive body, more than enough to accomplish what needed to be done around the Durango yards. (Otto Perry, Denver Public Library Western History Dept.)

The depot itself had been built in 1882—wooden, square-cornered and high ridge-roofed. The car they boarded also was wooden and had been built over 80 years before. This was one of ten coaches, painted in what McKinney's fellow railroaders at 1531 Stout Street in Denver called "Rio Grande Gold".

Up ahead was a fine little monster of power and symmetry, a 470-series K-28, breathing fire and ready to do what it had been doing since it came out of the American Locomotive Company back in 1923. It was known as a "sports model" mountain type narrow gauge engine.

At 8:30 AM, the train started up the valley. Nearly 700 other passengers could describe the wonders and delights of the day shared with the travel agents. So could over 51,000 persons who had ridden the little train the previous year. When the travel agents returned that evening to Durango, they called the trip—45 miles to Silverton and back again at speeds sometimes crowding 15 miles an hour—the highlight of their whole western expedition.

A few days later, a distinguished group of explorers, scientists, writers and educators rode the same car on the little train. They were members of the committee on research and exploration of the National Geographic Society. One of them, who had stood atop Mount Everest a few months before, hooked a leg over a back platform railing to lean out for a picture of the Animas gorge far below. Two former directors of the Smithsonian Institution shot countless rolls of film. An admiral took solitary command of an open vestibule and contemplated the mountain skyline from a non-nautical, but nevertheless rolling, deck.

In just short of a year and five months the D&RGW had established what was named Rio Grande-land and started to do something no major railroad had ever done before: to regenerate, operate and perpetuate an historic, pioneer rail line. History and fate already had worked through the years to single out *The Silverton* train as one which would outlive all its early day contemporaries.

As an emissary of the D&RGW who wore no railroader's cap, Doug Morrison, a Denver real estate broker, went to Durango and succeeded doubly well in a vital mission. He rounded up options on all the property in a block-and-a-half of Main Avenue completely surrounding the Rio Grande's old depot and narrow gauge yard, and he made and kept friends. Exercise of the options gave the railroad complete control of an area of ancient and drab buildings that had degenerated through the years into something between a skid row and a honky tonk.

As train passengers had increased, they had been subjected to more and more problems—impossible parking handicaps, panhandlers, peddlers, handbill-passers and even some train ticket speculators. By 1964 all this had changed. Five of the Main Avenue buildings that had deteriorated beyond restoration had been demolished. There was a commodious parking area right across the tracks that was not only convenient but made money for the railroad. In the middle of June 1964, what had been the third-rate Savoy Hotel was reopened as the General Palmer House, a motor-hotel that was plush and modern inside and decorously restored outside. Also separated from the depot by an expanse of green lawn was a new restaurant, the Grande Palace. It was opulent, elegant, and catching the fancy of the citizenry of the region as well as that of the visitors.

In 1964 the two-train schedule started nearly four weeks earlier, and with 772 seats now available, Amos Cordova, the agent, sold up to 800 tickets on some days. About that time, McKinney discovered a psychological trend which affected both business and tourist convenience in Durango and on the narrow gauge train.

It might be called the "weekend phobia" or perhaps the "Tuesday-Wednesday syndrome". It worked something like this. Many, if not most, of the people who planned trips to Rio Grande-land knew they wanted to ride the train as part of their vacation. When they started to arrange the date for their reservations, they would say, "We'll never be able to get tickets on Saturday or Sunday, because everybody will be wanting them on the weekend. So, let's ride *The Silverton* on Tuesday or Wednesday". As a result, it was possible almost any Saturday or Sunday to board the train. Everyone seemed to land in Durango on Tuesdays and Wednesdays, and so it was on those two days especially when up to 50 or more persons might be left at the depot after the second train pulled out.

On the trains in 1964 there were six more brand new all-steel coaches, built with resourcefulness and craftsmanship in the railroad's Denver shops during the winter. They were almost duplicates of the original 1880-vintage cars which were still going strong. What is more important, even the dyed-in-the-wool railfans thought they were wonderful.

So many things took place in McKinney's first 18 months. The last of the old and too-light 52-pound rail on the line was replaced that spring of 1964 with heavier steel. Now there was none lighter than 65-pound and some as heavy as 90 pounds to the yard. Gone were a few trees and an unsightly old telephone line that frustrated the photographers trying for spectacular viewing angles into the Animas gorge from the train. Instead of backing apologetically into Silverton as it used to do, the train now ran snorting right up to the center of town and created a twice-a-day pageant at the arrival times of noon and 1 PM.

Early in July an additional parallel track was built at Silverton to accommodate the second section of the train. So now, for 45 minutes each noon hour, two trains stood side-by-side, their engines commanding the intersection of Twelfth Avenue and storied Blair Street, a sight perhaps unique in the nation.

McKinney's handsome narrow gauge business car, the *General William Jackson Palmer*, was growing ever more popular as a charter car for those who like their pioneer railroading swanky. One hundred and fifty dollars would, in 1964, put your private car, with both platforms and everything, on the train, and you could take 17 guests along at that price. The ultra-plush 1880s private car *Nomad* and another classic car, the B-2, were added to the narrow gauge treasures at Durango. They, too, could be put on *The Silverton* train if someone wanted to entertain a board of directors in the grand manner.

A rewarding reciprocal program linked promotion of *The Silverton* with that of the other top-ranked vacation attraction of southwestern Colorado, Mesa Verde National Park. The theme was that you should not experience one without the other.

In Durango and throughout the area there was an obvious new spirit of confidence due to several developments, but principally two. One was the opening, late in 1962, of the Navajo Trail, the road that "had to be". It traversed the most magnificent part of the southwestern United States, linking the New Mexico-Arizona-California "sun country" with the mountain wonderlands of Colorado. It has become one of the favorite tourist routes of the west, and Durango sits astride the epicenter of it and its prime scenic crossroad, the Million Dollar Highway.

The second tremendous boost was the assurance of President Gus Aydelott and the directors of the Rio Grande that *The Silverton* was going to run on through the years. With more than a million dollars already in it, by mid-1964, the D&RGW removed the fear of years past that the rug might at any moment be pulled from under the regional economy.

Because the train, like Mesa Verde, was a national and even global attraction, there was a growing feeling in neighboring communities—Cortez, Mancos, Dolores and Pagosa Springs in Colorado, and Farmington and Aztec in New Mexico—that they were all part of a recreational empire in which intercity rivalries had no place. Durango, in turn, was promoting the Four Corners, Navajo Lake, Monument Valley, Canyon de Chelly, the Indian country, the Grand Canyon, the Great Sand Dunes, Aztec National Monument and other wonders within a couple of hours' driving radius.

It is possible to make an interesting comparison here. Those of us who watched Denver emerge as a major city

This is the way it was, but is no longer. On June 6, 1949, D&RGW 473 was stopped at Ah Wilderness with an excursion, each passenger car resplendent in coach green with gold lettering, then still the company standard.

in the post-war years can remember a strange conflict of emotions and predictions at the dawning of a new day. The trite but apt expression of those who foresaw what was happening, and what had to happen, was "bursting at the seams". Today in southwestern Colorado the seams are getting harder and harder to hold, and among its population are counterparts of all those who created the conflicts of hope and misgiving, optimism and foreboding in Denver in the late 1940s. In the Mile High City, many who had coasted along easily on earnings of old office buildings, unimaginative business, and ho-hum services were not too enthusiastic about the prospect of jet age competition from either hometown ventures or outside investors. But a tide was coming in, and nobody could stop it or even slow it down. The successful people of Denver today are those who saw that bigness and greatness were compatible, that a city could be both a front-runner in business and a happy place to live.

Durango and southwestern Colorado are not in line for skyscrapers and international airports for some years to come, but destiny is shaping there fast in a tourist and vacation business almost beyond contemplation. And while there are those who do not like it, there are more who are readying themselves for the roles they will have in the progress to come.

Favorite and secluded fishing spots are sure to become more crowded. Where oldtimers could pack all day without seeing another mortal, there are going to be more jeeps, more photographers, more hunters. The privately owned meadows and farms in the Animas Valley will be built upon. But there will be one slightly different note: land along the railroad tracks will sell at a premium; people love the narrow gauge.

Big motel and resort interests are looking at properties in town and out, and every week there is talk of another project. However, there are millions of acres of mountains and canyons, and all the people who are coming to the country could not really crowd it.

Durangoans and southwestern Coloradoans hope that their region will remain as beautiful and genuine as possible, and that commercialism will stay where commerce belongs and not exploit nature as it has in some other parts of the state. They are determined that tourists will not be charged for looking down into the Black Canyon of the Gunnison or for beholding spectacular Bear Creek Falls on the Million Dollar Highway. In Durango, they are looking for ways to beautify the river frontage and to eradicate a smelter dump that mars the landscape. In the meantime, there is great opposition to proposed scarring of mountainsides with new gravel diggings as has been done between the Air Force Academy and the Garden of the Gods along the Front Range of the Rockies.

In three years, McKinney proved that business progress and enjoyment of natural wonders need not be irreconcilable and they need not be compromised. Fortunately, the sight of a coal burning, cinder-and-smoke puffing locomotive chugging through the virgin wilderness with a long string of Rio Grande Gold cars behind it mellowed to one of beauty and not of commercialism.

To his lasting regret, McKinney was called back to Denver after less than three years in Durango, leaving the narrow gauge to continue its own progress on the impetus he had helped to generate. Rio Grande, involved at that time in a major railroad merger battle with the Union Pacific, promoted McKinney to director of public relations, a position he held until his retirement in 1973. Since then he has continued his association with railroading as vice president of the Colorado Railroad Historical Foundation and Museum in Golden.

Change had come to The Silverton; *tourists had discovered the train. Each summer day lines stretched out of the depot ticket office; potential patrons glancing at their watches and the slowly diminishing line. The days of green coaches and mixed trains were gone forever. (both, Robert W. Richardson)*

Doubleheaded train 463 was recorded on opening day, May 5, 1990, as it exited the Animas River bridge in north Durango. There is a permanent slow order for D&S's K-36 and K-37s over this span; no such restriction exists for the K-28s though. Blasting enough smoke and steam to the heavens to appease even the most hardheaded of narrow gauge gods, 476 and 473 are doing their best to bring their train up to track speed for the run to Silverton. (R.C. Farewell)

Mainline to Silverton

by R. C. Farewell

Through the 1950s the Silverton Branch was an integral part of Rio Grande's narrow gauge empire, a domain held together by a slim-rail mainline core that somehow managed to remain intact through rapidly changing times. Time, however, and a changing world extracted its toll on the once-extensive narrow gauge network. One active period of major narrow gauge abandonments and removals peaked during the 1950s. After the dust settled from this abandonment episode there remained a single narrow gauge mainline system that stretched southward from Alamosa to Antonito, Colorado, thence west over Cumbres Pass to Chama, New Mexico. From Chama, the mainline meandered further west through the rolling fringes of the southern San Juan Mountains to Durango, Colorado.

At Durango a pair of branches radiated from the mainline connection into the hinterland. The first of these two hub spokes was the Silverton Branch. From the Durango depot the Silverton Branch departed northward up the Hermosa Valley. Passing the hamlet of Hermosa, the branch climbed cliffside slopes to Rockwood, thence dropped down into the Animas River canyon and followed the serpentine gorge through the most rugged part of the San Juan Mountains reaching the one-time mining boom town of Silverton.

The second spoke radiating from the Durango hub was

(continued on page 184)

A summer's sunset finds D&S K-28s 476 and 478 being serviced at Durango. (R.C. Farewell)

Durango depot seemed to be a quiet place when Otto Perry pictured the structure during one of his railroad odysseys, in June 1948. The parking lot was empty, because the tourists had yet to discover the Silverton. There was still plenty of freight and passenger traffic through Durango to and from the east.

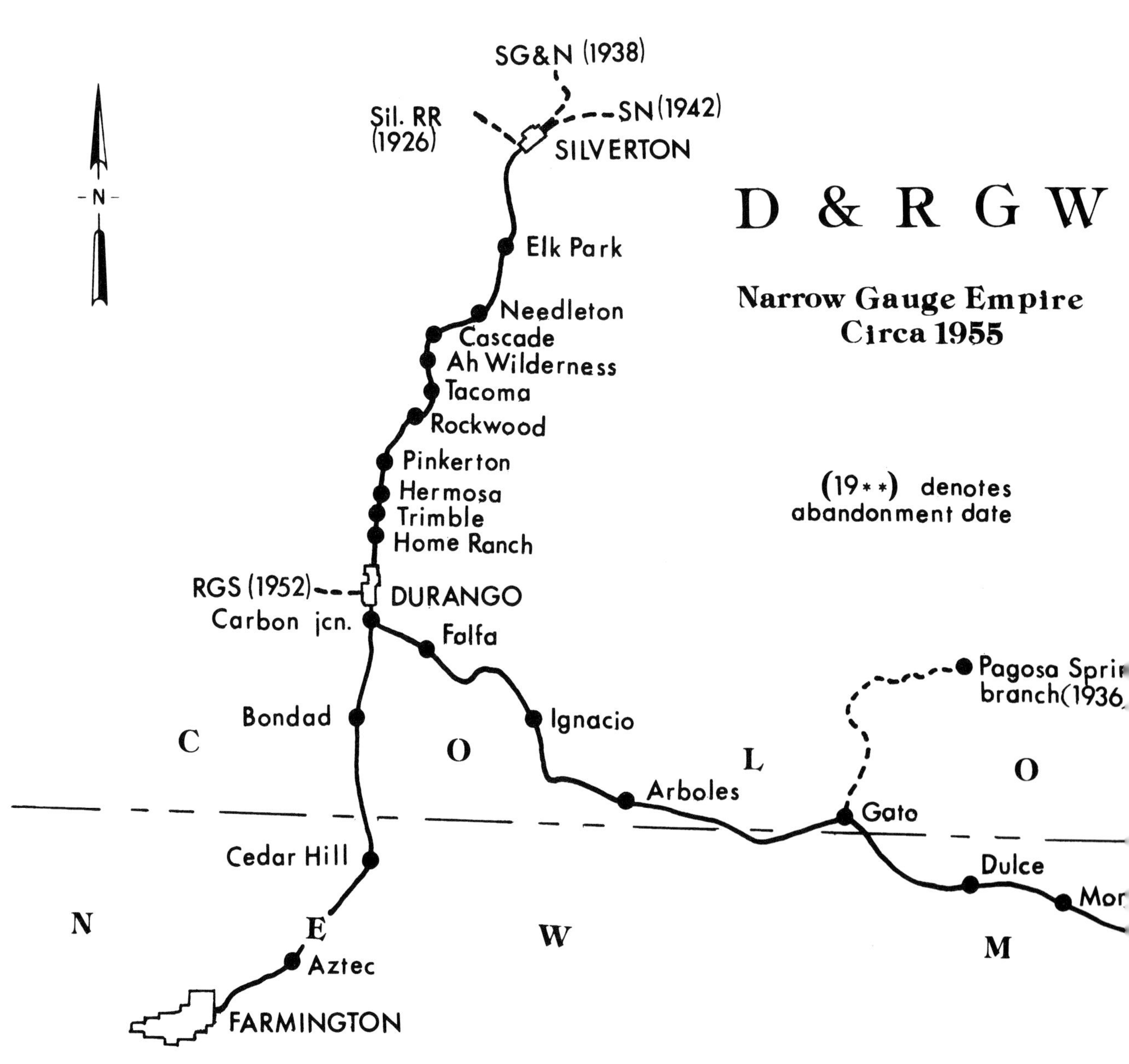

The first-class passenger San Juan *is seen above just east of Durango at Falfa on October 12, 1941. The* San Juan *was the assignment for Rio Grande's K-28s until discontinuance of the train in 1951. After its demise, the trio of remaining K-28s was assigned to Durango where they were utilized on the Silverton Branch. (both, Otto Perry, Denver Public Library Western History Dept.) (map below by R.C. Farewell)*

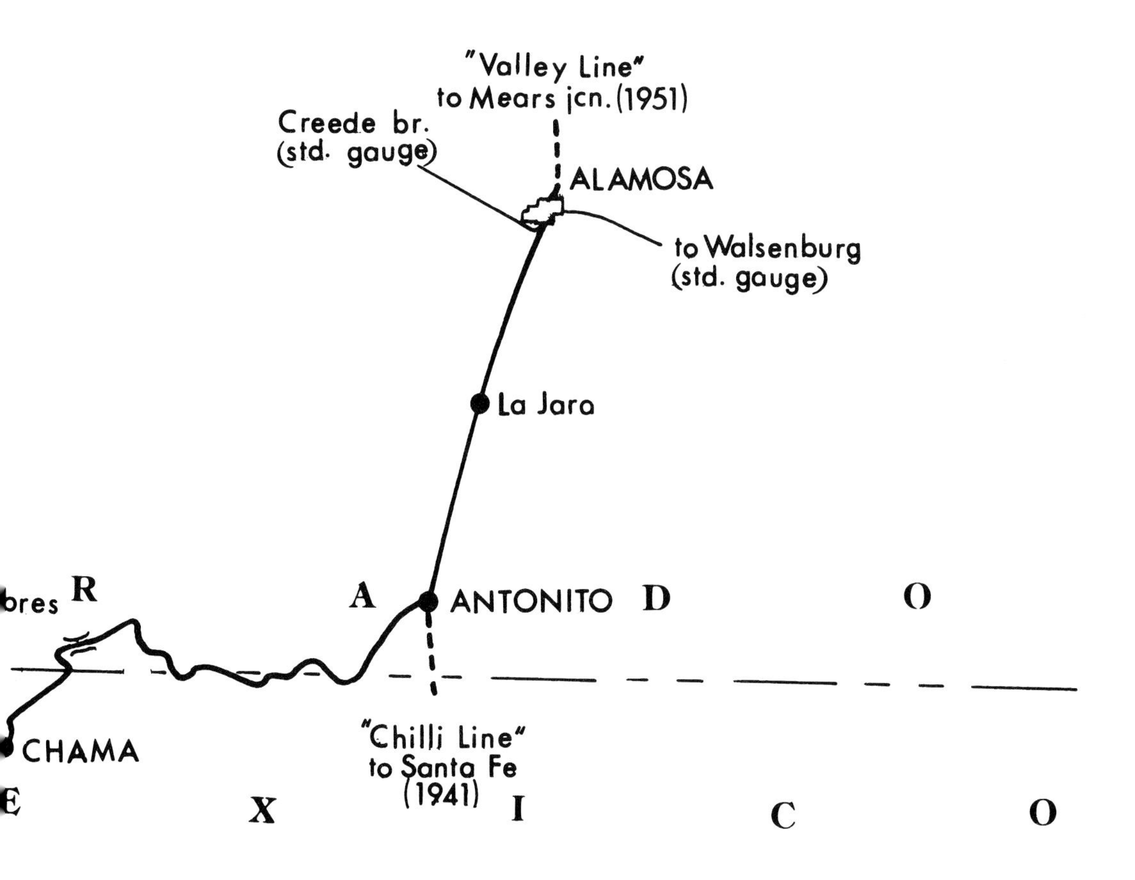

Rolling into Chama on the Durango-Alamosa mainline is an eastbound manifest under the care of K-36s 488 and 482. Just ahead are the wye and stock loading pens where 480 is working. The through freight train will receive priority; a prudent speed restriction is still in order. (Three photos, Robert W. Richardson)

JUST ANOTHER DAY AT CHAMA

At right, K-36 480 switches stock cars on the Chama wye in preparation for loading. The activity will be coming to a halt, however, for an eastbound manifest bound for Alamosa is rolling into town and will be tying up the mainline while a few setouts and pickups are accomplished. Note the condition of the wood siding on the stock cars, the various styles of board replacement on the upper levels. Compare, for example, adjacent cars 5582 and 5696. Repairs varied greatly; whatever size lumber was on hand at the time was used. Thus, each car came to have its own unique appearance; no two were alike.

It is September 10, 1946. Here at Chama the main focus is the Rio Grande's narrow gauge. Chama is a crew change point and the base of the nasty four percent ruling eastbound grade leading to a summit crossing at legendary Cumbres Pass.

Local yard switching is going on at the Chama stock pens. Nothing exceptional or out of the ordinary; stock movement was big business on Rio Grande's Alamosa to Durango narrow gauge. From the west a doubleheaded eastbound comes rolling into town. Again, nothing out of the ordinary; doubleheading is almost standard procedure on mainline freights and traffic was brisk in 1946.

Seen in the image above, Nos. 488 and 482 have pulled their train past the wye switch. No. 488 has uncoupled and pulled ahead to allow road engine 482 to accomplish some switching chores. Note the lumber flats, both steel and wood varieties. In the far background 488 quietly simmers next to an adjacent cut of stock cars. Out of view, No. 480 quiescently waits to accomplish its yard work, still coupled to the string of stock cars arcing behind the camera. Trainmen pass a few comments while the activity goes on; there is nothing special about what is happening here, it's just another late-1940s day in Chama.

Perhaps that is what makes this sequence of images so important. For what is seen here are a few short instants in the life of a narrow gauge railroad town in 1946. The focus, of course, is Rio Grande's narrow gauge. But there is the vintage vehicle at right, the clothing styles worn by the trainmen, the stock loading chute and pen. Finally, there is the mountain valley setting of Chama, so characteristic of country crossed by Rio Grande's narrow gauge.

In January 1958, K-37s 490 and 499 pause at Antonito to top off their tender tanks and change locomotive position within the train's consist before turning west toward Cumbres Pass and Durango. The traffic boom over the Alamosa-Durango mainline is in full swing; there is quite a lengthy string of high cars trailing No. 499's tender.

the Farmington Branch, which ran southward from Carbon Junction, located just south of Durango, downstream along the Animas River to Farmington, New Mexico. The branch was constructed to serve anticipated agricultural and coal business as well as to reach an interchange connection expected to be constructed by the Southern Pacific or its rival, the Santa Fe.

To serve its narrow gauge domain, the Rio Grande maintained a full and complete shop at Alamosa. This was active up through the final demise of the narrow gauge empire, servicing equipment running over the remaining mainline network. Of far greater importance to the faithful, however, was the fact that the narrow gauge shop complex was virtually a hidden and largely unknown mecca for any and all things to do with three-foot gauge operations. Alamosa was also the location of a connection with Rio Grande's standard-gauge outside world. From Alamosa, this connection climbed eastward over the Sangre de Cristo Mountains at Veta Pass to drop down the east side of the Rockies to Walsenburg. Most importantly, though, the Veta Pass connection at Alamosa served as a freight interchange lifeline for the final years of the narrow gauge.

Secondary shops and roundhouses survived at two locations through the final demise of the Alamosa-Durango mainline system. The first location, Chama, also served as a crew change point and attended to helper locomotive needs for the severe four percent ruling grade found on the west side of Cumbres Pass. The second main terminal and roundhouse was located at Durango. The Durango facility served the Silverton and Farmington branches, provided for Rio Grande crew, equipment and motive power needs for the western end of the narrow gauge system and, through 1952, furnished a narrow gauge helping hand, fixer-upper shop, locomotive rental service and interchange connection with quite legendary, but now-long-departed, Rio Grande Southern.

Enroute to Chama, K-36 No. 488 leaves the Antonito tank after a brief water stop.

Seen above, 483 and 484 are rolling tonnage south toward Antonito. The fact that there are two locomotives on the head-end plus the presence of tank cars in the consist infer that the train will be turning west at Antonito for Cumbres Pass and tank car loading at Chama. Just behind No. 484's tender are a pair of idler cars that must be cut out somewhere between Hartner, where this image was recorded, and Antonito, where the three-rail trackage and the need for Rio Grande's dual-gauge idler cars ends. (three photos, Robert W. Richardson)

Boom Times Precede Abandonment

In the early 1950s an oil and gas field discovery in the San Juan Basin near Farmington fueled a dramatic increase in traffic moving west from Alamosa to Farmington via the narrow gauge. Drill pipe tubing, oil field hardware, drilling mud and almost everything else that was bulky and associated with the exploration boom at one time or another moved west to the Farmington area over the narrow gauge.

Initially, the Rio Grande did not welcome the thought of rapid traffic growth on its aging narrow gauge mainline. Indeed, the railroad wished that traffic on the mainline would trickle away, giving legal weight to a desire to abandon the Alamosa-Durango trackage. Rio Grande insisted to El Paso Natural Gas Company, the requesting shipper, that the railroad had neither adequate motive power nor enough freight cars remaining in service to move large amounts of tonnage over the Alamosa-Durango line. It was suggested to El Paso that it consider moving its freight by way of the AT&SF to Gallup, New Mexico, thence north to the Farmington Basin by truck.

With badly-needed materials accumulating on standard gauge equipment at Walsenburg due to lack of transit to the Farmington area, El Paso was forced to take the shipping issue to the Interstate Commerce Commission. Requested was a decision to get Rio Grande and its narrow gauge into action. To help support its case, El Paso sent at least one special agent into the field to quietly determine just what Rio Grande *did* have in the way of usable narrow gauge motive power and freight equipment. Using the guise of a data-gathering model railroader, one of El Paso's agents was able to obtain very accurate and detailed information as to the status of Rio Grande's narrow gauge capabilities. El Paso's attorney presented this detailed information to Rio Grande's counsel; eyebrows were raised, the cards were on the table for all to see. The ICC ruled in favor of El Paso Natural Gas, and a directive was issued to Rio Grande to start moving the freight. The railroad suddenly found motive power and appropriate equipment to start moving El Paso's tonnage. The decision came none too soon, for at time the directive was issued, the Walsenburg accumulation of El Paso equipment had reached 125 loads.

(continues on page 193)

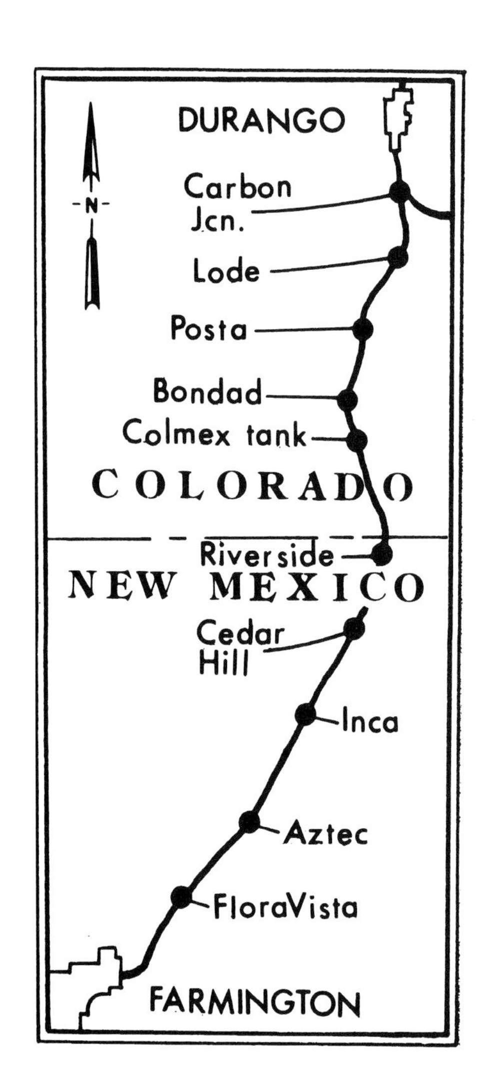

The Farmington Branch was the destination for the oil boom traffic which kept the narrow gauge mainline alive into the 1960s. The hamlet of Aztec and the town of Farmington were the focus of traffic moving to and from the branch. Seen obove, 493 switches cars into a siding at Farmington through the use of a stout pole; siding space was at premium during the boom years. Below, 495 rolls 58 cars of revenue tonnage across the Animas River bridge south of Cedar Hill on May 1, 1957. (photos, R.H. Kindig; map, R.C. Farewell)

A favorite haunt of leased USA diesel 4700N was the Farmington Branch. The black visitor was near Posta on a slag-dumping mission, February 24, 1954. Note the manual shovel work going on along the train; mechanized spreaders and tampers were not in vogue over Rio Grande's narrow gauge trackage.

SOUTH TO FARMINGTON

Smoking through Aztec on February 16, 1953 was K-37 493 and its assigned tonnage of 44 cars. Almost all of the traffic over the Farmington Branch during this time was oil field material shipped by El Paso Natural Gas Company, with destinations of either Aztec or Farmington proper. (both, R.H. Kindig)

Back in 1948 there was still a good deal of traffic to be moved over the narrow gauge mainline between Alamosa and Durango. Thus, when not on the point of the San Juan *D&RGW's K-28s could be found working freight. Seen above, on November 10, 1948, 476 and K-36 484 were bringing a string of revenue cars down the three-rail from Alamosa to Antonito. Note short reefer No. 74 and Chama-bound tank cars in the consist immediately behind the two head-end idler cars.*

At Antonito the train pauses to cut 476 and the two idler cars out of the train as well as take on water. Above, 484 has filled its tender and pulled south down the main with the pair of idler cars. No. 476 then backed up and pulled south to couple onto the idlers, backed up again, and then pulled down into an adjacent siding. The idlers will be left on the siding. In the meantime, below, No. 476 receives some minor mechanical attention while 484 couples onto the first half of the consist, and then pulls past the siding switch. Once 476 was ready to go, it would back up the mainline and couple to the remaining part of the train's consist and pull forward to No. 484's section. When the air test was completed, the train would depart Antonito for Cumbres Pass, Chama and Durango. (all, Robert W. Richardson)

Plow-equipped helper engine No. 487 was pulling onto the mainline in preparation for coupling onto No. 491's plow train. Out of sight behind 487's tender is a flanger, one of Rio Grande's more potent weapons in dealing with the winter white stuff that falls on Cumbres Pass. (all, Robert W. Richardson)

PLOW TRAIN

It is February 20, 1956, and narrow gauge country is locked in the cold grasp of winter. Here at Antonito, where this sequence was recorded, little snow falls. The reason is that Antonito, Alamosa and the rest of the San Luis Valley are in the rain shadow of surrounding mountain ranges.

To the west, however, is another story for the white stuff of winter can be found in the mountains in copious quantities. Rio Grande crossed the range to the west of Antonito at Cumbres Pass, a location noted for its wye covered by snowsheds for protection against the blowing drifts of winter.

Between Antonito and Cumbres lie broad, sweeping, rolling hills with few trees to slow the wind. When it blows the snow across these hills, drifts form in any hollows and especially across the narrow gauge's right-of-way.

To keep the mainline open over Cumbres and on to Durango, Rio Grande utilized plow trains and rotary snowplows. At the moment rotaries OM and OY were silenced, but the mainline remains in the midst of boom times. There is tonnage to be moved; the trains must go through. The solution used by Rio Grande was to run plow trains such as seen on these pages. Two engines with a flanger spliced between them pulling narrow gauge Jordan spreader OU and a caboose was the minimum equipment needed to battle the drifts.

Seen here is a somewhat more elaborate configuration assembled for what could turn out to be a major battle. Note the flatcar loaded with a bulldozer, a boxcar full of tools, auxillary water car, ex-postal car, and outfit car ahead of the caboose. Rio Grande is no fool when it comes to battling mother nature; the extra equipment could come in handy if things get nasty.

Water is taken on at Antonito; the plow train is switched into the order seen here, for just west of Antonito the first of the wind-blown snow drifts can be encountered. Above, Antonito is left behind as helper 487 and road engine 491 get a roll on their train. Forward progress will come to a halt before too long, though, for the cold air coupled with the wind and snowfall have produced some impressive drifts across the track not far ahead. In addition to the normal flanger train consist, this one included a five-car bulldozer outfit to be set out at Cumbres.

Westbound from Antonito the third rail is left behind. Indeed, the "End of Standard Gauge" sign says it all; ahead lies Rio Grande's undiluted narrow gauge empire with boom times in full swing. The narrow gauge is in its final heyday, and perhaps, ahead lies a trip back into decades long since past, times that should only be grandfather's memories.

K-36 487 was recorded on October 17, 1941 east of Carbon Junction enroute to Chama. Carbon Junction was the location where the Farmington Branch tied into the Alamosa-Durango line; the Durango yards and depot are a few miles to the north. (Otto Perry, Denver Public Library Western History Dept.)

K-37 491 is at the Antonito coaling dock after receiving a heaping load of "black diamonds." The mountain of coal in the tender will undoubtedly be diminished by a forthcoming run over Cumbres Pass. Note the drill rod loads, the rail-reinforced flatcars and the load of culvert pipe. All were prominent features associated with the Farmington Basin oil exploration-boom years. (Robert W. Richardson)

Eventually, Rio Grande proactively responded to the boom by building special narrow gauge drill rod flatcars out of surplus narrow gauge gondolas. Idler cars were constructed from cut-down narrow gauge box and stock cars and were later reinforced with sections of used rail. Although the traffic flow for loads during the final decades of the Alamosa-Durango mainline was largely westbound, eastbound tonnage was present in the form of finished lumber. In addition, oil from the Chama field moved eastward over the narrow gauge to a small refinery located in Alamosa. At the peak of the Farmington traffic boom, nine 70-car freights were being dispatched west from Alamosa over the narrow gauge mainline every week. Thus, the late 1950s and early 1960s were very good times on the remaining narrow gauge mainline. Unfortunately, the exploration phase in Farmington declined as the field became fully defined and drilled. With the end of exploration came a related dramatic decline in tonnage moving across the narrow gauge system.

Time slipped by; sand continued to flow out of the narrow gauge's hourglass. By the mid-1960s the boom times were over and freight traffic on the Alamosa-Durango line was declining toward an all-time low. Winter operation over Cumbres Pass ceased during the heavy snows of 1964–65. It was suspended thereafter whenever snow accumulated past the clearing capabilities of locomotive pilot plows on the highly irregular and infrequent freights or the occasionally-operated plow trains with their associated flangers and Jordan spreader. Toward the end of operation over the narrow gauge mainline the Chama-based rotary ceased to be used to clear Cumbres Pass.

Passenger specials, however, were being operated with increasing frequency; the outside world was beginning to notice the uniqueness of the narrow gauge operation. Unbeknownst to the faithful, the last revenue passenger run on the Alamosa-Durango mainline turned out to be a Epsilon Sigma Alpha Sorority excursion chartered on October 9, 1966. That particular run, the last of the year's fall foliage color season, was operated from Alamosa to Cumbres and was powered by K-36 No. 484 utilizing Silverton-service equipment. On January 6, 1967, Rio Grande announced that there would be no more passenger operations over Cumbres. The railroad felt the line was becoming too unsafe for passenger traffic. Mainline track maintenance

The last grains of sand were running out of the Alamosa-Durango line's hourglass when this scene was recorded. 498 and 493 are rolling tonnage bound for Chama and Durango just south of the crossing of the Conejos River. It is September 1967; Rio Grande's petition for abandonment would be submitted to ICC on the 18th of the month. By the end of December the last revenue train will depart Durango and work its way eastbound to Alamosa, in the process closing the final page on narrow gauge mainline operations. (Otto Perry, Denver Public Library Western History Dept.)

In 1961, Alamosa's locomotive dead line held some seasoned veterans. K-37 490, K-36 482, K-37 498 and K-36 481 were awaiting heavy repairs of one sort or another, with No. 481 to receive a complete rebuilding. Happily, all except No. 490 were to survive to the present day. (Otto Perry, Denver Public Library Western History Dept.)

continued to be deferred, and the handwriting was on the wall.

On September 18, 1967 Rio Grande petitioned the ICC to abandon the narrow gauge mainline between Antonito and Durango along with the Farmington Branch. December 1967 saw the last freight train operated over Cumbres Pass, dispatched eastbound with K-37 No. 493. Finally the hourglass sand ran out; the ICC approved the abandonment petition. During 1970 the Farmington Branch and the mainline segment between Durango and Chama were removed. The rest of the line between Chama and Antonito was spared for possible sale. The states of Colorado and New Mexico jointly purchased this trackage for its historical value, to be maintained and operated for the states by a designated third party.

Throughout the 1950s the Silverton Branch continued to see traffic, for the magnificent scenery found along its route was beginning to command attention. Operations continued in mixed-train format but were cut back in 1954 so that passenger service occurred during the summertime only. Prior to 1963, Rio Grande felt that declining revenues and increasing maintenance associated with operating a rolling steam-powered museum did not justify continuing the Silverton Branch. Indeed, years before actively pursuing a possible demise of the Alamosa-Durango mainline, the railroad was actively petitioning the ICC to abandon the Silverton Branch.

The ICC promptly turned down the petition in 1962, citing a public need to keep the branch running. Specifically, the significance of the decision was that "public convenience and necessity" encompassed the "sightseeing" function. Faced with that mandate, Rio Grande reevaluated its position and began to invest in the future of the branch, with an eye turned toward the positive financial return they felt that the operation could produce. Considering the big picture of the early-1960s narrow gauge network, though, the positive moves regarding the future of the 45-mile Silverton line were small indeed. The mid-

Dual-coupled, standard gauge No. 38 was switching narrow gauge cars at the Alamosa yards. One would have expected steam power to be accomplishing such mundane chores, but the winds of change were starting to blow toward Alamosa. Before long standard gauge steam would be gone from its last D&RGW stronghold here. (Robert W. Richardson)

At right, 490 and 484 are leaving Alamosa southbound with tonnage for Cumbres Pass, Durango, and Farmington. Included are tank cars which will be loaded with crude oil at Chama for a trip back to the refinery located here in town. Regardless of the consist, though, the early-morning light does a fine job of illuminating the narrow gauge toward the end of its heyday, the final curtain call before its demise. (both, Robert W. Richardson)

So poignant a view of the narrow gauge dismantling boneyard at Alamosa: About to meet the bone-chilling spatter and pop of the scrapper's torch is short reefer 59, its proud career ending in the grime of sooty soil and acetylene slag. After No. 59 is rolled on its side, its steel innards will be sliced away and its wood carcass trucked to some ranch for use as a storage shed, an unglorious reward for years of faithful service.

Pre-dawn at Durango finds D&S 481 being brought up to the depot from the ready track. In the foreground is caboose 0540 coupled to the customized "cat"-carrying flatcar. The immense ramp that allows the tractor access to the flatcar platform is just visible past the front caboose steps.

Below, No. 481 is illuminated by the first light of day as it moves toward its train. (all, R.C. Farewell)

Some scenes are timeless; No. 481's hogger awaits his 9:30 AM departure from Durango.

1960s came and went. When the mainline link between Durango and the outside world at Alamosa was suddenly gone, the Alamosa shops razed and most rolling stock in the process of being dismantled, the final curtain call had come for Rio Grande's once extensive narrow gauge. Thus, when the 1970s dawned the Silverton Branch stood alone as the last of the narrow gauge domain still more-or-less intact under Rio Grande's corporate umbrella.

Exit Rio Grande; Enter Durango & Silverton

As the 1970s progressed, Rio Grande made it increasingly clear that it was time to be out of the narrow gauge passenger business and more prudent to concentrate its resources on other ventures. Feelers went out regarding the possibility of giving the Silverton Branch to a foundation or selling the whole operation. One party interested in Rio Grande's rumblings was Florida citrus magnate Charles E. Bradshaw Jr. Bradshaw had a knowledgeable interest in railroads but was also an astute businessman. Specifically, the Silverton Branch was a nice relic, but business was business. An investment of the magnitude required to acquire the Silverton simply was not expendable pocket change; such as expenditure required a decent rate of return. During the late 1970s preliminary discussions between Bradshaw and the Rio Grande commenced. Bradshaw commissioned studies to determine what had to be done to increase the level of passenger service and the number of trains on the line, the first requirement toward turning the Silverton into an efficient business venture.

To increase the traffic density would unquestionably require the use of more motive power. All three of Rio Grande's K-28 2-8-2s remaining in existence were on the Silverton Branch and active; there simply were no more passenger engines available. Other Rio Grande narrow gauge motive power, however, survived the mainline abandonment and were available for rebuilding. Included were larger and more powerful K-36 and K-37 freight locomotives. Unfortunately, under Rio Grande's tenure those particular 2-8-2s were restricted from operating west (north by the compass) of Rockwood because of rock cut clearances and bridge strength limitations. Thus, the most scenic part of the Silverton Branch was off limits to the big engines.

Bradshaw evaluated the results of his studies and targeted costs associated with traffic increases. A projected rate of return was calculated for possible purchase and operation of the Silverton Branch. The results must have been favorable; Bradshaw entered into a formal purchase agreement with the Rio Grande in July 1979 to acquire the entire Silverton Branch and all its associated railroad-related structures and equipment.

On March 25, 1981, Bradshaw closed the deal with Rio Grande. For $2.2 milion in cash he acquired nine locomo-

Right, No. 481 has pulled forward through the yard leads north of the depot and has switched onto the mainline. Sunrise streaming horizontally down a Durango side street illuminates the locomotive and its conductor as the K-36 works its way back to the depot much as it has done for the past 60 years or so.

497 is a class of 1930 Burnham Shop graduate, a hybrid locomotive whose boiler began its existence in 1902 on D&RGW standard gauge C-41 No. 1003 and whose running gear was constructed new by Baldwin in 1930 for the conversion project. Regardless of origin, the highly-successful K-37 continues in operation on D&S today and was recorded crossing the bridge over the Animas River in central Durango bound toward Silverton with train No. 463's combine and coaches in tow, its girth exceeded only by its ability to haul maximum tonnage. (all, R.C. Farewell)

A quiet spring afternoon finds No. 480 simmering at the coaling dock; the D&S's flanger awaits a call to action. In the background is the new roundhouse and maintenance shop, built after the February 1989 fire which leveled the previous 1881-vintage structure.

tives, all remaining structures, rolling stock and work equipment on the property. There was, however, one immediate problem. Four of the nine locomotives, or rather the remains of those locomotives, were stored in Alamosa. Unfortunately, the narrow gauge connection between Durango and Alamosa via Cumbres Pass had been torn out 11 years earlier. The four in question were K-36 No. 480 and K-37s 493, 498 and 499. The solution was to use a heavy-duty low-boy trailer and haul each locomotive from Alamosa over the divide at Wolf Creek Pass to Durango. The rusting carcass of No. 480 was the first locomotive to be moved, leaving Alamosa on May 3, 1981; the three K-37s soon followed.

Bradshaw continued and enlarged upon Rio Grande's most recent scheduling of two trains each summer day between Durango and Silverton. Specifically, the final Rio Grande listing of Silverton Branch operations, formally known as subdivision 12, appeared in official timetable No. 4 issued on February 24, 1980. That yellow document specified westbound train No. 461 with an 8:30 AM Durango departure followed by train No. 463 with a 9:30 AM departure. D&S not only kept the same Durango departure schedules but continued Rio Grande tradition by retaining the same train numbers for each respective round trip.

As years under D&S control began to roll by, Durango-Silverton passenger patronage skyrocketed. In response, two additional morning trains, a winter train, and an afternoon/evening train were added. The morning addition, No. 115–116, has been labeled the *San Juan Express*. As an express train it is exempt from carrying a head-end box car for LCL shipments in its consist. Moreover, the train will not stop at any of the designated flag stops enroute to Silverton; indeed, the *San Juan Express* stops only for water. Durango departure time has been set at 7:30 AM. The second additional train to run up the canyon each day during the peak of summer has been designated No. 465–466. This train was added for the 1986 season. Durango departure for No. 465 is at 10:15 AM. Thus, during the mid-summer season there are four departures for Silverton each morning: 7:30 AM for train 115, 8:30 AM for train 461, 9:30 AM for train 463 and 10:15 AM for train 465.

An afternoon run was added, later dropped and is to be reinstated for the 1991 operating season. In the past it has been referred to as the *Cascade Canyon Mixed*. For 1991 it is to depart Durango in the late afternoon and will be operated only as far as Cascade, where it will wye and return to Durango in the evening. Train numbers assigned to the operation are 265 westbound and 266 eastbound. Finally, winter operations to Cascade wye and back, when run, fall under assigned train numbers of 261 westbound and 262 eastbound.

When reservations increase train length significantly past 12 cars per scheduled run, a second section of a given train may be operated. If run, it follows the first by a 15-minute interval. This does not affect following trains; they adhere to their stated departure times. Thus, if train No. 461 has a second section assigned, departures occur at 8:30 AM for No. 461, 8:45 AM for second 461, and at regularly scheduled times if No. 463 or No. 465 are to be operated. The result is that the single track mainline to Silverton can become a very busy place, especially during the mid-summer season. Special chartered operations are common in the fall. They are usually dispatched as the second section of a given train currently in operation. Less commonly they can be operated as a later train fitting one of the departure times not in use at that time of year.

The Animas River Railway

Part of D&S's charter included acknowledgment that some D&S trains would serve selected flag stops along the upper reaches of the Animas Gorge to detain or pick up backpackers, picnickers, or anyone else wishing to visit an otherwise nearly inaccessible area. Stopping here and there on a random basis, however, wreaks havoc on a tight schedule such as that maintained by D&S during the busy summer season. Thus was born the concept of the Animas

The day's run for No. 473 is over; the tourists have left. It works up and down the depot leads, shuffling cars to various tracks before moving deep into the D&S complex. Through all this acivity, the north end of the depot is quiet, devoid of all except the faithful, a few souls who are witness to the uniqueness of this happening in so recent a time.

River Railway, a satellite operation that could run up and down the canyon to pick up and drop off passengers as needed, thereby reducing delays for the regular Durango-Silverton trains. Sidings and wyes located within the canyon would allow sanctuary to keep the operation out of the way of steam trains.

Thus the Animas River Railway began running from its home terminal at Rockwood as far up the canyon as Elk Park wye and back once each day. A second trip was run daily during the peak of mid-summer traffic. This trip, however, made its turn-around at Cascade wye rather than Elk Park. The Animas River Railway utilized a motorized railbus and trailer, a combination that allowed just enough capacity to handle peak season demands to and from the inner canyon. Conceptually the Animas River Railway was a great idea; the sensation of riding through the crisp snap of early morning canyon air in the open railbus trailer while enroute to one's destination was an excellent way to get to know the secrets of the inner gorge on an intimate basis. Albeit not as well-known as its big-brother operation downgrade at Durango, the railbus was nonetheless discovered and patronized by the knowledgeable and adventuresome.

Unfortunately, the extremely high maintenance costs needed to keep the power section of the railbus in service made it financially unattractive for continued operation. September 23, 1990 saw the last canyon excursion of the railbus. When it returned to Rockwood the Animas River Railway ceased to operate. According to D&S management, the railbus and trailer are to be kept at Durango as backup in case of problems with the steam trains. The inner canyon flag stops have again become the responsibility of the regular trains.

Highball the mainline! No. 480 kicks up some smoke as the fireman pours on the coal after leaving the Durango depot with train 463. On the right are two yard tracks lined with seemingly derelict narrow gauge freight cars. Looks are deceiving; the cars have been serviced by D&S in the recent past and are fully operational, their state of decay arrested, their preservation insured. (R.C. Farewell)

Recorded in pre-D&S days, train No. 463 was rolling through the same part of Durango as on the previous page. The date was June 12, 1945, and K-27 "mudhen" No. 453 was assigned the duties of piloting the three freight cars, combine and wood caboose to Silverton. (Otto Perry, Denver Public Library Western History Dept.)

From D&RGW Branchline to D&S Mainline: the Physical Plant

Rio Grande began to upgrade the Silverton Branch starting with its 1963 "Rio Grande-land" project. As part of that effort, the four-span (three Howe truss, one steel truss) bridge at milepost 490 was replaced with a new two-span, 222-foot steel deck plate bridge in 1964. Initially prompted by the decomposition of one of the bridge's mid-stream span footings, part of this project included significant relocations of trackage leading to each end of the new bridge. Specifically, the new bridge was positioned some distance east of the old crossing to take advantage of lessened susceptibility to high-water damage and to allow for more stable footing. The old bridge spans were left in place with only approach trackage and bridge rails removed. Next, in 1972 Rio Grande replaced the short south member of the two-span bridge over the Animas River at milepost 477.8 with a steel unit.

Later, under D&S direction, more extensive physical engineering changes were accomplished on all bridges. Included were changes to the high bridge over the Animas River gorge south of Tacoma at milepost 471.2. This legendary span was upgraded in 1981 as part of a clearance and capacity enhancement project. The objective was to allow K-36 and K-37 series locomotives to run the entire distance to Silverton. The project was completed in late-summer 1981; on August 7th, K-36 No. 481 and a caboose were able to make the trip to Silverton and back to validate results. No problems were encountered; the trip was successful. The larger locomotives were then cleared for use over the entire Silverton Branch; they adhere to the same set of restrictions applied to the K-28s.

Worthy of note is that although the high bridge east of Tacoma has been strengthened, D&S maintains Rio Grande's traditional five mile-per-hour speed restriction while crossing the span. Moreover, double-headed locomotives are not allowed to cross the bridge coupled together. If a doubleheader is dispatched up the canyon, a fairly common occurrence, then the train must stop before the bridge to allow the helper to uncouple and cross singly. The helper then waits a short distance up the track on the opposite side of the bridge for the road engine to bring the train across for recoupling and thence doubleheading continues up the gorge to Silverton.

Considering locomotive weight cautions, even the three-span Animas River bridge on the north edge of Durango is not exempt from restriction. Through the end of its tenure, Rio Grande allowed the K-36s and K-37s to be operated as far north as Rockwood. Enroute up the Hermosa Valley the big engines had to cross the Durango bridge at milepost 452.4 on all but the shortest in-town switching capers. While crossing the bridge, the locomotives were restricted to ten miles-per-hour without exception. Doubleheaded K-28s, however, were not required to cross the span singly. D&S has continued Rio Grande's restriction on the Durango span; thus, when a westbound exits the ten mile-per-hour permanent slow order, a smoke and steam show worthy of appeasing the narrow gauge gods is produced as the hoghead pulls back the throttle to get the train up to normal Hermosa Valley track speed.

During the mid-1960s, rail on the Silverton Branch consisted of a venerable hodgepodge of sizes and weights. Present as late as 1963 were stretches of 65-pound rail between Durango and Rockwood with additional occurrences of the lighter rail between Tacoma and Cascade. Here and there within the latter stretch of light rail were replacement sections of heavier 85-pound rail. The line

HERMOSA WATER STOP

The hamlet of Hermosa lies toward the north end of its namesake valley. Between Durango and Hermosa the wide, lush and almost level valley gives an initial false impression as to the character of D&S's passage up the Animas Canyon to Silverton. Long, linked tangents and gentle curves imply the trip ahead to be little more than a stroll in the park.

After leaving Hermosa, however, all that changes. Just past the water tank the track alignment leaves the valley floor and begins a sinuous climb up cliffside slopes in an attempt to gain altitude. The 2.5% ruling grade is felt immediately. Gone are lush fields, ever so quickly replaced by Ponderosa pines, mountain foliage and outcropping rock ledges. Rio Grande responded to the serpentine grade from Hermosa to Rockwood by installing a water tank at Hermosa Creek. The location was a wise one; the water stop is utilized by D&S today.

Seen above, D&S No. 497 is crossing Hermosa Creek and slowing for a water stop at Hermosa tank. Next, at left, the train is inched forward to align the tender hatch with the tank spout; hand signals give critical directions.

Once the tender hatch is aligned, it is time to get the spout down and into position.

Not all D&S trains stop at Hermosa for water; K-28 or K-36-powered trains usually pass by. However, if No. 497 is assigned to a run that contains maximum tonnage, then odds are that the thirsty K-37 will stop at Hermosa for a drink. The reason is that 497 is really a hybrid locomotive, consisting of a standard gauge 1902-vintage boiler mounted on a 1930 narrow gauge frame and running gear. As such, it will consume a good deal of water while dragging maximum tonnage up the 2.5% grade between Hermosa and Rockwood. (all photos, R.C. Farewell)

If someone opens the tank outlet valve before the spout is positioned into the tender hatch, water will go everywhere.

Above, No. 497's tank is full when water runs out of the top of the filler hatch; there is no water level gauge.

At left, an anxious conductor checks why it is taking so long to get the tank spout up and out of the way and getting the train moving toward Rockwood; precious little leeway exists in the scheduling of mid-summer mainline operations.

between Cascade and Silverton consisted of 85 and 90-pound rail, as did the high line between mileposts 468.2 and 478.9. As the 1960s rolled on, Rio Grande initiated a project to replace the lighter rail, and this was completed under D&S management. Additionally, a flange lubricator was installed just west of Rockwood Cut to help with rail wear around sharp curves found on the highest section of the high line. As of 1990, then, all the light rail has been removed; without exception, the mainline consists of 85 to 90-pound rail. Perhaps some lighter rail still exists in some hidden corners of the Durango yards.

The Durango & Silverton projected future traffic density, and it anticipated problems of running greatly increased traffic on a single track mainline. One solution was to add passing sidings in critical areas. The first new siding was installed north of Durango at milepost 457.2 during 1982 and named Home Ranch. This was built with a tangent length of 1000 feet. The second new siding was located between Hermosa and Rockwood on the 2 1/2 percent ruling climb out of the Hermosa Valley. Named Pinkerton, this curving track was installed in 1982 with a length of 800 feet. In 1986 the need for extra capacity on short passing sidings became critical and thus Pinkerton was lengthened 200 feet around the curve to the north. Tacoma siding, built during the early years of the Rio Grande's domain, also received attention. Tacoma was lengthened from 900 to 1300 feet by adding to its north end. A second siding track at Tacoma was stubbed off at its north end and turned into a house track which in 1990 contained a string of derelict and decaying stock, high-side gondola, and work-train outfit cars. In addition, under D&S ownership, Tacoma has become the staging area for maintenance performed to the north in the most rugged part of the Animas Canyon. Thus, all sorts of heavy-duty equipment can commonly be found there during the summer trackwork season.

D&S's K-28s are somewhat frugal with their water consumption; they usually can run all the way from Durango to Tank Creek deep in the Animas River gorge before taking on water. Seen below, double-headed 476 and 473 are the motive power for this particular train No. 463. All Hermosa tank will rate is a good dusting of coal cinders and a quick blast of sooty steam. (R.C. Farewell)

Turn the clock back to October 1941. Rio Grande's mini-mudhen, alias C-25 No. 375, is rolling train 461 to Silverton. Long a fixture on the Branch, 375 still had eight years of service left in its distinguished career before being dismantled at Alamosa in 1949. (Otto Perry, Denver Public Library Western History Dept.)

High Water Induces Changes

A "one-hundred year" flood roared down the Animas River Canyon from Silverton during very heavy rains on September 10, 1970. This wall of water was instrumental in forcing Rio Grande to rework and upgrade its inner canyon alignment from north of Tacoma to Cascade Canyon and in the vicinity of Needleton. Specifically track, rip-rap, ballast and most everything else not securely bolted down was knocked out of position. In many places the flood waters scoured the right-of-way clear of anything and everything all the way down to bedrock. A section of track along the Canyon's east bank within a very narrow section of the gorge just north of Tacoma was left suspended over the rivercourse, its ballast and sub-base washed away. Long stretches of bolted rails complete with spiked ties were left hanging in mid-air. Short sections of this rusty "snap-track" still remain in the Animas watercourse today, a grim reminder of the potential fury of high water.

Rio Grande promptly set about rebuilding the trackage through the canyon, and by opening day of the 1971 season trains were able to roll, albeit with a number of slow orders related to the settling of new roadbed. D&S has taken the line reconstruction even further, with reinforced concrete retaining walls put in place and heavy steel netting and used-rail rip-rap retention grids filled with boulders installed north of Tacoma. The latest of these projects continued through 1990 and utilized work train equipment based at Tacoma siding for the efforts to the north.

During 1981 D&S added a wye north of Tacoma and south of Tefft at milepost 477.5. The wye was laid out in the small, almost-level meadow located near the confluence of Cascade Canyon and the main Animas Canyon. Named Cascade wye, this location is the destination for the summer afternoon/evening passenger run, as well as occasional winter operations up the canyon. Cascade wye is not to be confused with the much older but since-removed Cascade siding, which existed under Rio Grande's tenure a little less than a mile north at milepost 478.4. Rio Grande used this now-departed siding for occasional cattle loading, and it was also the location of a section house.

One of the biggest long-term projects undertaken by D&S on the Silverton line is the replacement of infirm and disintegrating ties. This low profile, yet incredibly important project, is ongoing; there is no end yet in sight. The high line south from the Animas River crossing at milepost 471.2 was one focus of this work during 1990. In places along this section almost all ties require replacement. Broken and missing tieplates are being attended to as well, with the result that the finished track will support heavy traffic levels for quite some time.

In 1982, to accomplish required high levels of track maintenance and enhancement, D&S acquired a narrow-gauge Pettibone machine, a do-it-all self-propelled track maintenance unit. At the same time, four narrow gauge coal hoppers were acquired from East Broad Top Railroad in Mount Union, Pennsylvania. These hoppers are utilized for ballast dumping and are usually to be found at Hermosa siding when not in use. Indeed, the 11 miles from Durango to Hermosa lie on the relatively level flood plain of the Animas River and have in the past been subject to occasional inundation. One major project just completed involved adding ballast to the alignment between Durango and Hermosa so that flood-prone sections of track could be raised about six inches. It was not uncommon during late 1989 to see a steam-powered work train on this stretch, with the four ex-East Broad Top hoppers involved in ballast dumping and tamping activities. Home Ranch and Hermosa sidings offered sanctuary to the lowly K-28-powered work train when one of the passenger trains was due to pass. This was indeed a sight. D&S also acquired a one-of-a-kind narrow gauge track tamping machine in 1983. This piece of equipment was instrumental in the Durango-Hermosa roadbed raising project and has been used elsewhere, most recently to stabilize new ballast on the mainline in the Cascade wye area. Finally, D&S has modified an ex-D&RGW standard gauge all-steel flatcar by installing a rather immense ramp at one end. This flatcar allows a "Cat" bulldozer to be loaded, moved to where on-line needs dictate, and be unloaded with ease.

Structures: New, Rebuilt or Otherwise

Durango's ten-stall roundhouse, originally built in 1881, had the roof and doorways of stall Nos. 4, 5 and 6 raised by the Rio Grande in 1965 so that K-36 and K-37 series locomotives could be backed all the way inside. Unfortunately, the Rio Grande's policy during the later stages of its tenure was to tear down or dismantle anything needing repair or in the way which was not absolutely essential to the railroad's operation. Thus in 1971 stall Nos. 7-10 were removed, and stall Nos. 1-3 were converted into a machine shop. At that time a new roof was added over the remaining structure. When D&S took over operations, it quickly found that additional roundhouse capacity was needed. New stalls could be utilized to restore locomotives needed for the expansion of operations. As a result, in 1985, stall Nos. 7-10 were rebuilt.

Unfortunately, on February 10, 1989, the roundhouse caught fire and was destroyed. The fire started in the machine shop area and rapidly spread through the entire structure. By morning the structure was reduced to a pile of charred beams and fallen bricks. Inside at the time of the fire were all operatable locomotives: K-28s 473, 476 and 478 along with K-36s 480 and 481 and K-37 497. All received varying degrees of damage. By May 5th, opening day of the 1989 season, Nos. 476 and 497 had fire damage repaired and were available for assignment. By the end of the season all other locomotives involved in the fire were repaired and restored to service.

A new roundhouse was constructed of cinder block with a brick facade using original bricks salvaged from the roundhouse debris. Included in the structure is a full machine shop. As of late 1990, the only problem related to the new building occurred when a hostler forgot to offset a new spark arrestor attached to the stack of No. 481 before

Exactly 15 minutes after the first section of train 461 rolled by, second 461 steams around the open curve just east of the US 550 overpass. Chasers followed first 461; only the faithful remain to admire K-36 No. 480 on as it grinds its way up the 2.5% grade to Rockwood. (R.C. Farewell)

backing the locomotive into its stall. The result was a "dinged" roundhouse roof and door frame, along with a badly dented spark arrestor.

Durango Yards Revised

In 1963, the Rio Grande determined, with a little prodding from Durango businesses, that some sort of parking area was badly needed for the ever-increasing number of patrons who desired to ride to Silverton. Thus, the Durango yards were revised. The westside trackage, other than the depot leads, was removed and the area turned into a parking lot. A balloon track to turn passenger trains was constructed around and across the south half of the south yard. The south yard leads and other track were not needed after the 1970 dismantling of the mainline to Chama and were removed as part of a highway construction project.

Other major changes in the southern yard area included removal of the double-spout water tank in 1967 and the dismantling of the massive wooden coaling tower in 1968. The dismantling program also included the car shop. D&S, however, planned on restoring and rebuilding a fleet of passenger cars which was needed for increased train capacity. Thus, during late-1981 and into early 1982 a new 200-foot-long car shop was built on the site of the departed Rio Grande building. To maintain some sort of storage capacity for equipment not immediately needed or awaiting restoration, storage tracks were built along the southern curve of the balloon track. Thus, Durango's yard layout was greatly altered from its earlier days as a mainline terminal; in essence it became a compact stub-end facility. All was not restoration and rebuilding under the D&S regime, however, for in late 1989 the old storage buildings and ore loading bins adjacent to the Silverton depot were leveled and the resulting debris removed to eliminate a potential safety hazard.

The Silverton: Motive Power Migration

From the 1930s through the 1968 demise of its mainline, the backbone of the Rio Grande's three-foot gauge operation was unquestionably its relatively modern K-28, K-36 and K-37 series 2-8-2s. In the background, however, was smaller power of much older vintage which was used on the plethora of light rail branches, in yards, or wherever track of questionable stability was present. As late as the 1940s and 1950s, a few of the D&RGW's venerable narrow gauge 2-8-0s were kept in operation to service the remaining light rail branches.

Habitats of surviving 2-8-0s included Durango; C-16 No. 271 was assigned in 1939 as the resident yard switcher. However, in 1941 the 271 was sold to the Montezuma Lumber Company, where it was finally retired in 1947, the victim of a scorched crown sheet. C-19 No. 346, later to become a centerpiece at the Colorado Railroad Museum, was the Durango switcher from 1941 through 1945. C-18

The departed Animas River Railway's railbus and trailer were recorded, above, on a summer's day as they snaked through the cuts bordering the east end of the high line just east of their home base of Rockwood. Unfortunately, the unique operation ended on September 23, 1990, a victim of exceedingly high maintenance costs. (R.C. Farewell)

class No. 315 finished its career assigned to switching chores there, as well; it was retired in February 1950 and donated to Durango for display. In June 1950, C-19 No. 345 became the regular switcher. In July 1951 345 and 319 were used as operational props for the movie *Denver & Rio Grande* which involved a head-on collision staged at milepost 475. Both locomotives were heavily damaged in the collision and were scrapped two months later.

In 1916 the Denver & Rio Grande acquired three narrow gauge outside frame 2-8-0 locomotives from the Crystal River Railroad. The two smaller ones spent their Rio Grande careers on the west end of the Marshall Pass mainline rolling tonnage through the Black Canyon of the Gunnison River. The third locomotive, Crystal River No. 103, was larger and more powerful than the other two. Built by Baldwin in 1903, it developed 24,641 pounds of tractive effort at a working boiler pressure of 170 pounds-per-square-inch. Thus, upon acquisition by Rio Grande, the 103 was classified as the sole occupant of class 112. Initially renumbered 432, it became class C-25 No. 375 in the system revision of 1924. Interestingly, 375's rather impressive tractive effort was almost as much as that produced by larger "mudhen" 2-8-2, 450-464.

At the time, the Rio Grande needed lightweight, high tractive effort locomotives for the Silverton Branch. Thus

Rio Grande restricted its big K-36 and K-37 2-8-2s from operating north of Rockwood because of bridge capacities and rock cut clearances. The latter problem is shown here, as 497 cautiously squeezes through the vertical rock cuts guarding the entrance to the high line just past Rockwood. Bridges were strengthened; cuts were widened. D&S now runs the big Mikes to Silverton, albeit with a good dose of caution while passing over critical trackage. (R.C. Farewell)

the mighty outside-framed 2-8-0 was assigned to Durango for service. For many years it was a local fixture rolling tonnage back and forth to Silverton as a helper or on the headend of mixed-train 461. Finally, in June 1949 time ran out for the 375; it was retired and dismantled at Alamosa.

Other locomotives that rated Silverton Branch service are not to be forgotten. Through the 1940s and 1950s Rio Grande's K-27 2-8-2 "mudhens" worked secondary mainline jobs and snowplow assignments as well as holding things together on the west end of the Marshall Pass line from Montrose to Cimarron. During 1952 three K-27s (453, 463 and 464) were assigned to Durango on a long term basis following the dismantling of the west end of the Marshall Pass mainline. Noteworthy is the fact that during 1948–49 Nos. 463 and 464 had received complete overhauls at Alamosa. One would have expected that the 1903-vintage mudhens would have followed their siblings to the scrapper's torch rather than be given a new lease on life via the backshop. Following service at Durango the 453 was scrapped in 1954 and the 463 was sold in 1955 to actor Gene Autry. The latter engine was to ultimately return to Rio Grande territory through donation to the city of Antonito in 1972. No. 464 remained in Durango for snowplow and other secondary chores until retirement in 1962. It was not scrapped but was kept at the Durango roundhouse, finally being sold to Knott's Berry Farm in California in 1973.

To ease Durango switching chores after the retirement of No. 464, a diesel of diminutive proportions was acquired. This Caterpiller-powered mini-monster was purchased in late 1963 from Edward Hines Lumber Company. Numbered D&RGW 50, this locomotive was a midget-sized powerhouse that developed a very respectable 20,550 pounds of tractive effort, more than enough to accomplish what was needed to be done around the Durango yards. As such No. 50 was utilized until February 1970 when it was sold, the demand for its switching services having declined following the demise of the narrow gauge mainline to Chama. No. 50 now resides at the Colorado Railroad Museum.

Delivered to Rio Grande during 1923 by the American Locomotive Company of Schenectady, New York, was a fleet of ten outside-frame 2-8-2s. Tractive effort for each of the new locomotives was rated at 27,540 pounds at a working boiler pressure of 200 psi. The ten were classified as K-28 and assigned numbers 470 through 479. The K-28s, affectionately known as "sport models", served Rio Grande primarily as passenger power but were not unknown in freight service. All remained in Rio Grande service through mid-1942. In October of that year, the US Army appropriated seven as a war effort measure for use on Alaska's White Pass and Yukon Route (that's right, not "Railroad" nor "Railway", but "Route"). Shipped from Colorado were 470-472, 474, 475, 477 and 479. On the WP&Y the K-28s were numbered 250-256. At the end of the war six were shipped to Seattle, where they were sold as war surplus and scrapped during 1946. The exception was 472 which was damaged in 1944 while in WP&Y service. It was repaired by the Northern Pacific at its Tacoma, Washington shops and then shipped to Ogden, Utah where it was put up for sale. Following purchase, it was also scrapped in 1946.

Thus remaining in Rio Grande service as of late 1942 were K-28s 473, 476 and 478 This trio held down headend duties on daily narrow gauge Alamosa-Durango passenger train No. 115-116, the *San Juan* through discontinuance of the train in 1951. Following the demise of the legendary *San Juan*, the trio was moved to Durango for service on the light rail of the Silverton Branch. Because of their relatively narrow clearance requirements and the fact that bridges on the Silverton Branch could tolerate their weight, the K-28s became the mainstay of Durango-

Silverton operations. Through the end of Rio Grande's tenure on the branch the three were all that were needed to maintain a well-defined level of service. Specifically, one locomotive for each of a maximum of two trains per day between Durango and Silverton allowed the third to be shopped, serviced, or held as a backup if troubles developed with one of the others. Interestingly, the third K-28 could also occasionally be found working freight from Durango east to Chama. At Chama, however, an arriving K-28 was quickly wyed and dispatched back to Durango with whatever freight was on hand. The only exception to this turnback procedure was if the eastbound 470 happened to be enroute to Alamosa for a shop date. Rio Grande's regard for the trio was shown by the high degree of care the engines received during their careers. When acquired by D&S, they were in excellent mechanical condition.

Following acquisition of the Silverton Branch, D&S relied exclusively on the three K-28s. Initial changes made included removal of the psuedo-diamond stack covers from around the authentic stacks of each engine. All three receive rigorous maintenance D&S and are kept in immaculate condition by Durango shop forces. In line with that philosophy, No. 473 received a complete overhaul in 1988. Unfortunately, all were involved in the February 1989 roundhouse fire, with the 473 receiving a great deal of damage. All were rebuilt. No. 476, the least-damaged, was returned to service in time to make an April test run up to Cascade wye and back with a string of empty coaches prior to the beginning of the 1989 season. As of the end of 1990, all three K-28s are in excellent condition and remain in active service.

In 1925 Baldwin delivered ten narrow gauge outside frame 2-8-2s to Rio Grande to help ease the motive power crunch developing on its narrow gauge mainline network. As delivered they each produced 36,200 pounds of tractive effort at a working boiler pressure of 195 psi. These locomotives were thus classified as K-36s and were targeted for heavy freight service over both Cumbres Pass between Alamosa and Durango and over Marshall Pass between Salida and Gunnison. Rio Grande assigned them road numbers 480 through 489. The overall design was instantly successful; the K-36s proved themselves worthy of whatever task needed to be done. Indeed, along with

D&S 497 has train No. 463 well in hand as it rolls along the high line beyond Rockwood. The pace here is leisurely; a permanent 8 MPH slow order assigned to the length of high line trackage keeps everything slow and sure. (R.C. Farewell)

473
DURANGO

478
478
478
478

soon-to-arrive K-37s, they were heavily relied upon by the Rio Grande through to the final demise of the narrow gauge. Of the ten K-36s, only one has been scrapped. No. 485 had the unfortunate distinction of being backed into the Salida turntable pit without the benefit of the turntable bridge being aligned. As a result of this sudden elevation change, No. 485 was heavily damaged. However, rather than repairing and returning the locomotive to service, the carcass was instead turned into a parts source to keep the others operating. The boiler and bent frame were scrapped at Pueblo in 1955.

D&S received two K-36s as part of its acquisition of the Silverton Branch. The first, No. 480, had been retired by the Rio Grande in 1970 and was stored at Alamosa. Initially, No. 480 had been kept inside the Alamosa roundhouse. Later, it was pushed out into the weather and by the time it was acquired by D&S in 1981, the locomotive had become a rusting hulk. In mid-1981 it was trucked to Durango via low-boy trailer. Over the next few years No. 480 was completely rebuilt. Following this restoration, it made its first revenue trip in 1985 and was released to active service under the D&S banner.

The second K-36 acquired by D&S was No. 481. Following a complete overhaul by the Rio Grande in the 1960s, the 481 was not put into active service but was placed in storage in the Alamosa roundhouse. It remained in preserved cold storage within the dark confines of the roundhouse until it was moved dead-in-transit to Durango in December 1967 as part of the last westbound freight over the Cumbres Pass mainline. After arrival at Durango, No. 481 was put into outside storage next to the west side of the roundhouse. After acquisition by D&S, inspection revealed that the years of residing outside through the rigors of Durango winters had created a major problem. The boiler had not been drained and had frozen. Thus, extensive repairs were necessary before 481 was returned to service in August 1981. Both 480 and 481 were in the 1989 roundhouse fire and were repaired and returned to active service during that year's operating season.

It became obvious soon after delivery of the K-36s that more of the powerful freight locomotives would be required to keep tonnage moving over the narrow gauge mainlines. In response, the Rio Grande had Baldwin build frames and running gear to K-36 specifications. The railroad then took boilers from 1902-vintage standard gauge C-41 2-8-0s and, using the Baldwin-built running gear, assembled its own hybrid locomotives at the Burnham Shops in Denver. The resulting narrow gauge locomotives

(Previous two-page photo) D&SNG Nos. 478 and 473 are westbound on the high line enroute to Silverton with a special excursion, September 22, 1990. Above, D&S train 463 was rolling across the Animas River bridge at the south entrance to Baker's Park. This bridge is new turf for the K-37 with a capacity and clearance upgrade project accomplished by D&S in 1981. (all, R.C. Farewell)

were rated at 37,100 pounds of tractive effort at a working boiler pressure of 200 psi. Thus the locomotives were classified as D&RGW K-37s. Rio Grande assembled two batches of the K-37s. The first, assigned numbers 490 through 495, entered service in 1928. The hybrid locomotive building effort was successful; four more were completed in 1930. The latter quartet were assigned numbers 496 through 499.

Following construction the 490s were assigned to the Marshall Pass mainline. Then all K-36s were used to work the mainline west of Alamosa. Following the dismantling of the Valley Line between Mears Junction and Alamosa in 1951, six K-36s were reassigned to Salida in exchange for five K-37s sent to Alamosa for service west over Cumbres Pass to Durango. The reasoning was that the K-37s slightly higher tractive effort would allow one additional car per locomotive to be moved over Cumbres; this capability was badly needed on Durango-bound freights. The six K36s assigned to Salida—Nos. 480, 481, 482, 485, 486 and 489—were used on the Monarch Branch and over Marshall Pass.

Only two K-37s have felt the scrapper's torch. In the early 1960s, No. 490 was set aside and utilized as a parts source to keep other locomotives running. The remains were finally dismantled during 1962–1963 at Alamosa. The other K-37 to depart the roster was No. 496. During a routine inspection its boiler was found to be cracked. At that point the locomotive was also utilized as a parts source; its tender was assigned to No. 491. In 1954 the cannibalized remains of 496 were transported to Pueblo for scrapping; it was officially written off in January 1955. Worthy of note is the fact this was the only D&RGW narrow gauge locomotive in later years to have three-way coupler pockets. As so equipped, it could couple to and switch either narrow or standard gauge equipment. Because of this feature, 496 was utilized as the Salida switcher for a period of time.

Durango & Silverton acquired four of the ten K-37s (493, 497, 498 and 499) as part of its Silverton Branch purchase. At the time of the 1970 dismantling of the Durango-Chama mainline, the 497 had received a recent shopping by the Rio Grande and was stored in serviceable condition at Durango. It remained at Durango, but was not operated, through the end of Rio Grande's tenure. D&S rehabilitated and restored 497 to operating condition, and it entered D&S service in 1984. After being

It is an overcast and grey late September day at Silverton, nestled in the middle of Baker's Park. The south edge of the expanse has a steep-walled exit to the outside world where the Animas River leaves the meadows and the branch enters the almost level valley for its final dash to town. 478 and 473 are blasting up the final grade into Baker's Park, the diffuse light backlighting copious smoke and steam as the locomotives cross the Animas River and begin to get a roll on their train.

damaged in the 1989 fire, it was rebuilt and returned to service later in the year. As of 1990 the 497 remains one of the six primary passenger locomotives, kept in excellent operating condition and maintained to exacting standards.

Concerning the other three K-37s acquired by D&S, all had been retired by the Rio Grande in 1970. Prior to D&S acquisition, Nos. 493 and 498 resided within the securely locked Alamosa roundhouse, while 499 sat rusting outside in the weeds. All three were trucked to Durango following D&S acquisition in 1981. They remain in storage pending rebuilding if passenger levels dictate the need for additional motive power.

D&S acquired one additional locomotive in 1983. This vintage item is a 2-8-0 originally built for the Denver & Rio Grande in 1887 as No. 420. It was assigned class 71 due to its 17,100 pound engine weight and a working boiler pressure of 145 psi. In 1916 No. 420 was sold to the Rio Grande Southern and became No. 42. The veteran 2-8-0 had the sad distinction of being the last RGS locomotive under steam, running from Grady siding east to Durango in the spring of 1953, just ahead of the RGS dismantling crew. Rather than being scrapped, No. 42 was acquired by the Narrow Gauge Motel in Alamosa. It later moved through additional owners at various locations before D&S was able to obtain the historic relic. Current plans include a full restoration when passenger levels dictate. A hydro test has already been completed; although the boiler is not perfect, it has been determined that the 42 is completely rebuildable.

Passenger Cars

The fleet of D&S passenger equipment consists of 46 cars. Of that total, two are not in service. The remainder can be divided into two categories. The first, closed cars, consists of 24 pieces of equipment. Twelve of these were initially built during 1879–1889. All were extensively rebuilt by the Rio Grande over the years, and D&S has brought the cars up to state-of-the-art specifications. Others include eight built in Rio Grande's Burnham Shops during 1963–64 for Silverton Branch service. The final four closed passenger cars were built by D&S during 1984–86. All are completely interchangeable in service regardless of construction date and possess two independent braking systems. Indeed, the differences between cars are indistinguishable to the untrained eye.

Sixteen open observation cars, numbered 400-409 and 411-416, round out the fleet. All were built utilizing frames and roofs that originated from either standard gauge box or stock cars. Of the group, Nos. 400-405 have a multi-faceted history. In 1953, Rio Grande cut down a number of standard gauge boxcars and rebuilt them into narrow gauge open-end gondolas designed specifically for hauling large culvert pipes and oil field drilling rods. These special flatcars went into use on the Alamosa to Farmington line which at that time was in the midst of a traffic boom. In 1963, following the end of the oil field traffic surge, six of the pipe cars were reworked, this time to create open observation cars for use on the Silverton

Departing Silverton with train 464, No. 481 rolls past the quiet depot. Little activity goes on here now for passenger loading and unloading is accomplished downtown. No matter though; the depot has been preserved for tomorrow and the ticket office remains open. Concern about front-loaders which leveled so many earlier Silverton railroad structures can be put to rest. (all, R.C. Farewell)

At left a front-loader lifts the first stack of lumber onto an ex-D&RGW standard gauge steel flatcar. Converted to narrow gauge for use during the 1950-60s oil field boom, the flatcar is now part of D&S's rolling stock. Once the Dodge pickup was loaded and securely chained down, the rest of the load could be put on board. Note the emphatic hand signals. Below, the last stacks of lumber are loaded.

FREIGHT SERVICE

D&S is a passenger operation, no question about it. Freight service is not forgotten; it is just that there is usually not very much freight to be moved. Once in a great while the situation arises when a carload needs to be transported somewhere on the system.

This sequence shows just such an occasion. A flatcar load is being assembled at the Silverton "piggyback ramp," the house track just northeast of the depot. First to be loaded, via a stout pair of wood planks, was the Dodge pickup, followed by the freezer at the near end of the flatcar and finally several stacks of lumber.

Baker's Park at its best. Doubleheaded 476 and 473 are rolling train No. 461 into the broad open expanse while the snow-covered West Elk Mountains loom overhead in the near background. (R.C. Farewell)

The final rays of a summer afternoon sun highlight train 464 as it drops down the 2.5% grade between Rockwood and Hermosa. Few patrons are leaning out the windows now; the day's experience is almost over. Even No. 481 seems to be drifting in a lull, coasting down the serpentine trackage, contouring in and out of every hidden hollow and gulch that descends the west side of the valley. (R.C. Farewell)

Branch. As such they remain in operation, albeit modernized and brought up to current D&S specifications.

One Does Not Ride the D&S; One Experiences It

Reams have been written on *The Silverton*, and uncountable rolls of film exposed trying to capture the fabric of its image. The bottom line is that this cannot be done. One simply has to ride the train, savor the operation, feel the sting of coal cinders in the eyes and the tang of coal smoke in the air. One must watch the morning operation in the chill of a Durango pre-dawn, stand bone-tired in the late afternoon sun as the day's trains are switched and put away, stare with bloodshot eyes through the protective cyclone fence as the locomotives are loaded with coal and run to the roundhouse for the night. You go through these motions not because you have to, or because it is expected of you, but because you *want* to.

Some call this Silverton addiction symptomatic of narrow gauge fever. Others do not know what to call it, but all of a sudden it is there, ingrained in your mind forever. It sneaks up from within subconscious memory when least expected, bringing narrow gauge scenes into the forefront of the mind for idle daydreaming. It is perhaps not unlike the pleasant anticipation induced by the drifting scent of frying bacon and fresh biscuits on a Sunday morning. Thus, when all is said and done, when the cameras are put away and the recorders silenced, one realizes that one just does not ride the Durango & Silverton, one *experiences* it.

It is June 1942 as Rio Grande's train No. 462 rolls out of the Silverton valley with 11 cars, caboose and a combine destined for Durango. In the intervening 48 years precious little has changed. No. 478 still rolls tonnage across the river; the view of Anvil Mountain is the same. Passenger cars have replaced the concentrate-service boxcars and high-side gondolas. To be able to come back to Silverton today and watch the narrow gauge in action, however, makes the few changes quite bearable. (Otto Perry, Denver Public Library Western History Dept.)

1956 promotional folder (Museum collection)

(left, above) One day in the summer of 1963, Alexis McKinney arranged for a photographers' special to run to Rockwood where it was turned on the wye and backed to a point above the high line. The train then returned south allowing morning photographs along the rock ledge high above the Animas River. Up to that time, this had been impossible, as the train always passed this location in the late afternoon shadow. No. 478 is shown here crossing the high bridge. The photographs taken on this occasion remained unique until Durango & Silverton began regular morning trains in the 1980s. (Alexis McKinney) A commercial newsreel company filmed an educational travelogue on the branch in the late 1950s. Alexis, who was executive editor of The Denver Post *at the time, rode a motor car ahead of the day's regular train and obtained the fine view (left, below), which he titled "Ah Wilderness Rolls Out The Carpet."*

The Silverton *would not have survived to enjoy its second century of service to the citizens of Colorado and visitors from around the world had it not been for the efforts of the three gentlemen pictured above: Alexis McKinney, Charles E. Bradshaw Jr. and Robert W. Richardson. This historic portrait was taken next to the brass-railed observation platform of the car* Nomad *at Silverton on May 21, 1988. (Ronald C. Hill)*

Pausing for water at the town of Gwanda on the West Nicholson Branch, this Class 16A Beyer Garratt is hauling a train of limestone to the cement plant at Colleen Bawn on May 31, 1990.

An international passenger train nears Plumtree behind NRZ's only blue-painted locomotive. The device at the left is a switchstand; the yellow lines indicate that the switch is lined into the siding.

Zimbabwe Steam Safari

by Ronald C. Hill

Once upon a time, Colorado was widely acclaimed as the "Narrow Gauge Capital of the World." Of course, that was not true then, and it certainly is not true now; although Colorado is fortunate today to have a number of authentic narrow gauge steam railroads such as the Durango & Silverton, Cumbres & Toltec and Georgetown Loop.

Probably the vast African continent is much more likely to be the home of the "Narrow Gauge Capital" because of the numerous meter gauge railways there. A few pockets of narrow gauge steam lines remain in Africa, but Zimbabwe and South Africa still boast numerous steam railroad operations. While steam has declined drastically in South Africa during the past decade, the National Railways of Zimbabwe (NRZ) has actually added rebuilt steam locomotives to its impressive roster, which makes sense in view of the fact that Zimbabwe has abundant coal supplies but no oil. At present Zimbabwe undoubtedly deserves the title "Narrow Gauge Steam Capital of the World." The situation there is even more appealing because all of the steam engines in service on the NRZ are distinctive Beyer Garratts, a type not seen elsewhere in substantial numbers.

A brief article in a recent issue of *Locomotive & Railway Preservation* magazine on steam in Zimbabwe spurred my interest, and eventually I decided to journey to Africa. A trip to South Africa in 1985 had been both pleasant and successful, and I looked forward to Zimbabwe and its Beyer Garratts with great enthusiasm. This time I was accompanied by my friend, Markus Frick, the son of Martin Frick, who is not only the president of the Manitou & Pike's Peak Railway but also a longtime board member of the Colorado Railroad Museum. Mark and I relied upon Leonard "Buz" Tobin of ACS World Travel in Denver, a true expert on African travel, to make our travel arrangements. His advice and assistance were both accurate and important, as we wanted to allow time for wildlife photography as well as railway photography.

Travel to Zimbabwe can be long and tedious, as it is ordinarily necessary to fly first to a European city and then

On the next page, an international passenger train from Botswana and South Africa, powered by "Double Hudson" Garratt No. 423, rolls through Sandown, Zimbabwe, on the Plumtree Branch en route to Bulawayo on June 2, 1990.

Class 16A No. 602 is trying desperately to start a heavy string of cars upgrade in the yard at the cement plant in Colleen Bawn on June 1, 1990. First the front engine would slip with a dramatic display of smoke and steam, and then the rear engine followed suit, but, after many attempts, the powerful Beyer Garratt slowly pulls the cars out of the yard.

catch a flight to Harare, the capital of Zimbabwe. Our experience revealed that perhaps the best service is provided by Air Zimbabwe which offers nonstop 767ER flights from London and Frankfurt to Harare. Harare itself does not have any significant railroad attractions, as all lines in that region of the country are either dieselized or electrified.

When we arrived in Harare, we really did not know what to expect from a "third world country" such as Zimbabwe. Formerly known as Rhodesia (after Cecil Rhodes), Zimbabwe gained its independence from Britain in 1980 following years of armed conflict which saw tourists kidnapped, an airliner shot out of the sky and open warfare throughout the country. The Zimbabwe African National Union of Robert Mugabe won the first independent election in 1980, and the popular Mugabe continues to serve as President of Zimbabwe today. He not only led his country to independence but also ended the civil conflict, and he is greatly admired by his countrymen. Zimbabwe, now a popular tourist destination because of its superb wildlife preserves, is both safe and hospitable. Everywhere Mark and I went, we found the people to be friendly, pleasant, helpful and not a little surprised that Americans would come all the way to their country in pursuit of steam locomotives. Unlike many foreign countries where steam still serves, Zimbabwe is both extremely gracious and convenient. Hotels are plentiful and comfortable, the food is good, tap water is safe to drink throughout the country and highways are excellent with little traffic (even though it may take a little while to adjust to driving a car with right-hand drive on the left side of the road). Automobiles may be rented from Hertz or Avis or a local rental company; however cars are in very short supply and should be reserved well in advance and confirmed in writing.

Bulawayo, a modern industrial city in the southern part of the country with a population of 650,000 persons, is the capital of Matabeleland province and the headquarters of the National Railways of Zimbabwe. More importantly for us, Bulawayo is also the center of all NRZ steam operations in Zimbabwe. At the time of our visit in June 1990, the steam shedmaster there told us that 89 steam locomotives were either in service or undergoing heavy repairs. These are divided into five different classes:

Class	Wheel Arrangement	Number Series	Dates Built
14A	2-6-2+2-6-2	500	1953
15A	4-6-4+4-6-4	370 to 424	1948-52
16A	2-8-2+2-8-2	600	1952-53
20th	4-8-2+2-8-4	730	1954
20A	4-8-2+2-8-4	740	1954

Interestingly, the 15A and 16A classes share the same boiler and cab. The only difference between the 20th and 20A engines are the diameters of the pony truck wheels. Except for the last order of 15A locomotives which were constructed in Belgium, all of these Beyer Garratts were built up by Beyer Peacock in England. All but the 20 class

A Class 16A Garratt steams peacefully outside the Bulawayo shed (enginehouse). This atmospheric nocturnal portrait was made with natural lighting—no flash was used.

(opposite, top) Made up entirely of South African Railway cars, a long passenger train powered by Class 15A (4-6-4+4-6-4) engine No. 423 accelerates smartly away from Figtree on its journey to Bulawayo on June 2, 1990.

(below) Returning from Colleen Bawn, a Class 16A (2-8-2+2-8-2) Beyer Garratt roars up the steep hill toward Gwanda and, eventually, Bulawayo on June 1, 1990.

423

No
605

Class 15A Beyer Garratt No. 372 takes on coal from the massive coaling tower at Thomson Junction on June 6, 1990. Soon the locomotive will haul a train up the mainline to Bulawayo.

engines are hand-fired, which often makes a monumental job for the hapless fireman. It is anticipated that some steam power will probably remain in operation until the year 2000, as diesel locomotives are gradually making inroads.

Bulawayo is also home to a magnificent railway museum owned and operated by the NRZ. It displays 15 beautiful locomotives, some of which are operable and occasionally used on excursion trains. The museum, located near the railway station, is a splendid tribute to the railways of Zimbabwe and is surely one of the finest rail museums anywhere.

Photography permits are absolutely essential for railway photography anywhere in Zimbabwe but are easily obtained by writing to the NRZ public relations office in Bulawayo. Permits for cab rides are also given freely by the railway headquarters as well as some stations along the line. It seemed ironic to us that the NRZ was so gracious and friendly toward railfans while many U.S. railroads are openly hostile. That is especially true in Colorado, which is as dependent upon tourism as is Zimbabwe. The result, of course, is that a large number of persons go to Zimbabwe just to see and photograph the wonderful Beyer Garratts. During our brief visit we encountered eight rail enthusiasts form Britain, two from Germany and two from South Africa. With our photo permits in hand we were welcome at trackside or at any NRZ facility, including the huge steamshed in Bulawayo, day or night. And our cab permits were good for the entire system.

The months of June, July and August are probably best for a rail-oriented trip to Zimbabwe. Since the country lies well south of the equator, that time of the year is actually winter—with crystal clear days and moderate daytime temperatures (in the 70s and low 80s) the norm. During June and July, early morning temperatures are often cool enough for spectacular steam effects; although the countryside is not as attractive in July and August when most of the foliage has fallen from the trees.

Bulawayo, a 45-minute flight from Harare via Air Zimbabwe 737, is the natural spot to begin a steam safari in Zimbabwe because it is the major rail center for the entire country. Two interesting branch lines, which are mostly steam-powered, radiate from Bulawayo. The West Nicholson Branch runs southeast to the town of West Nicholson; although most trains run only as far as Colleen Bawn, the site of the only cement plant currently operating in Zimbabwe. The line, which follows the highway from Mbalabala to Colleen Bawn, usually sees trains on weekdays only. When we were there, the West Nicholson Branch was about 75 percent steam-powered, normally with Class 16A engines but with a 14A often assigned to the Mbalabala turn. The other notable branch extends from Bulawayo southwest to Plumtree, the last town before the Botswana border. The Plumtree Branch features several international passenger trains each week which run from Zimbabwe through Botswana to South Africa and which utilize South African Railway cars exclusively. The Beyer Garratts do not run through, however, and the international trains are diesel-powered in Botswana and South Africa. The Plumtree Branch was entirely steam while we were there, and a major highway parallels the whole line. Thus, photography is fairly easy on both branches, and the West Nicholson line features some steep gradients.

But the mainline from Bulawayo to Hwange and Victoria Falls is clearly the most spectacular line in Zimbabwe. It is the longest steam line, has the most trains (about 60 to 70 percent steam-powered), passes alongside the world-famous Hwange National Park and terminates at Victoria Falls, one of the great natural wonders of the world. Unfortunately, most of the line from Bulawayo to Dete is difficult to reach, and there are no parallel roads. The area around the town of Hwange (formerly Wankie) probably offers the finest scenic and most interesting lo-

A caboose hop powered by a Class 15A 4-6-4+4-6-4 rushes around the dramatic horseshoe curve above Tajintunda (on the mainline between Thomson Junction and Hwange) on June 5, 1990. Visible in the distance in the huge electric power plant at Hwange which provides electricity to much of southern Zimbabwe.

NRZ No. 731, a giant Class 20th locomotive, works upgrade near Deka as it climbs from Thomson Junction toward Victoria Falls on June 6, 1990. (opposite) The fireman is taking a much-needed breather from his laborious duties as Class 15A Garratt No. 372 climbs around the base of Baobab Hill near Hwange on June 6, 1990. The world-famous Baobab Hotel sits atop the hill which is visible at the right.

cations for railway photography anywhere in Zimbabwe. The world-famous Baobab Hotel, situated atop Baobab Hill near Hwange, is a favorite hostelry for railway enthusiasts, and its splendid "Steam is Best" t-shirts are worn by railfans around the world. Indeed, one can sit on the hotel terrace under an 800-year old baobab tree and watch with rapt fascination as steam-powered freight trains struggle around the base of Baobab Hill! The only railway tunnel in Zimbabwe is nearby, and the fantastic horseshoe curve above Tajintunda (between Thomson Junction and Hwange) is a magnificent location for photography. Class 20 and 15A Beyer Garratts are most often seen on the mainline. In fact, the big Class 20 engines do not operate elsewhere. One passenger train in each direction between Bulawayo and Victoria Falls runs only at night and is not likely to be seen during daytime unless it has been severely delayed. As an added bonus for those who prefer more conventional steam locomotives, the Wankie Colliery Company at Hwange utilizes a fleet of green 19th class 4-8-2s to haul coal from the huge mine and processing plant down to connect with the NRZ at Thomson Junction.

Nearby is the incredible 10,000-square mile Hwange National Park. Established in 1928, the world-renowned game preserve is home to more than 20,000 elephants (which are not endangered in Zimbabwe) along with countless lions, zebras, giraffes, impalas, hippos and rhinos. Wildlife is easily seen and photographed from numerous viewing areas and the highway which traverses the park. We encountered several huge elephants strolling along the main park road late one afternoon, and a particularly large one inexplicably chose to charge our rental car and chase us down the road as we made a hasty retreat! Even the most dedicated steam fanatic will want to spend some time in Hwange National Park.

It seems that one group of engines runs exclusively between Bulawayo and Thomson Junction (near the town of Hwange), while another group operates only between Thomson Junction and Victoria Falls. In other words, a locomotive will run from Bulawayo to Thomson Junction and then turn around to return to Bulawayo, while a different engine will take the train on to Victoria Falls. The railway line from Thomson Junction is surprisingly rugged and dramatic but very difficult to photograph well due to

limited access.

Victoria Falls marked the end of our safari, as we planned to take an immaculate Air Zimbabwe BAe 146 from Victoria Falls back to Harare to connect with the long night flight to London. However, we had some spare time in Victoria Falls and decided to make use of our cab permits while we were there. With much enthusiasm we climbed aboard Class 15A No. 381 which was hauling a mixed freight consist to Thomson Junction. We had an uneventful ride, mostly downgrade, to Matetsi, where all trains pause for the engines to take on water and have the fire cleaned. An opposing coal train, powered by Class 15A No. 402, was already in the siding at Matetsi when we arrived. The fireman had just finished shaking down the grates, and No. 402 was ready for departure. We hurriedly climbed down from the cab of No. 381 and up the steps into the cab of No. 402, where we were greeted by the engineer, an amiable and skilled man named Albert. We soon learned that Albert obviously took great pride in his work and enjoyed obtaining as much performance from his locomotive as possible. No. 402 started up quickly with an authoritative bark from the exhaust. We met another train at the next siding up the line, but then it was clear steaming all the way to Victoria Falls. After the meet, No. 402 surged forward and began to thunder up the grade around curves and through dramatic rock cuts. There were some wonderful photo locations but all appeared to be quite inaccessible. Albert adjusted the cut-off a couple of times to make certain that No. 402 was climbing the steep grade as well as possible, and then he elected to relieve the exhausted fireman. I sat in the engineer's seat to watch the track ahead while Albert skillfully maintained full steam pressure. The "Double Hudson" Garratt ran very smoothly on the meter gauge track, which is a tribute not only to the design and maintenance of the locomotive but also to the excellent quality trackwork which exists throughout the NRZ system. Another engineer had previously told me that some of the Beyer Garratts had been run as fast as 75 MPH, which seemed phenomenal for such heavy engines on narrow gauge track. All too soon we steamed into Victoria Falls, and one of the finest experiences of our trip had ended. It was definitely anticlimactic to board the Air Zimbabwe BAe 146 for the tame flight to Harare! However, even the short flight proved to be very entertaining, as the BAe 146 flew at relatively low altitude and followed the railway line most of the way from Victoria Falls to Hwange and passed directly over Thomson Junction where several Garratts were steaming contentedly in the afternoon sunshine.

Zimbabwe proved to be an exciting, friendly and gracious country with an abundance of both steam locomotives and wildlife. It is not without a certain degree of adventure, which should be a part of every African safari. One morning as we were climbing the rugged hillside above Tajintunda siding to take a picture of a coal train on the horseshoe curve, Mark spotted large, fresh cat prints, And another day we saw a deadly puff adder snake crawling along the side of the road, but a little common sense and caution will avoid all potentially serious problems. Alan Miller, who has gone to Zimbabwe in pursuit of steam several times, summed it all up when he simply advised us "to keep an eye out for the odd lion." It seemed to us that the vast rewards of a steam safari to Zimbabwe are much greater than any possible difficulties. Mark and I thoroughly enjoyed our trip and the African experience, and we both want to return to Zimbabwe again soon.

(left) The unique design of the Beyer Garratt locomotive is shown to good advantage in this side view of NRZ Class 20A No. 741 as it traverses a high fill south of Hwange on June 9, 1990. Interestingly, the NRZ Class 20 engines proved to be both more powerful and more efficient than almost identical Garratts used by the South African Railway. (above) One of the most spectacular railway photo locations in Zimbabwe is the splendid horseshoe curve above Tajintunda. Here, NRZ Class 20A ((4-8-2+2-8-4) Beyer Garratt No. 741 steams magnificently around the curve during the early morning of June 9, 1990, with a coal train headed for Bulawayo. (right) NRZ Class 15A Beyer Garratt No. 372 is busy making up a freight train in Victoria Falls on June 14, 1990, after bringing in the overnight passenger train from Bulawayo, whose cars are still standing on the track adjacent to the station. The "Double Hudsons" are among the most popular and trouble-free steam engines in service on the National Railways of Zimbabwe.

Bursting dramatically through a steep rock cut near Entuba, Class 20A No. 741 is hauling a coal train to Bulawayo on June 9, 1990. For many miles in this region, the railway runs parallel to Hwange National Park, one of the foremost game preserves in the world, and it is not unusual for train crews to see lions and elephants at trackside.

SECTION	CLASS 14th	CLASS 15th	CLASS 16A	CLASS 20th	CLASS G MAM	CLASS D.E. 9		CLASS D.E. 9A			CLASS D.E. 10A	
						Single	Tandem	Single	Tandem	Triple	Single	Tandem
Gweru to Bulawayo	735	905	1000	1500	1200	500	1000					
Gweru to Somabhula						500	1000					
Bulawayo to Gweru	735	1000	1270	1500	1200	500	1000					
Somabhula to Gweru	905					500	1000					
Bulawayo to Mbalabala			680									
Mbalabala to Colleen Bawn			590									
Bulawayo to Gwanda	545											
Gwanda to West Nicholson	475											
West Nicholson to Colleen Bawn	580											
Colleen Bawn to Mbalabala	725		955									
Mbalabala to Heany Junction	475		650									
Heany Junction to Bulawayo	735	905	1000	1500	1200							
Bulawayo to Sawmills		1000		*1270	1100	650	1300	800	1600	2400	1450	2400
Sawmills to Bulawayo		1080		*1640	1300	750	1500	800	1600	2400	1550	2400
Sawmills to Dete		1000		*1270	1100			800	1600	2400	1450	2400
Dete to Sawmills		1080		*1640	1300			800	1600	2400	1550	2400
Dete to Thomson Junction		1000		*1270	1100			800	1600	2400	1450	2400
Thomson Junction to Dete		1080		*1640	1300			800	1600	2400	1550	2400
Thomson Junction to Victoria Falls		905	1300	*1590	1200						1700	2400
Victoria Falls to Thomson Junction		815	1000	*1450	1150						1300	2400

SECTION	CLASS D.E. 2 D.E. 4		CLASS D.E. 3		CLASS D.E. 6		CLASS D.E. 9A			CLASS D.E. 10A		CLASS B.D. 1	CLASS 15th
	Single	Tandem	Single	Tandem	Single	Tandem	Single	Tandem	Triple	Single	Tandem	Single	
Bulawayo to Plumtree	1000	2000	1050	2100	950	1900	700	1400	2000	1200	2400	1100	950
Plumtree to Bulawayo	1000	2000	1050	2100	950	1900	700	1400	2000	1200	2400	1100	950

*** May be reduced by 10% at the Area Manager's discretion**

HOURS OF DUTY FOR TRAINS WORKING

Station	*Open*	
Heany Junction	As required.	
Zvishavane	As required.	
Rutenga	As required.	
Mbizi	As required.	
Triangle	As required.	
Chiredzi	As required.	
Beitbridge	As required.	
Chicualacuala	As required.	
Mbalabala	As required.	
Colleen Bawn	As required.	
West Nicholson	As required.	
Khami	Continuously.	Daily.
Marula	Continuously.	Daily.
Plumtree	Continuously.	Daily.

SPECIAL INSTRUCTIONS

MAXIMUM LENGTH OF TRAINS

The maximum length of trains must not exceed the following, except when otherwise authorised:

Gweru—Bulawayo	160 axles
Somabhula—Bannockburn	160 axles
Bannockburn—Rutenga	200 axles
Rutenga—Beitbridge	200 axles
Rutenga—Chicualacuala	148 axles
Rutenga—Chiredzi	148 axles
Chiredzi—Mkwasine Loading Zone No. 3	184 axles
Bulawayo—Thomson Junction	152 axles
Thomson Junction—Victoria Falls	160 axles
Bannockburn—Zvishavane	120 axles
Heany Junction—West Nicholson	52 axles*
Bulawayo—Plumtree	112 axles

***NOTE:** Providing permission is obtained from the Traffic Superintendent a maximum of 80 axles (empties only) for Class 14A and a maximum of 96 axles (empties only) for Class 16A locomotives is permitted.

POINT TO POINT DISTANCES AND TIMINGS

Bulawayo to Plumtree

Distance from Bulawayo	STATIONS, SIDINGS, ETC.	Point to Point Distances	Passenger	MIXED BOGIE STOCK ONLY (LOAD 700 tonnes)	GOODS* LOAD (950x76)	Passenger	MIXED BOGIE STOCK ONLY (LOAD 760 tonnes)	GOODS*	GOODS*
km		km	Mins	Mins	Mins	Mins.	Mins.	Mins.	Mins.
0,000	**Bulawayo**	—		—	—	—	—	—	—
2,052	**Westgate**	2,052	6	6	—	—	—	—	—
9,883	Umganin Siding	7,831	11	15	20	15	17	16	14
17,763	**Khami**	7,880	9	12	13	9	11	12	11
27,413	Westacre Siding	9,650	11	13	14	11	13	14	14
37,706	Figtree Siding	10,293	12	14	15	10	12	13	13
52,033	Leighwoods Siding	14,327	22	23	25	21	22	24	22
59,401	Sandown Siding	7,368	8	9	10	8	9	9	9
69,380	**Marula**	9,979	11	13	13	11	14	14	14
79,249	Syringa Siding	9,869	11	14	14	12	13	14	14
93,157	Coldridge Siding	13,908	14	18	18	13	15	17	16
102,220	**Plumtree**	9,063	9	12	12	11	11	13	13
112,169	**Botswana Border**	9,949	—	—	—	—	—	—	—
OVERALL RUNNING TIMES			124	149	154	121	137	146	140
MAXIMUM TESTED SPEED km/h			50	45	35	80	75	60	60
CLASS OF LOCOMOTIVE			15th	15th	15th	D.E.2	D.E.2	D.E.2	D.E. 10A

*Based on "Run Through" Times at Sidings.

Pages 233-235 are reproduced from National Railways of Zimbabwe-Southern Area Working Time Table No. 68 effective September 18, 1988. (Ronald C. Hill collection)

Plumtree to Bulawayo

STATIONS, SIDINGS, ETC.	Point to Point Distances	Passenger	MIXED BOGIE STOCK ONLY (LOAD 750 tonnes)	GOODS* LOAD (950x76)	Passenger	MIXED BOGIE STOCK ONLY (LOAD 760 tonnes)	GOODS*	GOODS*
	km	Mins	Mins	Mins	Mins.	Mins.	Mins.	Mins.
Botswana Border	0,493	—	—	—	—	—	—	—
Plumtree	9,949	—	—	—	13	15	15	15
Coldridge Siding	9,063	10	13	13	10	12	14	12
Syringa Siding	13,908	16	19	20	17	19	21	19
Marula	9,869	10	13	13	11	12	14	13
Sandown Siding	9,979	12	15	14	12	13	15	14
Leighwoods Siding	7,368	8	11	10	8	10	10	9
Figtree Siding	14,327	16	18	18	15	17	17	16
Westacre Siding	10,293	12	14	15	11	13	13	13
Khami	9,650	10	13	13	10	11	12	11
Umganin Siding	7,880	10	12	12	9	11	10	10
Westgate	7,831	10	12	16	—	—	17	14
Bulawayo	2,052	6	7	—	16	16	—	—
OVERALL RUNNING TIMES		120	147	144	132	149	158	146
MAXIMUM TESTED SPEED km/h		50	35	35	80	75	60	60
CLASS OF LOCOMOTIVE		15th	15th	15th	D.E.2	D.E.2	D.E.2	D.E. 10A

*Based on "Run Through" Times at Sidings.

POINT TO POINT DISTANCES AND TIMINGS

West Nicholson Branch

STATIONS, SIDINGS, ETC.	Point to Point Distances	GOODS
	km	Mins.
Bulawayo	.....	.....
Mpopoma	5,794	13
Northolt	5,291	7
Cement	9,999	15
Heany Junction	12,255	20
Rogers Siding	5,068	9
Imbizo Siding	4,859	10
Ntunteni Siding	8,523	17
Bushtick Siding	5,844	12
Tank	5,206	13
Esigodini Siding	3,507	8
Mulungwane Siding	10,553	20
Mbalabala	12,735	28
Swazi Siding	10,766	21
Glass Block Siding	12,839	27
Stanmore Siding	5,477	10
Lumane Siding	13,131	22
Sabiwa Siding	15,459	27
Gwanda	4,765	10
Antenior Siding	11,370	20
Eagle Vulture Siding	6,845	11
Colleen Bawn	10,350	23
Jessie Siding	14,135	24
West Nicholson	5,569	12
OVERALL RUNNING TIMES		379
MAXIMUM TESTED SPEED km/h:—		
Bulawayo to Heany Junction		60
Heany Junction to Esigodini		50
Esigodini to Sabiwa		60
Sabiwa to Colleen Bawn		40
Colleen Bawn to West Nicholson		60
CLASS OF LOCOMOTIVE:—		14th, 14A

STATIONS, SIDINGS, ETC.	Point to Point Distances	GOODS
	km	Mins.
West Nicholson	.....	.....
Jessie Siding	5,569	14
Colleen Bawn	14,135	27
Eagle Vulture Siding	10,350	21
Antenior Siding	6,845	12
Gwanda	11,370	22
Sabiwa Siding	4,765	11
Lumane Siding	15,459	28
Stanmore Siding	13,131	24
Glass Block Siding	5,477	12
Swazi Siding	12,839	26
Mbalabala	10,766	27
Mulungwane Siding	12,735	26
Esigodini Siding	10,553	20
Tank	3,507	8
Bushtick Siding	5,206	12
Ntunteni Siding	5,844	16
Imbizo Siding	8,523	21
Rogers Siding	4,859	9
Heany Junction	5,068	10
Cement	12,255	16
Northolt	9,999	13
Mpopoma	5,291	11
Bulawayo	5,794	13
OVERALL RUNNING TIMES		399
MAXIMUM TESTED SPEED km/h:—		
West Nicholson to Colleen Bawn		60
Colleen Bawn to Sabiwa		40
Sabiwa to Esigodini		60
Esigodini to Heany Junction		50
Heany Junction to Bulawayo		60
CLASS OF LOCOMOTIVE:—		14th, 14A

About the Authors

WILLIAM F. GALE was born in Philadelphia in 1922 and grew up in a house next to the four-track mainline of the Pennsylvania Railroad. After graduating from Dickinson College in Carlisle, Pennsylvania, he served during World War II in the 76th Infantry Division in Europe. Beginning in 1948 he had a 27-year railroad career with the Pennsylvania, Delaware Lackawanna & Western and Erie-Lackawanna. He subsequently retired after nine years with the Interstate Commerce Commission's Chicago regional office and divides his time between Carlisle and a winter home in Texas. Bill has studied the history of Colorado railroads since the early 1930s and has visited the state frequently. He and his wife, Peg, have been married 45 years.

THOMAS J. NOEL is a professor of history at the University of Colorado at Denver and chair of the Denver Landmark Preservation Commission, which has endeavored to preserve some of Denver's streetcar suburbs. Since 1980 Tom has conducted the Smithsonian Institution's week-long Colorado tour, "Railroading the Rockies." Tom has received his B.A. in history and M.A. in library science from the University of Denver and his M.A. and Ph.D. in history from the University of Colorado at Boulder. He is the co-author or author of nine books, including *The City and the Saloon, Colorado Catholicism, Denver: The City Beautiful and Its Architects* and *Denver: Mining Camp to Metropolis.*

ROBERT W. RICHARDSON was born in Rochester, Pennsylvania, in 1910. He grew up in Akron, Ohio, and frequently rode passenger trains and electric interurbans around the Buckeye state. He developed a lifelong interest in stamps and printing and was editor of *Linn's Stamp News* for four years. In 1931 he began photographing trains with a special emphasis on narrow gauge, electric railways, short lines and branchline mixed trains. This avocation was aided by his employment as a sales representative for Seiberling Rubber Company.

After World War II service with the US Army Signal Corps in Iran, Bob returned briefly to Akron before moving on to Colorado in 1948. There he purchased Denver & Rio Grande Western narrow gauge locomotive 346, which became the nucleus of the collection that eventually formed the Colorado Railroad Museum in Golden in 1959. The museum's co-founder, along with Cornelius W. Hauck, Bob has served as executive director since 1966, when the non-profit Colorado Railroad Historical Foundation was created.

He has been responsible for preserving more artifacts, documents and records dealing with Colorado rail history than any other individual. Bob has always shared this history with others who are interested in it, primarily via the columns of the *Iron Horse News,* which he has published for over 30 years. Moreover, his continued effort, in the face of formidable resistance, to save *The Silverton* from abandonment was instrumental in saving the branch. Bob was there with his camera, in snow and cold as well as during the warmth of summer, preserving for the future the history of Rio Grande's operation.

JOHN S. WALKER JR., a Denver attorney, was associated with the Missouri Pacific, Chicago & North Western and Denver & Rio Grande Western for over 40 years. His professional responsibilities mainly involved state regulatory agencies ranging from Nashville, Tennessee, to Portland, Oregon, and the Interstate Commerce Commission. He retired in 1989.

R.C. FAREWELL's interest in Rio Grande narrow gauge began with a business trip through Colorado's narrow gauge country in 1973. He has since returned many times to Durango, which he considers to be the Mecca of narrow gauge steam. His association with Bob Richardson planted a seed which grew into "A Silverton Trilogy." Since 1979, R.C. has edited the monthly Rio Grande column in *Pacific RailNews.* His interest in the modern aspects of the Rio Grande culminated with the 1988 publication of *Rio Grande: Ruler of the Rockies.*

RONALD C. HILL was born in 1937 and spent the first ten years of his life in Fox Lake, Illinois. His first glimpses of trains occurred at the Fox Lake depot, which was on the Chicago Milwaukee St. Paul & Pacific line from Madison, Wisconsin, to Chicago. He holds fond memories of summer rides on the Santa Fe *Chief* from Chicago to the family farm near Lawrence, Kansas. In 1947 his parents moved to Denver where his father taught English at the University of Denver. During the 1950s an interest in ghost towns fostered enthusiasm for the railroads of Colorado. At the same time he became an accomplished photographer. One thing led to another, and he soon became a familiar figure at trackside as he photographed trains. A practicing attorney, Ron became a member of the Board of Trustees of the Colorado Railroad Historical Foundation in 1966 and has served as its president for the past several years. He has authored or coauthored eight railroad photographic books and has contributed photographs and articles on railroading to countless magazines and books. Early in his photographic career, Ron learned that the finest, sharpest images demand the finest cameras and lenses. He has photographed trains throughout North America and in Europe and Africa.

a Journal of Rail History in the Rocky Mountain West
from the Colorado Railroad Museum

the Colorado Rail Annual

We have been publishing our COLORADO RAIL ANNUAL at intervals since 1963. Our objective has been to fill the role of an active journal of rail history in the Rocky Mounatin West, covering interesting aspects of railroading in the region with a balance of carefully researched text and the best available photography. Growing acceptance by rail history enthusiasts has established the COLORADO RAIL ANNUAL series as one of the nation's leading sources of western railroad history. Popularity of the series has enabled us to expand our offerings and, at the same time, keep prices affordable—thanks both to the economics of our large press runs and the fact that much of the effort of producing our ANNUALS is volunteer. We are continually seeking suitable manuscripts to consider for future Annuals and would welcome hearing from anyone who has or knows of such.

COLORADO : RAILROAD
: MUSEUM :

DOCTOR BROWNLIE
DENTIST
DOCTOR BROWNLIE
DOCTOR
DOCTOR
MIDLA D RAILWAY.